Cross-Cultural Studies in Curriculum

Eastern Thought, Educational Insights

STUDIES IN CURRICULUM THEORY

William F. Pinar, Series Editor

For additional information on titles in the Studies in Curriculum Theory series visit www.routledge.com

Cross-Cultural Studies in Curriculum

Eastern Thought, Educational Insights

Edited by

Claudia Eppert • Hongyu Wang

Lawrence Erlbaum Associates
Taylor & Francis Group

New York   London

Lawrence Erlbaum Associates
Taylor & Francis Group
270 Madison Avenue
New York, NY 10016

Lawrence Erlbaum Associates
Taylor & Francis Group
2 Park Square
Milton Park, Abingdon
Oxon OX14 4RN

© 2008 by Taylor & Francis Group, LLC
Lawrence Erlbaum Associates is an imprint of Taylor & Francis Group, an Informa business

Printed in the United States of America on acid-free paper
10 9 8 7 6 5 4 3 2 1

International Standard Book Number-13: 978-0-8058-5674-3 (Softcover) 978-0-8058-5673-6 (Hardcover)

Library of Congress Cataloging-in-Publication Data

Eppert, Claudia, 1962-
    Cross-cultural studies in curriculum : eastern thought, educational insights / Claudia Eppert and Hongyu Wang.
        p. cm.
    Includes bibliographical references and index.
    ISBN-13: 978-0-8058-5673-6 (hardcover : alk. paper)
    ISBN-13: 978-0-8058-5674-3 (pbk. : alk. paper)
    1. Comparative education 2. Education--Curricula--Cross-cultural studies. 3. East and West. 4. Philosophy, Asian. I. Wang, Hongyu. II. Title.

LB43.E67 2008
375--dc22   2007017206

Visit the Taylor & Francis Web site at
http://www.taylorandfrancis.com

For Bill and Bill

CONTENTS

FOREWORD: "THE SICKNESS OF THE WEST"

Understanding is the expression of the affinity of the one who understands to the one whom he understands and to that which he understands.

—Hans-Georg Gadamer, *Reason in the Age of Science*

What is this affinity that seems to have developed over the past few decades between the interpretive disciplines in contemporary curriculum theory and, shall we say, the ways of the East? What is the affinity that has allured this wide array of teachers and scholars here, to this place, to this wonderful book you hold in your hands, coming, as they do, from East and West, to meet here, over East and West?

The authors of the present volume will give answers to this cluster of questions in their own ways in the chapters that follow. These answers, like these questions, are mighty and prophetic. As "globalism" raises its Hydralike nest of heads, one thing is for sure: this moment, this juncture, feels monumental. East and West just might be on the verge of tearing themselves to pieces all over again, as we have witnessed so often in the course of human affairs. The tragic singular logic that underwrites the West and shapes and directs its relationships with others—"you are either for us or against us" being only the latest formulation—seems to be sadly inevitable.

Or, maybe, this time, a bit more of the real conversation that we need to have *among* us will have time to occur, to ripen, to heal—even just a bit, just for now. Maybe the conversation can go on. Maybe we can breathe a little while longer. And yet, maybe not. Either way, this book steps into a vital breath.

We Westerners have had this dance before—countless times. In the mid-19th century, Arthur Schopenhauer gobbled up new German translations of Buddhist texts and found his own Kantian face: things "in themselves" are "will" and when things in themselves become tethered to our will, the result is a world of representation, a world that only exists in relation to our willing, a world, Schopenhauer (1963) suggests, of *illusion*:

> "The world is my representation": This is a truth valid with reference to every living and knowing being, although man alone can bring it into reflective, abstract consciousness. If he really does so, philosophical discernment has dawned on him. It then becomes clear and certain to him that he does not know a sun and an earth, but only an eye that sees a sun, a hand that feels an earth; that the world around him is there only as representation, in other words, only in reference to another thing, namely, that which represents, and this is himself. (p. 63)

The only remedy to getting caught in this web of illusion was, weirdly, almost Buddhist: the will must be denied. Willing is the source of desire, desire is the source of illusory attachment (or, better, an attachment to illusions), and attachment is the source of suffering.

This is, of course, only one step away from Richard Wagner's *Der Ring Des Nibelungen* immolation scenes where will is heroically broken and willful gods find their twilight. Even the musical motifs in this work suggest nature and desire with undulating, rising E-flat harmonics and the power of Wotan's staff descending down the same tonal sequence with great, triumphal, patriarchal willfulness.

And, of course, we get, as happens in the for-or-against logic of the West, the exact inverse of this denial of the will. Friedrich Nietzsche (1975) calls such denials sheepish Christian meekness and proposes instead a triumphal *affirmation* of the will (compare this thread of Nietzsche's work with the current Triumphal Willfulness of the Christian Right and their Christian Soldiers). For Nietzsche, every proposition of truth hides a common theme: *whatever* is proposed as true, as basic, as originary, as real, it is the proposing itself, rather than the content of the proposing, that is an attempt to affirm willful dominance. Therefore, Nietzsche suggests that it is the will-to-dominate (the "will to power" over things) that is in fact most true, most basic, most originary, most real.

Rather than denying such will, therefore, we should affirm it (we are told), because it is our true (Western) nature and we need only gobble up into our self-affirmation any who resist.

This, of course, is the logic of war. And I can't resist mentioning the endgame: The triumph of the will is an indirect, unintended outcome of a terribly recent East/West flirtation. So anyone who thought that flirtations with the East or romantic orientalism are adequate in these matters or that there is only good news to be had is sorely mistaken. This book faces up to these facts and thus requires such facing and effacing on the part of its readers.

Something in me still deeply believes the truths that this book opens before our eyes, that a conversation between East and West is a spot of perennial hope (and, of course, equally perennial suffering). But the teacher in me knows that, as Hans-Georg Gadamer (that most beautiful of "un-Eastern" men), said, "every experience worthy of the name involves suffering" (1989, p. 356). Even in such suffering, when these conversations work, when the courage is there, myriad strong and generous voices emerge. That is what we find in this book—spots of hope borne of suffering. They are strong, generous voices, each resisting in its own way the gobbling up of East by West or West by East. Let's remember, too, Jacques Derrida's caution that even here, we still presume will, albeit good will (see Michelfelder & Palmer, 1989). But this is the good news. A real conversation entails that I am always ready to hesitate and cup my ear again, not just toward the voice of another, but again toward the ghosts howling in my own voice.

This text moves "in-between," in a spot of great fecundity, a locus of interpretation ("*The true locus of hermeneutics is this in-between*" [Gadamer, 1989, p. 295])—a locus, one might say, of pedagogy itself. Under the sway of the voices in texts like this one, how one gets to think about classrooms, kids, and teachers gets more vigorous and difficult. Curriculum topics lose their Protestant-Eurocentric isolation and loneliness and burst open and outward into all their relations. When these conversations work, both East and West can understand their character, their power, and their foibles in ways that each could have never experienced through simple self-reflection. When it fails— when each side deafens, fundamentalizes, and literalizes—well, we get what we seem to have quite a lot of these days: a post-9/11 pedagogy, premised on paranoia, surveillance, incarceration, and interrogation; schools called "Foundations for the Future," "No Child Left Behind" uttered as a threat (however well meant), and so on.

Shh! We're in a wee bit of an entrenchment currently in North American culture and North American schools. This is one reason, among so many, that this book is so timely.

In the articulations of the ways of the East, many of us have found ways we might, if not cure, then at least care for the great illness of the Euro-Enlightenment project of (self-)consciousness and its consequent violence. This is why this book is so vital. It is an old pedagogical adage: We don't listen to others simply in order to understand *them*; we listen to others also in order to understand *ourselves*, because others can read our lives, and our deafness and blindness, back to us in ways that we cannot read them alone. This book's authors do not simply run with abandon to some exotic other, but use anotherness as a moment for a more generous and expansive self-understanding. The Buddha calls this "the emptying of self," and St. Augustine says that, as we learn, the self becomes "roomier" (quoted in Carruthers, 2005, p. 199). We find our limits in each other, and in those spots of liminality, well, there is sometimes a sharp intake of breath, and, as the Buddha and Gadamer have said, there is likely pain to pay in the venture.

In a conversation between Paul Geneson and Gary Snyder, the price of not venturing is finally named, a price that flows easily from the citation above from Schopenhauer's *The World as Will and Representation*:

Geneson: So when [Jean-Paul] Sartre . . . goes to the tree, touches the tree trunk and says, "I feel in an absurd position. I cannot break through my skin to get in touch with this bark, which is outside me," the Japanese poet would say . . . ?

Snyder: Sartre is confessing the sickness of the West. At least he is honest. The [poet] will say, "But there are ways to do it, my friend. It's no big deal." It's no big deal, especially if you get attuned to that possibility from early in life. (Snyder, 1980, p. 67)

It is good to see that right at the cusp of the confession of sickness, pedagogy as attunement is invoked and a path is almost laid out.

So at this terrifying end of the idea of self-containedness let's take one more step toward putting into sharper light the timeliness of this text and its wisdoms.

The affirmation of the constructs of a willful subjectivity are at the heart of contemporary pedagogy in the guise of constructivism, and the profoundly colonial character of this epistemology has been recently documented (see

Bowers, 2005; Jardine, 2006; Johnson, Fawcett, & Jardine, 2006; Smith, 2006). As Western consciousness has so often portended, if we hold in hand the conditions of reasonableness, morality, and civility, it is our duty, as Westerners, to impose such matters on the world, and to "construct" it in our own image without hesitation or apology, *without heed.*

An unnamed senior advisor to the administration of President George W. Bush affirmed the terrible truth we already know, that the sickness of the West is full bore: "'We are an empire now, and when we act, we create our own reality. And while you're studying that reality—judiciously as you will—we'll act again, creating other new realities, which you can study, too, and that's how things will sort out'" (quoted in MacMillan, 2006, p. A19). We can hear the mockery of studying and the (sometimes subtle and schooled, often literal) death of others. Under the sway of Empire, what, after all, is there to study when another is only what I understand and allow them to be?

These days, who needs a book on East and West if we create our own reality of what the East can be? As Bush has declared with great clarity, the United States already understands what the East can properly think about the West, and therefore it need not listen.

Sickness.

My own work, writing, and teaching—my own life and breath—have been intimately shaped by the ways of the East and the ways that those ways have helped me understand my own Western raising better. The trouble is, I'm feeling a bit like Sartre lately: encased, enclosed, entrenched, far away from that jeweled heart. When you are living with war, things start to shut down, possibilities narrow, conversations cease. And in the ensuing silence, "untruth" (Smith, 2006) is perpetrated under what Alice Miller (1989) has identified as a "black pedagogy": we are lied to, as the title of one of her books suggests, "for our own good." Untruth becomes truth because it is willed to be so.

Worse yet, perhaps, war makes those who might have a conversation more alike in their exaggerated unwillingness to listen to another, their inability to imagine or tolerate anything beyond the world they have constructed. This is not just a sickness of the West. It is the sickness of fundamentalism and the deafness, fear, and war footing it feeds upon, supports, aggravates, and declares as necessary always and only because of *the other's* deafness. It is no coincidence, speaking of East and West these days, that *both* are armed and dangerous, the meeting of Crusade and Jihad:

War tends to make cultures alike whereas peace is that condition under which each culture flourishes in its own incomparable way. From this, it follows that peace cannot be exported; it is inevitably corrupted by transfer, its attempted export means war. (Illich, 1992, p. 17)

This is one last reason, for now, that this book is so amazing, so timely, so true. "War, which makes cultures alike, is all too often used by historians as the framework or skeleton of their narratives" (Illich, 1992, p. 19), and the same may be said, too often, of curriculum, pedagogy, and education. In this book, East and West have, instead, been "left in peace" (Illich, 1992, p. 16).

Thus we have here in our hands the possibility that a real conversation might begin again. It is this possibility, in all its myriad ways and dependent co-arisings, that is at the heart—and that defines the hope—of pedagogy. Enjoy it. Savor it. And do not turn away from the suffering.

David W. Jardine
University of Calgary

References

Bowers, C. A. (2005). *The false promises of constructivist theories of learning: A global and eco-logical critique*. New York: Lang.

Carruthers, M. (2005). *The book of memory: A study of memory in medieval culture*. Cambridge, England: Cambridge University Press.

Gadamer, H. G. (1983). *Reason in the age of science*. Cambridge, MA: MIT Press.

Gadamer, H. G. (1989). *Truth and method*. New York: Continuum.

Illich, I. (1992). *In the mirror of the past: Lectures and addresses 1978–1990*. New York: Boyars.

Jardine, D. (2006). Cutting nature's leading strings: A cautionary tale about constructivism. In D. Jardine, S. Friesen, & P. Clifford (Eds.), *Curriculum in abundance* (pp. 123–136). Mahwah, NJ: Erlbaum.

Jardine, D., Friesen, S., & Clifford, P. (2006). *Curriculum in abundance*. Mahwah, NJ: Erlbaum.

Johnson, B., Fawcett, L., & Jardine, D. (2006). Further thoughts on cutting nature's leading strings: A conversation. In D. Jardine, S. Friesen, & P. Clifford (Eds.), *Curriculum in abundance* (pp. 139–148). Mahwah, NJ: Erlbaum.

MacMillan, M. (2006, February 2). What would Kissinger do? *The Globe and Mail* (Toronto, Ontario), A12.

Michelfelder, D., & Palmer, R. E. (1989). *Dialogue and deconstruction: The Gadamer-Derrida encounter*. Albany: State University of New York Press.

Miller, A. (1989). *For your own good: Hidden cruelty in child-rearing and the roots of violence*. Toronto, Ontario: Collins.

Nietzsche, F. (1975). *The will to power* (William Kaufmann, Trans.). New York: Random House.

Schopenhauer, A. (1966). *The world as will and representation* (vol. 1). New York: Dover.

Smith, D. G. (2006). *Trying to teach in a season of great untruth: Globalization, empire and the crises of Pedagogy.* Amsterdam: Sense.

Snyder, G. (1980). The real work. In *The real work: Interviews and talks 1964–1979.* New York: New Directions.

PREFACE: OPENINGS INTO A CURRICULUM OF THE WAY

Water, if not mixed with other things, is by nature clear, and if not stirred up, it is level. However, if it is blocked and cannot flow, it cannot remain clear.

—Chuang Tzu, "Rigid and Arrogant"

This book carries multiple aspirations. One is to initiate and deepen discussion of Eastern thought in the context of educational theory and practice. As J. J. Clarke (1997) points out in his book *Oriental Enlightenment: The Encounter Between Asian and Western Thought*, despite escalating globalization and a long history of East–West intellectual, cultural, and economic exchange, Eastern philosophical and spiritual traditions have yet to acquire a mainstream presence in contemporary Western society. Even with the dismantling of colonial structures, he notes that "endemic Eurocentrism" and "insularity of Western intellectual life" (p. 5) persist within public life and scholarly work. Clarke brings particular attention to the absence of oriental thought in education, stating that "while many educationalists have acknowledged the importance of a global outlook, our school and university curricula have often been slow to respond in practice" (p. 15). This situation presents a challenge to North American educators, to which our book can be read as one response.

At the same time that we recognize the continued marginality of Eastern thought, we also easily observe the extent to which Western scholarship on this topic has become increasingly popular within recent years, with new journals, academic organizations, programs, books and book series appearing at remarkable rates. Contemporary theory has illuminated the imperialism embedded within many Western institutions of knowing and being, and it has become evident that scholars in all academic disciplines are turning toward such traditions as Buddhism, Confucianism, Hinduism, Sufism, and Taoism in search of compelling and meaningful ways of conceiving relations among self, other, and environment. Moreover, a well-identified climate of alienation, stress, fear, violence, and exploitation has made all too clear the need for alternate insights and policy initiatives that will permeate the public sphere and support conditions for individual, communal, and global renewal and peace. This volume aspires to address some of the social and psychic problems we face today.

Within the educational field, attention to Eastern traditions is without doubt beginning to accelerate. Education constitutes the personal and social means for shaping and facilitating difficult transitions to deeper levels of being, knowing, and engagement. This understanding of teaching and learning, however, has become largely obscured in the current national and state obsession with standardization, measurement, and testing. Several scholars concur that contemporary American institutions of schooling are in nothing short of crisis (see, e.g., Purpel & McLaurin, 2004). Much educational research endeavors to respond insightfully and creatively to the recognition that past and current national mandates have contributed or are contributing to withering the spirit of educational structures and bodies. The recent emphasis on Eastern traditions and contemplative practices represents part of this struggle to reenvision frameworks for learning and living in the world.

While we employ the term *Eastern thought,* we are aware of the trouble with the signifiers *East* and *West.* Curriculum theorist Ted T. Aoki (1996, cited in Pinar & Irwin, 2005) is among those who identify *East* and *West* as narrow, reductive labels and points out the problematic of treating them as "two distinct cultural wholes ... each identifiable, standing distinctly and separately from each other" (p. 315). This essentialism is simultaneously mired in and obscures histories of psychic, social, and ideological construction, forged through processes of appropriation, oppression, exclusion, and idealization. Furthermore, contemporary social imaginaries of East and West gloss over centuries of deeply enmeshed global economic and cultural exchange and engagement, perpetuating myths of originality and authenticity. David Geoffrey Smith's provocative study, with which we begin our book, details an extensive and complicated past of oriental/occidental engagement, and deftly illustrates the very impossibility of articulating East and West as separate entities. East and West as grand narratives too easily serve to elide complex geographical, cultural, social, political, and religious differences, both across and within each label. We thus deploy the terminology of *East* and *West* in aspirations to foreground and deconstruct these binaries, aware that in so doing we also risk their reinscription. We embrace the language of "Eastern thought" in order to inclusively gesture toward religious and philosophical ideas and traditions connected with East and South Asia, to draw attention to convergences and divergences within and among these traditions, and to destabilize unitary and essentializing myths concerning East and West. Finally, we seek to recognize Eastern ideas and traditions as pluralistic and potentially subversive within both Eastern and Western historical and contemporary social, political, and educational contexts while also seeking not to romanticize them.

Furthermore, this edition intends to embed the subject of Eastern thought more deeply into the "complicated conversation" of curriculum theory, particularly into the increasing internationalization of curriculum studies. Current efforts in transnational curriculum inquiry to support scholarly exchange within and across national borders (Pinar, 2003) cannot probe beneath and reach beyond the surface of globalization (with its force and limits) without sustained intercultural dialogue on fundamental educational issues, including those raised by this volume's contributors. In this key, we offer an East–West dialogue as "wisdom (inter)text" in order to understand curriculum differently.

Yet, although we situate our dialogue within curriculum studies, this interdisciplinary edition discusses sage writings in Buddhism, Confucianism, Hinduism, and Taoism (as well as other traditions) and yields educational insights that invite new considerations for specific areas of scholarship, including critical pedagogy and social justice/social change education, environmental education, psychoanalysis, holistic education, character education, witness studies, professional ethics, women's and gender studies, peace education, literature and arts education, and the philosophy of education. Additionally, we cross boundaries of genre by including poetry and creative writing responsive to aesthetic aspects of Eastern thought. In putting these chapters together, we begin with David Geoffrey Smith's call to situate our studies in time and space, while letting other chapters proceed in thematically random order, hoping such an arrangement allows both (dissipative) structure and surprise.

While honoring the complexity and diversity of Eastern ideas, we take as our point of departure the awareness that many of these ideas share the outlook that educational endeavor extends beyond a preoccupation with knowledge acquisition. Ancient sages such as the Buddha, Confucius and his disciple Mencius, Kuan Yin, Taoists Lao Tzu and Chuang Tzu, and contemporary sages like Sri Aurobindo, Pema Chödrön, the Dalai Lama, Jiddu Krishnamurti, Sri Sri Ravi Shankar, Ravindrath Tagore, and Thich Nhat Hanh variously emphasize a predominant concern with the foundational educational question of how we might learn to live alone and with others and contend with our personal and social suffering. Indeed, while the overriding orientation of much Western educational theory and practice might be encapsulated in the indissoluble couplet of power/knowledge, ethics/wisdom/compassion might encompass a general identifying triplet for traditional Eastern educational philosophy, one that is enabled by (un)learning, a theme that echoes throughout this collection. In light of the pervasive "turn to ethics" (Garber, Hanssen, & Walkowitz, 2000) in recent academic scholarship, we might thus do well to bow to the insights of these sages and the traditions in which they are steeped.

We do not intend our edition to offer any comprehensive study of Eastern thought but hope it will inspire and open doors for further East–West inquiry and a dialogic search for educational and social renewal. Although Aoki (1996, cited in Pinar & Irwin, 2005) notably points to the limitations of the term *cross-cultural*, we have decided to retain it here. We appreciate the emphasis on *crossing*, in its evocation of a spiritual, psychic, and cultural movement to another shore, a dwelling of "interbeing," to follow Thich Nhat Hanh. We have titled this preface "Openings into a Curriculum of the Way" because this book reflects diverse individual and collective journeys at the same time that it defers to Eastern wisdom concerning paths toward renewal and peace. In this context we also invoke the image of water, an image that resonates throughout many chapters in this collection and is often gestured to metaphorically in much Eastern thought in order to illustrate the nature, challenges, and possibilities of "the Way." In its distillation, this book is about trying to become unblocked such that we might find a means to clearer and deeper waters.

We have faced numerous editorial challenges. As vigilant as we have been, we are aware that many of us approach our thinking about Eastern philosophies through Western lenses, so the colonizing trace is difficult, if not impossible, to evade. In efforts to address this concern, we invited our authors to position themselves in their particular journeys and foreground their perspectives at the outset. Practical issues also emerged, involving complexities of translation and different systems of scripts. For the most part we decided to leave these up to the contributors, and requested only consistency within individual chapters. Finally, the contributors herein have various backgrounds and engagements with Eastern thought, and our edition consequently reflects us as participating in a continuum of learning from and living with Eastern insights. But we acknowledge ourselves collectively as educators engaged in ongoing processes of inquiry and dialogue, on our way to new insights. May we invite you to participate in this journey, too?

Acknowledgments

This book would never have come to fruition without the support of many people. First, we would like to thank our contributors for their willingness to participate, their openness to ongoing repositioning, and their wonderful work. We are so very grateful to the reviewers of our manuscript; our editor, Naomi Silverman, for her support of this project and for patiently guiding us through the complications of editing; and project editor Takisha Jackson. Our many thanks go to David Jardine for agreeing to write the foreword and to Mary Aswell Doll for her commitment to the afterword. We are infinitely indebted to doctoral candidate June Newman Graham for her acute eye and engaged help. We wish to acknowledge the writings of Ted Aoki for widening the possibilities for East–West studies within the field of curriculum theory. And last, but certainly not least, we want to express our warm and deep appreciation to William F. Pinar and William E. Doll Jr.; without them the editors of this volume never would have met at Louisiana State University, Hongyu Wang as a graduating doctoral candidate and Claudia Eppert as an incoming assistant professor, and this book would likely never have come into existence. Both Bills, codirectors of the Curriculum Theory Project, have recently departed from LSU, and, in addition to our appreciation for their work toward the internationalization of curriculum studies we are enormously grateful to them for their commitments to the cultivation of an intellectual space that is rigorous and open, for the caring attention and generous support they have shown us over the years, and for their unique individual and complementary presences. We dedicate this book to them.

Claudia Eppert
Louisiana State University / University of Alberta

Hongyu Wang
Oklahoma State University

References

Aoki, T. T. (2005). Imaginaries of "East and West": Slippery curriculum signifiers in education. In W. F. Pinar & R. L. Irwin (Eds.), *Curriculum in a new key: The collected works of Ted T. Aoki*. Mahwah, NJ: Erlbaum. (Original work published 1996)

Clarke, J. J. (1997). *Oriental enlightenment: The encounter between Asian and Western thought*. New York: Routledge.

Garber, M., Hanssen, B., & Walkowitz, R. L. (Eds.). (2000). *The turn to ethics*. New York: Routledge.

Palmer, M., with Breuilly, E. (Trans.). (1996). *The book of Chuang Tzu*. London: Penguin.

Pinar, W. F. (2003). *International handbook of curriculum research*. Mahwah, NJ: Erlbaum.

Purpel, D. E., & McLaurin, W. M., Jr. (2004). *Reflections on the moral and spiritual crisis in education*. New York: Lang.

CHAPTER 1

"The Farthest West Is But the Farthest East"
The Long Way of Oriental/Occidental Engagement

David Geoffrey Smith
University of Alberta

Preamble

When the leaders of the neoconservative movement in the United States were planning their takeover of the U.S. government in the late 1990s, one of their primary fears was that "the idea of the West" was in serious jeopardy and in need of defense by any means necessary (Halper & Clarke, 2004, p. 94). Many factors undergirded this fear. The fall of the Berlin Wall had been a powerful semiotic event, a moment when a visible border dividing East and West in Europe lay in ruins. And Russia, with its ancient mystical Byzantine traditions deeply rooted in early Syrian and Persian spirituality, was now open to the West in new ways. The "-stans" of Central Asia (Kyrgyzstan, Tajikistan, etc.), now unprotected by the dismantled Soviet Union, exposed the proximity of China to the new Europe as part of a single land mass. The gross inefficiencies of the U.S.–Western European alliance of the North Atlantic Treaty Organization (NATO) during the Balkans War (1991–2001) revealed the full difficulties of such an alliance ever operating as a unified entity.

If Europe and America could no longer define "the West" in the singular way they had (basically since Christopher Columbus's landfall in 1492), then what remains of "the West" in the new global configuration of things? And if fear of the demise of the West is a preoccupation of Western political elites, what precisely is it that is feared? If it is "the East," as the nemesis to the West's hubris, then what is revealed in the current fear is the erosion of what historian John Hobson (2004) has called "an iron logic of immanence" (p. 3) that inhabits the Western imagination through all of its historical, political, and cultural self-renderings.

The logic of immanence is the logic that most of us in the Western tradition have been inducted into since we were children. In response to the basic question of how the West rose to a position of global power, the answer is given in self-contained Eurocentric terms. The Euro-American nexus, we have been told, is constructed through an autonomous genealogy according to which, as Eric Wolf (1982) describes it,

> Ancient Greece begat Rome, Rome begat Christian Europe, Christian Europe begat the Renaissance, the Renaissance the Enlightenment, the Enlightenment political democracy and the industrial revolution. Industry crossed with democracy in turn yielded the United States, embodying the rights to life, liberty and the pursuit of happiness. (p. 5)

As Wolf puts it, echoing G. W. F. Hegel, this rendering turns the very idea of history into a "moral success story" in which "the virtuous (i.e., the West) win out over the bad guys (the East)" (p. 5). What is missing in such an account, of course, is the multiple ways in which the very identity of "the West" is dependent, for its self-construction, on a vast history of relations with "the East"; that indeed there is no West without an East, and vice versa; and that the most fundamental requirement of a global age is a recognition of this fact so that a real conversation can begin about the necessary conditions of mutuality that will inevitably form part of all human futures.

In what follows I will try to trace many of the ways in which East–West engagement has been part of the human story since before the dawn of the first millennium of the Common Era. Largely, I limit the discussion to a kind of history of ideas, showing the deep inhabitation of the Western imaginary by oriental thought, sequent to the various forms of cultural exchange through trade and missionary endeavor. I do not engage the new scholarship that argues that indeed Asia was the center of the global economy until the 19th century (Frank, 1998; and, to a lesser degree, Abu-Lughod, 1989; Fernandez-Armesto, 1996); nor do I engage the kind of historical work undertaken by Hobson (2004) and others (Chaudhuri, 1990; Hodgson, 1993) who have detailed in unequivocal terms the multiple scientific and technological dependencies of the West on Chinese, Indian, and Muslim sources. All of this work, of course, will be of immense value in the future for teachers, teacher educators, and curriculum developers as a new kind of educational imagination comes into being as the result of it.

Indeed, the last remark points in an important direction, through a question concerning the relevance of this entire discussion. As one of my most challenging graduate students is always asking me, "So what ...?" In response I say that the landscape through which the Western imagination has been shaped for the last 500 years is changing radically and inexorably. As Westerners, we need to "face our relations" much more than our exclusivist tradition has allowed us to do for the last 2,000 years, and this is not something to be feared. It is not to be feared because the "Other" is in us already, if only we could see it. Our received logics prevent this perception, so the pedagogical and curricular tasks must involve a critique of those same logics, with the very means for such a critique available precisely through what until now has been so aggressively silenced and repressed.

May what follows mark a small contribution to a new kind of conversation regarding who we think we are as a species.

Drawing Some Contexts

The fragment in the chapter title is from Henry David Thoreau (as quoted in Fields, 1981, p. xii) and it underscores how East and West are relative positional terms that eventually conjoin, given the circular, global nature of our planetary home. Similarly, whatever your site of origin on the planet, leave it, go in a single direction, and eventually you will end up where you started. These two observations—that "the farthest east is but the farthest west" and that to set out on a long journey can begin the process of coming home—in a very general way define what will be attempted in this chapter. I write as a Westerner, an academic formed in the traditions of European scholarship. But I was born in China, and over the past 15 years or so I have sought better comprehension of what a deeper appreciation of oriental traditions might mean for Euro-American self-understanding. This chapter is a product of that labor. As will be apparent, there is an emphasis on recovering the Eastern influences on the Western imagination, not so much the other way; that is, how the East has seen and responded to the West. (For an interesting recent treatment of that side of things, see Guo, 2002.)

If this is the age of globalization, not just in the somewhat parochial sense of global economic integration as in the perhaps more important sense of unprecedented cultural interfacings, then the question of what it means to "meet" another assumes special relevance. My suggestion will be that to truly meet or encounter another, individually or collectively, is to meet and encounter oneself, individually and collectively. It is a kind of homecoming that involves both pain and pleasure, loss and profit. Through every encounter we find ourselves to be different from what we were before the encounter. In a sense, the other is now "in" me, and I "in" him/her/them, and this mutual indwelling is not something that can ever be surgically rectified or "purified out." This is very profound: because we are always constituted *through* one another, so in a sense we *are* the other. There is an ancient Hindu saying (in Sanskrit), "*Tuam sat asi*" (That thou art). To understand this can signal a foundation for ethics in global times.

Of course, it is a disturbing thought for the West, which is self-built as an edifice of difference to which all others are exhorted to aspire (but not really). To avoid the pain of deep encounter, the West raises the exhortation, "Our traditions of science, religion, philosophy and art have taught us what it means to be human, so if you want to be human, become like us. If you choose not to, then we have a right to destroy you, for the sake of our broader universal truth. And even if you do choose to be one of us, we still have the right to destroy you if we can. This is the law of life." In its most current iteration, this is the doctrine of the U.S. administration of President George W. Bush, but the legacy goes back 2,000 years to Roman Emperor Theodorus who, reinventing earlier Jewish and Greek sentiments, declared that anyone who is not a Christian is a pagan—that is, heathen and unenlightened. Europe entered the Dark Ages as Christendom binarized truth from myth, faith became linked to empire, and a parochial history became mythologized as History (Harpur, 2004). To this day, people who stand outside what has become the Euro-American empire stand outside of History (Dussel, 1995, 1996; Wolf, 1982); and as we shall see, this is no small matter.

Setting the stage in such stark terms may seem uncreatively exaggerated until one looks around at the contemporary global situation and sees how deeply divided it is along racial, cultural, and economic lines, with the West, now through the American empire, controlling everything. This is sometimes called "the 20/80 problem" (McMurtry 1998)—that is, 20% of the world's population controls, through various administrative, military, and financial mechanisms, the other 80%. This situation is about to pass, however, as all things must; an older order is dying and a newer one coming into being. Asia, through China and India, is now assuming a more equal partnership in the global power nexus, ironically by occidentalizing their own economic policies; although, as we shall see, contemporary economic theory found some of its earliest basic assumptions in the orient, and until the 19th century Asia was still the center of the global economy (Frank, 1998). The point, though, as historian Michel Beaud (2001) has noted, is that today the world is suffering from "A-cracy: the inability of government to carry out effective action at the level demanded by the problems we are facing" (p. 330). As a species we are confronted with the question of how we shall proceed together as the master narrative of Western superiority gradually dissolves in the face of newly emerging processes of globalization. What shall be the basis of dialogue between the West and non-West, or, in the context of this chapter, between the occident and the orient? What *way* shall define our life together? How shall we search for it? These are some of the questions guiding the remarks that follow.

That such a book as this one is now entering the occidental conversation surrounding education and curriculum theory is an interesting development in itself. It speaks of the emerging willingness of the Western academy to entertain ideas from outside its own historical traditions, not just as exotica but as part of a new, serious interlocutionary partnership over matters essential to human survival. This is related, I suspect, to a certain dissatisfaction within the Western academy, and in the humanities especially. This dissatisfaction is not only a condition that is self-constructed through the self-enclosure of the humanities' basic paradigmatic assumptions (see Dussel, 1995, 1996; Smith, 2003a, 2003b, 2005a, 2005b) but it is also a condition inflicted upon it by the new imperial money-circuited regimes of science and technology that are reducing the university to a tool of global capital (Slaughter & Leslie, 1999; Titley, 2005). That reduction assumes that science and technology are "value neutral" and hence can be delinked from any necessary critical discussion about everything else that deeply matters to human beings—religion, spirituality, philosophy, sex—except as those aspects can be made accountable to a calculus of wealth creation. Under the new dispensation, everything is indeed just a "thing" to be bought, used, or sold (Kuttner, 1999). Clearly, this is a completely inadequate axiological basis upon which any society or culture might meaningfully survive, and such current academic work as this represents at least one attempt to articulate alternatives that are more faithful to the full catholicity (from the Greek *kata*, "in respect of" + *holos*, "whole") of human experience.

A good way to understand the problem of the limits of Western intellectual paradigms is to examine the relationship between underlying cultural assumptions and their embodiment in various forms of cultural pathology. All cultures suffer illness, but different cultures suffer different illnesses; as well, similar illnesses are "suffered" differently in different places (Payer, 1988). In North America the most common diseases are heart attack, stroke, and cancer. Heart attack and stroke are the consequence of hypertension and stress (among other things); many cancers are the result of pollution of the food chain, for example, in turn a consequence of the corporate rationalization of agriculture. All of these have origins in assumptions about life. Primarily, life is seen as a matter of human control and domination, with the downside being an almost complete incapacity to "let go." If accumulation and consumption define the "good life," it is understandable that security and storage services are the fastest growing industries in the United States (Chandler, 2002; Hays, 1997), and obesity has become a great social concern (Gard, 2005). Within all of these understandings there is no place for emptiness, which is ironic because many lives feel empty even though they are so full. What the turn to oriental thought represents, then, on a very profound level, is a search for a way to creatively empty out so much of the accumulated baggage cultivated through the West's various philosophies of control.

Related to the above point, as contemporary academics in the Western academy, we work out of the inheritance of Immanuel Kant and the European Enlightenment of the 18th century. This tradition privileges critical thinking in the name of Reason, and its aim is emancipation from unthinking bondage to received knowledge and tradition and their institutional embodiments in the name of monarchy, ecclesia or, today, the state. The fruit is to be forms of knowledge that themselves are genuinely free of prejudice and self-will. The lived result, however, is a kind of "knowledgeism"—that is to say, a way of knowing that implies no connection between knowledge and knower. This is the logic of the "New Knowledge Economy" (Peters & Humes, 2003) and what Roszak (1994) has called "the cult of information." Knowledge now requires no embodiment; it just is, in itself, a kind of independent cultural currency. So the lived feeling of much academic work is that it is disconnected from any necessary connection to "my" life and how I live. The emerging and thriving interest in Asian traditions in the West serves as a counterpoint to this tradition and its personally alienating qualities, because if Asian traditions have one thing in common it is that they are concerned with the Way of life as a whole, not just its rationalizable aspects. To gain attunement to this Way, knowing "the way of the Way," is not just emancipating in the Kantian sense but is most profoundly a finding of Life—that is, the life that lives and breathes over, under, around, through, behind, above, and beyond anything we might say and do about it from our own inevitably limited perspectives of time and place. Of course, as will become clear, it is important not to romanticize Asian traditions or idealize them uncritically; it is valuable, however, to *re-cognize* them, to allow them to be seen and understood as relevant to the shared human situation.

If living the Way, then, is not just the end goal of seeking, but itself a manner of being in the present, this means that the end goal of education can never be knowledge in some independent and discrete sense, something to be accumulated for an anterior purpose such as status and other forms of social capital. Instead, the purpose of education is to learn how to live well, to be free of delusion, and to be attuned to the deepest rhythms of Life so that one is living Life according to its fundamental nature. If this sounds like mysticism, indeed it is, and for this there should be no apology, because it simply means that there is an essential unity to the whole of life that cannot be violated by human thought or action and that, indeed, to act *on* life as a projection of sheer will is a recipe for disaster on many levels.

Hindu and Buddhist traditions are united in their understanding that the root of all human suffering is ignorance (Sanskrit *avidya*), and by this is meant not "lack of knowledge" in the Western sense of "not having enough," but in the sense that any form of knowledge tied strictly to the phenomenal world, as the Western empirical traditions of science and technology are, misses a very essential point: that the phenomenal world is inextricably linked to the noumenal world—that is, to everything else. The visible and the invisible, the spoken and the silent, the implicate and the explicate, the latent and the manifest—all of these are always everywhere at work together, and to focus on only one at the expense of the others is to invite delusion or ignorance of a most unhealthy kind. The point is, then, that the present turn in the Western academy to Eastern thought is not strictly an academic interest. It arises, I believe, from a desire to be healed, personally and collectively, from the delusions that have come to so narrowly define the work of scholarship in the contemporary academic context.

As will become apparent in what follows, the turn of the West toward the East is also a form of homecoming that involves a recognition of the fact that some of the deepest roots of Western culture, even within Christianity itself, have early connections in the East, but that this has never been allowed to be acknowledged because of the exclusivism and philosophy of difference incipient in ancient Jewish and later Christian self-definitions of divine chosenness, and consolidated in Greek philosophy through such theories as

Aristotle's principle of noncontradiction (*a* cannot be *a* and *b and* still be *a*). Primarily though, as we shall see, it has been a political decision.

Ironically, these constructs of uniqueness and difference are themselves relational in origin—that is, they depend for their self-identity on the existence of an Other to which they are inexorably tied, and in many instances the tie is to the orient. For example, Abraham, the original patriarch of all three of the world's great monotheistic religions, has a name linkable to the Sanskrit, *a-brahman*, or "not Brahman," defining himself against the great Vedic traditions of Hinduism (Riley, 2000). Indeed, for Western scholars today one of the great and necessary intellectual challenges is to recover the "lost" dependencies of so much of our coveted traditions, because without such work we become forgetful of our deep and common human contingencies and end up behaving in ways that assume that others don't matter to who we think we are. That kind of assumption involves a hubris hiding from its nemesis, as 9/11 serves in reminder.

How is it that today we speak of East and West? If those of us living in Europe and North America are Westerners, by what "orientation" is this so? Well, there is the answer that we are "Western" in relation to the Orient, and this relation has a history of its own. For the last 500 years we have been living within what Samir Amin (2003) has called "the 1492 World System." The year 1492 marked Columbus's landfall in the Caribbean and the beginning of Eurocentrism, when, as a consequence of the massive fortunes accumulated through its "Latin" American conquests, Spain and eventually most of Europe shifted the center of global power away from the eastern Mediterranean and Central Asia, which had been under the control of Muslim caliphates for the previous 500 years. Before 1492, however, *Europe* meant "West" relative to Central Asia, which controlled the spice and silk routes from India and China, respectively. To this day China has never understood itself as "East." Translated into English, the character, or ideograph, for *China* means "Middle Kingdom," a self-definition that originally imagined all other peoples of the world as living in a condition of tribute to itself.

The Long Way of Oriental/Occidental Engagement

In the first part of this section I attempt to highlight some of the more profound points of engagement between West and East, starting from the ascendancy of Alexander (c. fourth century B.C.E.) to the fourth century C.E. My interest in this particular period is twofold. First, the time is pivotal for understanding how Europe became distinctively "Christian" in its self-understanding, setting up a political architecture of exclusion so that the many Asian influences that were part of Europe's early identity formation became almost entirely submerged—even silenced—under the weight of a homogenous orthodoxy that was a condition of the marriage of convenience between Roman imperial authorities and the Church in the fourth century. My second interest, therefore, is to resuscitate a sense of the "melting pot" character of the Middle East and Central Asia during this period, which encompasses both the apex and the decline of the Roman Empire. Not unlike today, it was a time of great multicultural interfusion, social experimentation, and religious pluralism. The early Christian church, which eventually became the sacral power of empire, was in its origins a polyglot, a loose and multicultural network of communities, each of which borrowed from the social, linguistic, and intellectual milieus in which they found themselves the requisite hermeneutic tools to describe what they were about (Harpur, 2004; Mack, 2001). The fact that the Christian canon, which was not fixed until the fourth century C.E., identifies each of its apostolic accounts as being "according to" different people (Matthew, Mark, Luke, and John) signifies a recognition of the fact that the accounts themselves are highly interpretive and not definitive, as later Protestant ascriptions would prefer to declare. It was not until the fourth century, when the Roman Empire was falling apart, that "fundamentalism" reared its head and the political hammer came down on religious pluralism. One might speculate how contemporary critiques of multiculturalism, and the rise of fundamentalism, are related to a fear of loss of global position.

It must be remembered that in the ancient world the connection between religion and politics was intimate. Misfortunes on the battlefield, plagues, and scourges of any sort were blamed on the unhappiness of the various divinities that controlled human destiny. Appeasing the gods was an absolute requirement of responsible political leadership. A crumbling empire required religious unification as a condition of its survival and restoration. Hence in 365 C.E. Pope Damasus I and Emperor Theodorus I made a pact to rehabilitate an earlier Temple-State system whereby the state would elevate and protect the Christian church as the sole mediator between divine and human realms and the church would ensure the ethical purity of the state in the work of divine appeasement. Such a condition required the centralization of doctrine, the granting of all interpretive authority to ecclesial authority (the bishops), and the closing of the door to all religious competition. The critical blow fell when, under papal order, the world's largest library, in Alexandria, Egypt, was

burned to the ground by a Christian mob incited by Theophilus, Bishop of
Alexandria, in 400 C.E. (Harpur, 2004, pp. 61–62).

The library had been the special pride of Alexander and placed under the
supervision of one of his boyhood friends and foremost generals, Ptolemy I. Its
policy was to house a copy of every single book that had ever been published,
every significant manuscript and papyrus. In his journeys into Afghanistan,
India, and Persia, Alexander, who once aspired to be "King of Asia" (Hammond, 2003, pp. 136–147), had encountered not just the many astrological sciences and mystery religions that were part of the lands he invaded, but also the
teachings of Buddhism and Hinduism. Alexandria then became, for example,
the center of Buddhist studies for the Mediterranean region, with the library
housing one of the largest collections of manuscripts outside of India. Strongly
contributive to this were Buddhist missionaries inspired by the Indian king
Ashoka, who in the third century B.C.E. attempted to establish a "reign of
Dharma" after being revolted by the widespread human slaughter of his own
military campaign in the Indian province of Kalinga (Fischer-Schreiber, 1989,
pp. 19–20). Galilee, the province in which Jesus was born, was on the trade
routes between the Afghanistan/China/India nexus and the Mediterranean,
and there is some speculation (Amore, 1985) that during his so-called lost
years between the ages of 13 and 30 Jesus may have lived in Egypt and been
subject to Buddhist influence. One tradition, recorded in the Gospel of Matthew, insisted that the Messiah had to "come out of Egypt" (Matt. 2:15) as a
replay of the original story of Moses leading his people out of slavery in Egypt
to the promised land of freedom and prosperity.

Many aspects of the gospel narratives resonate with themes that have no
precedent in Greek, Roman, or Jewish culture, but do have strong precedents
in Asian traditions. The birth narratives of Jesus provide a most obvious
example. That "wise men from the East" should come to pay homage to the
"young child" (Matt. 2:1) is a restatement of the traditional manner in which
incarnate Buddhas are recognized, a tradition practiced even to this day.
That such men should claim that "we have seen his star" (Matt. 2:2) echoes
Zoroastrian astrological belief from Persia that a divine birth is signaled by
a special star.

For Jesus to describe himself—or, more accurately, to be described by Gospel writers—in such terms as "the Way" (John 14:6) is interesting also. To say,
for example, "I am the Way" is to declare that "the Way" is not to be found in
following a set of formal prescriptions, but as a manner of being that is consis-

tent with the deepest resonances and rhythms of life. Asian biblical translators translate this as *Tao*, with Jesus as exemplar of Tao, or Way.

It is interesting that the early church's foremost theologian, Paul, had almost nothing to say in all of his writings about what Jesus specifically said or taught. Instead, his instruction is saturated with language about Jesus as "the Christ," claimed to have existed since before the foundation of the world. Even though the term *the Christ* (*Christos*) is from the Greek *khrio*, meaning "anoint," and is a translation of the Hebrew *masiah* (messiah), which also means "anoint," as a theological formulation, *Christos* itself stands in the Indian tradition of avatars (Sanskrit *avatara*, "descent") who incarnate divine consciousness on earth to "establish new pathways for religious realization" (Friedrichs, cited in Schuhmacher & Woerner, 1989, p. 25). There is a link here with Krishna in Hinduism. In the classical Indian epic *Mahabharata*, Lord Krishna is referred to as "the supreme, universal consciousness, as divine yet present … as unborn yet omnipresent" (Friedrichs, cited in Schuhmacher & Woerner, 1989, p. 185). In Greek, *Krishna* is always translated as *Christos*.

Radhakrishnan's *Eastern Religions and Western Thought* (1939/1989) is probably the foremost authority on the matter of cultural interfusions (especially in religion and philosophy) between East and West in the ancient world, although other works by other researchers are also important, such as that of Rawlinson (1992) and Basham (2000). All of this work is replete with examples of parallels, common sources, and lines of influence in the development of Western philosophical and religious formulations. And although Radhakrishnan warns against any simple theory of "borrowing" (as in *a* took from *b* to embellish its ideas about *c*), the work serves as an excellent reminder that until the fourth century C.E., movement back and forth between the Greek and Roman worlds and the various emissaries of (spiritual and intellectual, as well as material) trade from Asia was widespread. Roman historian Pliny referred to an Indian embassy that arrived in Rome during the reign of Claudius. The naming of various imported products—camphor, sulphur, beryl, opal, and so on—show the linguistic influence of India. Such theological constructs as "deification in Christ," which even today is the goal of Greek Orthodox practice, works from the ancient Hindu idea that the human soul is on a journey to direct union with the divine. Similarly, the Greek Orthodox *hesychiastic* tradition (from the Greek *hesychia*, "stillness"), emphasizing the achievement of tranquility and silence as the best means for realizing ultimate truth, clearly has a basis in the meditative traditions so common throughout Asia well before their appearance in the Mediterranean region.

The point is—and to state it here is to repeat it from before—all of this kind of cultural interfusion came to an end with the symbolic act of burning the Alexandrian library in 400 C.E. Henceforth, the religion of Europe fell under the banner of "Christ," but in that act, the nature of the Christ became sealed within a limited envelope of political culture. Even more unfortunate, that same limited envelope now took upon itself the claim to universality. The doctrine that "there is no salvation outside of the Church" was pronounced by the church's foremost theologian of the time, Augustine, and this inevitably came to mean that there is no salvation outside of Rome. Recognition of Christianity's deep roots in Asia became disallowed under a monolithic order of doctrine and practice sought for the consolidation, restoration, and sanctification of empire. Asia became the mystical Other to Rome's self-defined position of preeminence in the realm of divine understanding. As late as the 19th century, Europe's foremost philosopher, Hegel, could announce, "[With Europe] the idea of Christianity has reached its full realization. . . . Europe is absolutely the center and end of universal history. . . . [Europeans] are the carriers of the world spirit, and against that absolute right, the spirit of other peoples has no right" (as quoted in Dussel, 1995, pp. 20–42). It is not difficult to show how such ideas underwrote the European drive for global empire in the 19th century. In contemporary Western academies and departments of religious studies, most other religions are "-isms" (Buddhism, Hinduism, Taoism, etc.), whereas Christianity provides for itself, in its very name (Christianity), a privileged status.

Later I will trace out some of the ways that the West has in fact writhed under the burden of its own self-enclosure, with the East as Other providing relief for dedicated sojourners who have sought answers to European questions not resolvable from within the grammar of received tradition. Let it be noted that such attempts at serious interlocution with Asian wisdom have often met with derision even today (Cole, 2004; Žižek, 2001).

In the meantime I wish here to digress briefly to reexamine the history of East–West relations through the lens of new archeological evidence currently accumulating on a significant scale to suggest that the first "discoverers" of the (North and South) American landmass, as well as of major landfalls such as Australia and New Zealand, were not in fact the Europeans, but the Chinese. A few quick examples from the 1421 (n.d.) website:

- According to geneticists Gabriel and Corina Novick, the only people whose DNA appears on both sides of the Pacific Ocean, in the South American Incas and in the Maori of New Zealand, are the Chinese.
- The first Europeans to reach South America by rounding Cape Horn found wrecked Chinese junks.
- Father Antonio del Calancha, one of the first priests to arrive in South America, found native paintings of Chinese cavalry.
- Explorer Vasquez de Coronado found Chinese junks with gilded sterns off the coast of Peru.
- Professor Tulio Arends has analyzed blood samples from the Yupa Indians of western Venezuela to find elements found only in Chinese people.
- Cedric Bell of New Zealand has discovered the remains of a massive Chinese smelter operation on South Island, dating from the Song dynasty of the 10th century C.E.

Maori DNA from New Zealand's North Island shows that female (mitochondrial) DNA was that of the Chinese from Taiwan, whereas male (Y-chromosome) was Polynesian. This corroborates longstanding Maori stories that in about 1600 C.E. Polynesians from North Island invaded South Island, murdered "the Waitaha [Chinese] men," and took their women. This new research also supports that conducted in the 19th century that claimed that Buddhist monks traveled to the Americas as early as the fifth century C.E., that America is the land called *Fusang* in ancient Chinese texts, and that there are deep linguistic connections, such as in the name of the Maya people, after Queen Maya, the mother of Shakyamuni Buddha (Vining, 1885). Other work on this general theme can be found (e.g., Leland, 1875; Bruer, 1972; Mertz, 1972; Hobson, 2004).

What is important about this research concerns the difference that it makes to know it, and the answer has something to do with the imagination, especially for those of us enculturated within the Euro-American imaginary. Most fundamentally, this information disrupts the assumption of there being an evolutionary progression of European expansion throughout the world, a heraldic line from an Old World to a New World, and, in the context of contemporary American foreign policy, from a New World to a universalized American World. Instead of Europe being *the* bearer of civilization to the world, the new evidence underscores the reality of the world always having been inhabited by concurrent civilizations. This in turn invites a reconsideration of how the human world might now be imagined. No longer is the world simply a collection of lesser mortals awaiting Europe's truth—the logic of "development" still operating in all of the world's major development agencies such as the World Bank and the International Monetary Fund. Instead, the world can be imagined as a cast of peoples of different traditions and experience, all of whom possess civilizational practices of one kind or another, characterizable by greater or lesser degrees of success or failure, and who always participate within a global community in which every member can be held to a certain ethical accountability in relation to every other member. In a sense, such a view is resonant with the Buddhist understanding of interdependent coarising or "interorigination" (Nhat Hanh, 1988, p. 88). That is, whatever arises does so through a dense network of relations with others who simultaneously are being coproduced through that same network. This will be discussed further below; for now, it is on the point of ethics that it is instructive to examine the influence on European political philosophy of a Chinese figure such as Confucius.

The 16th through 18th centuries in Europe were tumultuous because of the religious wars of the Reformation. The Peace of Westphalia in 1649 marked the beginning of efforts to think about arrangements of social and political life in terms other than through the theological and monarchial referents that had determined things to that date and had been responsible for so much human slaughter in the previous half century. Euphoric dreams of a new Europe united around principles of rationality and secular morality were widespread, particularly through the writings of the French philosophes such as Michel Montaigne and Voltaire and the emerging movement later known as the Enlightenment. One of the most important yet conventionally unrecognized figures in all of this was the ancient Chinese sage Confucius (551–479 B.C.E.) and the school of Confucianism developed through his disciples such as Mencius and Hsun-Tzu. Confucian ideas had begun circulating in European intellectual circles through the diaries of Jesuit missionaries such as Matteo Ricci (1552–1610) and Francis Xavier (1506–1552), who in turn had traveled and labored in China, and India and Japan, respectively. The philosophes engaged Confucian ideas with great sympathy, and Confucius became known as "the Patron Saint of the Enlightenment" (Clarke, 1997, p. 42).

The debates between Ricci and the Confucian philosophers of his time (see Chidester, 2000, pp. 434–440) are interesting and currently relevant because they reveal, even at this early stage of serious East–West conversation, some of the stark differences in basic operating assumptions between Chinese philosophy and the European mind.

Ricci presented himself not as a man of religion, but of letters, to engage the Chinese literati on their own philosophical ground especially regarding questions of morality. He mastered the Chinese language and memorized the Confucian classics while working to replace the "natural religion" of China with the "revealed religion" of Christianity through his book *The True Meaning of the Doctrine of the Master of Heaven*. Ricci had high regard for Confucian ideas, writing, "'Of all the pagan nations that are known to our Europe, I know of none which has made fewer errors contrary to the things of Religion than the nation of China in its early Antiquity'" (as quoted in Chidester, 2000, p. 435). The stumbling blocks emerged for Confucian philosophers through Ricci's doctrine of Paradise and Hell and his emphasis on the right of the "Master of Heaven" to determine who would go to one place or the other. Said Xu Dashou:

The books of the Barbarians say:

[I]f you have done good throughout your life but have not made yourself agreeable to the Master of Heaven, all your goodness will have been in vain. If you have done evil all your life but for one single instant did make yourself agreeable to the Master of Heaven, all the evil you have done will immediately be absolved. ... The Master of Heaven is just a rogue ... inciting people to flatter him." (Quoted in Chidester, 2000, p. 438)

Such flattery was seen ultimately as a form of self-interest, which contradicted the Confucian emphasis on controlling personal desires to obey the principle of universal order, or *li*, with which harmony was to be maintained by observing ritual performances and moral propriety through filial piety and civic responsibility.

For the Confucian philosophers, the basic problem with the European manner of reasoning is that it is constructed through various forms of binary thinking. Ricci's Aristotelianism made distinctions between substance and accidents, cause and effect, the physical and the spiritual, and all of these kinds of categorizations were judged to get in the way of a more complex, organic, fluid, and interwoven understanding of the universe.

After 1620, Chinese scholars generally lost interest in Ricci, perceiving him as having distorted the traditional connection between personal morality and universal harmony. The Christian view was interpreted as disruptive of the social fabric, with faith in the absolute right of the divine over the human leading to political instability, as when people refuse to give absolute priority to the demands of the state. It can be argued that this is the point at which Confucian philosophy produces conservative culture. Historically in China and Japan, except for minor episodes, Christianity has never been supported by the state precisely because of its insurrectionary potential.

The leading European sinophile of the 17th century was undoubtedly Voltaire (1694–1778), who used the "natural philosophy" of Confucianism to challenge the authority and social control of the Catholic Church, which he argued ruled through superstition, flamboyant ritual, and institutions inherently corruptible because of their claim of divine appointment, positioning themselves beyond criticism. This interest in "natural philosophy" over the "revealed religion" of Europe became the cornerstone of the new rationalism that was spreading under the influence of the French *Encyclopedistes,* and also especially under the German philosopher Gottfried Wilhelm Leibniz (1646–1716). Leibniz's concept of the complementarity of opposites and his theory of monads in which all aspects of the universe mirror all others and act together harmoniously by nature clearly parallel the Chinese system of "correlative thinking" (Clarke, 1997, p. 47), with roots in not only Confucianism but also Buddhism and Taoism.

Leibniz was also part of a larger movement in Europe that sought a solution to religious and political strife in the possibility of a new universal language. Part of this effort involved seeking the first "pre-Babel" language, and because of its ideographic writing, Chinese was thought to be closer to nature than the original Hebrew of the biblical account, and hence closer to the first language, even to that of Adam. Early scientists such as Francis Bacon and John Webb (1668; as cited in Clarke, 1997, p. 47) in fact fully worked out their case in a book titled *An Historical Essay Endeavoring a Probability that the Language of the Empire of China is the Primitive Language.*

Part of the requirement of a new universal language was for a new universal system of knowledge, or science, and here Leibniz was profoundly influenced by the ancient Chinese text, the *I Ching,* which describes precise methods for understanding human action based on a complementary binary symbolism derived from broken and unbroken lines. From this, Leibniz developed a binary number system that in the 20th century became the template language of most computer operations and thus, following Leibniz's dream, has indeed become a kind of universal language, although not an unproblematic one. Leibniz's work was not translated into English until 1977, and this reflects a condition lamented by historian N. P. Jacobson: "[Leibniz] remains what history books in philosophy have chosen to ignore, the chief transmitter of Asian ideas into seventeenth century Europe" (as quoted in Clarke, 1997, p. 48). His indirect influence through the philosopher Christian Wolff on Immanuel Kant and the establishment of Reason as the foundation of a new secular Europe in the 18th century, including the theory of separation of Church and State that came to define the new America, cannot be underestimated.

A final note about the sinophilia of 17th century Europe can be directed to the work of the physiocrats, and especially the economist Francois Quesnay (1694–1774). *Physiocracy* means "government according to the natural order" (Thompson, 1995, p. 1030) and comes from the Greek *phusis*, "nature." In keeping with the spirit of his time, Quesnay developed his economic theory on the oriental principle of "natural philosophy" that we have been discussing (see Clarke 1997, p. 49). Against the mercantilists of his time, who believed that money (in the form of gold and silver) was the source of wealth, Quesnay argued that a nation's wealth came ultimately from the land and agriculture and that full realization of this wealth depended upon the freeing of producers from government interference so that the "natural laws" of commerce could operate freely. This idea of course became the foundation of Adam Smith's theory of laissez-faire market economics, published at the end of the American War of Independence (1775), whose influence is still dominant in the economic theory of the present time, especially its neoliberal versions. Again, the oriental origins of this theory are ironic given the current ascendancy of China to global economic power (Frank, 1998).

For various reasons, Europe's love affair with China had eroded by the end of the 18th century, based as such an affair was on secondhand accounts only, and documentary evidence rather than actual experience of China. When this was coupled with the emerging spirit of democracy in Europe that celebrated the power of the common people to challenge despotic religious and political authority, well, China's reputation simply could not withstand the recognition of its own comparable corruption through the abuses of Confucianism and the oppression of the average person under strict codes of obedient behavior. Europe thus turned instead to the concept of the Noble Savage for its ideal, and to the Romantic movement of Jean-Jacques Rousseau. In the 19th century, reaction against the excessive rationalism of the Enlightenment found inspiration no longer in China but rather in India, precipitated by the arrival in Europe, as a consequence of British and French commercial venturing on the Indian subcontinent, of ancient Sanskrit texts such as the *Upanishads* and the *Bhagavad Gita*.

The term *oriental renaissance* was coined in 1803 by German philosopher Friedrich Schlegel. Along with other Romantics, Schlegel was concerned with finding an alternative to European obsessions with rational progress and technocratic science. As historian Raymond Schwab (1984) has suggested, the coincidental arising of romanticism and the orientalism in the 19th century was not just coincidence, nor was it unique historically. In fact, the coincidence reflects a pattern notable throughout European history, whenever 'technical rationality' (for want of a better term), with its preoccupations with management and control, has assumed inordinate cultural dominance. As early as the second century C.E., "'the vogue of oriental prophets'" (Jean Filliozat; as quoted in Schwab, 1984, p. 254) arose to support the mystical knowledge of gnosticism against Greek rationalism, and more recent eruptions of interest in the East have occurred in the West in the 1920s, the 1960s, and again today as a reaction against the hypermaterialism that technical rationality produces especially through its face of economism. Schwab suggested that this pattern reflects "an oriental irruption of the intellect" (p. 248)—in contemporary parlance, a refusal of the right brain to be severed from the left.

Following Rousseau's quest for the Noble Savage—that is, for an earlier form of humanity unpolluted by what the European imagination had conceived it to be—the 19th-century orientalists became convinced that India contained the secret of an original, universal religion that could unify and save humankind. Texts such as N. A. Notovitch's *The Unknown Life of Jesus Christ* (1834/1990) claimed that Christianity originated in India, with Jesus mentored there by Brahmins and Buddhist monks before beginning his own teaching career. Sir Edwin Arnold's (1884) *The Light of Asia*, a Romantic retelling of the life of Siddhartha Gautama, was instrumental in the creation of British Victorian manners and the character of the ideal gentleman as detached but benevolent, upright, truthful, and replete with manly fortitude. Linguistically, the discovery and recognition of the common roots of Indian and European languages severely undermined the myth of Europe's origins being in Greece, Rome, and Palestine. Under the influence of a certain Comte de Gobineau (see Batchelor, 1994, pp. 266–67), the search for a pure origin in India also led to the philosophy of Aryanism (from Sanskrit *arya*, "noble"), named after a prehistoric people who had settled in Iran and northern India, and regarded by Gobineau as responsible for all the progress of humankind. Gobineau defined Aryans as people who spoke Indo-European languages, who were morally superior to "Semites," "yellows," and "blacks," and regarded the Nordic or Germanic peoples as the purest Aryans. The 20th-century horrors inspired by this idea need no elaboration here.

The point is that the 19th century saw the beginning of the collapse of the sense of univocal uniqueness, indeed supremacy, of the Eurocentric self-definition that had been in place and protected against "Others" since the fourth century. Indeed, it can be said that the postmodern imagination comes into being not in the late 20th century, but the early 19th. As Buddhist historian Stephen Batchelor (1994) puts it, "For the first time in its history, Europe ignored the Greek prohibition against barbarism and overcame the Christian fear of idolatry to discover that there were other civilizations that had the power to question her" (pp. 252–253).

The 19th century also produced an interesting cast of European characters and visionaries whose work, imbued with Romantic orientalist sensibilities, established much of the psychic and cognitive infrastructure for the occidental imagination of the 20th century. The Theosophists, formed by American Colonel Henry Steel Olcott and the Russian noblewoman Helena Blavatsky, claimed to have discovered in a secret location in Tibet (one of the few remaining countries at the time still unexplored by Europeans) an ancient tradition of wisdom underlying all religious manifestations throughout the world. Their goal of establishing the Universal Brotherhood of Humanity foreshadowed later secular universalist organizations such as the League of Nations and the United Nations. Dutch painter Vincent van Gogh was deeply inspired by the woodblock prints of Japanese Zen artist Hokusai: "'We see a man ... who spends his time doing what? In studying the distance between the earth and the moon? No. In studying Bismarck's policy? No. He studies a blade of grass'" (as quoted in Batchelor, 1994, p. 262). This marks an appreciation of what can be identified as a new kind of "meditative sensibility" that found later expression, for example, in Dutch phenomenology.

Of special relevance for the 20th century are the works of philosophers Arthur Schopenhauer (1788–1860) and Friedrich Nietzsche (1844–1900). Schopenhauer's importance lies in his acknowledgement of the Buddhist influences in the work of his philosophical forebear Immanuel Kant, still the most influential shadow in contemporary philosophy. On Schopenhauer's study desk was a bust of Kant and a statue of the Buddha. Kant's (1781/1999) *Critique of Pure Reason* was seen to contain the Buddhist insight that reasoning alone, as a kind of pure analytic logic in the Greek sense, was futile for arriving at truth. Instead, what was necessary was linking the structures of consciousness, through perception, with the structures of the external world; that is, *how* I think is identical with how the world is *already* structured, and the aim of thinking, or reason, is to reveal that coextension and live on the basis of it. Of course, contemporary philosophers such as Enrique Dussel (1995, 1996) have shown how this philosophy is exactly what produces and sustains empire, because there is a conflation of one's own thinking about the world with its fuller (and hence largely unknowable) nature. This issue has been a persistent problem for Buddhism in, for example, the appropriation of Zen meditation by imperial Samurai culture in Japan. In such a system, meditation aids the ability to kill more effortlessly because the killing procedures are coextensive with the way life itself proceeds (see King, 1993; Loy, 2003; Victoria, 1997). Kantianism, as a distortion of deeper Buddhist realizations, is also a problem inherent in various contemporary philosophies of ecology whereby my own self-understandings are conflated with a projected understanding of the natural world: I am like the world; therefore the world is like me. Such a view easily evolves into a failing appreciation of the complexity of the Other and others' lives and the production of a highly selective form of consciousness.

In *The World as Will and Representation*, Schopenhauer (1818/1966) seeks to advance the Kantian position by again invoking a Buddhist position, this time from the philosopher Shantideva of the eighth century C.E. Appropriating the Buddhist concept of *Dharma*, a comprehensive term describing that which sustains our essential being (from Sanskrit; literally, "holding, carrying"), Schopenhauer suggests that life is driven by a blind and aimless energy that he calls *Will*. Because this will is unknowable as a thing in itself, but only through the phenomenon that it brought into being, people often confuse the phenomenon in its temporal and spatial manifestations with what it "represents." This results in endless striving for goals that are inherently unattainable: if I fall completely in love with *this* person, place, or thing, I am doomed to disappointment as the deep energy (will) of life produces infinite change and transience. Striving, or, in Buddhist language, *desire*, is therefore a form of delusion that, Schopenhauer suggests, is remediable only through contemplation of music, art, and—ultimately—mystical intuition. The fact that Schopenhauer would not sit in silent meditation but only listen to music signifies the way that his own philosophical project was profoundly constrained within his own cultural ambience, for as ethnomusicologist Stephen Feld (1990) has shown, sound structure is always related to social structure.

Nietzsche is important as both a prophet and a philosophical prefigure of much of what has transpired in the 20th century. The son of a Lutheran pastor, Nietzsche was convinced that deep within the psychic habit of Christianity was "an overwhelming desire to do harm, to discharge an inner tension in hostile actions and ideas" (1895/1968, p. 142). Like others of his time, he turned to Buddhism as a means of discrediting his inherited religion. Especially valued by Nietzsche is Buddhism's refusal of the God concept: "[In Buddhism] the concept 'God' is already abolished by the time it arrives" (p. 139). Furthermore, declares Nietzsche, "Buddhism is a religion for the end and fatigue of a civilization" (p. 142). Unfortunately, such views were also linked to the incipient nihilism of Nietzsche's interpretation of the European tradition.

At the age of 21 Nietzsche read Schopenhauer's *The World as Will and Representation,* and although he agreed with the idea of the primacy of the will, he extended this to mean the *will to power,* an idea originally articulated in the work of the pre-Socratic philosophers of ancient Greece and also became "the evolutionary drive behind [Charles] Darwin's survival of the fittest" (Batchelor, 1994, p. 264). The theory of the will to power allowed Nietzsche to project his work beyond the sentimental nostalgia of Romantic orientalism onto the prospect of a new kind of future superhuman, or *Übermensch.*

Both Schopenhauer and Nietzsche contributed to, again unfortunately for the tradition of Buddhism that they selectively drew upon, the rising cause of German nationalism in the 20th century. As Batchelor (1994) expresses it, their work, along with that of orientalist Romantics such as Schlegel, "gave the Germans an opportunity to counter the Latin bias of the Renaissance by claiming as their own an even earlier antiquity than that of Greece and Rome" (pp. 266–267). When this was allied to the new "Aryan philosophy," the conceptual stage was set for "an unprecedented eruption of violence from within the European psyche" (p. 267).

The convening of the first World Parliament of Religions in Chicago in 1893 marked the first time in the human story of an attempt by leaders of all of the world's religious traditions, East and West, to address each other. It signified an extension of the earlier Romantic hope for some form of universal human understanding now to be informed by better appreciation of religious experience and meaning. This parliament still continues to meet, most recently in Barcelona in 2004. Of course it was, and continues to be, an effort underwritten by certain largely Western prejudices, such as the very desirability of such a conversation (to know the Other more deeply also enables better "management" of the human space) or even its necessity (which assumes that nondialogic religion, or fundamentalism, is an impediment to "progress"), as well as its very possibility under the auspices of some theory of universal communication, which is the prejudice of Western science. Of course, as we have seen, even this prejudice of science owes more than a little something to Asia and the tradition of natural law extending from Buddhist, Confucian, and Taoist insights.

What may be the most significant development of all in the contemporary context is a new convergence of Western science and Eastern religion. This convergence may mark what was identified at the opening of this chapter as a completing of a circle in the Western imaginary, a kind of homecoming. The convergence is articulated in what is sometimes described as the "New Physics" (Capra, 2000, 2004), or post-Einsteinian quantum theory (Bohm, 1989; Heisenberg, 1938), as well as the philosophy of "Deep Ecology" (Devall, 1985; Naess, 1990) and the new ecology-based theories of human cognition (Bateson, 2000; Maturana and Varela 1991, Varela, Thompson, & Rosch, 1992) and economics (Schumacher, 1989). All of this science either parallels or explicitly draws upon insights central to Asian wisdom. Specifically, there are:

- A refusal of the Aristotelian basis of Western knowledge whereby things are known best through their separateness from other things, an assumption that inspires the Western theory of identity; instead, everything is accepted as being inseparable from, interconnected with, and hence implicated in everything else.
- An abandonment of the (Newtonian) 17th-century understanding of the universe as operating according to principles of mechanics, and an appreciation of life as being in a constant state of flux and ultimately therefore indeterminate, knowable only as now rather than future or past.
- An acceptance that all of Life is a unitary condition, in which human beings are fully participant in spite of any self-conscious presumption otherwise; the conventional Western dualism of world-as-object to human-as-subject is taken as impossible as well as delusional.
- A belief that everything in life is self-organizing and coconstructive— that is, everything is constructed through every other thing, and what happens to one somehow influences what happens to everything else in a movement of constant adaptation and change.

It can be easily noted that much of what is discussed in this new scientific literature has its analogues in formal philosophical work of the late 20th century, especially that of postmodern theory and deconstructionism. Jacques Derrida's (1980) understanding of identity as always arising through a relation of deferral and difference is a case in point, as is the insight that every form of presence contains an absence, and every absence a presence. What is interesting about much of the negative response to this work in the West (e.g., Groothuis, 2000) is its seeming inhabitation by a (Greek) sense of the tragic, or of loss—a painful difficulty in accepting that an earlier innocence about what it means to be human is gone forever, or, more accurately, now increasingly invisible and submerged by a newer understanding of reality. Of course, in the new paradigm nothing is actually "gone forever," for there is no exteriority to which it could be banished and literally extinguished and forgotten. No, everything is always everywhere already present, but whether or not it is in evidence is a matter of mind and perception conditioned by culture and politics.

In closing this section, I simply note that other work examining specifically Asian influences, parallels, and points of engagement in contemporary philosophy has been well supported through the efforts of the East–West Center in Hawaii and its journal *Philosophy East and West*. David Loy (2002, 2003) is a preeminent scholar who has linked Buddhist and contemporary Western philosophy.

Issues and Prospects for East–West Engagement and Educational Theory

The brief narrative history above suffers from the same limitation of all narratives, which is that in the name of clarifying a subject through a tidy rendering, the real messiness and complexity of life become obscured. Also, there is the issue of inclusion/exclusion, of why *this* was included and not *that*, which is largely a question of a narrative writer's own fundamental predispositions and background assumptions. In my own case a number of factors are involved. The most important is probably the fact stated at the outset that I was born in China. But I also grew up in Central Africa before coming to the West (Canada) as a teenager. So my deepest sensibilities are inevitably tuned to efforts of integrating the tensions of cultural differences in the unity of my own person. I don't want to have to choose among China, Africa, and Canada; these are all "in" me already, and to try to define any one as more "choosable" than the other diminishes my own lived sense of value of each. Any effort to define which tradition might be best over all others can only be a political move, surely, and contrary to the real needs of the times.

Another important influence is the work of Argentine philosopher Enrique Dussel (1995, 1996), now exiled in Mexico, whose powerful deconstruction of Western modernity (Euro-America since 1492) reveals the multiple ways that the basic operating paradigms of the Western tradition act according to a two-sided myth. The surface side is the myth of emancipative reason qua Kant paraphrasable as "Through our constructs of Reason, we are the carriers and defenders of liberty for the world," whereas the underside is the myth of sacrifice paraphrasable as "All those who do not comply with our myth of liberty, underwritten by reason, we have the right to destroy, either directly through military and colonial conquest or through strategies of exclusion, silencing, and denial." Dussel argues that in the contemporary context, it is the voices from the second myth that need to be brought to the table of deliberation regarding human futures; hence my interest in showing the interlocutionary character of East–West engagement from Europe's early beginnings.

The third factor pertains to the issue identified in the first section of this chapter: the deep phenomenology of exclusion in the heart of the Euro-American tradition, linked to its Christian roots, even as they have been expressed most recently in the preliminary version of the new *Draft Treaty Establishing a Constitution for Europe* in whose preamble Europe is self-described as a "Christian civilization"—a thinly veiled caveat to Turkey, perhaps, which is now seeking entrance into the Eurpean Union (Preamble, 2003). (This was later edited to read that Europe "brought forth civilization.") In the United States, the recent powerful resurgence of conservative Christian evangelicalism as a political force denying the ultimate validity of all other forms of religious expression is also a case in point. Recent biblical scholarship, however (Borg, 2002; Crossan, 1994; Harpur, 2004; Mack, 2001), has suggested that the politics of exclusion were precisely *not* what defined the earliest Christian communities, and that instead they were characterized by what Crossan has called "open commensality," or open sharing of meals and community life with strangers and others outside of the received tradition. This means that the politics of exclusion in the Western tradition needs to be carefully reexamined. Also, it should be recognized that an Asian interpretation would not render the full meaning of openness through a binary, such as closedness or exclusivity, because openness also means being open to the necessity, at times, for boundaries. This question is too big to consider in depth here, except to say that the meaning of the term *openness* is a critical one for an interlocutionary age.

What I have attempted to do in the brief foregoing narrative is to show that *in spite of* the exclusionary disposition of Euro-American sensibility, an engagement between East and West has *always already* been in effect for over 2,000 years, that most of the operating assumptions of the West are *already* inhabited by Asian influences, and that those who persistently criticize occidental interest in things oriental merely contribute to a logic of denial that itself is a denial of the West's own history. It needs to be recognized that such criticisms continue to be loud, frequent, and vociferous. Christian theologian Harvey Cox (1977) has argued that the East is nothing but a "myth that resides in the head of Westerners ... a convenient screen on which the West projects reverse images of its own deficiencies" (p. 149). Philosopher C. S. Peirce once referred to "the monstrous mysticism of the East" (as quoted in Clarke, 1997, p. 197). Writer Arthur Koestler, in *The Lotus and the Robot* (1960), has discussed the "logical monstrosities" of India, with its "indifference to contradiction" (pp. 49–50). Further, he posits, "India, with all its saintly longings for samadhi, has no spiritual cure to offer for the needs of Western civilization" (p. 162). Contemporary philosopher Slavoj Žižek (2001) has criticized Western interests in Buddhism as a symptom of late capitalism, with Buddhism offering both a palliative for and means of denial of the reality of the current crises within capitalism. British Marxist educator Mike Cole (2004) calls recent efforts at articulating the relevance of Buddhist insights for educators "hopelessly romantic" (p. 640). Again, such comments reveal an ignorance of intellectual and cultural ancestry and constitute a denial of the ghosts in the collective unconscious.

Still, in terms of prospects for what Pasha and Samatar (1996) have called "intercivilizational dialogue" (p. 200) between East and West, huge issues remain to be addressed, and here I name only a few. One concerns the sheer immensity of what is involved in even naming *East* and *West* as traditions, and facile use of the terms does disservice to the deep complexity of each. Even to call the West *Christian* deflects attention from the multidimensionality of what this might mean in actual practice, to say nothing of the multiple ways in which the world is now largely a "post-Christendom" phenomenon, American Protestant evangelicalism notwithstanding. The enormous complexity and diversity of religious traditions in Asia needs no further enunciation here either.

In the event that educators' and curriculum developers' wish to engage the East–West conversation as part of the consideration for "teaching in global times" (Smith, 2003), a serious question is "Where do I begin?" A visit to any bookstore will quickly reveal a dizzying array of titles on hosts of different topics in the field, many from a comparative religion perspective, others attempting to proselytize, some offered as forms of psychotherapeutics, along with many translations of ancient texts. A key point is that none of this should be taken as an invitation to conversion, as if one could simply abandon one's own tradition and take up another, like a new coat or pair of shoes. As Radhakrishnan (1939/1989) has suggested, conversion is a form of suicide (p. 149), a kind of psychological switch-flipping that can have devastating consequences both for the converter and for his or her abandoned and found communities. Besides, the issue today is not simply a matter of making pure choices for one tradition over another, which is psychologically and conceptually impossible anyway given that there is no such thing as a "pure" tradition. The real challenge is to face the truth that no one tradition can say everything that needs to be said about the full expression of human experience in the world and that what the global community requires, more than anything else, is mutual recognition of the various poverties of *every* tradition, now revealed by globalization in unprecedented ways and in new degrees.

The search to cure the poverty of one's own tradition clearly works in all directions at once. Students in Asia look to the West, often romantically and idealistically, to cure the pain of the lack of basic freedoms they may perceive that they suffer in their homelands. Western young people find in the Asian traditions of inner cultivation and meditative sensibility deep relief from the hyperactivism and personal striving that are celebrated as virtues within capitalist culture. None of these moves requires conversion in the usual sense, but instead a simple new openness to that which lies beyond one's current understanding of things and then taking up the work of integrating it creatively into one's prior practice. Once this journey has begun, then the work of deepening understanding of Others can follow, with reading and study producing not repudiation but wisdom.

In the entire discussion of East–West engagement, it is important to acknowledge that vastly different axiological assumptions lie at the heart of it and that these differences cannot simply be woven into some new tapestry of globalized consensus. Neither, on the other hand, in a globalizing world is it enough simply to "let differences be" as if there could never be any points of address between them. As mentioned at the outset of this chapter, if globalization means anything beyond the parochial Euro-American vision of economic integration, it has something to do with unprecedented experiences of human "encounter" and the great possibilities that these hold for an emerging sense of globalized community no longer binarized by those policies of inclusion/exclusion that continue to control the minds of those controlling the systems of global power.

To illustrate an example of "difference" that cannot be easily entertained in the Western imaginary, followed by an example of how a new hermeneutic of understanding might ensue, I offer the following statement from a contemporary Vedantist philosopher in India, Swami Atmaswarupananda (2001):

> The scriptures and the great spiritual masters tell us that our central problem
> is desire. So, if we are still trying to attain something new, even if it is God-

realization, we are not changing our desire nature at all. The true purpose of the spiritual life is a dropping away of that which constantly wants something new, something else. It is not bringing something new into our consciousness that we need, as much as getting down to the root of it. (p. 3)

Clearly, this indictment of desire so central to both Hindu and Buddhist understanding runs counter to almost every intuition and virtue that Western "civilization" might ascribe to itself. In the West the very desire to fulfill desire is the inspiration for art, is the muse of love, represents the anticipation of heaven, and is the foundation of enterprise. Without desire, and the anticipation of its future fulfillment, can life be said to be "worth" living at all? Neoliberal economists would argue, How can poverty in Africa be overcome without the creation of desire?—of course, without being willing to put up for challenge their own interpretation of what people actually need to live well, nor being willing to face the fact that it has been precisely Euro-American economic policies based on desire that have created poverty in Africa since the beginning of the colonial period in the 16th century (Rodney, 1981).

What is interesting about Swami Atmaswarupananda concerns his birth name and the fact that his statement above has a story behind it that is relevant to the full discussion of this chapter, and indeed the entire book. Swami's original name was Bill Winford,[1] and for 20 years he worked as an investment advisor for one of Canada's most prestigious brokerage houses. A devout Christian, in his 40s he had to have two-thirds of his stomach removed because of chronic ulceration caused by stress and worry. One day during lunch at a large downtown hotel in Vancouver, he noticed that a certain Swami Provenanda from India was giving a series of evening lectures at the hotel on the subject of mind and consciousness. Bill attended the lectures, and he and the swami became friends. After a year of study, Bill moved to the swami's ashram in northern India, where he has lived for the last 40 years and is now a teacher.

Two things about his written oeuvre are interesting. One is that, probably in spite of himself, his hermeneutic of the Vedantic tradition is still imbued with an elemental Christian consciousness, giving evidence of Radhakrishnan's (1939/1989) theory about the improbabilities of conversion, and the more healthy labor of constantly reworking one's own tradition in the light of new evidence and experience. The second thing relates to Atmaswarupananda's quotation on *desire*, above, now understandable as written by a person who had a career *managing* desire—not just his own, but also that of others—and now, after more than 40 years, has come to see its futility as a raw form. Of course, in terms of Vedantic theology, as well as Buddhist and Taoist philosophy, to desire to put an end to desire only extends desire and thus is not the point. Instead, the challenge is to *see* desire for what it is, a product of mind susceptible to infinite chains of suggestibility that need to be carefully deconstructed and monitored so that one does not spend one's life chasing phantasms that are incapable of being realized (made real) in any meaningful sense. To be free of desire, therefore, is not to eliminate it (which is impossible) but to no longer be enslaved by it. There is a time for desire and a time to put desire to rest, and to know the difference is the basis of wisdom and true freedom. It is not difficult to see how such an understanding contradicts the fundamental requirements of consumerist cultures, thereby also announcing that wisdom traditions are inexorably political.

Getting down to "the root of consciousness," as Atmaswarupananda (2001) has suggested, has its own requirements, the most important being the cultivation of what can be termed *meditative sensibility*, and it is on this point that I believe the most profound point of convergence in East–West engagement can be achieved. Meditation is not only a central practice— perhaps *the* central practice—within Buddhism, Hinduism, Taoism, and, indirectly, Confucianism; in various ways it also is central especially in the mystical traditions of the great monotheistic expressions of religious experience. Of course, as we have seen, it can suffer abuses, particularly when used as a technique to perfect psychological readiness in the service of limited nationalistic or other political goals. This, however, has little to do with meditation's primary purpose, which the great Thai teacher Ajahn Chah (1982) articulated some years ago: "Meditation is the way of developing the mind so that it may be a base for the arising of wisdom" (p. 20). Notice that the purpose of cultivating the mind is not to produce yet more knowledge—for example, to feed the insatiable demands of "the New Knowledge Economy" (Peters & Humes, 2003)—but precisely to produce the capacity to discern and judge the true nature of that economy within the real economy of actual human requirements. Such is the practice of wisdom, and any suggestion that meditation is a flight from the "real world" has already lost sight of what a fuller notion of the "real" might actually involve.

For a concrete example of how teaching might be explored as a practice of wisdom, I refer to a graduate seminar I currently conduct at the University of Alberta titled "Teaching as the Practice of Wisdom." The course is organized around the theme of *Encounter*—seeing the practice of teaching as a constant and unfolding series of encounters that invite consideration of one's own and one's students' assumptions about how life is best lived, a kind of call to wisdom and maturity. This is true whether the encounter is with a formal curricular text or with another person, in the classroom, the hallway, the staff room, or the playground. Explorations of examples of daily encounters are refracted through weekly readings of Aboriginal, Buddhist, Confucian, Sufi, and Taoist literature, as well as the wisdom literature from the Bible (Job, Proverbs, Ecclesiastes). Every class begins with simply sitting together in silence for 10 minutes, itself a practice that nicely interrupts the hyperverbalism so characteristic of graduate seminars in Western academies. One overwhelming result of these practices, and especially the practice of silence, is the emerging awareness that so many of the pedagogical problems that preoccupy us as teachers can be, and in fact need to be, reinterpreted. Meditation makes possible the ability to "see" so many of the problems for what they are—struggles for power; defense of one's own predetermined teacherly identity; students' agony over the endless hours, indeed years, spent fulfilling other people's requirements; symptomatic of our mutual and sublimated addiction to consumerist fantasies that can never be satisfied, producing all those unconscious forms of self-hatred well understood within the symptomatology of addiction; and so on. In short, meditation affords the possibility of seeing and naming what is going on in the pedagogical situation *for what it is*, not for what it is supposed to be according to the hyperbolized prescriptions of state and nation, or even according to the prescriptions and registers of psychology and formal philosophy. This gaining of the freedom to see the world as it actually is is the deepest meaning of *wisdom*, such that the gaining of wisdom is in fact the mark of true liberty (Trungpa, 1988). Of course, as Confucius might have said, "Anyone who thinks they are wise, isn't" (Lau, 1998, p. 21), a reminder that wisdom is not simply a skill or a commodity to be acquired for an anterior purpose so that one can self-consciously declaim it. Instead, wisdom is known chiefly through its most mature characteristics, which are compassion and generosity, and which arise consistently through the emerging awareness of one's own mortality and the endless revelation of one's own laughable propensity for human foolishness.

In closing, I turn again to a claim made at the beginning of this chapter that to begin a journey can mark the beginning of a homecoming. This can now be read in reference to Hobson's (2004) earlier suggestion that the Western tradition is inhabited by a "logic of immanence" (p. 3). Hobson meant to address the sense of self-containment by which the West has perpetually kept at bay its debts to all those traditions through which it has constructed itself.

May this chapter serve the purpose of revealing another meaning of *immanence*, which relates to the manner of mutual "indwelling" (Thompson, 1995, p. 678) now better understandable as characterizing virtually everything we do and say as human beings. Whether we live or whether we die as a species, we live or die together.

Note

1. Swami Atmaswarupananda is a personal acquaintance of the author. The names used in this discussion—Bill Winford and Swami Provenanda—are pseudonyms.

References

Abu-Lughod, L. (1989). *Before European hegemony*. Oxford, England: Oxford University Press.

Amin, S. (2003). *Obsolescent capitalism*. London: Zed Books.

Amore, R. (1985). *Two masters, one message: The lives and teaching of Gautama and Jesus*. New York: Abingdon.

Arnold, E. (1884). *The light of Asia*. New York: Crowell.

Atmaswarupananda, S. (2001). *Trust God: Early morning meditation talks*. Shivanandanagar, India: Divine Life Society.

Basham, A. (2000). *The wonder that was India*. Delhi, India: South Asia Books.

Batchelor, S. (1994). *The awakening of the West: The encounter of Buddhism and Western culture*. Berkeley, CA: Parallax Press.

Bateson, G. (2000). *Steps to an ecology of mind*. Chicago: University of Chicago Press.

Beaud, M. (2001). *A history of capitalism: 1500–2000* (T. Dickman and A. Lefebvre, Trans.). New York: Monthly Review Press.

Bohm, D. (1989). *Quantum theory*. London: Dover.

Borg, M. (2002). *Reading the Bible again for the first time: Taking the Bible seriously but not literally*. San Francisco: HarperSanFrancisco.

Bruer, H. (1972). *Columbus was Chinese: Discoveries and inventions of the Far East*. New York: Herder and Herder.

Capra, F. (2000). *The Tao of physics*. Boston: Shambhala.

Capra, F. (2004). *The hidden connections: A science for sustainable living*. New York: Anchor.

Chah, A. (1982). *Bodhinyana: A collection of Dhamma talks*. Redwood Valley, CA: Abhayagiri Monastery.

Chandler, D. (2002). *Worldwide and U.S. storage services*. New York: IDC Research.

Chaudhuri, K. (1990). *Asia before Europe: Economy and civilization of the Indian ocean from the rise of Islam to 1750*. Cambridge, England: Cambridge University Press.

Chidester, D. (2000). *Christianity: A global history*. San Francisco: HarperSanFrancisco.

Clarke, J. (1997). *Oriental enlightenment: The encounter between Asian and Western thought*. New York: Routledge.

Cole, M. (2004). U.S. imperialism, transmodernism, and education: A Marxist critique. *Policy Futures in Education, 2*(3–4), 633-643.

Cox, H. (1977). *Turning East: The promise and peril of the new orientalism*. New York: Simon and Schuster.

Crossan, D. (1994). *Jesus: A revolutionary biography*. New York: HarperCollins.

Derrida, J. (1980). *Writing and difference* (A. Bass, Trans.). Chicago: University of Chicago Press.

Devall, W. (1985). *Deep ecology.* London: Gibbs Smith.

Dussel, E. (1995). *The invention of the Americas: Eclipse of the 'the other' and the myth of modernity* (M. Barber, Trans.). New York: Continuum.

Dussel, E. (1996). *The underside of modernity: Apel, Ricoeur, Rorty, Taylor, and the philosophy of liberation* (E. Mendieta, Ed. and Trans.). Atlantic Highlands, NJ: Humanities Press.

Feld, S. (1990). *Sound and sentiment.* Philadelphia: University of Pennsylvania Press.

Fernandez-Armesto, F. (1996). *Millenium.* London: Black Swan Books.

Fields, R. (1981). *How the swans came to the lake: A narrative history of Buddhism in America.* Boston: Shambhala.

Fischer-Schrieber, I. (1989). Ashoka. In S. Schumacher & G. Woerner (Eds.), *The encyclopedia of Eastern philosophy and religion* (pp. 19–20). Boston: Shambhala.

1421. (n.d.). *The year the Chinese discovered the world.* Retrieved November, 4, 2005, from http://www.1421.tv/pages/content/index.asp?PageID=89.

Frank, A. (1998). *ReOrient: Global economy in the Asian age.* Berkeley, CA: University of California Press.

Friedrichs, K. (1989). Krishna. In S. Schumacher & G. Woerner (Eds.), *The encyclopedia of Eastern philosophy and religion* (p. 185). Boston: Shambhala.

Gard, M. (2005). *The obesity epidemic: Science, morality, and ideology.* New York: Routledge.

Groothuis, D. (2000). *Truth decay: Defending Christianity against the challenges of postmodernism.* Los Angeles: Intervarsity Press.

Guo, Y. (2002). *Chinese translation of the West: A history for a global era.* Unpublished doctoral dissertation, University of Alberta, Edmonton, Alberta, Canada.

Halper, S., & Clarke, J. (2004). *America alone: The neo-conservatives and the global order.* Cambridge, England: Cambridge University Press.

Hammond, N. (2003). The kingdom of Asia and the Persian throne. In I. Worthington (Ed.), *Alexander the Great: A reader* (pp. 136–147). London: Routledge.

Harpur, T. (2004). *The pagan Christ: Recovering the lost light.* Toronto, Ontario: Thomas Allen.

Hays, R. (1997). Charting security's management. *Security Management, 41*(4), 22–24.

Heisenberg, W. (1938). *Physical principles of the quantum theory.* London: Dover.

Hobson, J. (2004). *The Eastern origins of Western civilization.* Cambridge, England: Cambridge University Press.

Hodgson, M. (1993). *Re-thinking world history* (E. Burke III, Ed.). Cambridge, England: Cambridge University Press.

Kant, I. (1999). *The critique of pure reason* (P. Guyer and A. Wood, Trans. & Eds.). Cambridge, England: Cambridge University Press. (Original work published 1781)

King, W. (1993). *Zen and the way of the sword: Arming the samurai psyche.* New York: Oxford University Press.

Koestler, A. (1960). *The lotus and the robot.* London: Hutchinson.

Kuttner, R. (1999). *Everything for sale: The virtues and limits of markets.* New York: Knopf.

Lau, D. C. (Ed.). (1998). *Confucius: The analects.* Harmondsworth, England: Penguin.

Leland, C. (1875). *Fusang, or the discovery of America by Chinese Buddhists priests in the fifth century.* London: Traubner.

Loy, D. (2002). *A Buddhist history of the West: Studies in lack.* Albany: State University of New York Press.

Loy, D. (2003). *The great awakening: A Buddhist social theory.* Boston: Wisdom.

Mack, B. (2001). *The Christian myth: Origins, logic, and legacy.* New York: Continuum.

Maturana, H., & Varela, F. (1991). *Autopoesis and cognition: The realization of the living.* New York: Springer.

McMurtry, J. (1998). *Unequal freedoms: The global market as an ethical system*. Toronto, Ontario: Garamond Press.

Mertz, H. (1972). *Pale ink: Two ancient records of Chinese exploration in America*. Chicago: Swallow Press.

Naess, A. (1990). *Ecology, community, and lifestyle: Outline of an ecosophy*. Cambridge, England: Cambridge University Press.

Nhat Hanh, T. (1988). *The sun, my heart: From mindfulness meditation to insight*. Berkeley, CA: Parallax Press.

Nietzsche, F. (1968). *Twilight of the idols and the Anti-Christ*. Oxford, England: Oxford University Press. (Original work published 1895)

Notovitch, N. (1990). *The unknown life of Jesus Christ*. London: Leaves of Healing. (Original work published 1834)

Pasha, M., & Samatar A. (1996). The resurgence of Islam. In J. Mittelman (Ed.), *Globalization: Critical reflections* (pp. 187–201). London: Lynne Rienner.

Payer, L. (1988). *Medicine and culture*. New York: Penguin.

Peters, M., & Humes, W. (2003). Education in the knowledge economy. *Policy Futures in Education, 1*(1), 1–5.

Preamble (2003). *Preamble, Draft treaty establishing a Constitution for Europe*. Retrieved January 7, 2006, from http://europa.eu.int/constitution/futurum/constitution/preamble/index_en.htm (now defunct).

Radhakrishnan, S. (1989). *Eastern religions and Western thought*. London: Oxford University Press. (Original work published 1939)

Rawlinson, H. (1992). *Intercourse between India and the Western world: From the earliest times to the fall of Rome*. Delhi, India: South Asia Books.

Riley, G. (2000). *One Jesus, many Christs*. Minneapolis, MN: Fortress Press.

Rodney, W. (1981). *How Europe underdeveloped Africa*. Washington, DC: Howard University Press.

Roszak, T. (1994). *The cult of information*. Berkeley, CA: University of California Press.

Schopenhauer, A. (1966). *The world as will and representation* (E. F. J. Payne, Trans.). London: Dover. (Original work published 1818).

Schuhmacher, S., & Woerner, G. (Eds.). (1989). *The encyclopedia of Eastern philosophy and religion*. Boston: Shambhala.

Schumacher, E. (1989). *Small is beautiful: Economics as if people mattered*. San Francisco: Harper Perennial.

Schwab, R. (1984). *The oriental renaissance: Europe's rediscovery of India and the East, 1680–1880*. New York: Columbia University Press.

Slaughter, S., & Leslie, L. (1999). *Academic capitalism: Politics, policies, and the entrepreneurial university*. Baltimore: Johns Hopkins University Press.

Smith, D. (2003a). On enfraudening the public sphere, the futility of empire, and the future of knowledge after 'America'. *Policy Futures in Education, 1*(3), 488–502.

Smith, D. (2003b). *Teaching in global times*. Edmonton, Alberta: Pedagon Press.

Smith, D. (2005a). Not rocket science: On the limits of conservative pedagogy. In K. Cooper and R. White (Eds.), *The practical critical educator* (pp. 68–75). Dordrecht, Netherlands: Kluwer.

Smith, D. (2005b). Troubles with the sacred canopy: Global citizenship in a season of great untruth. In G. Richardson and D. Blades (Eds.), *Troubling the canon of citizenship education* (pp. 125–135). New York: Peter Lang.

Thompson, D. (Ed.). (1995). *The concise Oxford dictionary of current English* (9th ed.). Oxford, England: Clarendon Press.

Titley, B. (2005). Campus Alberta Inc.: New directions for post-secondary education. In T. Harrison (Ed.), *The return of the Trojan horse: Alberta, Canada, and the new world order* (pp. 91–112). Montreal, Quebec: Black Rose Press.

Trungpa, C. (1988). *The myth of freedom and the way of meditation.* Boston: Shambhala.

Varela, F., Thompson, E., & Rosch, E. (1992). *The embodied mind: Cognitive science and human experience.* Cambridge, MA: MIT Press.

Victoria, B. (1997). *Zen at war.* New York: Weatherhill.

Vining, E. (1885). *An inglorious Columbus; or evidence that Hwui Shan and a party of Buddhist monks from Afghanistan discovered America in the fifth century a.d.* New York: Appleton.

Wolf, E. (1982). *Europe and the people without history.* Berkeley and Los Angeles: University of California Press.

Žižek, S. (2001). *On belief.* New York: Routledge.

CHAPTER 2

Breathing Qi (Ch'i), Following Dao (Tao)
Transforming This Violence-Ridden World

Heesoon Bai
Simon Fraser University

Avraham Cohen
University of British Columbia

The Human Presence Today

If we were to choose one word to describe the present state of the natural world, it would be *holocaust*; we are experiencing an apocalyptic moment on the planet. Humanity's twelve billion hands and six billion mouths are tearing apart the earth piece by piece—and devouring it. Eighty percent of the original forests of 200 years ago, which covered the earth like a protective and nourishing skin, have been ripped, burned, and torn off; the rivers and streams that course through the earth like arteries and veins are disturbed, ruptured, drained, and poisoned; the oceans are so depleted that they cannot sustain the presently remaining and struggling marine life forms; the thick layer of atmosphere protectively blanketing the entire planet has been thinned, punctured, and poisoned; the bowels of the earth are being gutted by oil and metal extraction; fresh water, the earth's vital fluid, has become so scarce through overconsumption that this situation may be the trigger that will start a chain reaction toward a final shutdown. The list of environmental devastation goes on. To this list we must also add an equally appalling record of exploitation and violence toward fellow human beings, which although not exclusive to contemporary society has reached new heights of clinical precision and efficiency in recent history. Notwithstanding all the beauties and joys that we still can encounter everywhere on the planet, these horrific pictures of the human presence on earth we presented here are undeniable truths of our reality today.[1]

How can present-day humanity be so reckless, destructive, cruel, and heedless? Responses vary to this question. Some postulate a "human nature" that is fallen and egregious. A variation of this is a genetic hypothesis that we have selfish and possibly cruel genes. Both of these explanations rely on reification, and therefore an essentialism, of what humanity is and neglect to consider the decisive contribution of the *metaphysical* ("beyond physical") dimension of culture, history, ideology, societal modes of production, and social organizations to humanity's anthropological self-concept. Human animals are psycho-conceptual beings subject to the metaphysical functions of beliefs, feelings, perceptions, desires, hopes, and dreams. For human beings, the physical or biophysiological and the metaphysical dimensions are bound up like the "two" sides of a möbius strip, seemingly distinct yet inseparable. In responding to why we are so damaging to the planet and to each other, it is not enough to point to allegedly innate biophysiological features like animal aggression and territoriality or to such physical conditions as overpopulation and resulting overcrowding in a world of scarce resources; we should also inquire into the historically and culturally established metaphysical views that shape the way we see and experience ourselves and the world.

This chapter begins with the recognition that a dualistic consciousness that categorically separates the self from the world and mind from matter is probably the deepest source of humans' environmental degradation and exploitation of each other.

Psychic Autism That Hears Not the World

David Loy, along with many other thinkers, has located the central problem of humanity's exploitive and rapacious behavior in the dualistic, hence, alienated consciousness. He states,

> The ecological problem seems to be the perennial personal problem writ large, a consequence of the alienation between myself and the world I find myself

in. In both these dualisms, the self is understood to be the locus of awareness and therefore the source of meaning and value. This bifurcation devalues the objective world, including all of nature, reducing it to the sphere of activity wherein the self labors to fulfill itself. The alienated subject feels no responsibility for the objectified other and attempts to find satisfaction through exploitative projects that, in fact, usually increase the sense of alienation. (Loy, 2003, p. 172)

To experience the world in the frame of a dualistic consciousness is to see the world as other-than-self or not-self. In Buddhism—some of whose concepts and terminology we adopt in this essay, as well as those of Daoism—such consciousness is understood as constituting *ego* and is viewed as a self that sees itself as categorically separate from the world—what lies "out there" beyond one's portal of consciousness. To the ego, the world is fundamentally alien or foreign. Ego consciousness defined in this way is categorically and substantively separate from the world. In particular, this fundamental separation and alienation includes person-to-person relationships. The self sees itself as the subject, in which case the other is, even if near and dear, objectified and seen as an object upon which the subject exercises and projects its will and desires. What the objectifying ego is not readily and amply capable of is intersubjectivity, the mode of being aptly characterized by Moustakas's (1995) book title *Being-In, Being-For, Being-With*, explained as

> *Being-In* oneself and *in* the world of others, *Being-For* oneself and *for* life, and *Being-With* others are ways of being open to the possibilities of creative life, being receptive to new rhythms, and finding ways of expressing individuality, wholeness, and essence. (pp. xx–xxi)

Moustakas's use of these three prepositions combined with the word *Being* captures a holistic vision of intersubjectivity in the human realm and describes the antithesis of the ego consciousness, which, as we have described it above, is alien from other, whether human, nonhuman, or nonsensate.

Let us probe a little deeper into the affective consequences of the ego consciousness and its dualistic ways of being. A certain spectrum of affective experiences is available to the ego consciousness, all the way from fear and hostility at one end to greed and domination at the other, with indifference somewhere in the middle. In more primal, visceral terms, the ego, because of its categorical separateness, can only experience the other in the form of threats of being swallowed and eaten (ego annihilation) or the desire to swallow and eat the other (ego domination). Indifference, the attitude and experience of "I don't care," or "it doesn't matter to me," is what the ego experiences when it is momentarily free from the threats of annihilation or the desire for possession and domination.[2]

Given the logic of unbridgeable separateness between self and other, what is not readily and abundantly available to the ego self are intersubjective experiences of being able to partake, empathetically, in others' experiences. The other's joys and sorrows become one's own. The Buddhist notion of the "heavenly abode" (*brahma-viharas*) refers to such intersubjective experiences and includes sympathetic joy (*mudita* in Pali), compassion (*karuna*), and loving kindness (*metta*).[3] Being able to experience intersubjectivity is also celebrated by Confucians and is given the name *humanity* or *humaneness* (仁). In Chinese thought, psychic and affective resonance that facilitates intersubjectivity is called *kan-ying* (感 應: literally, affect and response). *Kan-ying* is a function of human sensitivity and receptivity whose workings depend on an ontological sense of continuation of being between the self and the other (Tu, 1989). The alienated consciousness of the ego self is not readily capable of being more than superficially touched and moved by the other. Proper sensitivity and receptivity are lacking.

Thomas Berry, a contemporary ecotheologian, likens the dualistic consciousness's compromised function of being touched and moved by the other to psychic "autism" (1996, pp. 410–414). Noting our psychic autism toward the natural world after the Cartesian coup de grace of radically severing the ontological tie between the order of mind and the order of matter,[4] he writes, "The thousandfold voices of the natural world suddenly became inaudible to the human. The mountains and rivers and the wind and the sea all became mute insofar as humans were concerned (p. 410)."

When the world we encounter is objectified—that is, rendered a "collection of objects" (Berry, 1996)—it does not have the *power* to release in us feelings and perceptions of resonance. The world objectified is mute, dumb, and numb to us; we therefore do not hear, see, or feel it. The trees do not speak; the wind does not sing; the mountains do not call. We do not hear the trees and the wind; we do not hear the mountains. When we do run into people who are capable of hearing trees and mountains, we see them as primitive animists in need of further cognitive development toward scientific rationalism. Worse, we may see them as crazy and suspect that something is wrong with their brains. This kind of rationalism inhabits an *objectified* consciousness—that is, a consciousness that sees the world as inanimate, a mere "collection of objects," and thus treats it as such. The objectified is there to be taken and used but not held sacred and befriended. We can do whatever we want with it, including destroying it. It is only made up of things—mere *stuff*. Do we have to wonder why we have a throw-away economy, and a society of conspicuous consumption?

Breathing Qi (氣)

If we acculturate and educate people in this mold of dualistic, objectified—hence, alienated—consciousness, which naturally results in their turning the world into a source of exploitation and a dumping ground, and then we turn around and tell people not to do that, where is the logic? What use is there in telling people, however urgently, not to be disrespectful and destructive toward aliens, enemies, things, and "stuff"? Such moralistic injunctions only exhibit ignorance about human psychology. Intrinsic respect for people and things, or *reverence for life*, as Albert Schweitzer called it, comes out of a mode of understanding and perception, and not just an espoused belief or doctrine that this universe and all its inhabitants are "alive" and sacred. Thus, the task for us engaged in promoting the well-being of the planet and humanity is not to deliver moralistic injunctions and threats, but to introduce views and practices that will help people to inhabit a nondualistic, intersubjective consciousness. In this essay, we introduce the reader to the Daoist *qi* philosophy and practice as a way of understanding experientially these ideas. We hasten to note and emphasize here that there are, even to our limited exposure, many other world philosophies and ways of being that proffer essentially the same or similar ideas about sacred aliveness. The qi philosophy is only one of them.

Now, before we even get started on our exploration of the consciousness change through qi practice, a few words of caution are due to the reader who is, we suspect, like ourselves: keen to adopt new ways and see results. Skeptics and enthusiasts alike, please be warned. Babies and little children learn to see the world and inhabit a certain corresponding consciousness naturally, with little conscious effort and with utmost ease just by the fact of being immersed in the given cultural environment, but to change an older person's established way of seeing and doing is a difficult and time-consuming effort, and often a struggle. (We would also add that we do not wish to romanticize the mind of the child, which, while delightful to witness and partake in, usually does not have to any substantial degree the witnessing and self-reflective capacity of adult consciousness.) Part of an adult's difficulty lies in the peculiarity of the task: to shift and change one's consciousness while inhabiting the same consciousness. This may sound like a mission impossible. Not quite. The key is that we do not think of the task as a discontinuous change in which one thing is replaced by another en masse. We think of it as a slow and gradual process of change during which small parts are transformed continually, bit by bit, over time, and there is awareness that these small parts are connected to the whole, which is also affected by these ongoing changes. It is very much like renovating a house room by room while one is living in it. In the case of consciousness change through qi practice, "room by room" becomes "breath by breath." Needless to say, this kind of change of consciousness takes a strong commitment to practice and immense patience with the process—commitment and patience we often lack in our fast-food and quick-fix culture.[5]

The qi ontology is an excellent example of a nondualistic worldview, and, most important for us, it comes with a whole range of embodied practices, from martial arts to brush painting. The qi philosophy posits that the whole universe, both what we in the modern West conventionally divide into animate and inanimate, or mental and material, is made up of qi. What is qi? Zhang Dainian, the author of *Key Concepts in Chinese Philosophy* (1989/2002), explains,

> *Qi* is the life principle but is also the stuff of inanimate objects. As a philosophical category *qi* originally referred to the existence of whatever is of a nature to change. This meaning is then expanded to encompass all phenomena, both physical and spiritual. It is energy that has the capacity to become material objects while remaining what it is. (pp. 45-46)

The first significance of qi for us is that it is psychophysical, meaning that it encompasses both the psychical (mind) and the physical (matter). This integration is etymologically reflected in the Chinese character for qi, 氣,[6] as it is composed of two parts: steam (气) rising from rice (米) as it cooks. Perhaps there are alchemical allusions of transformation and creation in this etymology. Through the cooking of hard-to-digest rice grains, they become nourishing food that vitalizes the one who eats them. This line of interpretation shows a connection, made in human *experience*, between matter and vital energy. Zhang (2002) posits that "the best translation of the Chinese word *qi* is provided by Einstein's equation, $e=mc^2$" (p. 45). It may indeed be that there is an empirical scientific basis to qi as matter energy. We support the notion of people doing scientific research on qi; however, in this essay, we are not pursuing the cause of scientific verifiability. We take the stance that qi is foremost a philosophical understanding that human beings can entertain *and* an experiential phenomenon that human beings sense and feel. We are creatures of psychophysical phenomena, meaning that in our experience, the mental/spiritual is not separate from the physical. This is a radically different philosophical perspective from the Western one that draws a categorical divide between mind/spirit and matter.[7] For example, classical Chinese thought is based on and centralizes human experience (Ames & Hall, 2003). In this worldview, we cannot separate what is mental from what is physical. Characteristically, classical Chinese thought insists on the standpoint of experience. We will return to this important point later.

In common usage, qi means both "air or breath" and "energy." As a philosophical understanding, qi is the basic "substance" of the entire cosmos, including human beings. The mental/spiritual and the material, or the animate and the inanimate, are all manifestations of qi. To quote Tu Wei-ming, a contemporary leading authority on Chinese philosophy (Tu, 1989), "Mountains, rivers, rocks, trees, animals, and human beings are all modalities of energy-matter [qi], symbolizing that the creative transformation of the Tao is forever present" (p. 72).

Here, however, a point of clarification, or perhaps a correction, is necessary in reading Tu's comment. Mountains and rivers being modalities of energy matter do not just *symbolize* qi's transformative power. They are, as far as our experience is concerned, qi's concrete manifestations. Thus, in this way of understanding, what there is (ontology) coincides with what we experience (phenomenology). This, we should note, is very different from the classical Western philosophical paradigm that dualistically separates ontology (reality) from phenomenology (appearance). In this paradigm, reality (*noumena*) is always hidden behind appearance (*phenomena*).[8] From the nondualistic perspective of qi philosophy, it makes little sense to draw the kind of categorical distinction that we in the West conventionally draw between mental and physical, animate and inanimate.

In saying and accepting, collectively and individually, that something is an *inanimate* object we are prescribing to ourselves how to experience and relate to this object—namely, without the evocation and involvement of feelings and personal regard for it. If we were to be cued into experiencing these so-called inanimate things in terms of the flow of qi that animates everything we perceive, it is altogether possible to feel the pulsating energies in all things and see them in their inner vividness. It goes without saying that this cue must have immanent personal meaning that is constituted by integrated thought-feeling. This kind of vividness and vital energy is potently present in what are known as "enlightenment poems" by Chinese and Japanese masters. As we move toward enlightenment—that is, a way of being that is characterized by nondualistic consciousness, the charge and vibrancy of life becomes more and more apparent.

Qi Practice and Consanguinity

From the perspective of qi perception, plants and rocks, animals and streams, have something very fundamental in common with human beings in that we all share and manifest the vital breath of the cosmos. All beings are, to repeat Tu Wei-ming's phrase, "modalities of energy-matter [qi]." In this interpretive seeing, a great sense of "continuity of being" or consanguinity, with "the ten thousand things" (to borrow the Chinese expression for the "phenomenal world") may arise. Humans are distinct—but not radically separate—from other beings such as mountains and forests, animals and flowers, for everything is a qi manifestation. When we can truly perceive and feel, not just intellectually understand, the qi in all beings and things, the resulting sense of universal interconnectedness would be strong enough to overcome the usual sense of the categorical otherness about human and nonhuman others. The neo-Confucian philosopher Chang Tsai (1020–1077) feels consanguinity and companionability with all beings: "Heaven is my father and earth is my mother, and even such a small being as I finds an intimate place in their midst ... all people are my brothers and sisters, and all things are my companions" (as quoted in Tu, 1989, pp. 73–74).

Philosophically, qi is the principle of life; phenomenologically or experientially, qi is vital energy that enlivens our perception so that all that is phenomenologically presented to us comes alive to our senses and sacred to our moral sensibility. Thus, when we say that qi is the principle of life, what we mean is that qi has the transformative power to turn our alienated perception of the objectivist consciousness (seeing things merely as objects) into animated perceptions that see the whole world as being suffused by a vital and sacred life force. We do not mean to suggest a causal linkage here. What we are saying is that awareness of qi is synonymous with this altered and unified consciousness. This perception is the ethical basis of the emerging and deepening consanguinity that one feels with the whole phenomenal world. The following passage from Ch'eng Hao (1032–1085) well illustrates the ethical implication of the qi philosophy (Tu, 1989):

> A book on medicine describes paralysis of the four limbs as absence of humanity (*pu-jen*). This is an excellent description. The man of humanity regards

heaven and earth and all things as one body. To him there is nothing that is not himself. Since he has recognized all things as himself, can there be any limit to his humanity? If things are not part of the self, naturally they have nothing to do with it. As in the case of paralysis of the four limbs, the vital force (*ch'i*) no longer penetrates them, and therefore they are no longer parts of the self. (pp. 75–76)

Qi is not simply a life principle; it is a *universal* life principle in that, when qi is the experiential basis of each moment of perception, one feels interconnected with everything and every being on the planet and in the universe.

Joining and Harmonizing Qi: Aikido

Earlier we indicated that in order to experience the world in the modality of qi, it is not enough to only theoretically adopt its philosophy. For the former to happen, the concept or philosophy we are adopting has to become embodied, meaning that the practitioner has to actually see, sense, and feel in certain ways pertaining to the concept. As noted earlier, that the process of embodiment takes time and dedicated effort—daily, with body, mind, heart, and spirit (in the sense of the felt "charge" and "sparks" of energy)—as part of the living of life is a given. In the entire process of embodiment, however, the most important guide is the "sensing-feeling": Do I sense-feel some sensations of energy, in the form of tingling or heat or vibrations in the fingertips? Do I sense-feel this "bright" *yang* energy of the sun ("heaven")?[9] Do I sense-feel this "surging" qi while I breathe like this?[10] Do I feel the stagnation and blockage lifting as I stand firm on the ground, my toes spread wide and in contact with the soil, and breathe deep down into my belly and sense-feel "vast" qi moving through my entire body?[11] The practitioner becomes able to identify certain sensations, perceptions, and feelings as dynamic phenomena of qi. Further, the practitioner has to be able to become sensitized to the ever shifting ebbs and flows of qi, and the nuances of shifts that can be described as increasing, decreasing, turning, sending, receiving, integrating, harmonizing, and so on. This is no weekend practice, and overnight results are rare. Without this kind of embodied work, however, qi remains merely a philosophical concept. With this point about embodiment in mind, we turn to the exemplary practice of *aikido*, a modern Japanese martial art first devised by O-Sensei, Ueshiba Morihei (1883–1969).

In Far Eastern traditions, many practical arts have been developed as ways of embodying and working with qi. From martial arts to calligraphy, working with the flow of qi is the central objective of learning. In this section we will explore the example of aikido to learn more deeply about working with qi. We choose aikido as an example for three reasons:

1. Aikido is a qi practice that specifically aims at restoring peace to ourselves and to the world. As we may recall, the concern that has brought us to write this essay is, precisely, today's "violence-ridden world" of conflict and malaise. Our quest is to find an exemplary philosophy and practice that may help us to transform the way we think, perceive, and act.
2. Aikido provides clear and concrete illustrations of what it is like to work with qi.
3. One of us has been a student of aikido and can speak about working with qi from experience.

The core of aikido and of what we are trying to convey here is an idea, formulated by Ueshiba, that our goal is not to defeat an opponent but to change our opponent's heart. A further delineation of the basis of qi—or, as the Japanese say it, *ki*—is captured in Ueshiba's *The Art of Peace*:

> Morihei was asked if his miraculous powers were due to spirit possession. "No," the master replied. "The divine spirit is always present within me—and you too, if you delve deeply inside—so I am just obeying its commands and letting the awesome power of nature flow through me." (M. Ueshiba, 2002, p. 25)

There is much of interest in this brief quote. Of particular interest is the idea that the divine spirit, ki (qi), is always present. The divine spirit as qi is not something transcendental that lies outside humanity and its earthly context. That never is the meaning of "divine" in the context of Daoism or, for that matter, Buddhism or Confucianism. In these philosophies the divine is the mundane and the mundane is the divine. Qi is never *not* there, but—and this is, in our view, crucial—how well we can manifest it in ourselves and in our lives is a matter of our own cultivation. To this end, first of all, we must delve deeply inside, into our psychophysiology, into the depth of our mind-body-heart-spirit. We must do our "inner work" (Cohen, 2002, 2005), the self-reflective and self-embodying practice that explores who one is and removes barriers to its integrity and authenticity.

The goal of aikido is harmony or peace, as the literal meaning of the three Chinese characters show: *ai* (合; "converging, bringing together, harmonizing"); *ki* (氣; qi); do' (道; "the way, the path, the art"). Ueshiba wanted to develop a martial art whose goal was achieving peace rather than fighting and winning battles. In Morihei Ueshiba's understanding, people get into battle situations precisely because they are lacking *aikido*, the art of bringing together and harmonizing ki (qi) in the body/self in connection with the universe, and thus his aikido is about teaching people how to practice this art. His son Ueshiba Kisshomaru notes,

> This body is the concrete unification of the physical and spiritual created by the universe. It breathes the subtle essence of the universe and becomes one body with it, so training is training in the path of human life. In training the first task is to continually discipline the spirit, sharpen the power of nen [awareness or consciousness or spirit], and unify body and mind. ... Nen is never concerned with winning or losing, and it grows by becoming properly connected to the ki of the universe. When that happens, nen becomes a supernatural power that sees clearly all things in the world, even the smallest movement of hand or foot. (K. Ueshiba, 1984, p. 36)

Kisshomaru Ueshiba, successor to his father in becoming chairman of the Aikikai Foundation, elaborates the relationship between nen and ki:

> Nen, the single-hearted concentration seeking the unity of the order in the universe and the principle of change, becomes the wellspring of the subtle working of ki. When this subtle working, rooted in nen, is manifested in the heart and mind of a practitioner, he becomes free and open, and his insight becomes penetrating. When it works through the body, the result is spirited, dynamic movement in circular and spherical rotation. In short, nen is the line that connects ki-mind-body and the universal ki. (p. 37)

Morihei Ueshiba himself left the following poem that speaks of his connection to ki:

> Standing amidst heaven and earth
> Connected to all things with ki,
> My [mind-heart] is set
> On the path of echoing all things. (K. Ueshiba, 1984, p. 39)

In the following we have reconstructed a short narrative to illustrate phenomenologically what it is like to work with qi, or ki, in aikido practice.

> "Watch" the following: I am standing on a tatami mat wearing my *gi* (traditional practice uniform). My opponent moves toward me with his right arm upraised and his hand over his head, with the knife hand[12] edge facing me and

coming down toward the top of my head. I am standing sideways with my right foot forward. I am standing with my weight equally distributed. I feel light and inwardly still. I am alert and capable of moving in any way at any moment. I can feel the ki within me, pulsing. It can be described as a sense of anticipation in the moment, with no idea that anything has to happen. As he comes close and his knife hand descends, I step slightly toward the right side of his body and just slightly to one side. I detect a feeling and "see" a small light stream that seems to be leading his next move that will be toward me. I move in such a way as to join with the light and its direction. I initiate a turning motion to the left. As his hand comes down I complete my turn. With one motion that is directed by the inner feeling of ki, which I experience as heat and a sense of being simultaneously pushed and led by something, my left hand comes over top of his descending arm near his wrist and joins with his movement. I am now moving with my opponent. I feel a sense of oneness within myself and with my partner, who now no longer seems like an opponent. I can feel the joining of his ki and mine. In a singular and swift motion I grasp his wrist and, going with his movement, continue his downward motion with him while simultaneously moving my right hand into position under his elbow. I feel a slight push within from my ki and I accelerate his movement, lock his elbow and in a flash he is turning in the air and landing on the mat on his back. As he is descending I have a firm hold on his arm that transcends the physical. I maintain the physical connection, which is based in the connection of ki. I am able to slow his descent sufficiently so that he will not be injured by the landing. I maintain my hold on his wrist with both hands. I continue the move until he is immobilized. The action is effortless. I hold him on the mat. The wristlock that I have now applied is firm and held with only sufficient pressure to ensure his immobility. The pressure is equal only to any resistance that comes from him. I feel the profound ki-based connection between us. I have inflicted no injury. I have turned an attack move into a joining and care-full experience. I am not injured, nor is he.

Being in the flow of ki, it seems as if I have not *done* anything. The ki itself has flowed in such a way to bring things to the right place. I have looked after both myself and my opponent. I have allowed this to happen by being in touch with the movements and intent of my opponent in this corner of the universe. Throughout the experience my breath has coincided with my movements. I have gathered my ki in my hara.[13] I have exhaled in concert with my movements to join with and make safe my opponent. I have unified my breath with my body and joined with his energy. I am at one with my experience, which includes my opponent and the environment. The experience has been guided by the ki that I was experiencing in the moment. I have learned to step aside and allow ki to pursue its natural path. It is effortless, as I am not doing anything. I have allowed ki to work through me.

Qi (氣) Is Superabundant in Dao (道)

Peace reigns when we can fully participate in "the vitality that sustains all life" (M. Ueshiba, 2002, p. 49). For too long a time humanity has been living according to a model of life that says that we have to compete with, dominate, exploit, and devour each other because there is a dearth of resources. It is scarcity, not abundance, that we picture as the model of reality. And it is deficit that characterizes the human consciousness said to be unavoidably dualistic and objectifying. Again, we are not disputing that the world is running out of fresh water, clean air, petroleum, arable land, forests, fish, and the list goes on. Nor are we disputing that most of us are operating out of a dualistic consciousness most of the time. But, let us be careful about what conclusions we draw based on these events. It is fallacious reasoning to confuse a symptom with a cause. If the world is being depleted and we are running out of vital resources, which is by all accounts factually correct, could it be that this is because humanity has been operating with a model of scarcity and deficit? The latter is said to be the original condition of human life, "the state of nature," as Hobbes (1651/1969) pictured it for us: "solitary, poor, nasty, brutish, and short" (p. 85). In the state of nature we conduct ourselves in the manner of "every man, against every man" (p. 84). Violence becomes the chief method for securing what we need. We suggest that the world of depletion we are facing is at this point both result and cause of the scarcity and deficit mentality. Had the model of abundance and fulfillment for reality and human consciousness prevailed and more people lived by this model, then we would be living a very different existence. While the deficit model is dominant, both models exist in the field of human consciousness, and there is an unresolved tension between them, which itself is indication of a lack of awareness about what exists in the field. We suggest that qi philosophy transformed into practice conduces an awareness of the state of the world and that this awareness allows the possibility of a change, individually and collectively, toward a deep feeling of humanity that will obviate the need for violence.

Classical Chinese thought describes a model of reality, *Dao* (道), which is likened to an "empty vessel" that never depletes:

> The Dao is like an empty vessel,
> but its use is inexhaustible.
> Oh, unfathomable source of the myriad beings!
>
> —*Dao De Jing*, chapter 4

Dao is usually translated as "Way" or "Path." The Chinese character for it, 道, is composed of two parts: "head" (首) and "foot" (足). Together, they signify the processual reality in which humans can be endlessly creative. It is the infinite field—the cosmological playground—of creativity for all beings, human and otherwise. Humans, as bipedal beings—with their heads pointing to "heaven" and receiving the heavenly *yang qi* and their feet touching the ground and drawing the earthly *yin qi*—are joyous and fulfilled. This is a very different model of human reality from the one given to us by thinkers like Hobbes.

In his provocative essay on the historical significance of *Dao De Jing* in terms of the evolution of consciousness, William Irwin Thompson (1996) alludes to the contrast between the Hobbesian model and the Daoist model of reality. He contrasts the masculine, fixed, rigid, geometric, dominating, expansionistic, territorial, possessive, and militaristic mind-set with the flexible, fluid, chaos dynamic, process-oriented feminine mindset of Daoism. In picturing what a Daoist society is like, Thompson states,

> This is not a vision of capital-intensive economies of scale and state transport systems but rather of autonomous individual villages saturated with a sense of the larger process of circularity of the Tao [Dao]. And what empowers the release of possessions and possessiveness is the practice of a yoga that enables the completely autonomous individual to connect directly with the Tao. (p. 256)

Dao, the path of qi, is a road to superabundance, open to individuals who practice the art of gathering and harmonizing qi. When individuals find their source of abundance, they are content and peaceful inside and outside. They do not see the world as a battlefield of competition, struggle, exploitation, and rapacious consumption. According to the qi philosophy, the world is a place of abundant creativity and an unfailing source of wonder and mystery. However, unless and until individuals directly access, connect with, and work with qi in the field of Dao, all this is a theory, and a utopian discourse. Fortunately, what we are presented with is not just theory but praxis: methods of how we may turn theory into living practice. The key to this translation is the practice of working with qi.

Chapter 10 of the *Dao De Jing* reads:

> Cultivating and embracing the unity of spirit and matter,
> Can you prevent their separation?
> Concentrating vital energy,
> Can you make it soft like the newborn's suppleness?
> Wiping and cleansing your inner mirror,
> Can you make it free of blemish?

Governing common people in your kingdom through love,
Can you reach *wu-wei* (无为)?
When the gateway to Heaven opens and closes,
Can you hold on to femaleness?
Understanding everything throughout the four corners of the world,
Can you comprehend it without conscious effort?
(The leader does not dominate and control people. Such, then, describes the mysterious and profound power of virtue.)

To elaborate, we quote Ames and Hall's accompanying commentary to the above chapter:

Early Daoist [Taoist] cultivation certainly involved a meditative regimen that seems to be the central issue here. In fact, much of the *Dao De Jing* [Tao Te Ching] can be read as a metaphor for breathing exercises. It is the thorough integration of the physical and spiritual aspects of our experience in the concentration of our *qi* that enables us to maximize our potency and invigorates our minds. Penetrating insight is not inspired by some instrumental, enabling, "tried and true" wisdom, but is rather an immediate and fundamentally creative activity out of which fresh and efficacious intelligence arises to guide the way. ... The dynamic field of experience is the locus in which the stream of phenomena is animated and achieves consummation, but all of this pageantry occurs without the presence of some controlling hand. The energy of transformation lies within the process itself rather than in some external agency. It is the very nature of the world to transform. (pp. 90–91)

As Ames and Hall point out, breathing exercise or meditation is key to the transformative practice of qi. Each breath is like a brush stroke that captures and articulates qi. Each breath delicately shapes and colors consciousness, to the form and hue of the nondual, animated consciousness. Breath by breath we dissolve dualistic thinking and perception, and transform consciousness.[14]

The human body need not be a rapacious organism that devours the world. The human psyche need not be starved and malnourished, suffering from insatiable hunger and thirst. The human body-psyche becomes the site for manifesting a superabundance of joy, ecstasy, love, and peace. We cite once again Morihei Ueshiba (2002) for what he has to say about the importance of individuals connecting with qi:

The Art of Peace functions everywhere on earth, in realms ranging from the vastness of space down to the tiniest plants and animals. The life force is all-pervasive and its strength boundless. The Art of Peace allows us to perceive and tap into that tremendous reserve of universal energy. (p. 47)

For Thompson (1996), too, individuals' connecting with qi is not simply an act of individual salvation, important as such is; connecting with qi has colossal significance for the shape and destiny of our civilization:

> Over two thousand years ago, humanity chose the militarist and hierarchical path at the fork in the road. Now here we are again, and I, of course, hope that the road not taken 2000 years ago will be the road we take this time for this axial shift of the year 2002. (p. 262)

Civilization is in crisis—at a fork in the road. In one direction, a broad, multilane superfast highway that we have been on for recent millennia leads to violence and destruction; in the other direction—somewhat hidden and, some might even say, esoteric, but nonetheless an unmistakable path—leads to a Daoist vision of the world where "the unique individual, through the immediacy of his or her own breath and awareness, can connect to the universal *Tao* and the Zen of their original nature" (Thompson, 1996, p. 262).

Educing Humanity

Through Daoist qi philosophy and practice, or other differently named philosophies and practices that integrate the self with the universe, mind with matter, and intellect with feelings, individuals *can* enter into a process of movement toward *existential* security and fulfillment. As individuals become increasingly ensconced in this process they will tend to feel increasingly peaceful and loving toward the world. No amount of moralizing talk and imposition of rules and principles, threats of punishment and losing out, or even promises of survival and gain, can turn us into truly peaceful and loving human beings, free from rapaciousness. Nothing less than a thorough transformation of human consciousness will bring substantial and enduring peace on earth; it is a transformation wherein "individuals live in a supersaturated solution in which they all have access to an interior yoga through which they can connect with the cosmos" (Thompson, 1996, p. 261). True, population control, pollution control, and all manners of conservation measures will be helpful, just as eyedrops soothe eyes that are red and sore from lack of sleep. But let us not confuse a remedy with a cure, a symptom with the cause of a disease process.

Education today faces a most critical challenge: to either become germane to the solution and cure or continue to be part of the problem and disease. Education that is premised in the worldview and practices of dualism of self and other, mind and matter, intellect and affect sponsors the continuance of human alienation and existential insecurity, which in turn educes in varying degrees of severity the inhumanity of exploitation and violence that is manifest in rapacious behavior. Educationally, too, then, we are at a turning point. If we want a world of peace, love, compassion, caring, and joy in life, then the project of education is to educe, evoke, and provoke learners toward nondualistic, intersubjective consciousness. To this end, education has to design and develop institutions that offer learners three kinds of empowerment: First of all, it enables them to undertake a critical examination of dualistic worldviews and practices as reflected and embodied in their own everyday lives and the world around them (criticism); second, it enables them to entertain and inhabit different ways of being and living in the world (creativity); and third, it enables them to function nondualistically and intersubjectively in a world that is dualistic and objectified, thereby becoming practitioners and models of the art of peace (ethics). In this chapter we have described these three empowerments. We have critiqued the damaging works of the dualistic consciousness, explored the alternative worldview of Dao and qi, and through aikido presented an example of practice that facilitates the practitioner to successfully intersect with the dualistic world in a way that is potentially transformative for the practitioner and the world.

In terms of curriculum and pedagogy, we conceive of classroom practice at any level as enacting the above three empowerments: criticism, creativity, and ethics. The intellectual component of the curriculum is supported especially, but not exclusively, by criticism, while the creative component is especially supported by a wide range of arts, crafts, and practices that are contemplative, aesthetic, psychological, somatic, and intersubjective. In this context, we recommend particularly that schools include various forms of contemplative arts, including meditative practices, yoga, prayer, Zen drawing (Franck, 1993), or journal writing, to name a few possibilities. But possibilities are limitless, and creativity knows no bounds. Finally, we would like to see education as a process of empowerment wherein students learn to meet the world of instrumentalism with the courage and creativity of nondual and intersubjective consciousness.

There are a few last thoughts to share. Objectified—that is, dualistic—consciousness is always into trying to do things *to* the world, *to* the other. Even "doing good" falls into this mode. The objectified consciousness of the educator does the same, always working on learners by telling them what to do, how to be, how to improve; "teaching" them how to fix their problems; fixing students who are seen as problems; and so on. Educators embodying the nondual, intersubjective consciousness take a different approach. First, they teach others by being an authentic and living embodiment of what they deem to be valuable and potentially meaningful to learners. They realize that teaching is not merely a matter of telling, however persuasively and urgently, and that it is crucial to be a model in one's own being and one's own life. We echo Mahatma Ghandi's beautiful line, "My life is my message," and add to it, with all due respect, *moment to moment to moment*. Second, teaching from the mode of nondual consciousness is *participation* in the learning process of students. When the usual duality between teaching and learning, being a teacher and being a learner is overcome, teaching and learning become dynamically and seamlessly interconnected, and thus become a mutual process of transformation by participation. Chapter 17 of the *Dao De Jing* speaks of such teachers (leaders) and their effect on the learners (the governed): "Indeed, the sage-ruler, relaxed and retiring, seldom issuing orders. When affairs of state are completed, the people all say: 'We are like this naturally.'"

Notes

1. We are well aware that many readers might find our characterization of the natural and human world today as "holocaust" unreasonable and even untrue, pointing out that there is just as much cause to celebrate humanity and nature as there is to grieve over human mistakes, destruction, and loss. Fair enough. The authors of this paper feel in fact quite privileged to enjoy relatively clean air and water where we live, and live in modest comfort and security. We enjoy our lives, are grateful for our lot, and feel tremendous responsibility to use our privilege well toward healing the earth and ourselves. However, personal circumstance and good fortune aside, the fact remains that countless lives in the world, including in our own neighborhoods, but especially in the so-called underdeveloped nations, suffer from compromised and abject lives in environmentally devastated and socially unstable regions. As well, extensive and increasing environmental devastation is an undisputable state of the world in which we are all, privileged and underprivileged alike, mired. Let anyone who thinks that we are exaggerating our claims about the environmental devastation read well-documented books and reports, such as the annual publication *State of the World* from the Worldwatch Institute.

2. It is of more than passing interest to us that the foregoing description in the context of developmental processes places a person at the level of, approximately, a three-year-old (or younger). To the extent that our child-rearing practices do not nurture and facilitate development toward and into the capacity for empathy (understanding of the other's experience in a way that does not consume the empathizer, provides a meaningful sense of the other's experience, and facilitates a fitting response, which includes appropriate emotion), to that extent we must and will draw very simple lines between what *I* need and what *the other* has. The primary issues then becomes, Can *I* get what *I* want, or defend against what is threatening?

3. The fourth brahma-viharas is equanimity (*uppekha*), which is said to be the foundation for the other three in the sense that it supports their unimpeded workings. Without equanimity or enlightened state of "disinterest" or "impersonality," it is hard to be loving and kind

toward all sentient beings, for we can become jealous of others and thus ill-willed. Without equanimity, we also find it difficult to be compassionate or sympathetically rejoicing, for we may get too distressed about—and then recoil from—others' suffering.

4. Thomas Berry attributes the decisive turn to this kind of psychic autism to René Descartes's philosophy of dualism that divided reality into mind and matter and reduced the order of matter strictly to the property of extension in space. Accordingly, the only qualification for matter is that it occupies space and can therefore be measured. This way of seeing, of course, de-animates Nature and objects.

5. To give an idea about what this change of consciousness looks like, consider the following example of intersubjective consciousness that can emerge through dialogue (again, we emphasize that the emergence of such consciousness takes time and practice through substantial inner work):

    A: I am sad. You are happy.
    B: I am happy. You are sad? Hmmm. … I feel both happy and sad now. I feel happiness and sadness flowing back and forth between us. Both your happiness and my original sadness pervade me, and I feel like I'm more than one person.
    A: Yes, I do, too, now. It is as though the solid and rigid sense of who I am, separate from who you are, has dissolved, and I have become more of a fluid point of view than a solid entity. Now, exchanging a visual metaphor for an auditory one, I feel as though I am a flute through which air moves in and out, this way and that way, creating different sounds and melodies. I hear the happy song; I hear the sad song. I can hear all songs.

6. In this essay we have adopted the Pinyin system of Chinese character spelling. Thus 氣 is *qi* (Pinyin) rather than *ch'i* (Wade-Giles). We shall also note that the same character, 氣, is written and pronounced *ki* in Japanese and Korean. Also, 氣 is translated in a variety of ways, as "vital energy," "energy-matter," "vital power," and "vital force," among others.

7. The Western tradition of thought is decisively dualistic in ontology. To wit, look at just about all of the major thinkers in classical Western thought, from Plato to Descartes. It is only during the modern times, mainly starting with Friedrich Nietzsche, that this dualistic ontology is called into question and critiqued.

8. The separation of the phenomenal (appearance) and the noumenal (reality) began with ancient Greek philosophy and reached the crowning perfection in Immanuel Kant's philosophy that made the noumenal (*Ding-an-sich*, the "thing-in-itself") completely inaccessible and unknowable to human beings.

9. In this essay we will not, because of space and focus, get into the *yin-yang* (陰 陽) theory that is central to qi philosophy. *Qi* can be classified into two types: *yin qi* and *yang qi*. Roughly speaking, yin (陰) is the quality of darkness, moistness, coolness, and expansiveness; yang (陽) is the quality of brightness, dryness, warmth, and concentratedness. See the section on Qi in Zhang's (2002, pp. 45–63) for more details on yin and yang.

10. The reference to "surging qi" comes from Mencius (in Zhang 2002, p. 47).

11. This is Mencius's terminology (in Ames and Hall, 2003, p. 19).

12. *Knife hand* is a term used in martial arts to describe a technique where the strike attempt is made with the side of the hand and not a closed fist.

13. *Hara* is the Japanese term for "center," and refers to a point located two fingers below the navel and midway between the belly surface and the back, from which the experienced and accomplished martial artist moves and is moved by ki.

14. Here we give a small example of a "breath-by-breath" qi meditation in action—that is, each moment as a lived meditation:

I am sitting still and quietly at my computer. My attention is focused and yet relaxed. I am not seeking any particular experience. I am attending to what crosses my consciousness. I am aware of a thought: "What should I write here?" Then, "Who writes? Who thinks?" I feel my feet touching the ground. I feel very relaxed. I hear a sound outside, a truck driving by. I am inhaling. I am exhaling. I am aware of the center in my belly. I feel a small energy, qi, that is like a tight little ball in my hara. I feel the electricity-like energy spreading. I hear silence. I am aware of being bigger than I am. My consciousness is extending and expanding. My qi is extending and expanding. I am me, who is everything (every thing) and nothing (no thing). I am complete and a part of everything.

References

Ames, R. T., & Hall, D. L. (Trans.). (2003). *Daodejing: "Making this life significant:" A philosophical translation*. Toronto, Ontario: Ballantine.

Berry, T. (1996). Into the future. In R. S. Gottlieb (Ed.), *This sacred earth* (pp. 410–414). New York: Routledge.

Cohen, A. (2002). *Whole person meditation: Introductory manual*. Vancouver, British Columbia: Life Force.

Cohen, A. (2005). *Contemplations and rumours about the inner life of the educator: That which we are we shall teach*. Unpublished manuscript, University of British Columbia, Vancouver, British Columbia.

Dainian, Z. (2002). *Key concepts of Chinese philosophy* (E. Ryden, Trans. and Ed.). New Haven, CT: Yale UniversityPress/Foreign Languages Press. (Original work published 1989)

Franck, F. (1993). *Zen seeing, Zen drawing: Meditation in action*. New York: Bantam.

Hobbes, T. (1969). *Leviathan*. London: Washington Square. (Original work published 1651)

Loy, D. (2003). *The great awakening: A Buddhist social theory*. Boston: Wisdom.

Moustakas, C. (1995). *Being-in, being-for, being with*. Northvale, NJ: Aronson.

Stryk, L., & Ikemoto, T. (Eds. and Trans.). (1977). *The Penguin book of Zen poetry*. London: Allen Lane.

Thompson, W. I. (1996). The road not taken. In *Coming into being*. New York: St. Martin's Griffin.

Tu, W. (1989). The continuity of being: Chinese visions of nature. In J. B. Callicot & R. T. Ames (Eds.), *Nature in Asian traditions of thought: Essays in environmental philosophy* (pp. 67–78). Albany: State University of New York.

Ueshiba, K. (1984). *The spirit of Aikido* (T. Unno, Trans.). Tokyo: Kodansha International.

Ueshiba, M. (2002). *The art of peace* (J. Stevens, Trans.; J. Stevens, Ed.). Boston: Shambhala.

Zhang, D. (2002). *Key concepts in Chinese philosophy*. New Haven and London: Yale University Press.

CHAPTER 3

Fear, (Educational) Fictions of Character, and Buddhist Insights for an Arts-Based Witnessing Curriculum

Claudia Eppert

Louisiana State University*

They fear
    They fear the world.
They destroy what they fear.
They fear themselves ...
They will kill the things they fear
    all the animals
  the people will starve ...

—Leslie Marmon Silko, *Ceremony*

Have you ever held fear? Do you hold it, not move away from it; not try to suppress or transcend it, or do all kinds of things with it, but just see the depth of fear, and its extraordinary subtleties?

—Jiddu Krishnamurti, *On Fear*

In the tradition of British writers such as Charles Dickens or Evelyn Waugh, Booker Prize winner Jeannette Winterson's characters are vehicles for satiric

---

* This chapter was written while the author was at Louisiana State University. She is now associate professor at the University of Alberta, Canada.

comments on human nature. In her remarkable 1995 novel *Art and Lies: A Piece for Three Voices and a Bawd,* Winterson describes Miss Mangle as follows:

> Miss Mangle, who had lived so long beneath the bells of St Paul's … could hear nothing at all. Having an ordinary desire to appear both sociable and wise, she answered any address to her with the words "Very Right. Very True". In this way, she retained a large circle of friends, none of whom guessed that their tolerant confidante was stone deaf (p. 6).

Winterson's characterization of Miss Mangle reveals wisdom and harmony to depend upon an agreeable and compassionate listening. Yet, for Miss Mangle's friends, appearance is disturbingly sufficient. Themselves not listening, they do not notice that she cannot hear. In contrast to Miss Mangle's case, however, their inattention seems motivated by choice or force of habit rather than physical disability. This paper approaches Eastern philosophical perspectives on attention as a contribution to the difficult question of how educators might further conceive an arts-based curriculum of witnessing. I address this question in this chapter by situating the challenges of attention and witnessing within Eastern philosophy—specifically, Buddhism—and within what appears to be a pervasive undercurrent of fear and anxiety in the American public sphere. I also consider the national press for character and literature education as responses to this fear and anxiety.

There does seem much to fear in this new millennium, which started out surrounded by warnings of "Y2K" doom. Within the last few years, in public and private life, I have been feeling increasingly vulnerable to communal and collective expressions of aggression and violence, environmental damage, and disease: wars, terrorism, the SARS virus, the West Nile virus, violence against women, global warming, flesh-eating bacteria, water shortages, AIDS, anthrax, sniper attacks, food poisoning, school shootings, gang violence, the owning and using of guns. Here in Baton Rouge, Louisiana, we were subject for two years to the presence of a serial killer. Fear and anxiety appear to suffuse every aspect of our lives. In addition to never-ending concerns about violence, there are also the less notorious but equally affecting fears about loss or lack of jobs, wealth, recognition, achievement, physical and mental health, possessions, security, kinship, freedom, independence, and love. The energy of fear projects itself in experiences of frustration, blame, anger, worry, insecurity, distrust, and sorrow; in thoughts of protection, superiority, judgment, hatred, and evil; and, finally, in actions of physical and/or symbolic defense, aggression, withdrawal, and flight. The 20th-century Indian philosopher Jiddu

Krishnamurti reflects upon the indiscriminate nature and disabling consequences of fear. He asserts:

> A mind that is afraid, that has deep within itself anxiety, a sense of fear, and the hope that is born out of fear and despair—such a mind obviously is an unhealthy mind. Such a mind may go to temples, churches; it may spin every kind of theory, it may pray, it may be very scholastic … and behave righteously outwardly; but such a mind that has all these things and its roots in fear—as most of our minds have—obviously cannot see things straight. (1995, p. 56)

These last six to seven years I have been studying Eastern thought, predominantly ideas in Buddhism, Daoism (Taoism), and Hinduism. I first approached these traditions and ideas in order to further my re(search) concerning the complexities of witnessing, via literature and the arts, what Kleinman et. al. (1997) describe as "social suffering"; namely, the "results from what political, economic and institutional power does to people and, reciprocally, from how these forms of power themselves influence responses to social problems" (p. ix). It was with some astonishment that I realized the profound insight Eastern thought offers into the human condition, human frailty, and human possibility. Why, in my formal educational history, was I not exposed to this vast resource? As stated in the preface to this volume, North American educators are challenged to intervene in our ongoing reluctance to accept, as J. J. Clarke (1997) notes, "that the West could ever have borrowed anything of significance from the East" or that Eastern thought is anything but "evanescent and intellectually lightweight" (p. 5; see also Clarke, 2000). As I have increasingly come to learn, Eastern thought has given great consideration to the subject of fear and to attention as its antidote. That this literature fulfills a contemporary need among many is evident in my own browsing of North American bookstore shelves, which are well-stocked with such contemporary works as Krishnamurti's (1995) *On Fear*, Pema Chödrön's (2002) *The Places that Scare You*, and Thich Nhat Hanh's (2002) *No Fear, No Death*. Although I draw from these texts, especially Krishnamurti's writings, a central focus is Theravāda Buddhism—the earliest of the traditions to develop following the Buddha's death. Through an introduction to Buddhism, we can ascertain the full human dimensions of fear (and its companion, anxiety) and recognize fear not only as an individual character trait or—often—heroic flaw, but also as a social and cultural phenomena, a "structure of feeling" to deploy Raymond Williams's (1977) oft-quoted term. We can discern relationships among fear, schooling, and society in Western contemporary and historical times; investigate the responsibilities of educational theory and practice to address individual, communal, and collective fears; and consider new possibilities for a curriculum of witnessing.

Since the publication of Felman and Laub's groundbreaking study *Testimony: Crises of Witnessing in Literature, Psychoanalysis, and History* (1992), testimony and witnessing have emerged as central concepts in the humanities and educational theory (see, e.g., Berlak, 1999; Boler, 1999; Carey-Webb and Benz, 1996; Douglass and Vogler, 2003; Eppert, 1999, 2004b; Hesford, 1999; Malpede 1996; Maclear, 1999; Oliver, 2001; Ropers-Huilman, 1999, 2003; Simon, 1994, 2005; Simon and Eppert, 1997; Zembylas and Vrasidas, 2005). They provide a fertile means for a (post)modern working through of how we might ethically engage with historical and contemporary events of trauma, oppression, violence, and exploitation in recognition of the extent to which our current age is one of a deep crisis of response and responsibility. Witnessing thus encompasses engagements with such events as well as commitments to social change.

Yet, for many, our imaginations are conflicted as we are faced with fears and sometimes overwhelmingly complex social and, indeed, global challenges. In times when we are overburdened with "busy-ness," many of us are pulled between desires, on the one hand, for social responsibility and action and, on the other hand, for denial, escape, and retreat in the pursuit of our own happiness and liberty. How, in our contemporary world, do we negotiate such conflict, anxieties so deeply embedded in our psyche? It is a question we must address in light of current global issues, but also in recognition that it is one that has been wrestled with throughout Western history in epics, legends, myths, and even such popular tales as *Star Wars* and the *Lord of the Rings* trilogy. In this latter sense, it is a question that haunts Western literature, and even one that constitutes the nature and structure of what counts as story—as drama or narrative, comedy or tragedy—and what counts as (heroic) character. This question penetrates the very heart of the self in relation to the world and is fundamentally intertwined with debates about morality and ethics. And it is a question that cannot escape the binding of literature, philosophy, and education. In other words, the challenges of witnessing are struggled with, not only within story, but also within sociopolitical perceptions of the educational role(s) of literature, the arts, and the imagination.

While contemporary writing on witnessing is wonderfully diverse and complex, we can identify some shared perspectives. Particularly, writing informed by the frameworks of 20th-century philosopher Emmanuel Lévinas, postmodernism, and psychoanalysis communicates resonant insights concerning the challenges witnesses face. Very generally, these include:

1. Learning one's relationships to the experience of the suffering of self, others, and environment
2. Negotiating what is knowable with what is unknowable
3. Experiencing and working through difficult and conflicting emotions
4. Critically interrogating the personal and the political
5. Opening oneself to the pedagogical possibility for deep transformational insight, one that potentially threatens the very psychological coherence of the *I* witness

A curriculum of witnessing that wrestles with these challenges (through the arts, for example) sets the stage for the realization of a dire pedagogical hope among most educators—namely, that a deeper insight will emerge among witnesses, one that promises to translate into a positive transformation not merely of self but also of society.

Yet, since my forays into Eastern thought, I have come to realize the increasing need to more fully foreground, for myself, a spiritual dimension to what so far has been a predominantly Western philosophical and psychoanalytical understanding of a witnessing curriculum. Indeed, the question that haunts literature also haunts religion. Witnessing as a concept carries deep spiritual roots. We find the concept in the Hebrew Bible and in the New Testament—in *Genesis,* for example, or in the Gospel of John, in which John comes "as a witness / to bear witness to the light." Witnessing entails not merely observing "light" but bringing a deep personal commitment to that which is being witnessed. In this respect, witnessing carries within it dimensions of relationship and the seeds of social change within the context of walking a spiritual path. One might say that the witness participates in a search for, engagement with, and communication of an inner and outer experience that is intimately linked with larger struggles for fuller connection and with the question of how to live (and die) in the world.

Witnessing is thus bound up not only to ethics and identity in a secular frame but also to "spirit," to the self's search to awaken consciousness to, for lack of a better expression, a relational place in the universe. We can identify in witnessing what David G. Smith (1999) describes as an individual or collective journey variously motivated by the question of meaningful existence, an inner call, the escape of oppression, and search for divine purpose (p. 1). This journey is reflected in not only Western but also Eastern spiritual literature. For example, we can find it in the myths and legends surrounding the Buddha's awakening. As Prince Siddhartha Guatama sits beneath the bodhi tree in the final stage of his awakening, the demon *Māra,* lord of death and selfish passion, tries to tempt and terrify the soon to-be Buddha from his goal of becoming enlightened as to the nature of human suffering. However, in response to numerous dire temptations, the Buddha, with firm resolve, touches the ground with his right fingertip, determined not to be swayed, whereupon the earth responds, "'I bear you witness', with a hundred, a thousand, and a hundred thousand thunderous roars" (Smith and Novak, 2003, p. 10; see also Easwaran, 1985, p. 27). The story of the Buddha's awakening is a journey—of spirit and *Bildung*—that demands the Buddha's encounter with fear and emptiness. In *The Hero With a Thousand Faces,* Joseph Campbell (1949) details the extent to which this *Bildungsroman* of spiritual witness, for inner enlightenment and path to maturation and responsibility, reverberates cross-culturally, in many ancient myths and religions.

Yet, in *Joseph Campbell and the Power of Myth* (Konner & Perlmutter, 2001) Campbell also observes how this story of education, and this educational story, appears to be eroding in our modern and postmodern age, disappearing from our contemporary landscape of engagement and ritual. With the exception of such films as *Star Wars,* he notes that today's popular stories and films predominantly highlight physical challenges, and heroic identity is more generally defined by attainments of secular happiness: fame, fortune, love, possessions. Other humanities and education scholars similarly voice this concern, and some contend that we are currently living in a state of moral and spiritual crisis (Loy and Goodhew, 2004; Needleman, 1976, 1994; Purpel and McLaurin, 2004; Smith, 1999). Philosopher Jacob Needleman (1976), for example, considers how these searches that were elemental to ancient traditions have become largely unheard/ignored/stamped out in the midst of modern scientism, educational theory, technology, psychology, and even religion, all of which, influenced by the age of reason, describe a rationalistic universe. Contemporary Western life, Needleman maintains, has lost "ideas and practices that were meant to penetrate behind the screen of one's automatic thoughts and motivations" (p. 57) and, consequently, we increasingly live our lives on automatic pilot, searching for worldly happiness with an unacknowledged tension between this search and the one of awakening. This shutting off and shutting down from the spiritual search, I suggest, limits our capacities for human(e) witnessing.

This chapter takes a rather circuitous route to illustrate this point. It introduces Buddhist explanations of fear and points to connections between fear and processes of thought. It subsequently considers how Western, and specifically Anglo-American, educational practices have throughout history supported the "automization" that Needleman describes. Fear has played a significant role in this long educational process, and public debates about literature education, for example, can be seen as outward expressions of inner psychic conflict. In this chapter I will show how past fears change shape but basically continue into the present, and how literature education, within the frame of character education, continues to reflect these fears. These fears foster a troublesome sociopolitical conception of (heroic) character. The formation of Western, and particularly American, individualism in several ways was forged out of and sought to address fears. Yet, the mythos of individualism—particularly as it has morphed into a mythos of the autonomous, rational, materialistic, and secular individual in the last two centuries—may have exacerbated our fears rather than solved them. And possibly it is making us, and our environment, ill. Western and American society is challenged to (learn to) attend and heal, particularly if the projects of social change are to be productive. Perhaps in contrast to certain contemporary educational initiatives (e.g., some of character education), Eastern thought, particularly Buddhism and its journey of awakening, provides an avenue.

Buddhist Insights into Fear

Commonly, our first impulse is to perceive fear as externally produced: the emotional effect of an encounter with an animate or inanimate entity that we find threatening. At any rate, popular wisdom, which asserts that "there is nothing to fear but fear itself," encourages us to recognize fear as located in our perception, and to rationalize and heroically master our fears. Except with cases that warrant psychotherapy, this is usually as deep into fear as we (dare) go. Buddhism (as well as Hinduism and Daoism), however, goes a good stretch further. It also embeds fear in our perception—our perception not just of the object of our fear or fear alone but more centrally of the very nature of human reality and existence. More specifically, it attributes fear (and suffering) to our naive everyday understanding and experience of time and space.

Much Buddhist literature (e.g. Bresnan, 2003; Easwaran, 1985; Nhat Hanh, 2002; Strong, 2002) draws attention to how, as human beings, we tend to live our lives as though there is such a thing as permanence and a contained/containable self. Psychically and emotionally we invest ourselves in these views and what unfolds from them. Our temporal perception causes us to engage with the world in a preferential way. We develop investments in emotions and concepts, favoring, for instance, life over death, sameness over difference, good over bad, pleasure over pain, beauty over ugliness, significance over insignificance, and love over hate. Our spatial perception allows for the illusion of a permanent, fixed, or separate "ego" self, and subsequent attachment to notions of superiority, possessions, validation, and our thoughts and emotions. *Samsara* is the Buddhist word for the unending cycle of suffering (in Pali, *dukkha*; in Sanskrit, *duhka*) that comes from our false perceptions. Because our ego self is bent on consolidating our sovereign identity and on achieving lasting pleasure (the perceived positive side of the dualisms), it is inconsolably insecure about possible threats to its survival and the fulfillment of its desires. The chase for security, for "me" and "mine," in the belief that obtaining these will lead to permanent happiness and will bring relief from restless desire, inevitably breeds a paradoxical insecurity that inspires dynamics of fear. Fearing what we might lose or not be able to acquire, we spend a great deal of our time worrying, strategizing, fantasizing, forever contemplating the future, bound to restless mind energy about what has (not) occurred, what is (not) occurring, and what might (not) occur. The Buddha specifically outlines three cravings or thirsts (in Pali, *tanha*; in Sanskrit, *trishna*) from which we universally suffer: the desire for sense pleasure, the desire for birth in a world of separateness, and the desire for self-oblivion or self-destruction (momentary or extended) prompted by our negative experience of the other two cravings (*Samyutta-Nikāya*, 2005). These cravings never distinguish or subside; the satisfaction their fulfillment brings is only ever temporary.

These views we have of the nature of reality and existence are fundamentally misguided. Buddhism encourages us to look deeply at the world and to realize that not only is everything impermanent but also that the notion that we can isolate the self in space and time is an illusion. Closer study of our selves and environment shows, in fact, that we are part of universal processes of change, of cause and effect, and that we are thoroughly interconnected with each other, with nature, with the universe. The five aggregates (in Sanskrit, *skandhas*) represent the processes by which the ego identity appears solid and separate to us. These include form (that is, sense of being), feelings, perception, concept, and consciousness. Through the passage of years and life events, patterns of perception, emotion, and belief entangle and solidify. They coalesce into an interminable and habitual stream of chatter that serves to reinforce an image or life narrative of "this is me." The recognition that this life narrative that "I am" is based on false perception encompasses the Buddhist doctrine of no-self. There is no abiding substantive self, only interdependence and a "constant flow of patterns of energy" (Bresnan, 2003, p. 217). While the doctrine of no-self is central to Buddhist thought, it is also the subject of ongoing debate. Several scholars have pointed out that while the Buddha admitted the harm that can come from believing in a self, he himself was cautious to posit the existence of neither a sovereign soul or "self" (in Sanskrit, *atman*) nor "no-self" (in Pali *annata*; in Sanskrit, *anatman*) (Easwaran, 1985, p. 120; Epstein, 1995, pp. 63–65; Safran, 2003, p. 12; Strong, 2001, p. 96). In the *Samyutta-Nikāya*, the Buddha, in dialogue with his disciple Ananda, explains his silence upon being asked about this by a wanderer named Vacchagotta, stating that an answer either way would have been to justify either eternalism or nihilism, and thus perpetuate a dualistic worldview mired in attachment. Buddha's enterprise was instead to doubt and to dismantle any attachment whether to self or to no-self (Easwaran, 1985, p. 120; *Samyutta-Nikāya*, 2005; Strong, 2001, p. 96). To understand the doctrine of no-self, it might be constructive to acknowledge the hyphen as symbolic of nonattachment and a nondualistic "middle way" consciousness.

While we generally feel fear, Buddhism understands it also as a thought process. An example commonly drawn upon to illustrate the intricate relationship between mind and fear is the story of the snake. One encounters a snake in a dark room and experiences spontaneous fear. However, when one turns on the light, one recognizes that there is no snake but only a coil of rope. Fear thus is the consequence of the mind's thought of a snake and a threat to the disintegration of self. As Patrick Bresnan (2003) describes it, this story makes apparent that "fear (as distinct from fright) ... is a form of thought ... a creation of the thinking mind ... [and] is at the heart of suffering" (pp. 226–227). In order to counteract the consequences of fear, we must understand its processes, and this means developing an understanding of the machinations and limitations of the conceptual mind and the transformation of thirst into spiritual growth.

In the secular West we have long invested ourselves in the philosophy that through autonomous thinking we can access reality. Yet, as Lévinas (1961, 1991) has also indicated, the products of the thinking mind (what Lévinas calls the "said") are self-referential and cannot directly access truths located in the dimension of the unknown. Toni Packer and Swaebe (2002), as influenced by Krishnamurti, observe that the "unknown" isn't what we think it is! Unknown means not knowable. For the thinking ego-mind, the unknown is still something known—namely, something imagined, speculated about, and feared. Thought (ego) cannot have any direct experience of the unknown because of the very fact that it is unthinkable! Thought can only think hypothetically about 'the unknown' but what it thinks about comes out of the known—imagining what could happen. And the 'known' is full of illusion. (p. 64)

They note that

to solve the problem of the ego there has to be *direct insight* into the whole movement of thought that is creating the ego—discovering time and time again how it is functioning in ideas and stories, and the pain and pleasure triggered by those stories. ... Thought itself isn't insight and can't have insight. Thought only thinks: it constructs or deconstructs images, ideas, and narratives. Insight illuminates the thinking process: it sees through constructs; it sees constructs as constructs, not as truth. (p. 66)

This is, indeed, the direct other side of René Descartes famous dictum, "I think, therefore I am."

Buddhism's critique of thought not only places into question a Western philosophical tradition that has prioritized reason, but also challenges Western educational practices in which truth is epistemologically based and ascertained. It invites educators to initiate questions about what the development of mind—through, for example, Bloom's taxonomical focus—can really accomplish. Within the Buddhist view, much of thought is connected to opinion making, which in turn is attached to comparisons, evaluation, judgment, agreement and disagreement, and control and mastery, all of which inhibit our ability to truly pay attention. Chödrön (1997) points out how "all ego really is, is our opinions, which we take to be solid and real and the absolute truth about how things are" (p. 110). Krishnamurti (1995) states that

one cannot give attention if one is interpreting or translating or comparing what is being said with what one already knows. One has to listen—an art one has to learn, for normally one is always comparing, evaluating, judging, agreeing, denying, and one does not listen at all. (p. 53)

Buddhism's suspicion of thought is expressed in such practices as, for example, Zen's embrace of koans, riddles intended to draw attention to the limits of reason.

However, one should not take this hermeneutics of suspicion to mean that faculties of reason and analytic inquiry are disavowed. As the Dalai Lama (2003) points out, in Buddhism, faith is not enough. Faith arises in conjunction with reason and logic, and any faith-based claims must be backed up by logical analysis (p. 12). The Tibetan tradition has a strong history of oral debate, critical analysis, and book study. Theravada Buddhism similarly emphasizes the analytic study of the Pali canon. Smith and Novak (2003) tell the story of one monk who stressed that "to seek liberation through meditation alone, without study, is like trying to climb Mt. Everest with one arm" (p. 75). Yet, this study serves the larger focus of self-study. Buddhism maintains that if we can gain deep insight into our cognitive and emotional processes—identify the nature of reality—and gradually loosen (in body and mind) the grip of our attachments to our false views, we can alleviate our suffering and participate more fully and harmoniously in the world. Chödrön (1997) emphasizes this point, noting that "the reason we are here at all in this world is to study ourselves. In fact, it has been said that studying ourselves provides all the books we need" (p. 73). This study, undertaken through practices of mindfulness and meditation (which I will discuss more fully in subsequent sections) illuminates the self to the point of self-forgetfulness. Self-deception becomes so skillfully exposed that there's no mask to hide behind anymore (Chödrön, 1997, p. 26). As the 13th-century Japanese Zen master Dōgen stated:

To study the Buddha way is to study the self
To study the self is to forget the self
To forget the self is to be authenticated by the myriad things

(quoted in Safran, 2003, p. 23)

Self-study and self-forgetfulness encompass the path of awakening.

Several cultural theorists (e.g., Di Paoloantonio, 2000; Mitscherlich, 1975; Santner, 1990) have proposed that institutions and nations are an extension and reflection of psychic identifications and investments. Samsara can be seen as similarly operating on communities and nation-states. Nations are equally intent upon securing their identity and on achieving lasting pleasure. They are potentially insecure about possible threats to their survival and to the fulfillment of their desires, and participate in actions that help to mitigate this insecurity. Eknath Easwaran (1985) contests that "[t]he Buddha would trace every conflict, even war, back to [the] basic selfish drives [thirsts], occasionally couched in self-righteous language or elevated into national or corporate policies" (p. 181). Michael Moore's (2003) film *Bowling for Columbine* illustrates well a collective samsaric dynamic. Moore examines what he identifies to be a deep-seated historical and cultural fear in the dominant American imaginary that can be in part held responsible for school-related teen violence, such as the 1999 shootings at Columbine High School in Littleton, Colorado, and the American obsession with gun ownership. In an inventive seven-minute cartoon inset, Moore reveals an entrenched past of American aggression and suggests that deep fear and the ongoing perception of imminent danger has driven and continues to drive American rallies, attacks, and crusades. The cartoon suggests that the Puritan colonization of America was tied to traumas of persecution and emigration, and that dominant American memory harbors anxieties of potential repeated helplessness and persecution at the hands of an indeterminate generalized other. This generalized other is sublimated into specific others (e.g., indigenous peoples, African Americans, witches, communists, terrorists, aliens, immigrants, youth). Moore theorizes that the collective American psyche by and large holds the belief that it is better to protect oneself and fight now than to wait and suffer an inevitable death. Even in peaceful times, his film suggests, America and Americans experience anxiety and participate in protective actions, such as the belief in the right to bear arms. While I complicate Moore's thesis about the origins of American fears, his film nevertheless offers a compelling entry into a fuller study of expressions of fear and anxiety embedded within Western and American history and formal education.

Literacy and the Haunting Spirit of Control

Historical research on Western and American formal education draws attention to the spirit of control that characterized schooling initiatives during the 18th and 19th centuries. William Doll brings a haunting genealogical perspective to his historical study of this spirit of control, asking readers to consider how ghosts inform contemporary curriculum and, from the other side, invoke us to remember what we have forgotten or repressed, to bear witness, as in Dickens's *A Christmas Carol*, to what was, what is, and what might be (Doll, 2002, p. 27). He introduces a positive spin to fear by observing how specters overcome our consciousness, pursuing "us as actors until [we see] the reality that lies beyond mere perception" and initiate change (p. 28). Doll observes how the educational emphasis on control, however, originated much earlier, as early as the late 16th and early 17th centuries in Europe. Curriculum during this time became infused with a protestant (and Calvinist) desire for rigorous control and investments in method, order, discipline, and the erasure of uncertainty (pp. 30–31). He attributes this shift to a social climate of turbulence: religious conflicts; technological advances such as printing presses; war; and unprecedented scientific challenges introduced by Copernicus and Galileo, among others (p. 33). This European curriculum, initiated by Peter Ramus, came to mark a paradigm shift in perceptions of the role and purposes of education that continues today. The protestant zeal for control traveled the Atlantic to lay much of the foundation for American public schooling. Yet, the question this zeal compels is that of what lies underneath, and what interweaves with it. This chapter holds fear as one possible answer. In the face of fears exacerbated by social upheaval and uncertainty, control and order offer (the illusion of) comfort and security.

American educational history manifests several expressions of social fears, and these are intimately linked with national vision. If Moore contends that it was Puritan fear of persecution following the Protestant reformation that laid the foundation for American schooling, Douglas McKnight's (2003) research offers a different view. He argues that following the Great Migration of 1630, Puritan colonists were driven by a moral and spiritual errand into the American wilderness to construct what they identified biblically as "a city on the hill," a land of conversion and salvation that all of Europe would come to applaud. Challenged by the struggle of good against evil and a belief in predestination, Puritans relied heavily on willpower, moral fortitude, and the interaction of faith and reason (prayer and study) to achieve their goals. Their fervent hope for transcendence, and also the burden of deliverance, was accompanied by a great fear of failure (McKnight, 2003, p. 3). McKnight believes that it is this fear, rather than the fears about persecution as is commonly taught in contemporary schools, that dominated the colonial imagination (p. 24). The Puritans voiced their passions and fears about this symbolic narrative through the *jeremiad,* a lyrical crisis sermon, which McKnight asserts, "still haunts the national consciousness" (p. 3). Indeed, McKnight quotes Bercovitch (1993) to illustrate how fear and anxiety, or "crisis thinking," sustained the Puritan's errand: "'Anxiety became their chief means of establishing control. The errand, after all, was by definition a state of unfulfillment, and only a sense of crisis, properly directed and controlled, could guarantee the outcome'" (as quoted in McKnight, p. 29). What thus emerges in the mythic American consciousness is not only the drive to establish a national identity based on fear-inspired vision but also a rhetoric of fear and anxiety that operates as the means for the realization of this vision. McKnight further observes how the Puritan fear of failure was also connected to the fear of a disobedient public, whether in the form of families who embraced religious commitments with less rigor or new immigrants who brought with them alternative worldviews.

Fears of an uncontrolled/uncontrollable society are readily illustrated in Western historical debates about morality and literacy. As many have documented (see, e.g., Brantlinger, 1998; Gee, 1988; Graff, 1987; Manguel, 1996; Willinsky, 1991), for centuries literacy, and particularly literature, has been viewed as a double-edged sword, a practice that either inevitably threatened individual and social corruption or, just as inevitably, could initiate a higher moral and social consciousness. In his *Republic*, Plato illustrated this ambivalence. On one hand, he argued that story was useful in communicating morals and, on the other hand, he exiled poets from his ideal society in his belief that they bear false witness (being at a third remove from reality), support emotional disequilibrium, and ignite sociopolitical upheaval (Bogdan, 1992; Edmundson, 1995; Hamilton and Cairns, 1961; Havelock, 1963). Fears that the reading of nonregulated texts might unleash an unruly imagination and rebellious action prompted censorship, not only by Plato but also by many others. Alberto Manguel specifically describes an extensive global history of censorship: the burning of Pythagoras's works in Athens in 411 B.C.E., Chinese emperor Shih Huang-ti's book burning efforts in 213 B.C.E., the burning of the Jewish Library in Jerusalem during the Maccabean uprising, the banning of Ovid's works by Augustus in the first century C.E., the banning of books composed by Homer, Virgil, and Livy as ordered by the emperor Caligula, and so on (Manguel, 1996, p. 283). Carlo Ginzburg's (1989) *The Cheese and the Worms* tells about the repeated capture and execution of a 16th-century miller named Mennochio at the hands of the Roman Inquisition because of his unorthodox reading practices. Fears of social unrest by England's working class in the 18th century caused Parliament to close down reading rooms and other sites of working-class literacy, learning, and social action (Willinsky, 1991, p. 23). In response to slave revolts in the 1820s and abolitionist publications, laws were passed in southern U.S. states prohibiting slave literacy in fear that it would produce strivings for emancipation (Kaestle, 1983, pp. 196–197).

Yet if fear motivated censorship, it equally initiated fervent efforts to create a literate, well-educated, and moral public. In North America and England, panic concerning the decline of the moral fabric of society due to 18th- and 19th-century industrialization inspired the controlled in-school reading of the Bible, proverbs, and moral fables (Brantlinger, 1998; Eagleton, 1983; Graff,

1987; Kaestle, 1983, p. 70). Into the 18th and 19th centuries, anxieties that had dictated a curriculum and pedagogy of control throughout Europe and North America continued, their sources changing shape in some cases but not in others. These subsequent centuries were riddled with worries about the widespread growth of cities, increasing industrialization, and economic expansion, the emergence of an urban working-class mass population, diseases and epidemics supported by population density, and a developing immigrant population (Doll, 2002, p. 34; Kaestle, 1983, p. 70). Fears were sublimated into visions of education as factories emphasizing order, discipline, and work. School literacy practices, particularly the institutionalization of English as a separate school subject, were founded in the belief that such practices would reduce crime, drinking, infidelity, the vices of immigrants, and pregnancies and cultivate morally refined and obedient citizens who would participate in the realization of national democratic aims (Eagleton, 1983; Graff, 1987; Kaestle, 1983, p. 70). Reading the great books was touted as integral in ensuring that youths would not be corrupted by popular fiction and social ills in an era of printing presses, newspapers, dime novels, and generally widespread availability of diverse reading material (Brantlinger, 1998; Eagleton, 1983). Strict disciplinary measures, including physical punishment, were enforced in classrooms for purposes of "moral suasion" (Kaestle, 1983, p. 19). It thus seems fear in the powerful begets fear in those not powerful—it was instilled through threats of corporal punishment in order to assuage (hidden) fears among the governing elite of social rebellion and chaos.

The Effects of Fear

From a Buddhist perspective, then, fears concerning social disorder mask more foundational fears about threats to the self's coherence. What becomes readily evident are the consequences of unacknowledged fear. While fear can indeed motivate some change, in the measure that it remains hidden or repressed, masked by rhetoric of control and order, it can do considerable psychic and social damage. Moreover, fear and wisdom take alternate roads in terms of decision making. Krishnamurti (1953) posits that

> education must take into consideration this question of fear, because fear warps our whole outlook on life. To be without fear is the beginning of wisdom, and only the right kind of education can bring about the freedom from fear in which alone there is deep and creative intelligence. (p. 34)

Krishnamurti moves beyond discussions of literacy and morality to emphasize how Western education supports rather than addresses dynamics of fear. In his *Education and the Significance of Life* (1953), he maintains that his travels all over the world have shown him the extent to which education globally is increasingly producing human beings whose primary interest is in obtaining security, achieving worldly success, and having a good time (p. 9). The educational emphasis on conformity, on regulation as opposed to spontaneity, on training and efficiency, on competition and worldly success, he pointedly elaborates, "breeds fear; and fear blocks the intelligent understanding of life" (pp. 9–10).

Surveillance and Character Education Initiatives

More than 50 years after Krishnamurti's published critique of education and society, we might do well to wonder how far we have come in our understanding of life. Contemporary American times signal at minimum the continuation of past investments. Recent years have shown a marked increase in school surveillance practices (for example, requirements that students and faculty wear identification badges) and "zero-tolerance" programs, combined with government-sponsored funding and research into school violence. National documents have been produced, such as *Early Warning, Timely Response: A Guide to Safe Schools,* that provide guidelines for school communities to recognize signs of "troubling behaviors" among youths and respond to a crisis (Early Warning, n.d.).[1] In addition, there has been renewed nation- and statewide emphasis on moral/virtues or character education, as a separate subject or integrated within literature or social studies classrooms.

While, as we have seen, character education was strongly advocated in the early age of institutionalized education in Anglo-dominated nations, in the mid-to-late 20th century it was much diminished, until about two decades ago (McClellan, 1999). Tianlong Yu notes how, since the 1980s, Democratic and Republican politicians and educators, such as William Bennett, secretary of education during the administrations of U.S. presidents Ronald Reagan and George H. W. Bush, have advocated a renewed attention to the cultivation of tradition and "traditional (American) values," virtues, and literacies in public schools (Yu, 2004, p. 58; see also McClellan, 1999). In 2002, the White House held a one-day character-education conference in efforts to respond to a perceived youth crisis. Character education emphasizes normative personal and social virtues such as responsibility, respect, commitment to truth, wisdom, honesty, tolerance, and, in some cases, citizenship, patriotism, heroism, and obedience. Its beliefs follow an Aristotlean view of "virtue education" as teachable and comprising attention to behavior, feeling, and reason (Noddings, 2002, pp. 4–5). As Nel Noddings (2002) points out, central to character education is a literature curriculum that supports the inculcation of values through fables and narratives that provide heroes and inspirational accounts (p. 2).

At the heart of surveillance and many character-education initiatives is the view that contemporary youth, subjected to unregulated familial and social pressures, are increasingly aberrant and criminal. Proponents make their arguments by drawing upon accounts that indicate increases in the number of youth who are no longer reading; significant increases in school violence as media accounts document an era of pervasive bullying, hazing, and school shootings; and marked growth in apathy and alienation. They are riding a political tide of strong public sentiment. If, in the past, there was widespread acknowledgement of education as an instrument in containing youth, current research reflects the public belief that educational institutions are failing or have failed in this endeavor and that youths are out of control. Behre, Astor, and Meyer (2001) observe that opinion polls indicate that the major perceived contemporary problem facing U.S. schools is school violence (pp. 131–153).

Popular films also support the public perception of youth as out of control. Films such as *Stand and Deliver* (1988) and *Dangerous Minds* (1995), for example, offer romantic and idealized narratives that rescue audiences from their fears by indulging us in myths of visionary teachers who motivate students and transform unruly and apathetic classroom and school environments (Grant, 2002, pp. 77–95). At the other extreme are films such as *187* that refuse to reassure audiences. Written by former teacher Scott Yagemann and directed by Kevin Reynolds (1997), *187*, the police code for homicide, portrays contemporary urban schools as war zones filled with graffiti and surveillance cameras, the educational system as impoverished in resources, principals as paralyzed with fear of lawsuits, minority students as largely apathetic and criminal, and teachers as unsupported and variously numb, angry, anxious, and fatigued. Fear dominates *187*'s educational body, although it is not fear that students will become corrupt but that they are already so and that teachers and administrators are powerless in the face of it. In contrast to traditional school environments in which students largely experience their own fears of curricula, teachers, and administrators, the students in *187* show little fear beyond that of peer encounters. Fear of unleashed student power by underclass minority youth in a morally askew,

unsupportive social and educational environment translates into traumatized teachers whose testimonies the audience acutely experiences.

Several educators (Noddings, 2002; Purpel, 1997; Yu, 2004) have commented upon the limitations of conventional character-education programs
to address contemporary social and educational failures. These programs,
they illustrate, by and large contradictorily argue that moral education is an
inevitable component of schooling but that, in light of contemporary ills, it
needs to be reintroduced. Its critics also detail how certain character initiatives
tend to promote exclusively Western renderings of values, and present these
values as universal, decontextualized from variables such as gender, race, and
class. In addition, they tend to emphasize either the secular or the evangelical,
seek obedience to rather than critique the status quo, express commitments to
social change, emphasize individual qualities and goals (and, thereby, detract
attention from larger sociocultural issues), base their curricula upon the
ascertainable belief that virtue can be directly taught, and rely on education as
a form of indoctrination.

What becomes readily apparent in both surveillance strategies and character-education programs is that the fault of the current educational state of
things lies less with the system than with individual children—youth that
need to be watched at all times and trained in behavior and perspective. In
other words, these initiatives generally contend that the problems plaguing
society—poverty, crime, failure, and apathy—are the result not of social structures and inequities but of the individual; thus, the individual, the student, is
found lacking in character. Purpel (1997) writes:

> implicit in such discourse [of character education] is the assumption that our
> social problems are *not* so much rooted in the failures of our social, economic,
> and political structures as in the attitudes and behaviors of individuals. The
> thrust of this approach is to move the discussion away from the extremely con-
> troversial realm of ideological dispute toward the safer and presumably more
> consensual realm of desirable personal traits, to convert social and political
> issues into educational and pedagogical ones, and to focus on stability rather
> than transformation. (p. 140)

Rather than represent a new frontier in educational possibility, the discourse of character education appears to echo the language and ideologies of
early Puritan America. Purpel notes that the moral rhetoric of today is more
coy and subdued than that of colonial and 19th-century education as a result
of legal constitutional restrictions that support the separation of church and

state, a more pluralistic economy, and a positivistic paradigm that emphasizes objectivity and neutrality (1997, p. 142). However, beliefs concerning the moral impoverishment of youth and the direct, unambiguous teaching of virtues abide. Purpel also points out that the values of obedience, hierarchy, and hard work "overlap nicely with the requirements of an economic system that values a compliant and industrious work force, and a social system that demands stability and order" (p. 146). Indeed, the emphasis on obedience supports the automization of which Needleman and Krishnamurti speak. One might then consider if fear of youth is socially and culturally perpetuated as an industry and supports the reproduction of existing hegemonies.

Moreover, surveillance and character initiatives not only emanate from fear but saturate their curriculum and pedagogy with fear. Julia Webber (2003) observes the irony, noting that "in their efforts to make schools 'safe,' policy-makers and school workers have rationalized an atmosphere of fear and mistrust among students by subjecting them to routine forms of monitoring and discipline" (p. 12). While, on some level, the rhetoric informing surveillance and character education initiatives might function as the continuation of the jeremiad thinking McKnight discusses, I wonder that if, from a psychoanalytic and Buddhist perspective, it might not also exhibit a "fear effect"—that is, a fight and flight reaction to fear produced out of thought-alarms that are the consequence of a samsaric worldview. As Freud (1959) details, the immediate common response to not only a perceived fearful event but also fear itself is to experience anxiety and to fight or flee. The wording of the subtitle of Bennett's book *The De-Valuing of America: The Fight for Our Culture and Our Children* (1992) certainly seems to betray one of these reactions. Not only psychoanalysis, but also neuroscience literature, illustrates that we commonly experience fear before we are able to take an objective and reasoned stance on a situation (Johnson 2003, p. 38). To this extent, one might infer that the experience of fear diminishes our capacity for well-reasoned and wise actions. As we shall see, Buddhism makes clear that before we can respond soundly and wisely to what is happening in our world, we must turn inward and face our fears. In this process, we must also face the ontological truths about (our) (attachment to) "character."

Hungry Ghosts

Yet, while I assume a critical approach to the dramatic rhetoric and conservative positions of some character-education proponents, it does seem that contemporary times are at least somewhat out of joint in several respects. Rather than cite statistics, it is enough to make this one observation: school shootings in today's world are no longer unimaginable. In tandem with this observation, valid research does indicate that youth—especially boys—in our increasingly visual culture are reading less literature (Smith and Wilhelm, 2002), although the links among conventional text-based literacy, crime, and morality remain highly debatable. Many educators do attest that apathy is one of the hardest challenges they face. Moreover, there is not only a global memory of an extensive past of violence with which we need to contend but also a contemporary global present of ongoing individual and social violence, oppression, destruction, and exploitation. And we are unequivocally destroying Mother Earth. In effect, our problems are not individual and isolatable as much as they are social and interconnected.

Scholars have been deploying the language of educational and sociopolitical "crisis" to describe our times for many years now. According to Deborah Britzman, the rhetoric of educational crisis emerged from the post-Holocaust writing of social theorists such as Adorno and Arendt (Britzman 2003, p. 8). For many, the language of crisis intermingles with descriptions of anxiety and trauma. Indeed, Felman and Laub (1992) contend that ours is a "post-traumatic century" while others such as Charles Jencks (1989) have identified ours as an "age of anxiety." Notably, in my readings to date of translated Buddhist sutras, and Eastern spiritual texts more generally, I often encounter the word *fear* but not the words *anxiety* or *trauma*. These terms (with their current personalized connotations) were largely introduced in Western psychoanalysis between the mid-19th and early 20th centuries. Anxiety (*Angst*) differs from fear in that fear's source is more identifiable, often a response to a concrete encounter, while anxiety lacks an easily nameable object and reflects doubt concerning one's capacity to cope with it (Freud, 1959; Heidegger, 1977). Anxiety may be inspired by a sense of chaos or lack of control, an uncertain memory of a past event, or an apprehension of some future event. Often, it is the effect of trauma, defined by an overwhelming—traumatizing—sense of physical and/or psychical helplessness or lack of control in the face of the magnitude of a situation (Freud, 1959, p. 102). In fact, Freud began developing his own interpretation of trauma from his studies of women "hysterics" in the mid- to late 1800s and soldiers returning from World War I who suffered from "combat neurosis" (Caruth, 1995). That anxiety especially captures a distinctly mid-1800s to present-day individual and collective voice of helplessness is also reflected in a range of artistic expression: Thoreau's (1854/1981) language of "quiet desperation," Edvard Munch's 1893 painting, *The Scream* (or *The Cry*), Francis Bacon's (1909–1992) pained figures, and Paul Klee's *Mask of Fear* (1932). It seems there is no end in sight to this voice and to all to which it is responding.

Buddhists such as the Dalai Lama (1999) and Thich Nhat Hanh (1994, 1998), as well as Buddhist psychoanalysts like Mark Epstein (1995), have observed a rather unique contemporary phenomenon among Westerners and comment upon how strange this phenomenon seems to them in light of the bountiful material resources of Western industrialized culture, and also the emphasis this culture places on the pursuit of individual happiness. They describe this phenomena as that of the "hungry ghost." In Buddhist cosmology, hungry ghosts are visualized as having bloated bellies that testify to an insatiable hunger and thirst—longing—and long thin necks that represent their incapacity to receive nourishment. These Buddhist teachers variously remark upon the frequency with which they encounter individuals who appear alienated from the world. These individuals desperately long to fulfill the emptiness and unworthiness they have experienced in their lives at the same time that they feel threatened by such fulfillment. Nhat Hanh (1998) notes the irony of estrangement in this present technological age, writing:

> Never in human history have we had so many means of communication— television, radio, telephone, fax, e-mail, the worldwide web—yet we remain islands, with little real communication between family members, individuals in society, or nations. There are so many wars and conflicts. (p. 73)

Elsewhere, Nhat Hanh (1994) links alienation to violence, and maintains that our incapacity to listen is to blame. He stresses, "As you feel no one [listens to you or] understands you, you become more and more like a bomb, ready to explode, and you spill your suffering all over the people around you. ... And you become more and more alone." Winterson's (1995) novel *Art and Lies* bears witness to the loneliness and isolation of not being heard. As any educator will readily and disturbingly testify, hungry ghosts are all too easy to see in our schools. School shootings exemplify this rampant alienation, as do bullying and apathy. In my view, testing classrooms of students about conservative Western virtues is unlikely to help or heal the heart of (the phenomenon of) the hungry ghost.

Several Buddhists locate this contemporary sensibility precisely within the rise of an individualistic and materialistic culture. The West, and mainstream America particularly, has fostered within its social beliefs and economic structures a heightened attachment to the notion of an autonomous and sovereign self with the risk of producing an egocentric culture increasingly alienated and unable to listen, and with the risk of the loss of democratic possibilities. Freedom here is envisioned as the pursuit of individual happiness and the fulfillment of desires (Safran 2003, p. 8). The hungry ghost syndrome is a consequence of this "me" and "mine" culture. By emphasizing attachments to a capitalist-supported and bred egocentrism, it seems we in the West might have unwittingly and ironically exacerbated rather than escaped from suffering and alienation. According to Epstein, while for many in Asia the challenges of Buddhist meditation involve (un)learning samsara in the context of a deeply "enmeshed" cultural and family history, for many in the West the starting point of meditation is a history of "estrangement." Epstein, for example, locates our estrangement in our society's "emphasis on individuality and autonomy, the breakdown of the extended and even nuclear family, the scarcity of 'good enough' parenting, and the relentless drive for achievement versus affection" (1995, p. 177). Drawing upon the work of several psychoanalysts, Safran also describes the potential negative effects of a heightened individualism: isolationism, an internal hollowness, a lack of personal conviction and worth, a chronic, undifferentiated emotional hunger, a culture of narcissism, a grandiose and hyperindividuated sense of self and one's uniqueness that defensively masks fragility and alienation, a desperate pursuit of intimacy in the face of isolation, an unrealistic expectation of intimacy in relationships as a spiritual substitute, and the incapacity to realize and maintain intimacy because of narcissistic defenses (2003, p. 7). I recently asked students in my graduate arts, aesthetics, and curriculum theory seminar to describe in writing what they see when they look at our contemporary age, and was surprised to see the similarities between their responses and what Safran details. I didn't quite expect negative descriptions to dominate to the extent that they did. "Success-driven," "instant gratification," "judgmental," "materialistic," "rushed," "despair," "complacency," "lack of questioning," "lack of responsibility," "struggle," "focus on convenience," "don't bother me with bad news," "crowded," "cyborg," "lost and found," "heartbreak," and "here and now" were some of the words and phrases they used.

Searching for Authentic Character

It is important to keep in mind that the individualism to which these psychoanalysts are referring is not static, but rather one that has evolved through the centuries and continues to shift. Notably, McKnight (2003) illustrates that the Latin origin of *individual*, in effect, means "indivisible," which McKnight interprets as being spiritually and socially connected (pp. 43–44). Individualism was part of the expression of a person's spiritual calling, which the institution was intended to serve. In America, individualism was realized through affiliation with a paternal ideal: first, in childhood with the family; then in professional apprenticeship, with an institution and community; and finally, with the spiritual father and nation, which symbolically represented a reunification (p. 44). (The language betrays a gendered religious and sociopolitical vision.) As McKnight describes it,

> [T]he institutional structure of Puritan society was not set up to oppress one's free will, but actually made one's individuality and identity possible. Without it, no spiritual or mundane life had any meaning, for it was believed that the person could not transcend his or her condition without a social form or language of interpretation and institutional guidance. (2003, p. 46)

Only in the 19th century did the modern self-reliant and self-possessive conception of the American individual emerge (p. 44). Primarily in the 19th and 20th centuries, with the birth of psychoanalysis, increased secularization and the denigration of religion, the intensification of capitalism, technological advances, mass public schooling, and an embedded scientific consciousness, we came to attach to a more autonomous individual and a recognition of institutions as hindrances to individual desire for personal expression or freedom (p. 47).

A changing lexicon exemplifies the cultural shift to a more isolated individualism and the evolution of narcissistic defenses. The *Oxford English Dictionary* shows, for example, that apathy began to acquire negative connotations in the mid- to late 1800s, moving from being considered a stoic virtue to being identified with indifference and sluggishness. Similarly, Patricia Meyer Spacks's (1995) research on British literature reveals that the word *boredom* did not significantly enter the English lexicon until the late 1800s, and its use began to increase dramatically in the mid-1950s (pp. 3, 13). Prior to the 1800s the emphasis on personal responsibility, combined with a sense of spiritual accountability, did not provide the opportunity for the introduction and indulgence of boredom. Spacks attributes its rise to an increasing cultural acceptance of individualism and subjective experience. The increasing focus on the self, and the gratification of the self, led to boredom being understood as the result of lack of external stimuli rather than an internal psychic dynamic. This narcissistic defense breeds a different cognizance of others, by which objects—others—might be perceived as boring, as uninteresting, as commodities, as irrelevant.

In several ways the psychiatric establishment contributed to the focus on self. As Safran (2003) documents, psychoanalysis emerged at a time when religious worldview was fading, taking shape as a "system of healing" when alliances to religion were thinning (pp. 3–4). Yet, according to Epstein, while Western psychotherapy has been able to identify the problem of the restless, estranged, and insecure self it has not been able to work with this problem directly and deliver freedom from narcissistic craving (pp. 6, 39). Epstein contends that part of the problem lies in continued psychotherapeutic investments in self-reconstitution—that is, analytic and interpretative listening practices centered upon the search for the discovery and narrative reconstruction of a true self (p. 65). Despite the insights of some Western psychoanalysts such as Winnicott, who has pointed out that there is little point in formulating such an identity except for the purposes of understanding the false self, Epstein (1995) notes that many psychotherapists largely still consider themselves custodians of a true self (p. 72). Moreover, the focus of much therapy is on the search not just for self-realization but also on happiness in the belief that these two pursuits are synonymous (Needleman, 1976; 1994). Safran (2003) similarly writes that "psychoanalysis and other forms of psychotherapy can perpetuate or exacerbate the pathology that they are attempting to remedy. By focusing on the enrichment of the self they can create pathological individualism" (p. 7). Education faces a similar dilemma.

The quest for identity is also evident in 19th- and 20th-century Western literature, which produced a very new literary genre of journeying. In these centuries, journeying includes the (quest)ion of whether one can determine one's own destiny. In this spirit, Dickens (1849–50/1966) opens his semiautobiographical novel *David Copperfield* with his protagonist wondering if he shall turn out to be the hero of his own life (p. 49). As literary critic Wayne C. Booth (1988) observes, "for complex reasons, much modern thought about the 'individual' … has stressed the search inward for the core of the real 'me,' the 'authentic' self, unencumbered" (p. 237). Authenticity in these terms means separation, the defining of oneself against something or someone else. Booth remarks that the modern search for one's true self involves peeling away the "inauthentic, insincere, alien influences that might deflect the self from its unique, individual destiny" (p. 237). He contends that these alien influences have been social and institutional ones, in recognition of the historical and modern failures of church, state, and nation to offer refuge from violence and abuse. Fear of rebellion among the masses against institutional authority thus meets fear among individuals of institutional absorption and constraints. Self-composition becomes a creative effort for many writers and artists in the face of the dangers of mass conformity and blind patriotism. Referencing modern novels such as George Orwell's *1984* and James Joyce's *The Portrait of the Artist as a Young Man*, Booth illustrates how the protagonists in these novels risk loneliness and persecution to struggle to develop their characters in an environment that threatens the very extinction of individual freedom.

Life's but a Tale

I have sought to foreground the hidden dimension of fear that motivates a spirit of control, censorship, and the construction of barriers and binaries. From within a Buddhist perspective, we can see how fears throughout Western history have contributed to the shifting shape and intensification of individualism as a concept signifying separateness. Economic, social, political, personal, and religious fears of rebellion and also of assimilation have fortified individual and collective psychic defenses. The present-day individual by and large continues a self-determined autobiographical pursuit for a differentiated, sovereign self and for a life of happiness. This search generally is confined to a continuum that ranges from conformity to nonconformity within the umbrella of larger normative social structures. Yoshiharu Nakagawa (2000) details the "catch-22" in modern Western principles of individualism and individual liberty: while Western principles applaud the realization of independent self-identity as an educational outcome, the "successful" formation of this identity ultimately depends upon a servile response to governing linguistic, cultural, economic, religious, and political bodies and norms. That is, individualism is accomplished through a complex process of learning to find oneself within an adherence to particular social structures. Even individuals who seek to rebel against educational and social structures conform to the degree that they measure their differences by and against prevailing social norms and continue to perceive themselves in ontological and dualistic terms, often negotiating life in ways consistent with a samsaric worldview.

In my view, the mythos of separate and secure individualism can consequently stir up an unhealthy dose of conformity and alienation—conformity in the guise or deceit of individual freedom to be different, and alienation through the processes of identifying one's unique character, which, in many respects, entails determining preferences of one over the other. There is little that ventures behind the screen of preferences. The greater the attachment to one's preferences (to *this* and not *that*), the greater the risk of isolation, division, and discord. Not only individuals, but also groups merge on the basis of *this us* and not *that other.* And separation develops. There is a dangerous dynamic at work here. Right and might can begin to attach as we draw increasingly firm boundaries around our self-image, and views become entrenched in the exigencies of tradition. We can hold on ferociously and fearfully, as if our very survival depends on it. And discrimination, prejudice, forces of conversion, oppression, exploitation, and annihilation can threaten to ensue. The pursuit for autonomous identity at minimum creates a tension between the instrumental use and abuse of another and environment for the attainment of one's own individual and collective happiness and a more democratic, caring, and interdependent worldview. This striving for a personal and national *I* thus actually and ironically produces rather than resolves the very question of one's responsibilities to another. In other words, without the insistent and unmitigated press for separate being (over and against what Nhat Hanh describes as our contrary underlying natural condition of "interbeing"), would ethics be the issue it is?

Buddhism reveals individualism to reside more deeply in egoistic machinations—in the mind's delusion of itself as a permanent, substantive "self." While the West has made cultures and nations out of the cultivation of varieties of different levels and shapes of individualism, it is important to note that Buddhism identifies the self's confusions about identity, time, and space, as a human—and thus universal—phenomenon. In this sense, everyone in the world experiences fear and desire and is inclined to perceive in egocentric ways. However, individuals, communities, and cultures negotiate and attend to these experiences and attachments differently in reference to their understandings and investments. Religions ideally serve as comfort and also as guideposts for a journey that deflates egocentrism. Ideally, they deconstruct the *I* and offer some constructive, holistic balance that enables the emergence and maintenance of inner and outer peace and nonviolence. It seems to me that what ultimately characterizes the secular West is not a belief in self per se but the intense and normalized *pursuit, attachment to,* and *entrenchment* of an *I*. The gratification, production, and consumption of individualism and identity is valued at the expense of the consideration and cultivation of another side. As we have seen, Buddhism stresses the consequences of attachment to figuring out the essence of who we are and the impossibility of once and for all satisfying desire (Epstein, 1995, p. 55). The search for a definitive self is in vain because the human condition is such that self as autonomous and fixed is a false construct. In baring this attachment to self as a constructed fiction, Buddhism shows life to imitate art. Because we firmly believe in a foundational and separate self, we compose ourselves as the lead characters in an autobiographical story. The story of our lives is at once tragic and comic in the sense of the needless suffering and antics that are produced by our misguided strivings to overcome our insecurities and to consolidate the *I* and live happily every after. Naively, we weave a plot of fear—Shakespearian echoes of sound and fury—replete with encounters with dualities (duels) and threats to the coherence of the self we have individually and socially created. Through this plot we come to define and settle in our selves. But, in the Buddhist view, this anxiety-filled story is one of samsara and rarely leads to fulfillment and peace, whether individual or collective.

Perhaps this is why the protagonist in the mythic narrative of the West eventually comes to experience the impossibility of the search and suffers a profound and pervasive melancholic sense of loss. As Booth (1988) maintains, "sooner or later one hopes to locate and remove all alien stuff and discover bedrock—but what one discovers is emptiness, and the makings of an identity crisis" (p. 237). This emptiness is not like the Buddhist sense of no-self, which ultimately illuminates fluidity and interconnectedness with others, with nature, and with the universe, but rather like a hollowness and the incapacity to know life and love.

Certainly, as Booth (1988) remarks, the arrival of the "posts-" in theory since the 1960s all stand as efforts to deconstruct the myth of individualism, aspiring to show us that "the isolated individual self simply does not, cannot exist" (p. 238). Contemporary theorists such as Foucault and Barthes have variously pinpointed the "death of the author" and shown subjects to be constructed through language and culture. Within (post)modern understandings, character becomes a matter of performance, the enactment of or resistance to socially constructed roles via pastiche and parody in order to reveal the deceits and conceits of identity. And yet, Booth (1988) and others (e.g., Wellmer, 1993) note the persistence of modernity and its trappings within and among a fragmented (post)modern sensibility. I wonder if part of the problem might not be that, in addition to sentiments of loss and emptiness that cannot be rationalized or played away, the (post)modern self wrestles with generations of fears that have not been faced, and that the self, moreover, simply does not know *how to face*. When we look at where we are now, we see what we are harvesting from the past—not just the continued spinning of individualism but also the psychic effects of generations of fear and imagined antidotes of denial, repression, and control. As poet W. B. Yeats (1921/1973) has written, "[t]hings fall apart; the center cannot hold." (Post)modern irony in this case might be regarded not only as a freeing venture (if momentary) but also as an intellectual 21st-century psychic defense. Abraham and Torok (1994) detail the generational suffering produced by unacknowledged and unexpressed events and emotions and illustrate how over time these events and emotions are encrypted, assuming returned forms difficult to decipher—the very stuff of anxiety. Krishnamurti (1953) describes how fear not only kills our spirit but also invites apathy and violence, commenting that

> fear perverts intelligence and is one of the causes of self-centered action ...
>
> fear dulls the mind and heart so that we are not alert to the whole signifi-
> cance of life; we become insensitive to our own sorrows, to the movement of
> the birds, to the smiles and miseries of others ....
>
> fear in whatever form prevents the understanding of ourselves and of our
> relationship to all things. (pp. 34, 57, 58)

As long as we have not given full attention to our fears, and the contexts that support them, selves and nations are inclined to continue their restless search for security, control, and riches, even to the point of participating in violence. In her novel *Ceremony* (1986), Leslie Marmon Silko (1986) writes of the injustices committed against Native Americans by Whites:

> They fear.
> They fear the world.
> They destroy what they fear.
> They fear themselves ...
>
> (pp. 135–136)

Within the public sphere and popular culture it seems that Western society has arrived at a crossroads, and new currents are afoot, in response to the question of "Where do I/we go from here"? For some, the answer has been a return to conservative safety nets of familiar ideas and divisions. Of fundamentalism, Safran (2003) writes, "In its extremity and rigidity, it involves a brittle and defensive attempt to revitalize a fragmented culture and shore up a sense of self under assault" (p. 20). But, for others, the failed search for an authentic self seems to be leading to a search for a more integrated and awakened self, a different kind of protagonist, one defined not by attainment and essentialism but by processes of letting go.

Beyond Asia, Buddhism is becoming an increasingly traveled road (Prebish and Baumann, 2002), and is being variously described as one among the healing arts that provides a "corrective" against individualism and alienation (Safran, 2003). Buddhism appeals to Westerners for multiple reasons: it isn't a religion demanding a leap of faith in the traditional Judeo-Christian model (although, as Safran carefully notes, the reality of this is very complex); its constructivist insights resonate well with (post)modern understandings; it is strongly self-reliant and, in large measure, embraces rigorous questioning of self and authority; it is accessible; and it offers a psychological, philosophical, and/or spiritual path. One central component of this path is the practice of mindfulness conjoined with meditation. While meditation styles are varied and numerous, as are Buddhist traditions, in what follows, I briefly outline the Vipassanā practice of the Theravādan tradition (as it is the practice with which I'm a little bit more familiar).

Vipassanā

Following the Buddha's passing, Buddhism branched into two dominant schools: *Mahāyāna* (or "great raft") and *Hinayana* (or "little raft"), the latter also becoming more centrally known as *Theravada*, the "Way of the Elders." Early Mahāyāna Buddhism was inclined to envision the Buddha as world savior who divinely inspires others to become Buddhas and placed its emphasis on the cultivation of compassion, on lay rather than monastic communities, on ritual, and on notions of grace and reverence. In contrast, Theravāda Buddhism tended to view the Buddha as a supreme sage and teacher who acquired insight through personal struggle and stressed the importance of self-reliance in the processes of spiritual cultivation, monasticism, and wisdom—from which compassion arguably naturally flows (Smith and Novak, 2003, pp. 63–73). Theravāda also sought to adhere more strictly to the traditional teachings of Guatama Buddha himself, as recorded in the earliest texts, the Pali Canon. Scripted in approximately 100 B.C.E. in a language close to the Buddha's own, the canon contains the *Sutta Pitaka* (a basket of discourses given by the Buddha), the *Vinaya Pitaka* (a basket of discipline or code of rules laid out by the Buddha), and the *Abhidhamma* (summaries and lists of teachings in the discourses). Theravādians view themselves as having two tasks: studying the Pali scriptures and practicing Vipassanā meditation.

Vipassanā meditation, according to Smith and Novak (2003), loosely translates as "insight" or "penetrative seeing"; it consists of two practices: Samatha meditation, which trains the mind in one-pointed concentration and tranquility, and insight meditation which succinctly provides practitioners with direct understanding of the nature of mind and reality. In the *Satipatthāna Sutta* (Discourse on the [Four] Arousings of Mindfulness), the Buddha maintains that meditators should train their one-pointed concentration on four objects of contemplation: body, feeling, consciousness, and mental phenomena. With regard to the first contemplation, they should monitor, for example, their breath, posture, and any bodily change. In the second contemplation, they should observe the coming and going of more subtle bodily sensations, particularly as these are associated with pleasure, displeasure, and indifference. The third contemplation involves attention to whether the mind is light or heavy, distracted or concentrated, and so on. The final contemplation is directed toward the nature of one's thoughts and emotions (e.g., the presence of desire, anger, fear, attachment, etc.) and their relationship to other Buddhist doctrines, such as the *Four Noble Truths,* the *Five Skandhas,* and the *Seven Factors of Awakening* (Smith and Novak, 2003, p. 206, n. 17).

As attention to these four objects becomes more concentrated, meditators become increasingly aware not only of the full dimensions of these objects but also of impermanence, no-self, and craving. Indeed, Vipassanā is nothing other than simply observing *what actually is* with increasing insight and capacities of attunement. At a meditation retreat I attended one summer, the monk asked us to describe what we hear when we invite a bell to sound. At first, practitioners hear only the most obvious reverberations. The more attention is cultivated, however, the more fine-tuned hearing becomes, until endless reverberations resound. So it is with the objects of meditation and mindfulness. Moreover, meditation involves bringing a scientific spirit of inquiry to practice, objective observations in which no attempts are made to judge or change anything. Buddhism acknowledges the physical and psychic dangers of repression or dissipation of emotion and affect (Easwaran, 1985, p. 146). Vipassanā encourages practitioners to instead skillfully touch and investigate fear as it arises, pulses, and passes in our bodies, to come to learn the multiple and highly subtle ways in which each of us denies, avoids, bypasses, or represses it; creatively weaves a distracting net of thoughts, ideas, images, and story lines around it; attaches an "I" to it, intellectually tries to rationalize and solve it; and so on (Goldstein and Kornfield, 2001). By and large we do everything with fear, but face that fear directly. Buddhism thus encourages confrontation with fear in the sense not of a reality TV show like *Fear Factor*—which requires contestants, for example, to stand in the midst of a swarm of bees—but of a deep reflective exploration into the highly complex nature and mechanisms of fearing as it moves (within) us. In so doing, the intricacies of how fears are embedded in delusion, are intertwined with aversion and attachment, and arise and pass like everything else become apparent. As meditators become more and more experientially intimate with fear, attending to it within the stillness and calmness of meditation, applying analytic insight to it and learning to channel it in positive ways, Buddhism holds that fear gradually loses its grip. Practitioners come to develop a new relationship to fear in which it becomes appreciated as a potential "sign of growth, as the membrane between what we know and something new. It tells us we are about to open to something bigger than the world we usually experience" (Goldstein and Kornfield, p. 222). Smith and Novak (2003) describe how, as the unskilled meditator's modes of conduct become revealed, new modes of conduct take "shape under the influence of the ethical ideals of the Eightfold Path [i.e. right understanding, right resolve, right speech, right action, right livelihood, right effort, right mindfulness, right concentration]" (p. 84).[2]

Vipassanā meditation slowly illuminates that far beneath conventional reality, beneath the hustle and bustle of everyday life, is an underlying reality in which there is no separateness but rather vast stillness and emptiness. With much perseverance and concentration, like the Buddha, meditators can come to fully enter into an experience of emptiness. Indeed, they can experience it because it is the natural state of our (non-)mind/being. Easwaran (1985) likens the mind to the mechanism of film projection. While we generally experience film as continuous, in effect, every moment of image is followed by a moment of nonimage or darkness/emptiness, and only when the projector is slowed down can we see a flicker of emptiness (p. 53). In successive stages, rigorously developed one-pointed concentration and mindfulness (rather than egoistic will) slow the mind such that contemplation is easier and the experience of emptiness becomes accessible. Ambition, goal making, willfulness, desire: all these commonly cultivated and institutionally supported aspects of contemporary character can't get one there. Rather, these stages involve the meditator in numerous (not to mention, difficult) acts of letting go. The meditator is challenged to slowly identify and subsequently relinquish all the heavy baggage associated with attachments to all the characteristic players of identity—the busybody, the chatterer, the thinker, the doer, the desirer, the striver, the worrier, the commentator, the comparer, the competitor, the clock watcher, the projector, the lecturer, the judger, the controller, and so on. Investments in all characters are discarded as their limitations and hindrances become evident, and obstacles such as fear and doubt are overcome bit by bit. In the end, there is no-character. Only emptiness. Only fluidity and interdependence. Letting go is immense and sustaining.

The deeper the meditation the more the conventional world and its ways becomes increasingly remote and nonessential, rather like the experience of the surface of an ocean when we are far below sea level (Easwaren, 1985, p. 51). Yet, instead of this being an oppressive or claustrophobic experience, it is described as profoundly liberating; indeed, meditation shows freedom in an entirely new light from the common Western notion of it as the exercise of attachment to individuality. Also, as skilled meditators venture further and further into the innermost reaches of the mind, they experience ever-intense layers of positive emotions such as rapture, loving kindness, compassion, joy, and equanimity.[3] Such emotions and capacities are opened up because all the baggage of being has been left behind. Now practitioners can really experience selves, others, and world—with eyes, ears, and heart all wide open. Therefore, with the unfolding experience of emptiness paradoxically comes an abiding experience of fullness and compassion, often recognized as an emerging radiance felt within and reflected without. As Easwaren (1985) describes, the Buddha journeyed into the very farthest reaches of the mind—nirvana, a realm of complete purity unbroken by any thought, entirely unaffected by pain/pleasure and craving, and where the experience of emptiness is not fleeting but infinitely lasting. He draws attention to the Buddha's description of enlightenment as a "chick breaking out of its shell," and adds that "we have no more idea of what life is really like than a chicken has before it hatches. ... For a moment the Buddha draws aside the curtain of time and space and tells us what it is like to see into another dimension" (p. 47).

Care Education

Buddhism contributes to educational theory and practice in two vital and closely knit ways: it offers a path/praxis, and a holistic vision and experience of self and world that issues forth emotional healing, "fellow feeling," and equanimity. While contemporary theory has in recent years turned its attention to ethics (Garber, Hanssen, & Walkowitz, 2000) alerted by the need for a greater consciousness of responsibility/responsivity, one defined in terms different from much of Western philosophy, debate occurs concerning poststructuralism's abilities to reach into the everyday. Poststructuralism has notably deconstructed the self, but some theorists contend that it has as yet neither been able to communicate with the public sphere nor offer a readily accessible practice of daily engagement. We are still living with too much fear, anxiety, anger, and greed, and our social problems remain. Essays in David Loy's (1996) edited collection *Healing Deconstruction: Postmodern Thought in Buddhism and Christianity*, for example, point not only to deconstruction's liberatory potential through its critique of logocentrism but also to deconstruction's difficulties in leaping from "*theoria* into a healing *praxis*" (Loy, 1996, p. 57; emphasis in the original). Contributors like Berry (1996) reflect upon the continued refusal of deconstructionists to engage the work of feminist theorists.

Yet, feminist theorists have been very attentive to concrete interconnections between inner and outer world, between theory and praxis. The work of feminist care theorists, especially, has gained momentum as a way of addressing contemporary issues concretely and in ways attuned to emotions and affect. Specifically in the field of education, care theorist Noddings (1992, 2002) has recently focused her attention on the problems of youth violence. She asserts, "Violence has many roots, but it seems obvious that people who feel cared for and who have learned to care for others will be less likely to engage in violent acts" (2002, p. 38). In emphasizing the educational need for a relational sense of care, Noddings draws attention to the boundaries of character education. While care theorists share with character educators the view that a better world depends on the presence of good people, Noddings (2002) maintains that care theorists differentiate themselves in significant ways. They are more relation-centered rather than agent-centered, concerned less with inculcating virtues directly than with establishing conditions that invite the best in students. They do not rely on eternal truths, but give considered attention to situational factors in discussing virtues. They emphasize dialogue, and invert the Kantian privileging of reason over feeling, stressing the cultivation of emotions and moral sentiments over principles (pp. 1–9).

Moreover, while care and character education cite literature as a means of accomplishing their aims, Noddings (2002) indicates key differences. Although both value stories as a vehicle for the discussion of virtue, care theorists prefer a literature curriculum that is less didactic, presents moral dilemmas, problematizes ethical decisions, allows for reflection on why literary characters make the choices they do, and generally wrestles with essential questions about existence. This contrasts sharply to a more didactic character-based curriculum celebrating Western heroes (p. 2). Noddings accepts the limits of ethical heroism, citing a scene from Orwell's *1984,* in which the protagonist Winston Smith "threatened with the thing that he most feared betrayed Julia, whom he loved" (Noddings, 2002, p. 9). Indeed, faced with extreme physical and psychological torture at the hands of a brutal regime, Smith is understandably unable to hold onto his integrity and his love for Julia. The novel ends with a bleak description of an aging Smith, whose entire spirit has been broken and who in the end fully succumbs to the brainwashing of the Big Brother government. Noddings maintains that because the personal and social events we experience can be so challenging to overcome, we need to concentrate on developing and maintaining an environment of care where moral life can flourish (p. 9).

Personal and sociostructural cultivation of care is without doubt crucial to individual and collective well-being, especially in America, where the "sink or swim" mentality seems so imprinted on the capitalist national dream at the expense of so much fear, anxiety, and suffering. In my view, institutionally supported expressions of care (e.g. Medicare, ecological care) are essential to the well-being of a people and country. How is it at all possible to have a healthy and peaceful society and environment if governmental bodies do not show a caring disposition through their policies and programs?

While, to me, the importance of a relational sense of care is beyond debate, it seems at least equally important to probe the depth and influential scope of our negative and destructive emotions if we are to be able to really care in the first place. Buddhism brings to care education an abiding awareness of just how difficult the cultivation of care and compassion can be, because our egoistic attachments to our identities and to permanence are so very deeply entrenched. At issue here is not Winston Smith's naturally impossible individual effort to withstand torture against a violent regime, but Big Brother's social acceptance of fear as a foundation for governance and relationship. Orwell's 1984 shows a government that breeds fear in order to retain power and control: "In our world there will be no emotions except fear, rage, triumph, and self-abasement" (Orwell, 1954, p. 215). The novel makes all too clear that fear and greed inhibit if not destroy capacities for care: care and fear are intimately connected, and so, in order to enable the former to thrive one is challenged to reckon with the latter, individually and socially to learn the origin, nature, and nuances of its regulative force. By doing so, one would hope, wisdom (including the wisdom of care and compassion) rather than fear can influence public decision making.

Getting to the true heart of one's no-self and of social transformation is a long, long journey that exceeds the time/space boundaries and formal curriculum/pedagogy of conventional educational enterprise. Noddings (2002) observes how philosopher and activist Simone Weil "said that the form of attention required by caring or living is very rare" (p. 29). Noddings believes it is more common than Weil contends, citing parenthood as an example. While I agree that parenthood illustrates exceptional capacities for love, I also tend to be sympathetic to Weil's view because Buddhism makes apparent how our fears, desires, and attachments are so very deep-rooted. It is so difficult to fully attend and be open to children, to let them go and not try to exercise control over them, because it is so difficult to let go of our selves. Perhaps it is because Weil was also influenced by Eastern thought (Eppert, 2004a) that she identifies caring attention as rare and emphasizes the pedagogical and curricular value of a "gymnastics of attention" (1952/1997, 1951/1973). Indeed, while Buddhism brings light to the complexities of attention in relation to an egocentric worldview, it also unearths fascinating nuances of care and compassion—identifying, for instance, different forms and possibilities. As Nakagawa (2000) observes, "the Buddhist idea of compassion can radically transform the meaning of care" (p. 232).

Literature and Arts Curricula

The current disconnections between educational theory/practice and many American educational structures are beyond belief. So many dynamic possibilities are sparkling in research and public cultural life in terms of individuals searching for and learning alternative ways of living and engaging with self, other, and environment. Yet, rather than be at the forefront of a transformational age of insight, wisdom, and compassion, a good deal of the public educational system remains largely entrenched within an outmoded web of beliefs and fears that makes genuine teaching and learning occur within fractured moments, through the persistence, patience, and passion of educators and students yearning and committed to bringing into the modern classroom arrangement some freeing breaths of air and thought. Purpel and McLaurin (2004) argue that we need to make the life journey for significance and the addressing of contemporary social problems the orientation, core, and content of our curricular and pedagogical endeavors. However, at this point in time, until educators can awaken politics (or politics awakens independently) from its national American Dream of what Pinar (2004) contrastingly identifies as the narcissistic "nightmare" of assembly-line corporate schooling, here in this fractured refuge lies one wellspring for significant conversation. One might ask what Buddhism (and other Eastern traditions) might bring to this specific space/time constellation to help us through our contemporary travails.

Krishnamurti invites education to awaken

> the capacity to be self-aware and not merely indulge in gratifying self-expression. ... The right kind of educator, seeing the inward nature of freedom, helps each individual student to observe and understand his own self-projected values and impositions; he helps him to become aware of the conditioning influences about him, and of his own desires, both of which limit his mind and breed fear; he helps him, as he grows to manhood, to observe and understand himself in relation to all things, for it is the craving for self-fulfillment that brings endless conflict and sorrow. ... Thus education, in the true sense, is the understanding of oneself, for it is within each one of us that the whole of existence is gathered. (1953, pp. 15, 17, 29)

For Krishnamurti, and much of Eastern thought, self-awareness rather than gratifying self-expression as the project of education is fashioned within the framework not of individualism and conventional reality but of emptiness and underlying interdependence. In Buddhism, the search for authenticity is the finding of no-self, a return that inscribes dissolution of attachments to both self and no–self. In fact, it seems multiple counter movements or reversals are at work in processes of Buddhist meditative educational inquiry: searching leads to the letting go of the will and desire, learning is replaced by the challenges of unlearning, the search for moral character gives rise to the ethical possibilities of "no-character," and the desire for significance gives way to the awareness of the significance of in-significance. Choosing gives way to embracing. Even the notion of crisis is undone, coming to appear as a time-bound concept and as a participant in and producer of fear and anxiety. Yet, these descriptions are weak—too singular, linear, and either/or. As Noel Gough (1990) emphasizes, the English language is limited, not getting out of dualisms easily, and English speakers can benefit from developing new words and new stories (p. 14). We need expressions that are less polarized, less aggressive, less one-directional, and more sustaining, integrated, balanced, more paradoxical; ones that embody and reflect our struggles as well as the possibilities of compassionate awareness, interdependence, farsighted wisdom, action, and equanimity—a nondualistic "middle way" language.

Our current global reality is very fragile; especially so is our environment. Our cities stand in danger of becoming concretized; our earth, a wasteland. Therefore, we need to care, learn compassion, and bring ourselves and our world more in balance through skillful means. To counter our samsaric orientation it might be productive to invite educational endeavors and communities that, in contrast to the current climate of testing and some of character education, favor self-reflection and self-understanding; cultivate care; and support searches for significance. And then we could encourage the tipping of the scales back even more toward holism through the introduction of a curriculum that exposes learners, via avenues such as literature and the arts, to Buddhist understandings—not only to complex dynamics such as fear but also to wisdom about attachment, compassion, impermanence, no-self, and the significance of in-significance.

I admit my own attachments to literature in advocating it and the arts as productive resources, here, and echo several of the justifications made by so many other past and present women and countless men throughout the centuries for the educational possibilities of literature in the wake of Plato's charges and his exiling of poets from his *Republic*. This is not, concurrently, to infer that literature is pure and can't reflect or contribute to violence. The work of many feminist, poststructuralist, and postcolonial literary theorists has shown how reading, writing, and language generally are culturally inscribed, are able to manifest bias and to wound deeply. Yet, as an avid reader, it seems to me that literature is one among other forms of human expression with (only) the potential "to make something happen" (Des Pres, 1988, p. 231). Literature and the arts at their most dynamic invite outside-the-box critical, creative, and contemplative engagements. Rather than hurry toward censorship, we might investigate the natures of that *something*, explore what literature might open up for those engaging it to learn about themselves and their world. My own preoccupation continues to be with the psychosocial dynamics of reading, viewing, and witnessing cultural texts about social suffering, as this constellation of engagement has long struck me as a potentially fertile site of entrance into a study of the heart of human relation, construction, confusion, and (educative) insight (Eppert, 1999, 2000, 2002a, 2002b, 2003, 2004b). Interactions between text and reader can shed valuable light on shared and also different situational human fears, attachments, and character traits as these intertwine with social issues. In this vein, as Des Pres suggests, with skillful reading, literature "allows me to know what I fear, to understand (by standing under) the burden of my humanness" (p. 231).

Literature is often censored out of fear. That said, karma, interbeing, and the general Buddhist awareness that thinking, hearing, seeing, reading, and writing resonates—affects like a stone thrown in water—also invite responsive caution.

This awareness is rooted in sensitivity, while the orientation of many who support censorship and propaganda is reactive. The reactive participates in what Mikhail Bakhtin identifies as a centripedal homogenizing force (1975/1990). Wisdom contrarily emerges from an "otherwise than being" (Lévinas, 1991). Humphries (1999) describes the U.S. media, which so frequently feeds upon fear, as motivated by the desire for domination and manipulation rather than a sense of responsibility and involvement (p. xvi).

How, more succinctly, might literature and the arts welcome a more balanced and cross-cultural dialogue that excavates possibilities beneath the surface of the self, and even beneath the contemporary fragmented self? It would be ideal if institutions of learning could simplify a little—and become more still and balanced generally, offering learners sustaining spaces for (re)creation and contemplative practices such as mindfulness and meditation. Vipassanā meditation is currently being taught to youths in prison and, according to Garbarino's (1999) research, with significant success. The challenge in such an offering is to include but also move beyond important basic stress-reduction strategies to pose questions of who we are (not) and how we are (not) living. While we could choose not to deploy any books, thought-provoking texts can, ideally alongside meditation, also supply nourishment for contemplation, conversation, and expression. Maxine Greene (1995, 2001) often speaks of the arts as a promising educational arena for awakening.

I follow Lévinas in recognizing the fault lines of prescription and method, and would like to paint just some broad strokes of possibilities for an integrated and more balanced literature curriculum. Pinar (1975) considers several productive components of a course of study in literature: archaeological investigations of the text's situatedness in literary and intellectual history's textual analysis; reader response; and reflections upon the reader's biography, intellectual gestalt, conceptual lenses, and psychology (pp. 418–422). Eastern ideas and conversations can suffuse and permeate all these components. Most immediately, a curriculum bent in this direction might deconstruct the myth of an original, self-enclosed Western and national literary canon and identity by illustrating the extent to which writers therein have themselves been influenced by Eastern thought. In the context of the traditional American canon, authors such as Whitman, Emerson, and Thoreau come readily to mind, among numerous others.

Furthermore, traditional Western canonical literature—through novels such as Orwell's *1984* or Joseph Conrad's *Heart of Darkness* (1902/1973)—offers compelling springboards for hermeneutic inquiry into individual and collective samsara. Orwell's *1984*, for instance, illuminates not only how a political body utilizes fear to maintain control and cultivate obedience but also how a regime of fear and terror impacts the spirit of individuals and creates complex and damaging psychosocial dynamics of acquiescence and resistance.

Mary Aswell Doll (2000) draws on Buddhist themes to envision a "mythopoetics of curriculum." She beautifully illustrates how Conrad's *Heart of Darkness*, in effect, reworks the Western hero ideal that developed from the Indo-European myth of Theseus and the minotaur, in which the protagonist slays the monster, conquers nature, and opens the world to the powers of reason. Doll (2000) discusses how this myth "forged the Western world's conception of dark as fearsome and led a long parade of tellings about the necessity to kill the dark" (p. 82). Conrad's protagonist Marlow, however, who "had the pose of a Buddha preaching in European clothes" (Conrad, quoted in Doll, 2000, p. 82), shows darkness not as something to be conquered or even conquerable. Rather, the character Kurtz's journey into the depths of the African jungle comes to entail witnessing darkness as a truth to be feared, in which fear is reconfigured with a trusting and reverential, spiritual connotation (Doll, 2000, p. 82). Marlow, the story's narrator, returns readers to a preconventional and mystical understanding of the "monster as something to be-friend, not to kill" (p. 82). Fear reconfigured within the social imaginary in sublime and reverential terms joins William Doll's (2002) productive description of fear as that which attends our encounters with specters that incite us to change.

This literature might interweave with stories that reveal an array of protagonists journeying for in-significance. Cyril Lanier's (1997) short animated film *The Master of the Carriage,* about a 19th-century carriage driver's mythic and allegorical series of adventures from the outer to the inner, is a tender and delightful example. Another is German author Herman Hesse's novel *Siddhartha* (1922/2003). Along his journey to finally face his fear of himself (p. 36), the protagonist's understanding of life becomes more profound, and he develops a capacity to listen that stands in significant contrast from the lack of attunement displayed by Miss Mangle's friends in Winterson's *Art and Lies.* Toward the novel's conclusion, Siddhartha arrives at a large river in the forest, the same one across which a man had once ferried him when he was a young man still in the early stages of his search. Newly awakened and gazing at the streaming water, he feels that it has something special to tell him, and hears an inner voice invoking him to attend to its teachings: "Love this water! Stay with it! Learn from it!" (p. 89). He recognizes the river carries many secrets, but has yet to be privy to more than one:

He saw the water running and running, constantly running, and yet it was always there, was always and forever the same, and yet new every instant! Who could grasp this, who could fathom this?! He did not grasp or fathom it, he felt only an inkling stirring, a distant memory, godly voices. (p. 89)

He continues his way upstream until he reaches the ferryman Vasudeva, whom he befriends and who invites him to live with him in his hut. Siddhartha expresses his gratitude to Vasudeva for the invitation and notes how intently the ferryman listens to his passenger's life story:

One of the ferryman's greatest virtues was that he knew how to listen like few other people. Without a word from Vasudeva, the speaker felt that the ferryman took in his words, silent, open, waiting, missing none, impatient for none, neither praising nor blaming, but only listening. Siddhartha felt what happiness it is to unburden himself to such a listener, to sink his own life into this listener's heart, his own seeking, his own suffering. (p. 92)

Siddhartha thanks the river man for hearing him so well, commenting, "'Rare are the people who know how to listen, and I have never met anyone who knew it so well as you. This too I will learn from you'" (p. 92). But Vasudeva reminds him about the pedagogical injunction from the river:

"You will learn it … but not from me. It was the river that taught me how to listen. … The river knows everything. … Look, you too have already learned from the river that it is good to strive downward, to sink, to seek the depth." (p. 93)

Eastern myths and sacred literature additionally portray struggles with fear and insights into relationships between nonegocentric awareness and social responsibility, and could be included in a world literature curriculum—a productive, emerging alternative to the traditional Western canon of English literature. In some of this mythical and sacred literature, fear and intimidation are represented allegorically in the form of supernatural evil or death. In the *Kathaka Upinashad* it is the god of death (Yama, Mrytu) who tries to tempt the Brahmin youth Nachiketa away from his quest for knowledge. And, we have seen how the mythic demon Mara haunts the Buddha-to-be, not just as he meditates beneath the bodhi tree but also, as Hajime Nakamura's *Gotama Buddha: A Biography Based on the Most Reliable Texts* (2000) emphasizes, for seven long years before his enlightenment. Following his attainment of nirvana, the Buddha wrestles with the question of his social responsibilities, debating whether to retreat from the world or return to it, in recognition that his teachings may neither be wanted, nor understood. He returns because of enlightened compassion—an important though sometimes neglected part of the story of departure and arrival.

Yet, as David Loy and Linda Goodhew (2004) point out, while this sacred literature is valuable, "new stories are needed that relate more directly to the experience of (post)modern people living in the twenty-first century" (p. 6). These authors look to popular science fiction and fantasy to uncover Buddhist themes. For example, they offer a fascinating reading of J. R. R. Tolkien's *Lord of the Rings* triology, showing Frodo to be the antihero who leaves home "not to slay a dragon or win some treasure but to *let go* of something. His renunciation of the Ring is not done for any selfish purpose but to save the world—the defining characteristic of a bodhisattva" (p. 8). *Lord of the Rings* reveals the karmic effects of the Ring of Power, showing how different motivations lead to different actions (p. 9). Apart from Tolkien, Loy and Goodhew also highlight the work of Ursula K. Le Guin and the animated films of Hayao Miyazaki. While they discuss Miyazaki's *Nausicaa of the Valley of the Winds* and *Princess Mononoke* to illustrate the worth of nonviolence, Miyazaki's recent animated film *Spirited Away* (2001) is a beautiful telling of a young girl named Chihiro and her reluctant willingness to confront and work through her fears and enter a world of spirits in order to rescue her parents.

Eastern, and specifically Buddhist, themes signpost *mindful readings,* bringing a different perspective to a contemporary kaleidoscope of Western theories of interpretation, such as reader-response theories and literary anthropology (Iser, 1989; Rosenblatt, 1968, 1995), hermeneutics (Gadamer, 1960/2005), and ethical criticism (Eaglestone, 1997; see also Attridge, 1999; Buell, 1999; Eppert, 1999; Newton, 1995). Some scholars and educators are already exploring the possibilities here. For example, curriculum theorist Dennis Sumara (2002), appreciating that access to information guarantees neither understanding nor deep insight, advocates that understanding be fostered through interpretative practices (p. xiv). Reading literature in school, he contends, still matters precisely because it can cultivate creative "opportunities for such practices to be learned" (p. xiv). Through his readings of such novels as Anne Michael's (1996) *Fugitive Pieces,* Martha Brooke's (1997) *Bone Dance,* and Mark Salzman's (2000) *Lying Awake,* Sumara eloquently conveys how mindfulness can support a close, committed, and sustained reading of texts.

And Jeff Humphries (1999), in his exciting work *Reading Emptiness: Buddhism and Literature,* also brings Eastern thought into Western engagements with literature and maintains that Buddhism invites an awareness "opposite to that of all Western literary theory" (p. xiii), which is riddled with dualistic thought and language. He does not articulate a Buddhist theory of literature per se, as he recognizes that there can be no such thing. Instead he seeks to illustrate how, in contrast to much conventional criticism, neither text nor reader has "any reified, static, or inherent existence, [but are instead] involved in a process of mutual 'projection,' two mutually reflecting sets of lenses or mirrors" (p. xiii)—in effect, caught in the web of Indra's net. He writes,

> [E]verything at any given moment exists in a relation of interdependence. Texts are like Zen gardens: What we see depends on what we bring to the seeing. ... To realize emptiness ... does not lead to denial, but affirmation ... in literary study, it does not shatter the text, but illumines it. (p. 36)

Humphries maintains that the unspecified loss that characterizes much of mainstream Western literature and art in the last two centuries as works of interminable mourning (p. 27) can also be positively regarded within a Buddhist context as processes of letting go, as "preliminary to ... enlightenment, which must bring an apprehension of occulted presence in and around us" (p. 28).

Currere and Witnessing

As I conclude this paper, two years after I began it, Hurricane Katrina—which devastated the Mississippi Coast and flooded much of southeast Louisiana, including the city of New Orleans—is two weeks past. And Hurricane Rita—which struck western Louisiana and its border with Texas—is one week past. Fear has naturally been in the forefront of these events. However, alongside so much amazing communal and collective attention, involvement, and activism, some reactive expressions of fear occurred that, in my view, served only to exacerbate rather than lessen anxiety, conflict, suffering, and isolationism. In Baton Rouge, for example, media accounts of the looting and lawlessness in New Orleans, and rampant local *rumors* of crimes committed by evacuees here in town, spawned the immediate shutting down of the downtown and the skyrocketing of gun sales at the local Wal-Mart. And, the other night, only two weeks after this current disaster that has left so many distraught and traumatized, unable to even yet register what has happened, national television was once again blasting the all-too-familiar question, "Are you safe?" Mainstream U.S. news devoted an hour to examining what might occur if the nation is hit by other disasters and what we in America can do to protect ourselves.

I register how all this news affects me, initiating ripples of fear. I feel the subtle ways fear enters me, and observe a cluster of thoughts: should I perhaps buy a weapon, a better alarm system, and secure my home and environment more fully in other ways? That I am even entertaining such questions is troubling and produces "dis-ease." Eastern thought provides me with a small bit of understanding, offering a view as to the origin and consequences of fear in self and society. It reveals how fear reproduces while it steals away from possibilities of personal and systemic vision, relationships with others, long-range change, and how one might begin to work to loosen fear's rhetoric and destructive grip.

Buddhist insights contribute to a curriculum and pedagogy of witnessing social suffering in several ways. In my view, these insights resonate productively with psychoanalytic educational awareness that "learning [is] a psychic event, charged with resistance to knowledge" and that the "wars within" are reflected in wars at large (Britzman, 1998, p. 118). Witnessing events of violence and suffering through testimonial engagements commonly elicit an unruly and charged terrain of difficult thoughts, memories, and emotions. As witnesses, we experience not only fear and anxiety but also anger, outrage, guilt, and shame, all of which limit our capacities to listen and respond. Long-held, cherished, and taken-for-granted knowledge, beliefs, mores, attitudes are placed into question, producing crises of identity and significance (Felman, 1992). Dynamics of melancholia and mourning are in play. Learners are confronted with the challenge of how to work with and through crisis, and several educators have wrestled with the pedagogical difficulties of witnessing in classroom contexts: how to negotiate the conflict and "discomfort" (Boler, 1999, pp. 175–203) that arises and facilitate ethical transitions? Discomfort is a terrific word choice because it highlights not only aspects of the nature of the encounter with social suffering but also our lack of facility and dis-ease with difficult and intense thoughts, memories, and emotions generally. Megan Boler (1999) and Michalinos Zembylas (2005) addresses the centrality yet surprising dearth of nuanced attention to emotion in scholarly and educational life.

Meditation supports emotional and cognitive literacy by providing opportunities for witnesses to "sit with" and allow a deeper understanding of the origins, nature, and consequences of what they are remembering, anticipating, thinking, and feeling to unfold. Indeed, in Buddhist meditation, discomfort is greeted as a good sign of our attachments and aversions, and welcomed as an opportunity to investigate its source and nature and practice acceptance and release. Even, for example, the simple discomfort at sitting for any length of time is instructive, providing a window into just how discomfort discomforts us and our restlessness to *do* something with it, in an immediate reactive sense: fix it, "tolerate" it, run from it, project it onto others, criticize it, and so on. Meditation can facilitate engagements with social suffering by attuning us to the intimacies of our psychic and physical landscapes such that when emotions arise, we don't as readily "act out" with repression, denial, aggression. It is also said to aid in the healing of trauma. Furthermore, meditation and mindfulness readily encompass "vigilance" (Simon and Eppert, 1997, p. 189) toward events and toward sentient and nonsentient others, exposing and guarding against egocentric engagements of voyeurism, spectatorship, identification, and projection. Nhat Hanh (1998) writes, "Whenever we hear a conversation or witness an event, our attention can be appropriate or inappropriate. If we are mindful, we will recognize which it is, nurture appropriate attention, and release inappropriate attention" (p. 33).

Diligent contemplative bodily practice, therefore, is essential. Body-mind are intertwined, laboring together. Richard Shusterman (2000) describes how Asian thought and practices, such as Tai Chi, yoga, meditation, support what he names "somaesthetics"; that is, "the awareness of our bodily states and feelings" for the pursuit of central philosophical aims—"knowledge, self-knowledge, right action" (pp. 268–267). He notes that while many ancient Greek philosophers emphasized the training of the body for the cultivation of wisdom and virtue, "a very sad curiosity of recent [Western] philosophy is that so much inquiry has been devoted to the ontology and epistemology of pain, so little to its psychosomatic management, to its mastery and transformation into tranquility" (p. 270).

Witnessing has been described by Roger Simon and I as calling for an "*embodied cognizance* within which one becomes aware of, self-present to, and responsive to something/someone beyond oneself" (Simon & Eppert, 1997, p. 183, emphasis added). Buddhism has heightened my appreciation that cognizance refers to insight rather than knowing or being aware as the product of thought and analysis alone. Critical thinking and analysis are vital but not enough to address fear, greed, and hatred, to heal, and to live in the world non-dualistically, connectedly, compassionately, and transformationally. To quote Packer and Swaebe again, from earlier in this chapter: "to solve the problem of ego there has to be *direct insight* into the whole movement of thought that is creating the ego" (p. 64). Insight and embodied experience walk hand-in-hand. Vipissana monk S. N. Goenka (1998) details different stages of a wisdom-based witnessing: the first is witnessing "what you have heard. It is someone else's wisdom, not yours" (p. 4); the second is "your intellectual reasoning, your understanding of someone else's wisdom" (pp. 4–5); the third is

> the truth you directly witness yourself. ... To listen and understand intellectu-
> ally is very helpful, but at the same time every teaching has to be witnessed.
> Belief in the Buddha's words is essential, but unless you yourself witness the
> truth you can never become enlightened. ... This is what is taught in the
> *Satipatthāna Sutta*. (p. 5)

Goenka's words stress the necessity of the inward-turned journey and how meditation can pierce the "entire field of mind and matter [so that] you can witness something beyond" (p. 4). The beyond that can be witnessed is "interbeing." Safran (2003) quotes Francis Cook: "There is no absolute reality beyond or distinct from this world of interdependent being. It is a place where the individual arises out of an extremely extensive environment of other individuals—parents, grandparents, culture, soil, water, stone, mist, and many, many more—and takes its place as one other individual. Once in the world, the individual is constantly and massively conditioned by the extensive environment of other individuals" (p. 23). Embodied witnessing not only answers but also, in effect, dissolves the question of whether and how we are our brothers' (and sisters') keepers, slowly illuminating universal connection and equipping us not just with insight but also with *capacities* to be fully—actively, wisely, and whole-heartedly in body and mind—responsive, responsible, and compassionate to the suffering of self, others, and the environment. It can constitute a healing resource.

The collection of the Buddha's essential teachings, the *Dhammapada*, recommends, "Before trying to guide others, be your own guide first. It is hard to learn to guide oneself" (*Dhammapada*, 1985, p. 121). Witnessing thus addresses the educator first and foremost. Before and/or as we embark on projects of social action, we are advised to turn inward, in the awareness that such a turn fuels transformation and reconstruction. Insight into no-self and in-significance can individually and collectively instruct and empower in ways that conventional contemporary Western identity construction cannot. We are invited to come to know ourselves fully, but the pedagogical injunction of self-knowledge and understanding, as this chapter has sought to illustrate, does not here denote an autonomous subject but rather the unpacking of the perception of and attachment to essentialism. Krishnamurti (1953) stresses,

> Surely, the teacher himself must first begin to see. He must be constantly
> alert, intensely aware of his own thoughts and feelings, aware of the ways in

which he is conditioned, aware of his activities and his response; for out of this watchfulness comes intelligence, and with it a radical transformation in his relationship to people and to things. (p. 103)

Autobiographical curriculum inquiry complements this exercising of attention, and one can readily identify relationships between Eastern thought and *currere*, "the running of the course" (Pinar, 1975, 1994, 1996, 2004). Pinar (1975) discusses the curriculum theorist/practitioner as on an educational journey or pilgrimage, rigorously engaged in questioning, studying, and reflecting upon his or her inner experience, his or her *Lebenswelt*. While he invokes a broad spectrum of writers in his contemplation upon the nature and possibilities of autobiographical inquiry, Pinar also attends to Zen's early influences upon him, linking processes of *currere* with contemplative investigations into one's attachments, fears, and, generally, the architecture of the self (1975, p. 411; 1994, pp. 146–147).

Furthermore, Pinar (2004) draws attention to the sociopolitical dynamics and implications of autobiographical educational inquiry: "only through a genuine democratization of one's interiorized elements, none of which gets deported (projected in psychoanalytic terms) to the bodies of others who then become 'others' can the body politic be reformed and the public sphere reconstructed" (p. 38). Both autobiographical inquiry and meditation/mindfulness recognize the subject as historically and ideologically constituted, and support Foucauldian analysis. If Pinar addresses misguided interpretations of *currere* as a solipsistic educational endeavor, Robert Hattam (this volume) tackles uninformed critiques that Buddhism is monastic and divorced from social concerns. Hattam illustrates how *engaged Buddhism*, for example, is fundamentally about the cultivation of mindfulness in contexts of social action. Both authors elaborate on the necessary intricate web of relationship between the personal/inner and the sociopolitical/outer, and such a web's educational implications.

While Buddhism is integrally tied to activism, at the same time it reveals certain concerns. Nhat Hanh (in Maida, 2005), for example, sheds additional light on dynamics of engaged (Buddhist) witnessing in contexts of advocating and acting for nonviolence, equality, ecological sustainability. He reflects upon antiwar protests during the Vietnam War, and observes how, even though activists sought peace, to a great degree their emotions, language, and actions reflected aggression. A more original paradigm shift, he maintains, involves loosening the tightness of our views and notions about what is "right." It is attachment—grasping and clinging—that is the deep structure of discord. Elsewhere (Nhat Hanh, 2002), he writes that there are no ideas or prejudices that are worthy to kill for, not even Buddhist ones, and quotes the Buddha's advice: "My teachings are a finger pointing to the moon. Do not get caught in thinking that the finger is the moon. It is because of the finger that you can see the moon" (p. 52). This challenges educators also, advising us away from rigid and too tightly enforced pedagogical agendas, whether agendas based on testing and reproduction of the status quo or on sociopolitical transformation. Instead, it encourages student-directed (un)learning and educators to sustain learners as they follow their own course/way.

Finally, notions of karma and rebirth point to the numerous difficulties of and barriers to personal and social transformation. Transformation can take many lifetimes. Fear and anxiety are productively replaced with extended mindful effort. In consideration of the time and enormous self-discipline that mindfulness and meditation require, perhaps it is sensible not to make too many claims and instead reinvite more quiet, reflection, unpacking, and modest action into a contemporary overburdened, unbalanced, and noisy knowledge industry and a world in haste to produce and consume. It's hardly likely that change can simply be thought, spoken, or written and then spontaneously acted upon. Structural changes initiated without deep and sustained, long-cultivated attentiveness, wisdom, and compassion are likely to reflect samsaric reactions rather than responses. At least, this is some of what I've been taking from what I've been studying so far.

None of this is to romanticize Buddhism or Eastern thought more generally. As any tradition, I imagine that Buddhism suffers challenges accruing from centuries of political intertwinement; dynamics of establishment and entrenchment; inevitable misinterpretation, misrepresentation, and misappropriation; and aporias (such as those of gender) wrought by virtue of immersion in a particular cultural time-space nexus. In *Terror and Transformation: The Ambiguity of Religion in Psychoanalytic Perspective,* James W. Jones (2002) explains the necessary and productive tension between processes of idealization and deidealization, processes which religious traditions themselves bear the responsibility of embracing and negotiating. Subject to realities of impermanence, Buddhism is itself changing, its rituals becoming redefined as it breathes in an increasingly global world and takes up greater residence in Western lands. As it continues to participate in an East–West dialogue it will continue to shift in shape. Perhaps it will keep growing. Perhaps it will eventually disappear and something new will emerge. That said, as I hope this chapter has illustrated, Buddhism and Eastern thought nevertheless seem to have a lot to offer for the (scary) places and times in which we currently find ourselves.

How shall I live?
The question presses on me through the thin pane. The question tails me through the dense streets. In the anonymous computer-face of the morning mail, it is the question only that I read in red ink, the question burning the complacent page.
"How are you Handel?"
(How shall I live?)
"What are you doing these days?"
(How shall I live?)

—Jeanette Winterson, *Art and Lies*

Notes

Earlier versions of this paper were presented at conferences of the American Educational Research Association (2002) and American Educational Studies Association (2004). My thanks to the Venerable Su Khanh Hy for his conversations with me about Vipassanā meditation.

1. *Early Warning, Timely Response: A Guide to Safe Schools* (Early Warning, n.d.) was produced by the Center for Effective Collaboration and Practice of the American Institutes for Research in collaboration with the National Association of School Psychologists under a cooperative agreement with the U.S. Department of Education's Office of Special Education and Rehabilitative Services, Office of Special Educational Programs.
2. In this sense, there is a strong emphasis on morality and ethics within Buddhism, one intimately connected with the larger picture of supporting the path and attainment of enlightenment.
3. Scientific research has undertaken neurological examination of Buddhist practitioners engaged in compassion meditation, and findings show significant neural changes among long-term practicing Tibetan monks as opposed to student volunteers with little experience. See Lutz, Greischar, Rawlings, Ricard, & Davidson, 2004.

References

Abraham, N., & Torok, M. (1994). *The shell and the kernel: Renewals of psychoanalysis* (vol. 1; N. Rand, Trans. and Ed.). Chicago: University of Chicago Press.

Attridge, D. (1999). Innovation, literature, ethics: Relating to the other. *PMLA: Publications of the Modern Language Association of America, 114*(1), 20–31.

Bakhtin, M. M. (1990). *The dialogic imagination: Four essays* (C. Emerson & M. Holquist, Trans.). Austin: University of Texas Press. (Original work published 1975)

Behre, W. J., Astor, R. A., & Meyer, A. (2001). Elementary and middle-school teachers' reasoning about intervening in school violence: An examination of violence-prone school subcontexts. *Journal of Moral Education, 30*(2), 131–153.

Bercovitch, S. (1993). *The rites of assent: Transformations in the symbolic construction of America*. New York: Routledge.

Berlak, A. (1999). Teaching and testimony: Witnessing and bearing witness to racisms in culturally diverse classrooms. *Curriculum Inquiry* 29 (1), 99–127.

Berry, P. (1996). Sky-dancing at the boundaries of Western thought: Feminist theory and the limits of deconstruction. In D. Loy (Ed.), *Healing Deconstruction: Postmodern thought in Buddhism and Christianity* (pp. 53–70). Atlanta: Scholars Press.

Bennett, W. (1992). *The de-valuing of America: The fight for our culture and our children*. New York: Summit.

Bogdan, D. (1992). *Re-educating the imagination: Toward a poetics, politics, and pedagogy of literary engagement*. Portsmouth, NH: Boynton/Cook.

Boler, M. (1999). *Feeling power: Emotions and education*. New York: Routledge.

Booth, W. C. (1988). *The company we keep: An ethics of fiction*. Berkeley, CA: University of California Press.

Brantlinger, P. (1998). *The reading lesson: The threat of mass literacy in nineteenth century British fiction*. Bloomington: Indiana University Press.

Bresnan, P. S. (2003). *Awakening: An introduction to the history of Eastern thought*. Upper Saddle River, NJ: Prentice Hall.

Britzman, D. P. (1998). *Lost subjects, contested objects: Toward a psychoanalytic inquiry of learning*. Albany: State University of New York Press.

Britzman, D. P. (2003). Introduction. In *Practice makes practice: A critical study of learning to teach* (rev. ed.). Albany: State University of New York Press.

Buell, L. (1999). In pursuit of ethics. *PMLA: Publications of the Modern Language Association of America, 114*(1), 7–19.

Campbell, J. (1949). *The hero with a thousand faces*. Princeton, NJ: Bollingen.

Carey-Webb, A. & Benz, S, (Eds.) *Teaching and testimony: Rigoberta Menchú and the North American classroom*. Albany: State University of New York.

Caruth, C. (Ed.). (1995). *Trauma: Explorations in memory*. Baltimore: John Hopkins.

Chödrön. P. (1997). *When things fall apart: Heart advice for difficult times*. Boston: Shambhala.

Chödrön. P. (2002). *The places that scare you: A guide to fearlessness in difficult times*. Boston: Shambhala.

Clarke, J. J. (1997). *Oriental enlightenment: The encounter between Asian and Western thought*. New York: Routledge.

Clarke, J. J. (2000). *The Tao of the West: Western transformations of Taoist thought*. London: Routledge.

Cook, F.H. (1989). *Sounds of valley streams*. Albany: State University of New York.

Conrad. J. (1973). *Heart of darkness*. New York: Penguin. (Original work published 1902)

Dalai Lama. (1999). *Ethics for the new millennium*. New York: Riverhead.

Dalai Lama. (2003). *Stages of meditation* (G. L. Jordhen, L. C. Ganchenpa, & J. Russell, Trans.). Ithaca, NY: Snow Lion.

Des Pres, T. (1988). *Praises & dispraises: Poetry and politics in the 20th century*. New York: Viking.

The Dhammapada. (1985). (E. Easwaran, Trans.). Berkeley, CA: Nilgiri Press.

Dickens, C. (1966). *David Copperfield*. Harmondsworth, England: Penguin.

Di Paolantonio, M. (2000). Loss in present terms: Reading the limits of post-dictatorship Argentina's national conciliation. In R. I. Simon, S. Rosenberg, & C. Eppert (Eds.). *Between hope and despair: Pedagogy and the remembrance of historical trauma* (pp. 153–186). Lanham, MD: Rowman and Littlefield.

Doll, M. A. (2000). *Letters like running water: Towards a mythopoetics of curriculum.* Mahwah, NJ: Erlbaum.

Doll, W. E. (2002). Ghosts and the curriculum. In W. E. Doll & N. Gough (Eds.), *Curriculum visions* (pp. 23–70). New York: Lang.

Donohue, E., Shciraldi, V., & Ziedenberg, J. (1998). *School house hype: School shootings and the real risks kids face in America.* San Francisco: Justice Policy Institute/National School Safety Center.

Douglass, A., & Vogler, T. A. (2003). *Witness and memory: The discourse of trauma.* New York: Routledge.

Eaglestone, R. (1997). *Ethical criticism: Reading after Lévinas.* Edinburgh, Scotland: Edinburgh University Press.

Eagleton, T. (1983). *Literary theory: An introduction.* Minneapolis: University of Minnesota Press.

Early Warning. (n.d.). *Early Warning, Timely Response: A Guide to Safe Schools.* Retrieved 16 February 2007 from http://www.ed.gov/about/offices/list/osers/osep/gtss.html.

Edmundson, M. (1995). *Literature against philosophy: Plato to Derrida.* Cambridge, England: Cambridge University Press.

Eppert, C. (1999). *Learning responsivity/responsibility: Reading the literature of historical witness.* Doctoral dissertation, Ontario Institute for Studies in Education, University of Toronto, Toronto, Ontario.

Eppert, C. (2000). Re-learning questions: Responding to the address of past and present others. In R. I. Simon, S. Rosenberg, & C. Eppert (Eds.). *Between hope and despair: Pedagogy and the remembrance of historical trauma* (pp. 213–230). Lanham, MD: Rowman and Littlefield.

Eppert, C. (2002a). Entertaining history: (Un)Heroic identifications, Apt Pupils, and an ethical imagination. *New German Critique, 86,* 71–102.

Eppert, C. (2002b). Reading relations, loss, and responsive/responsible learning. In M. Morris & J. Weaver (Eds.). *Difficult memories: Talk in a post-holocaust era* (pp. 45–67). New York: Peter Lang.

Eppert, C. (2003). Histories re-imagined, forgotten, and forgiven: Student responses to Toni Morrison's *Beloved. Studies in Reading and Culture, 10*(2), 185–194.

Eppert, C. (2004a). Altering habits of attention and inattention in education: Simone Weil and Emmanuel Lévinas. In H. A. Alexander (Ed.). *Spirituality and ethics in education: Philosophical, theological, and radical perspectives* (pp. 42–54). Brighton, England: Sussex Academic Press.

Eppert, C. (2004b). Leslie Silko's *Ceremony*: Rhetorics of ethical reading and composition. *JAC: A Quarterly Journal for the Interdisciplinary Study of Rhetoric, Writing, Multiple Literacies, and Politics 24* (3), 727–754.

Epstein, M. (1995). *Thoughts without a thinker: Psychotherapy from a Buddhist perspective.* New York: Basic Books.

Felman, S., &. Laub, D. (1992). *Testimony: Crises of witnessing in literature, psychoanalysis, and history.* New York: Routledge.

Freud, S. (1959). *Inhibitions, symptoms and anxiety* (A. Strachey, Trans.). New York: Norton.

Gadamer, H. G. (2005). *Truth and method* (J. Weinsheimer & D. G. Marshall, Trans.). New York: Continnuum. (Original work published 1960)

Garbarino, J. (1999). *Lost boys: Why our sons turn violent and how we can save them.* New York: Free Press.

Garber, M., Hanssen, B., & Walkowitz, R. L. (Eds.). (2000). *The turn to ethics.* New York: Routledge.

Gee, J. P. (1988). The legacies of literacy: From Plato to Freire. *Harvard Educational Review, 58*(2), 195–212.

Ginzburg, C. (1989). *The cheese and the worms: The cosmos of a sixteenth-century miller* (J. Tedeschi & A. Tedeschi, Trans.). New York: Dorset.

Glassner, B. (1999). *The culture of fear: Why Americans are afraid of the wrong things.* New York: Basic Books.

Goenka, S. N. (1998). *Satipatthāna Sutta discourses.* Seattle: Vipassanā Research.

Goldstein, J. & Kornfield, J. (2001). *Seeking the heart of wisdom: The path of insight meditation.* Boston: Shambhala.

Gough, N. (1990). Healing the earth within us: Environmental education as cultural criticism. *The Journal of Experiential Education 13* (4), 12–17.

Graff, H. (1987). *The legacies of literacy: Continuities and contradictions in Western culture and society.* Bloomington: Indiana University Press.

Grant, P. A. (2002). Using popular films to challenge preservice teachers' beliefs about teaching in urban schools. *Urban education, 37*(1), 77–95.

Greene, M. (1995). *Releasing the imagination: Essays on education, the arts, and social change.* San Francisco: Jossey-Bass.

Greene, M. (2001). *Variations on a blue guitar: The Lincoln Center Institute lectures on aesthetic education.* New York: Teachers College Press.

Hamilton, E., & Cairns, H. (1961). *Plato: The collected dialogues.* Princeton, NJ: Princeton University Press.

Havelock, E. A. (1963). *Preface to Plato.* Cambridge, MA: Belknap Press of Harvard University Press.

Heidegger, M. (1977). What is metaphysics? In D. F. Krell (Ed.), *Martin Heidegger: Basic writings* (pp. 89–110). New York: Harper & Row.

Hesford, W. S. (1999). *Framing identities: Autobiography and the politics of pedagogy.* Minneapolis: University of Minnesota Press.

Hesse, H. (2003). *Siddhartha* (J. Neugroshel, Trans.). New York: Penguin. (Original work published 1922)

Humphries, J. (1999). *Reading emptiness: Buddhism and literature.* Albany: State University of New York Press.

Iser, W. (1989). *Prospecting: From reader-response to literary anthropology.* Baltimore: John Hopkins University Press.

Jencks, C. (1989). *What is post-modernism?* (3rd ed.). New York: St. Martin's Press.

Johnson, S. (2003). Emotions and the brain: Fear. *Discover, 24*(3), 32–39.

Jones, J. W. (2002). *Terror and transformation: The ambiguity of religion in psychoanalytic perspective.* New York: Brunner-Routledge.

Kaestle C. F. (1983). *Pillars of the republic: Common schools and American society 1780–1860.* New York: Hill and Wang.

Kleinman, A., Das, V., & Lock, M. (1997). Introduction. In A. Kleinman, V. Das, & M. Lock (Eds.), *Social suffering* (pp. ix–xxvii). Berkeley: University of California Press.

Konner, J., & Perlmutter, A. H. (Producers). (2001). *Joseph Campbell and the power of myth* (DVD). South Burlington, VT: Mystic Fire Video.

Krishnamurti, J. (1953). *Education and the significance of life.* San Francisco: Harper.

Krishnamurti, J. (1995). *On fear.* San Francisco: Harper.

LaCapra, D. (1997). Lanzman's *Shoah:* "Here there is no why." *Critical Inquiry 23*(2), 231–269.

Lévinas, E. (1961). *Totality and infinity: An essay on exteriority* (A. Lingis, Trans.). Pittsburgh, PA: Duquesne University Press.

Lévinas, E. (1991). *Otherwise than being or beyond essence* (A. Lingis, Trans.). Dordrecht, Netherlands: Kluwer Academic.

Loy, D. R., & Goodhew, L. (2004). *The dharma of dragons and daemons: Buddhist themes in modern fantasy.* Boston: Wisdom.

Lutz, A., Greischar, L, Rawlings, N., Ricard, M., & Davidson, R. (2004). Long-term meditators self-induce high-amplitude gamma synchrony during mental practice. *PNAS, 101*(46),
16369–16373.

Maclear, K. (1999). *Beclouded visions: Hiroshima-Nagasaki and the art of witness.* Albany: State
University of New York Press.

Maida, G. K. (Producer and Director). (2005). *Peace is every step: Meditation in action: The life
and work of Thich Nhat Hanh* (DVD). Berkeley, CA: Legacy Media.

Malpede, K. (1996). Teaching witnessing: A class wakes to the genocide in Bosnia. *Theatre
Topics 6* (2), 167–179.

Manguel, A. (1996). *A history of reading.* New York: Viking-Penguin.

McClellan, B. E. (1999). *Moral education in America.* New York: Teachers College Press.

McKnight, D. (2003). *Schooling, the puritan imperative, and the molding of an American
national identity: Education's "errand into the wilderness."* Mahwah, NJ: Erlbaum.

Mitscherlich, A., & Mitscherlich, M. (1975). *The inability to mourn: Principles of collective
behavior* (B. R. Placzek, Trans.). New York: Grove Press.

Moore, M. (Director and Writer). (2003). *Bowling for Columbine* (DVD). Los Angeles: MGM/
UA Home Video.

Murdoch, I. (1999). *Existentialists and mystics: Writings on philosophy and literature* (P. Con-
radi, Ed.). London: Penguin. (Original work published 1950)

Nakagawa, Y. (2000). *Education for awakening: An Eastern approach to holistic education.* (vol.
2). Brandon, VT: Foundation for Educational Renewal.

Nakamura, H. (2000). *Gotama Buddha: A biography based on the most reliable texts* (vol. 1; G.
Sekimori, Trans.). Tokyo: Kosei.

Needleman, J. (1976). Psychotherapy and the sacred. *Parabola, 1*(1), 52–65.

Needleman, J. (1994). *The indestructible question: Essays on nature, spirit and the human paradox.* London: Penguin.

Newton, A. Z. (1995). *Narrative ethics.* Cambridge, MA: Harvard University Press.

Nhat Hanh, T. (1994). *The present moment: A retreat on the practice of mindfulness* (CD). Lou-
isville, CO: Sounds True.

Nhat Hanh, T. (1998). *Teachings on love.* Berkeley, CA: Parallax Press.

Nhat Hanh, T. (2002). *No fear, no death: Comforting wisdom for life.* Riverhead, NY: Penguin.

Noddings, N. (1992). *The challenge to care in schools: An alternative approach to education.*
New York: Teachers College Press.

Noddings, N. (2002). *Educating moral people: A caring alternative to character education.* New
York: Teachers College Press.

Oliver, K. (2001). *Witnessing: Beyond recognition.* Minneapolis: University of Minnesota Press.

Orwell, G. (1954). *1984.* New York: Penguin.

Packer, T. (2002). The state of entanglement: An interview with Toni Packer, by G. Swaebe.
Parabola: Myth, Tradition, and the Search for Meaning, 37, 2–68.

Pinar, W. F. (Ed.) (1975). *Curriculum theorizing: The reconceptualists.* Berkeley, CA: McCutcuhan.

Pinar, W. F. (1994). *Autobiography, politics and sexuality: Essays in curriculum theory 1972–
1992.* New York: Lang.

Pinar, W. F. (2004). *What is curriculum theory?* Mahwah, NJ: Erlbaum.

Pinar, W. F. (with Reynolds, W. M., Slattery, P., & Taubman, P. M.). (1996). *Understanding
curriculum: An introduction to the study of historical and contemporary curriculum discourses.* New York: Lang.

Prebish, C. S., & Baumann, M. (2002). *Westward dharma: Buddhism beyond Asia.* Berkeley,
CA: University of California Press.

Purpel, D. E. (1997). The politics of character education. In A. Molnar (Ed.), *The construction of children's character: Ninety-sixth yearbook of the national society for the study of education* (part 2, pp. 140–153). Chicago: University of Chicago Press.

Purpel, D. E., & McLaurin, W. M., Jr. (2004). *Reflections on the moral and spiritual crisis in education.* New York: Lang.

Ropers-Huilman, B. (1999). Witnessing: Critical inquiry in a poststructural world. *Qualitative Studies, 12*(1), 21–35.

Ropers-Huilman, B. (2003). Witnessing and advocacy in educational leadership. *Journal of School Leadership, 13*, 581–610.

Rosenblatt, L. M. (1968). *Literature as exploration* (rev. ed.). New York: Noble and Noble.

Rosenblatt, L. M. (1995). *Reader, the text, the poem: The transactional theory of the literary work.* Carbondale: Southern Illinois University Press.

Safran, J. D. (Ed.). (2003). *Psychoanalysis and Buddhism: An unfolding dialogue.* Boston: Wisdom.

Samyutta-Nikāya. (2005, June 11). Retrieved 3 January 2006 from www.metta.lk/tipitaka/index.html.

Santner, E. L. (1990). *Stranded objects: Mourning, memory, and film in postwar Germany.* Ithaca, NY: Cornell University Press.

Shusterman, R. (2000). *Pragmatist aesthetics: Living beauty, rethinking art* (2nd ed.). Lanham, MD: Rowman and Littlefield.

Silko, L. M. (1986). *Ceremony.* New York: Penguin.

Simon, R. I. (1994). The pedagogy of commemoration and formation of collective memories. *Educational Foundations, 9*(4), 5–24.

Simon, R. I. (2005). *The touch of the past: Remembrance, learning, and ethics.* New York: Palgrave MacMillan.

Simon, R. I., & Eppert, C. (1997). Remembering obligation: pedagogy and the witnessing of testimony of historical trauma. *Canadian Journal of Education/Revue cannadienne de l'education, 22*(2), 175–191.

Simon, R. I., Rosenberg, S., & Eppert, C. (Eds.) (2000). *Between hope and despair: Pedagogy and the remembrance of historical trauma.* Lanham, MD: Rowman and Littlefield.

Smith, D. G. (1999). *Pedagon: Interdisciplinary essays in the human sciences, pedagogy, and culture.* New York: Lang.

Smith, D. G. (2002). *Teaching in global times.* Unpublished manuscript, International Forum on Education and Society, University of Alberta, Edmonton, Alberta.

Smith, H., & Novak, P. (2003). *Buddhism: A concise introduction.* San Francisco: HarperCollins.

Smith, M. W., & Wilhelm, J. D. (2002). *"Reading don't fix no Chevy's": Literacy in the lives of young men.* Portsmouth, NH: Heinemann.

Spacks, P. M. (1995). *Boredom: The literary history of a state of mind.* Chicago: University of Chicago Press.

Strong, J. S. (2002). *The experience of Buddhism: Sources and interpretations.* Belmont, CA: Wadsworth.

Sumera, D. J. (2002). *Why reading literature in school still matters: Imagination, interpretation, insight.* Mahwah, NJ: Erlbaum.

Thomerson, J. (2000). *School violence: Ten things legislators need to know.* Denver, CO: National Conference of State Legislatures.

Thoreau, H. D. (1981). *Walden and other writings* (W. Hawarth, Ed.), New York: Modern Library. (Original work published 1854)

Webber, J. A. (2003). *Failure to hold: The politics of school violence.* Lanham, MD: Rowman and Littlefield.

Weil, S. (1951/1973). *Waiting for God* (E. Craufurd, Trans.). New York: Harper & Row.

Weil, S. (1952/1997). *Gravity & grace* (A. Wills, Trans.). Lincoln: University of Nebraska Press.

Wellmer, A. (1993). *The persistence of modernity: Essays on aesthetics, ethics, and postmodernism* (D. Midgley, Trans.). Cambridge, MA.: MIT Press.

Williams, R. (1977). *Marxism and literature.* Oxford, England: Oxford University Press.

Willinksy, J. (1991). *The triumph of literature/The fate of literacy: English in the secondary school curriculum.* New York: Teachers College Press.

Winterson, J. (1995). *Art and lies: A piece for three voices and a bawd.* Toronto, Ontario: Vintage.

Yeats, W. B. (1973). *Twentieth-century poetry and poetics* (2nd ed.; G. Geddes, Ed.). Oxford, England: Oxford University Press.

Yu, T. (2004). *In the name of morality: Character education and political control.* New York: Lang.

Zembylas, M. (2005). *Teaching with emotion: A postmodern enactment.* Greenwich, CT: Information Age.

Zembylas, M., and Vrasidas, C. (2005). Lévinas and the "inter-face": The ethical challenge of online education. *Educational Theory, 55*(1), 61–78.

CHAPTER 4

Socially-Engaged Buddhism as a Provocation for Critical Pedagogy in Unsettling Times

Robert Hattam

University of South Australia

Alternatives to Revenge in Unsettling Times?

We are living in "unsettling times"—times in which economic, political, and cultural factors are aggregating in new ways as cause and consequence of major shifts in global realities and sensibilities. The postindustrial nation-state is now faced with "ungovernability" pressures from both within and outside its borders (Offe, 1987). Inside there are pressures to deal with the effects of living under the conditions of a globalizing postindustrial economy (Stiglitz, 2002) and to recognize the social, cultural, and religious diversities that constitute complex multicultural societies (Gutman, 1994). The nation-state's recognition of ethnic, racial, and religious difference, however, seems to have stalled in recent years, and mistrust of it has intensified (Gilroy, 2000; Lash & Featherstone, 2002). For those postsettler societies, there are pressures to heal the effects of colonization with indigenous/First Nations peoples (Brennan, Behrendt, Strelein, & Williams, 2005; Pritchard, 1998).

Economically, under conditions of globalization, the nation-state struggles with the aspirations of its citizens for the "good life" in conjunction with the emergence of the "new poor" living in the margins of every large city

(Bauman, 1998; Castells, 1998). Simultaneously, economic globalization and Western models of development continue to exacerbate the contrast between "first world" affluence and "third world" poverty (United Nations Development Project, 2003). New information and communication technologies have contributed to changes in civil society, politics, and cultural practices, and the media now challenge families and schools as the most significant sites of social and identity formation (Castells, 1996; Kellner, 1995). The media have also arguably contributed to a loosening of the connection between identity and place, an "unsettling" mirrored in human terms by diasporic, expatriate, and itinerant communities swelled by global flows of asylum seekers and refugees, and the emergence of global terrorist and state surveillance networks (Castells, 1997; Kellner, 2003).

There is a lot at stake at this time. This new constellation has the potential to intensify divisiveness in our societies and hence damage the fragile network of relationships that holds them together. And while we mustn't fall for what Foucault (1983) calls "one of the most harmful habits of contemporary thought" (p. 206)—that is claiming, in our "analysis of the present," to be living in a "unique or fundamental or irruptive point in history where everything is completed and begun again" (p. 206)—we do need to think carefully about what the present means for ethicopolitics (Bauman, 1999; Beck, 1997). If we take Pinar's (2004) advice, then curriculum (and pedagogy) can be understood in terms of a "complicated conversation" (p. xiv) involving academic knowledge, the life worlds of students, society, and the historical moment (or the present). "Unsettling times" can be seen as a provocation for educators to (re)think what is appropriate curriculum and also to think through pedagogies for unsettling times.

Pedagogy for Unsettling Times?

This notion of "unsettling times" provides a frame for considering the question, What is "good" pedagogy? The question is one that is pertinent for not only those who are teachers in the formal sense but for all cultural workers involved in politicopedagogical work. This chapter takes up this issue within/ against "critical pedagogy," which is understood as a significant educational movement that is neither homogenous nor coherent, and one that is open to ongoing reflexivity (Peters, Lankshear, & Olssen, 2003; Trifonas 2000, 2003). The term *critical pedagogy* here invokes a range of views including the Freirian tradition (Shor & Freire, 1987), "feminist pedagogy" (Gore, 1993), "critical multiculturalism" (McLaren, 1997), and "multiliteracies" (New London Group, 1996). Critical pedagogy provides an "emancipatory" social vision for pedagogical work that rejects views of pedagogy that are ahistorical, depoliticized, and positivist. The critical pedagogue focuses on the way that power relations exert an effect on how knowledge is (re)produced and exchanged in any pedagogical act. Against critical pedagogy, there is still much to do to properly elaborate how we might learn to live together in societies of ever increasing cultural complexity. It is easy enough to say yes to the discourse of emancipation (Derrida, 1996, p. 82) but difficult to put it into practice (Torres, 1998). What I want to argue for here is ongoing reinvigoration of critical pedagogy that is especially interested in borrowing from those "traditions" that have a strong commitment to praxis. Unfortunately, in secularizing times, the so-called Eastern philosophical traditions have been either marginalized or mystified in these curriculum and pedagogical debates. This chapter aims to bring a Buddhist imaginary into conversation with these critical pedagogies.

Socially-Engaged Buddhism as a Resource for Reconciliation/Pedagogy

In this chapter I would like to suggest that socially-engaged Buddhism could be investigated as a resource for critical pedagogy. In one of the strands of my research (Hattam, 2004) I am attempting to map out, in broad terms, an emerging Buddhist critical social theory, or socially critical Buddhism, that is being shaped in a dialogic space between both "traditions." As a student of both critical theory and Tibetan Buddhism I understand them as dynamic, rejuvenating traditions—very much alive and involved in translation in an increasingly East–West globalizing culture. In my work, *critical theory now* is understood in terms of what Agger (1998) refers to as a "theory cluster" (p. 4). This metaphor attempts to represent the state of critical theory today. Critical theory is no longer defined in terms of its relationship to Karl Marx, even though I do have some sympathy for that sentiment. Critical theory today is also feminist (Benhabib, 1992; Benhabib, Butler, Cornell, & Fraser, 1995; Fraser, 1997), postcolonial (Said, 1978; Spivak, 1987; Young, 1990), queer (Sedgwick, 1991), antiracist (McCarthy & Critchlow, 1993), and postmodern (Best & Kellner, 1991; Flax, 1990; Kellner, 1988), poststructuralist (Poster, 1989), indigenist (Rigney, 2000), ecological (Gottlieb, 1996), and theological (Freire, 1972; Kovel, 1991; Wexler, 2000). Critical theorists work in every traditional discipline of the social sciences as well as having developed interdisciplinary spaces around such studies as new social movements, labor, women, diaspora, culture, and Aboriginal studies.

In terms of Buddhism, my focus lies in the Tibetan schools, and in particular the Gelugpa school, but I have an interest in all of the various strains and draw on all of these. (My meditation teacher was an Abbot in Sera Jey, one of the Gelugpa monasteries.) I am especially interested in what I understand to be an emerging social movement that goes by the name of socially-engaged Buddhism (Eppsteiner, 1988; Kotler, 1996; Queen & King, 1996). One important edge of this movement is found in the comparative philosophy (Loy, 1996a, 1996b) of those scholars who are willing to use modern thought to understand ancient thinkers from different cultures while also using ancient thought to understand our (post)modern world. The claim for socially-engaged Buddhism as a site for developing "reconciliation/pedagogy" is substantially based on the proposition that, by definition, Buddhist wisdom/knowledge provides resources for fostering coexistence rather than promoting fear, anger, and revenge. This chapter will sketch out some aspects of this socially-engaged Buddhist movement.

What Is Socially-Engaged Buddhism?

The term *engaged Buddhism*, according to Batchelor (1994) appears to have entered the discourse in the 1930s during the "monks' war" against the French occupation of Vietnam. But then, the idea of a socially-engaged Buddhism predates the actual use of the term. Being socially-engaged *and* Buddhist begins with Shakyamumi Buddha's life and teachings and might best be characterized by his work in developing a community of practitioners referred to as the *sangha*. His discourses had a revolutionary effect on the society of his time and his teaching dealt with "this-worldly" topics such as politics, good government, poverty, war, and peace (Rahula, 1985). The Buddhist sangha provides a model of community and community development based on a lifestyle that is "minimalist, nonacquisitive and noncompetitive" (Swearer, 1996, p. 215). The Buddha's teachings on social, economic, and political life are not well known but are scattered throughout ancient Buddhist texts. Rahula (1985) draws our attention to some examples. For instance, the *Cakkavattisihanada-sutta* of the *Digha-nikaya* clearly states "that poverty is the cause of immorality and crimes such as theft, falsehood, violence, hatred, cruelty etc." (p. 104). The *Kutadanta-sutta* provides other examples including the futility of suppressing such crimes through punishment. Instead, "the economic condition of the people should be improved," and "adequate wages should be paid to those who are employed" (pp. 104–105).

In the present situation, in which Buddhism is being translated from the East to the West, it is not possible to define one socially-engaged Buddhism, but for the sake of initiating the conversation I will outline a working definition. Kraft (1999) defines socially-engaged Buddhism in these terms: "Engaged Buddhism entails both inner and outer work. We must change the world, we must change ourselves, and we must change ourselves in order to change the world. Awareness and compassionate action reinforce each other" (p. 10).

Socially-engaged Buddhism might also be understood in terms of a practical spirituality in which "spiritual development and dedication to the pursuit of a more humane world necessarily go hand in hand" (Swearer, 1996, p. 212). The socially-engaged Buddhist rejects the idea that Buddhism is world rejecting, "world-denying, passive or socially inept" (Kraft, 1992, p. 3).

The argument for a contemporary socially-engaged Buddhism has been neatly summarized by Jones (1989), whose logic I will paraphrase here. Under the (post)modern conditions in which we now live, "socio-historical conditions … institutionalise alienation, ill will, aggressiveness, defensiveness, and acquisitiveness" (p. 194). In turn, "those societal conditions are kammically inherited by each new generation, whose delusive personal struggle for identity and meaning is socialized and super-charged by previously mentioned norms and institutions" (p. 195). Kraft adds:

> Greed, Anger, and Delusion—known as the "three poisons" in Buddhism—need to be uprooted in personal lives, but they have to be dealt with as social and political realities. Throughout the world today, large-scale systems cause suffering as surely as psychological factors cause suffering. Traditional Buddhism focused on the latter; engaged Buddhism focuses on both. (1999, p. 10)

Our own delusion and its institutionalization are now so interpermeated that contemplation and activism need to go hand in hand. But without some form of mind-transformative practice such as meditation that enables us to begin to heal our own alienation and delusion, we won't develop the necessary insight and our efforts to effect social change can only be undermined.

Engaged Buddhism Is Not New

Attempting to define a socially-engaged version of Buddhism suggests that there is an unengaged version, but that would contradict some of the basic principles of Buddhism. On this point the Dalai Lama posits that a world-rejecting or world-denying Buddhism would be a contradiction in terms. Such a view would certainly be an anathema to the Bodhisattva sensibility, a point that I will elaborate on later. On this same point, Thich Nhat Hanh (1987a) posits that even meditation is not an "escape from society" (p. 45). Rather than thinking that meditation is an escape from society, Nhat Hanh notes that meditation is in fact a process that "equips oneself with the capacity to reintegrate into society" (p. 48). Society is difficult to live in, but our suffering only increases if we succumb to its alienating effects. And if our alienation becomes too extreme, then "we can not help change society to make it more liveable" (p. 49). Meditation then, is not world-denying, but is a way of dealing with our psychosocial alienation, which enables us to stay in society.

To provide a little more specificity to my argument I turn to Jones (1989), who provides a model of three types of practice that can be considered as socially-engaged. He argues that socially-engaged Buddhist practice can involve

1. alternative societal models—for example, monastic or quasi-monastic communities;
2. social aid, service, and welfare, both in employment and voluntarily; and
3. radical activism, which is "directed to fundamental institutional and social changes, culminating in societal metamorphosis (p. 216)

Of course, in many instances, the social engagement involves all three of these. As an example, the Tibetan government in exile, in collaboration with a range of other institutions, is involved in rebuilding the great monasteries of Tibet in India (Drepung, Ganden and Sera) and also in establishing a range of other monastic or quasi-monastic communities. This government in exile also has in place programs to assist exiled Tibetans with health and other welfare services, especially for those of the Tibetan diaspora now living in India. The Dalai Lama engages in a nonviolent struggle with the Chinese government over reclaiming some version of Tibetan independence. It's the third version that is of most interest to me in the present discussion.

An alternative way of representing socially-engaged Buddhism, and the one I will use here, involves contemplating the sensibility of the socially-engaged Buddhist practitioner. Contemplating such a sensibility involves going after what makes someone both a Buddhist and an activist. How does a Buddhist (re)think practice in terms of social struggle? Nhat Hanh, as a Zen practitioner living in Vietnam during the early 1960s, frames such a question in this way:

"When a village is being bombed and children and adults are suffering from wounds and death, can a Buddhist sit still in his unbombed temple?" (Nhat Hanh, 1987b, p. 35). This can be reworded to make it less context-specific: How can I sit in the meditation hall when there is war on outside? The question has relevance to our present situation, given that we are part of an alliance that is waging a "war on terror." This question is suggestive of the way in which socially-engaged Buddhists are "working the hyphen" (Fine, 1994) between personal and social transformation and hence resisting the idea that Buddhism should be understood entirely in terms of a mystical quietism.

Most of this chapter is organized around the question, Where can we go for conceptual resources, inspiration, and advice about what it means to be socially-engaged and Buddhist? The are a number of options, including investigating the mode of being of the Bodhisattva (Hattam, 2000), drawing on scriptural sources (Nagarjuna, 1975; Thurman, 1985), examining the socially-engaged Buddhist sensibility of a few Eastern Buddhist scholar-practitioners, or reviewing some of the emerging scholarship on socially-engaged Buddhism by Western interpreters.

The *engaged* perspective has always been at the very heart of Buddhist theory and practice but at various times has been less evident in the community of Buddhist practitioners. Its recent manifestation might be seen as a strengthening of what has always been extant in the tradition but has come to the fore in light of contemporary social conditions. It may be that what we refer to as socially-engaged Buddhism is an artifact of the recent movement of Buddhism into Western culture, a process that has involved a "fresh" examination into what it means to be a Buddhist practitioner. This examination into what Buddhism means theoretically and practically may have concentrated our gaze on the engaged aspect. Perhaps what is "new" is the emergence of an international movement. In this sense engaged Buddhism as a new social movement is an expression of globalization. Perhaps ironically, the most significant contributions to this "fresh" examination into what it means to be Buddhist have been developed by Buddhist scholar-activists from Asia. I have chosen to focus on the Dalai Lama, Thich Nhat Hanh, and Sulak Sivaraksa. Before I begin, though, I need to emphasize that all three are scholar-practitioners whose lives are lived as experiments in ethical life, of how to live a life under extreme circumstances and hence provide some insights into both theory and practice. Not only their writing, but their lives, are sites for investigation and insight.

The Dalai Lama and Universal Responsibility

The Dalai Lama's writing on socially-engaged Buddhism is extensive, and I do not intend to review the corpus here. My more modest task is to outline briefly his advocacy of Buddhist social engagement. The Dalai Lama is most renowned for his work as the leader of the Tibetan government in exile and his struggle for the independence of Tibet. He is a Nobel Peace Prize recipient and travels the world as an ambassador, not only for his own people but also as an icon for peace in general.

The Dalai Lama's theory of social engagement is informed by his own Gelugpa education and might be understood to revolve around the idea of "universal responsibility," which is how he describes the Bodhisattva motivation, or *bodhicitta*. *Bodhicitta*, a term that is not well known in the West, refers to "the good heart" (Lobsang, 1997, p. 10) or "the awakening heart." Of course, the metaphor of the heart as the site of our love and compassion hides more than it illuminates. For Buddhists love and compassion, or concern for the welfare of others, are not feelings but types of awareness (Lati, 1980, p. 99). Love and compassion arise and abide in our minds. Love is understood as a "quality of mind," of "wanting others to be happy" (McDonald, 1984, p. 94). Compassion, being the other side of love, is also a type of mind: the wish that others are free from their suffering. In thinking about bodhicitta, the metaphor of mind/heart might be more appropriate.

There are extensive descriptions of how we might develop bodhicitta in foundational Buddhist texts and in the Dalai Lama's own writings. The idea is usually presented in terms of the wish to seek enlightenment as a means of alleviating the suffering of others. At a certain point in one's spiritual work there is a choice: to strive for enlightenment for oneself alone or to practice out of compassion for the suffering of others. Geshe Rabten (1984) describes this choice in these terms: "It is as if we and our elderly mother were in prison, and we took a chance to escape alone, just leaving our mother inside" (p. 139). To actually get at what this means requires studying some preliminary ideas that I haven't the time to elaborate upon here. Alternatively it's possible to explain *bodhicitta* in terms of what Chögyam Trungpa (1984) refers to as "connecting with your heart" (p. 42). Awakening one's heart involves living with the "tremendous sadness" when "we open our eyes to the rest of the world" (p. 45). It is living with one's heart "completely exposed" (p. 45). Bodhicitta is a heart/mind that spontaneously experiences love and compassion for all beings without exception; it is the mind/heart that is required if we are to get beyond the notion of "insiders" and "outsiders." The critical tradition has a lot to say about the distorting effects of othering but has yet to even imagine the mind that is postdeconstructive—"the subject after deconstruction, a determination that succeeds the duty of deconstruction without lapsing back into the pre-deconstructive or classical conceptions of the subject ..." (Critchley, 1996, p. 39)—and beyond experiencing duality or binaries. As well, the critical tradition has little to say about how we might cultivate such a mind. Bodhicitta is the mind that is beyond discriminations of friends, enemies, or those we hold as neutral. Bodhicitta is the mind that spontaneously experiences loving kindness, not only to our dear ones but also to those who harm us. The expansive form of loving kindness implied here is often defined in terms of the bodhisattva vow:

> For as long as space endures
> And as long as living beings remain
> Until then may I too, abide
> To dispel the misery of the world.

In another famous text on this topic, Geshe Langri Tangpa Dorje Senge's *Thought Transformation in Eight Stanzas*, it is asserted that we should even treat our enemies with loving kindness, holding those of wicked nature as a "dear one so hard to find as though discovering a precious treasure" (Rabten & Ngawang Dhargyey, 1977). Liberman (1986) suggests that a beginner to this sort of Buddhist logic "is likely to wonder if there is a misprint" (p. 116).

The Bodhisattva path is traditionally described in terms of a personal practice, or what Thurman (1985) calls "individualist transcendentalism" (p. 121). However, as I argue, such a view is not world denying, but can be understood in terms of "compassionate action." In the Dalai Lama's (1992a) own words, "when you practice you do not isolate yourself from the rest of society" (p. 91). What is significant in the Dalai Lama's recent writings has been his elaboration on the nature of "compassionate action" and his reworking of the idea of universal responsibility in the light of our increased interconnectedness.

Compassionate Action in Postmodern Conditions

The Dalai Lama's position follows a traditional view that proposes the cultivation of concern for others' well-being on an individual level. In part this is based on the idea that until we have actually stabilized some level of love and compassion we are under the influence of the afflictive emotions and hence can be of only limited benefit to others:

> In the beginning of Buddhist practice, our ability to serve others is limited. The emphasis is on healing ourselves, transforming our mind and heart. But as we continue, we become stronger and increasingly able to serve others. But until that time, we may get overwhelmed by the suffering and difficulties of other people. We may become exhausted and not able to serve others effectively, not to mention ourselves. So we must begin simply by doing as well as we can, trying to improve ourselves, and, at the same time, trying as much as we can to serve other people. It is natural to feel some limitation with both, and we just have to accept that. (Dalai Lama, 1992a, p. 94)

The aim is to develop an active form of compassion that goes beyond overcoming "the distortions and afflictions of your own mind, that is, in terms of calming and eventually dispelling anger and so forth" (Dalai Lama 1992a, p. 96).

He adds:

> When there is something that needs to be done in the world to rectify the wrongs with a motivation of compassion, if one is really concerned with benefit it is not enough simply to be compassionate. There is no direct benefit in that. With compassion, one needs to be engaged, involved. (Dalai Lama, 1992a, p. 96)

Such a view of compassionate action can only make sense if we are responding to the issues of our social context. Understanding the nature of contemporary society is essential for compassionate action. The Dalai Lama (1999) acknowledges that "[t]oday's [social] reality is so complex and, on the material level at least, so clearly interconnected" (p. 161) that conceiving of ethical practice only in terms of the need for individual transformation is no longer adequate. He cites the examples of the globalization of economics—that a stock market crash on one side of the globe can have a direct effect on the economics of countries on the other side—and the impact of technology on the environment. But what does it mean to cultivate universal responsibility under post(modern) conditions? From the perspective of universal responsibility, the Dalai Lama outlines some general directions and identifies some significant struggles that require urgent attention.

In outlining these directions he begins by reaffirming that universal responsibility infers a reorientation of our hearts and minds away from self and toward all others without partiality. The aim to cultivate and practice universal responsibility involves taking personal responsibility for the well-being of all others. The practice of universal responsibility, then, must be by definition counterhegemonic in the sense of countering those aspects of culture that harm others. Against the greed, envy, and aggressive competitiveness encouraged by "a culture of excessive materialism" (p. 165) the Dalai Lama recommends the cultivation of contentment. He notes that we need to counter the "culture of perpetual economic growth" that fosters discontent and contributes to the growing economic inequality that is emerging everywhere, and also seems to be "the source of damage to our natural environment" (p. 166). Universal responsibility also demands a commitment to honesty that helps "reduce the level of misunderstanding, doubt, and fear throughout society" (p. 168). Honesty also involves not being blind to the various injustices that distort societies and a commitment to speak out against them. A sense of universal responsibility means countering the urge to ignore the diseased and the marginalized, and to "ensure that the sick and afflicted person never feels helpless, rejected, or unprotected" (p. 169).

Central to the Dalai Lama's view of universal responsibility is the practice of compassion but, in a postmodern context, compassion must be extended to both the individual and society. In that sense, "compassion belongs in the political arena too" (p. 173), and will require that we engage in a number of significant social arenas. The Dalai Lama mentions especially education, the media, our natural environment, politics and economics, peace and disarmament, and interreligious harmony. Each of these arenas requires our engagement because the stakes are so high if we do not act. While the Dalai Lama does not provide any specific advice about how these arenas might be reformed, his position constantly shuttles along a dialectic of personal and social transformation, such as the need to "disarm ourselves internally," which then creates the conditions for "dismantling military establishments" (p. 207).

Thich Nhat Hanh and the Tiep Hien Order

While he is from a different Buddhist tradition, Thich Nhat Hanh's justification for socially-engaged Buddhism has many features similar to that of the Dalai Lama.

Thich Nhat Hanh is one of the most prominent socially-engaged Buddhist scholar-practitioners. He became a monk in the Zen tradition and played a significant role in ending the Vietnam War in the 1960s. His peace work was acknowledged by Martin Luther King, who nominated him for the Nobel

Peace Prize (Nhat Hanh, 1967). He founded the Tiep Hien Order, which aimed to respond to "the burgeoning hatred, intolerance and suffering" that "were forged in the crucible of war and devastation that was the daily experience" (Nhat Hanh, 1987a, p. 5) of the Vietnamese people. Their struggle for peace involved maintaining the strictest neutrality, which meant not taking sides with either the noncommunists or the communists. For Nhat Hanh, neither of the warring parties actually spoke for the people of Vietnam, and that was part of the problem. The Vietnamese people felt that they had been "effectively excluded from participation in the determination of their own country's future" (Nhat Hanh, 1993b, p. 50). Taking inspiration from Mahatma Gandhi, this group developed a range of nonviolent forms of struggle, including fasting and using literature and the arts as methods of challenging oppression. This commitment to nonviolence was paramount and was based on the realization that "the means and the ends are one" (Nhat Hanh, 1993b, p. 43).

For the Tiep Hien Order, the struggle to actually be heard among the killing was the most significant issue and this anguish eventually led many Buddhists to self-immolate. Rather than being seen as suicide, these self-immolations are understood as acts of courage by people who loved life to the point that they were prepared to suffer extreme pain to awaken others to the suffering of war. This form of nonviolent struggle was also predicated on the view that our "enemies are not human beings but the intolerance, fanaticism, oppression, greed, hatred, and discrimination that lay within the hearts of ... men and women" (Nhat Hanh, 1993b, p. 45).

The practice of nonviolence for Nhat Hanh was not a matter of prefabricated technique. The point was to have "the substance of nonviolence and compassion in yourself. Then everything you do will be in the direction of nonviolence" (p. 45). "To practice ahimsa [nonviolence], first of all we have to practise it within ourselves" (p. 65). To work for peace means to quell the violence inside us first. The practice of killing arises out of our minds. For Nhat Hanh, a violent mind arises in dependence upon "dividing reality into two camps ... and standing in one camp while attacking the other" (p. 65). To undermine our own violence, then, we need to abandon dismissing some people as our enemies, even those who act violently. "If we work for peace out of anger then we will never succeed. Peace is not an end. It can never come about through non-peaceful means" (p. 66). To undermine violence, Nhat Hanh recommends understanding our coresponsibility in that violence. Such a practice, of course, has to contend with our own anger and frustration and our tendency to blame those we see as the perpetrators. To go beyond violence, he posits that we need to understand that the weapons that harm us are our "own prejudices, fears, and ignorance" (p. 75). To go beyond violence demands that we go beyond the idea of the enemy and replace it with the "notion of someone suffering a great deal who needs our compassion" (p. 77). The idea of practicing compassion "within ourselves" is further elaborated when we consider the meaning of the name Tiep Hien.

Going Beyond Violence

Tiep means "to be in touch with" and "to continue." *To be in touch with* infers being in touch with "the reality of the mind as well as the reality of the world" (1993b, p. 12). For Nhat Hanh, to be in touch with the reality of the mind means not only to "be aware of the processes of our inner life, i.e. feelings, perceptions mental formations etc., but also to rediscover our true mind" (p. 22). A "true mind" is an enlightened mind undefiled by negativity, free from suffering and the causes of suffering, free from delusions such as hatred and attachment, and free especially from the ignorance of self-grasping. To be in touch with the reality of our minds is also to become aware of the reality of the world and hence to realize the unity of mind and world: "these are not two separate worlds; they belong to the same reality" (p. 12). To be in touch with our minds we simultaneously get in touch with the reality of the world. Invariably, our minds encounter all manner of phenomena, some wonderful and others dreadful. Nhat Hanh addresses this process in terms of seeing deeply into minds and simultaneously seeing deeply into the world. The term *tiep* also means "to continue," which connotes perpetuating the way of enlightenment of the Bodhisattva.

Hien translates as "to realize" and "to make it here and now." *To realize* directs us toward a process of transforming our understanding and compassion into real life. Realization is the process in which understanding and compassion become lived. In this way we avoid being trapped in doctrines and ideas: "Understanding and compassion must not become ideas about understanding and compassion. They must be real existing entities within life itself which can be seen, touched and experimented with" (Nhat Hanh, 1993b, p 13). For instance, to share joy we must have joy within us. To transmit serenity we need to realize this state in our mind streams. In this sense we need to do more than just talk about peace or compassion for others. It is not enough to have the mere idea of these states; we must have a peaceful and compassionate mind, or "one's actions could only cause more trouble and destruction in the world" (p. 14). And *to make it here now* reminds us that "only the present is real" (p. 14). As Nhat Hanh posits,

> To practice Buddhism does not mean to endure hard things now for the sake of peace and liberation in the future. The purpose of Buddhist practice is not to be reborn in paradise or a Buddha land after death. The purpose of the practice is to have peace, for ourselves and others, right now while we're breathing. Means and ends cannot be different. (p. 14)

It is important to understand that this means that every activity is an occasion for practice. We cannot wait until our lives are more conducive to practice, but must use our everyday lives as grist for transformation. For a Buddhist, there is nothing in life that is outside that transformative process. Nhat Hanh has also been experimenting with developing a form of Buddhist praxis that embodies that ideal.

Peace Work and the Malaise in Western Society

Nhat Hanh's Buddhist activism has been redefined as a consequence of living in exile since the signing of the Paris Peace Accords in 1973. His socially-engaged Buddhism has thus developed more expansive aims than just peace in Vietnam at that time. His trips to Paris during the peace negotiations had already alerted him to more profound problems or suffering arising from "the deep malaise in [Western] society" (Nhat Hanh, 1993a, p. 7).

He writes,

> When we put a young person in this society without trying to protect him, he receives violence, hatred, fear, and insecurity everyday, and eventually he gets sick. Our conversations, TV programs, advertisements, newspapers, and magazines all water the seeds of suffering in young people, and in not-so-young people as well. We feel a kind of vacuum in ourselves, and we try to fill it by eating, reading, talking, smoking, drinking, watching TV, going to the movies, or even overworking. Taking refuge these days in these things only makes us feel hungrier and less satisfied and we want to ingest more. (p. 7)

From Plum Village in France, Nhat Hanh now engages in an international community development project based on "right livelihood" as a context for both personal and social transformation. *Right livelihood* he defines in terms of the "art of living" (Nhat Hanh, 1994a, p. 242), which he understands to have "ceased to be a purely personal matter" but instead must be understood as a "collective matter." The livelihood of each person affects us all, and vice versa" (p. 245). His project can be understood as one of "developing and maintaining communities of resistance" (Berrigan & Nhat Hanh, 1975, p. 117). The very idea of communities of resistance arises out of the insight that we are engaged in a "long term struggle in which [people need to] stand up more visibly and perhaps with more risk" (p. 121), and that "a moral, individual action [is] no longer enough; there must be unity of effort which [is] more and more highly political" (p 121). His living in exile and learning about Western society has meant that he has had to expand his idea of the struggle for peace:

> It is a resistance against all kinds of things that are like war. Because of living in modern society, one feels that s/he cannot easily retain integrity, wholeness. One is robbed permanently of humanness, the capacity of being oneself. ... So perhaps, first of all, resistance means opposition to being invaded, occupied, assaulted, and destroyed by the system. The purpose of resistance, here, is to seek the healing of yourself in order to be able to see clearly. (Berrigan & Nhat Hanh, 1975, p. 122)

Nhat Hanh (1993a), along with a range of others, has proposed a Buddhist theory or theology of resistance that involves a rethinking of *sila*, or the practice of ethics. Such a theory is framed by a rethinking of the Buddhist lay precepts. These precepts traditionally define ethical practice in terms of what an individual should abandon. Simply put: no killing, stealing, lying, sexual misconduct, or intoxicants. But when these precepts are understood in terms of right livelihood in (post)modern conditions, ethical practice demands actively resisting the social conditions that give rise to these negative actions. Rather than view the precepts as negativities to avoid, Nhat Hanh has developed a rewording of each of them that adds also the practice of their antithesis. For instance, to avoid killing, we practice reverence for life and hence develop compassion for others. To avoid stealing, we practice generosity and develop loving kindness. To avoid the suffering of sexual misconduct, we practice responsibility in our relationships with others. To avoid lying, we practice deep listening and loving speech. And to avoid intoxicants, we practice keeping our bodies and mind healthy, which means being mindful of what we consume both materially and culturally.

Of course, each of these practices are interrelated. To practice one of them well involves practicing all five. The practice of ethics as experiments in the art of living in a postmodern society, as Aitken (1993) understands, is a path "uncharted by the old teachers" but one in which the "unholy alliance of greed, state ego, racism, androcentrism, and technology has made an imperative" (p. 105). But Batchelor (1993) reminds us that the practice of precepts has always involved a tension "between those who emphasize the literal meaning of the precepts and those who emphasize the values that underlie them" (p. 139). The underlying problem is the impossibility of solving our ethical dilemmas, especially with those uniquely complex situations, with any form of precepts. The practice of ethics demands that we "look deeply at the situation and then choose, with wisdom, what to do" (p. 139), and the wisdom that is required here is "beyond the wording of the precepts" (p. 139). Beyond the wording is a commitment to a set of values, which Batchelor defines as "clarity, stillness and freedom of mindfulness" (p. 140). With that in mind, Nhat Hanh's rethinking of the precepts goes a long way in identifying what these values might be, thus providing a practical and useful map for cultivating an ethicopolitical practice in an unjust world.

Sulak Sivaraksa and a Buddhist Vision for Renewing Society

Sulak Sivaraksa, too, provides a socially-engaged reinterpretation of living an ethicopolitical life that resonates strongly with the ideas of the Dalai Lama and Thich Nhat Hanh and also provides insights and inspirations for a post-colonial Buddhist theology/theory. One of Thailand's most prominent social critics and activists (Sivaraksa, 1998a; Swearer, 1996), Sivaraksa is renowned in the West for his work in the International Network of Engaged Buddhism, and his work is situated in the Thai Theravādan tradition. He is a valued partici-pant in the World Council of Churches, in Peace Brigade International, in the Gandhi Peace Foundation and was recently recognized for his work by win-ning the Swedish government's alternative to the Nobel Prize, the Right Live-lihood Award. His work encapsulates both a critical and Buddhist sensibility and is characterized by a Buddhist dialectical approach that he applies to all manner of binaries including local/global, theory/practice, and self/society. A theme that marks his writing and his activism is his commitment to rethink-ing what it means to be Buddhist. His work is ecumenical and catholic, and he is especially committed to defending a socially-engaged form of Buddhism.

Struggling for Social Justice in Thailand Demands a Global Outlook

The focus of much of Sivaraksa's work has been in response to the process of "development" in Thailand, which he understands in terms of a crisis. Against those advocates of Western-style economic globalization, Sivaraksa sees a degradation of the everyday life of the Thai people. His critique of contemporary Thai society is based on a view that "Thailand is in the midst of an identity crisis that began during the reign of Rama VI ..." (Swearer, 1996, p. 209). Since that time, Thai political elites have engaged in a wholesale appropriation of a Western lifestyle with the concomitant erosion of traditional cultural, religious, and social values. With a few exceptions, these elites have turned to a Western "development" model to transform Thailand.

"Such a framework," notes Sivaraksa,

> presupposes the concepts of capital markets, nation-state structures, the "free individual" (i.e. consumer), and the linear and unlimited procession of growth. These are foundations of a world view for the vast majority of the West, large segments of Japan, and increasing numbers of southern elites who study abroad. However, for the large percentage of the human race, these concepts are still alien. (Sivaraksa, 1998b, p. 1)

Unfortunately, while offering great promise, this top-down model of "development" has meant that the existing feudal elites have been able to use the modern nation-state to consolidate their power over their "clients" (the Thai citizenry). Instead of the ideal of material prosperity, democratic government and individual social mobility, the reality of contemporary Thailand is distorted:

> Material prosperity exists for a small group of patron elite in government and business circles; feudal cronyism is disguised as representative democracy; and a mass of disempowered citizens are increasingly cut off from their historical and cultural identities. These identities are replaced with modern consumer identities which they have few personal or communal resources for coming to grips with. (Sivaraksa, 1998b, p. 2)

The implementation of a paradigm of modern "development" is characterized by Sivaraksa as the degradation of a village lifestyle that was self-sufficient and involved naturally cooperative institutions to the emergence of urban slums that require government services to provide support:

Farmlands are usurped by monoculture agribusiness and those formally outside the money economy have no way to earn even enough to eat. The young
people go to the city to find work, and they end up working in sweatshops, as
prostitutes, as drug runners, or living on the streets not finding work at all.
These nonelite are not choosing to be poor, homeless, or violent. They have been
placed in the situation by the ["development" model]. (Sivaraksa, 1992a, p. 24)

Meanwhile, feudalistic leaders embezzle large amounts of developmental
aid money for their personal business interests, and this "has had a cascading
effect" on all sectors of society, "especially government officials who seek to get
their own slice of the pie at the expense of public welfare" (Sivaraksa, 1998b,
p. 2). In traditional Thai culture, people are taught that personal growth is
related to social well-being. People are "taught to respect other living beings"
and that "personal achievement at the expense of others is frowned upon";
"[e]xploitation, confrontation, and competition are to be avoided, while unity,
communality, and harmony are encouraged" (pp. 5–6). The breakdown of traditional cultural values and their replacement by an unbounded consumerism
has resulted in intolerable environments from industrial waste and consumer
pollution and an explosion of HIV/AIDS from the booming sex industries.
"The department stores have become our shrines," comments Sivaraksa, and
"have replaced the Buddhist temples as centers of social life" (1992a, p. 4).
Also, crime and religious fundamentalism have emerged as people attempt
to respond to the ensuing alienation of "development." Being forced into the
world market and global consumerism by the structural adjustment packages
on the World Bank and the International Monetary Fund are rationalized
by the rhetoric of self-determination, but in reality they involve a process in
which indigenous cultural systems are overwhelmed by the power of foreign
transnational corporations. The traditional values of Thai society have been
unable "to resist the pressures of consumerism" (p. 8).

Sivaraksa (1992a, p. 24) provides a unique Buddhist critique of this "think
big" strategy for development in Thailand, which has been called *economic
rationalism* in the West (Saul, 1997). From his Buddhist perspective, this
model is a materialist development theory that "measures development in
terms of physical results, such as increased income, more factories, schools
hospitals, or food, or a larger labour force" (Sivaraksa, 1992a, p. 35). But
this theory assumes wrongly that development can be understood only in
material terms. What is missing is any sense of the development of human
potentiality. Through quantifying development, the theory has ignored the

"quality of humanity" (p. 35). A materialist theory of development has no way of thinking about what it means to live fully and assumes these issues are "metaphysical or religious" (p. 26). These issues are existential, not economic, and they are "related to our needs for leisure, contemplation, love, community, and self-realization" (p. 37). A development theory that is sensitive to the existential requires a multidisciplinary approach that involves "ecologists, sociologists, political scientists, anthropologists, philosophers and others" (p. 37). Under the think big strategy for development people are perceived only as a labor force and as consumers. Whether they are exploited, their environment is degraded, or the quality of their lives deteriorates is irrelevant. As an example, Sivaraksa (1992a) draws special attention to the construction of a "modern" factory in a "developing" country:

> The sole function of a factory like this is to accumulate money for foreign investors, and for those few local investors who are willing to oppress their own countrymen [and women] and obstruct them from exercising economic and political power at or near their own level. ... The producer's motive is to invest money in a way that will bring him the greatest financial return. He cannot be concerned with the disappearance of natural resources. He may be producing luxury goods of little utility, while the majority of the people struggle for the basic necessities of life. (p. 38)

This model of development is, for Sivaraksa, an expression of the logic of capitalism, which privileges "catering to the physical pleasures of the wealthy ... rather than the welfare of the general public" (p. 39–40). Such logic has little resistance in Thailand. Unlike the reality of the developed countries, which have labor unions with some power, government officials are fairly honest, and consumers have their own organizations, the "developing" countries have to tolerate rampant dishonesty and exploitation. Sivaraksa argues that the adoption of this model of development places Thailand in a "vicious cycle" (p. 42). The critique of this development model is treated with contempt and has little or no voice. The model is obviously unsustainable even in the short to medium term. The solution is not a matter of continuing with the idea of "more production is better, as long as there is a just distribution" (p. 42). Under the conditions of "fast capitalism" (Agger, 1989), "new problems are appearing faster than ... can be solved" (Sivaraksa, 1992a, p. 42). The addiction to economic growth, along with little concern for the consequences, ultimately means an unsustainable exploitation of natural resources that cannot go on forever. Sivaraksa traces this problem back to the lifestyle of those living in the richest nations. "Unless the citizens of the richest nations seriously change their life-styles, and do it soon, there is little hope" (Sivaraksa, 1992b, p. 134).

For those of us living in the richer nations, Sivaraksa's demand can only be realized if we can get beyond thinking of ourselves as separate and self-exist-ing. We need to think about how we are "co-responsible" (1993b, p. 84). If we reject the illusion of separateness, then we are implicated in everything that happens, the good and the bad. We cannot then blame another but must see ourselves as involved. "We are all victims of violence, anger, misunderstand-ing, and the lack of respect for our human dignity" (Nhat Hanh, 1993b, p. 84), but we are also the perpetrators. Beyond the duality of our own separateness we cannot take sides with victims against the perpetrators. "Taking sides is too easy" (p. 107) but we can take sides with those who are suffering the most, and that will mean transforming our own lifestyle.

Buddhism for the Contemporary World

A parallel theme for Sivaraksa's critique has been his interests in the relation-ship between the Buddhist community and the state. For Sivaraksa (1992a), this relationship needs to be always in tension. The religious traditions need to nurture a prophetic aspect "that calls for a more just and peaceful society on Earth, here and now, and stop postponing justice for some future existence" (p. 57). Unfortunately, in Thailand, segments of the Buddhist Sangha became dependent on state patronage. The growth of monastic wealth was accom-panied by the integration of the Sangha into society; often the priestly class became another sector of the elite, with its own social power, cultural influ-ence, and selfish interests. "The institutionalization of the Sangha was typi-cally linked to state control, so that instead of holding the state to the ethics of nonviolence, the Sangha was increasingly called upon to rationalize violence and injustice," notes Sivaraksa (1992b, p. 128). Rather than being the spiritual advisors of the nation's leaders, the Sangha now perform ceremonies that have little or no relevance to the society: "The 'new' spiritual advisors," comments Sivaraksa, "are from the Harvard Business School, the Fletcher School of Law and Diplomacy, and the London School of Economics" (1992a, p. 4).

In this context of a perverted form of Buddhism, Sivaraksa attempts to rethink what it means to be a Buddhist practitioner. He is very clear that tra-ditional Buddhist approaches need to be rethought in order to make sense of life in contemporary societies, but "without compromising the essentials" (Siv-araksa, 1994, p. 2). He is especially sensitive to avoid thinking about Buddhism as a form of escapism and rebukes Buddhist thinking that considers dharma only in terms of the personal. In a clear exposition of his position in the context of thinking about world peace he notes that a Buddhist approach "demands self-awareness and social awareness in equal measure," and this requires "not just a counter-psychology, but also a counter-culture, a counter-economy, and counter-politics" (Sivaraksa, 1992b, p. 127).

Sivaraksa's Buddhist perspective is not about the shunning of the material aspects of life, such as food, clothing, shelter, and medicine. Instead, these are understood as the means to building a mental and spiritual ecology, not as ends to be accumulated. His writing is replete with examples of projects in which communities are mobilized as both "a political force and protest movement" and also as "a creative new venture of self-reliance and sustainability. Both streams being committed to incorporating spiritual practice and a goal of contentment rather than material wealth" (Sivaraksa, 2001, p. 2). There is a Buddhist alternative to the "think big" version of development. Development must aim at the reduction of fostering greed and hatred and increasing power: "It is the reduction of desires that constitutes development. This is the opposite of the materialist notion that dominates our conventional thinking" (Sivaraksa, 1992a, p. 44). Thus, for Sivaraksa, this process of reducing selfishness involves two realizations: "an inner realization concerning greed, hatred and delusion, and an outer realization concerning the impact these tendencies have on society and the planet" (p. 47).

Buddhism as a Resource for Critical Pedagogy

By way of conclusion I'd like to make a few suggestions for critical educators, as socially-engaged Buddhism offers a range of possibilities for both curriculum and pedagogy.

Buddhism offers "new" cultural resources to critical pedagogy, and to countercultural and counterhegemonic movements in general, and might be considered as a "resistance narrative" (Moore, 1993, p. 6) that enables us to rethink ethicopolitical practice. I agree with Clarke (1997) who argues that ideas and practices coming "East of Said" (see Fox, 1992) have "for three centuries assumed a counter-cultural, counter-hegemonic role, and become in various ways a gadfly plaguing all kinds of orthodoxies, and an energiser of radical protest" (Clarke, 1997, p. 27).

In terms of curriculum, it would be possible to study socially-engaged Buddhism as a "resistance narrative," choosing any of the Buddhist inspired political struggles in many Asian countries with large Buddhist populations, such as Burma (Aung, 1991, 1997a; 1997b); Tibet (Adhe, 1997; Dalai Lama, 1997; Dawa, 1997; Kelly, Bastian, & Aiello, 1991; Palden, 1997); Thailand (Watts, Senauke, & Bhikkhu, 1997); Sri Lanka (Macy, 1983a); and Vietnam (Berrigan & Nhat Hanh, 1975; Nhat Hanh, 1967), to name the most famous ones. In each of the stated countries, significant political struggle is or has been conducted by Buddhist practitioners committed to working a dialectic between inner and outer work. These Buddhist activists have also been inspirational at a time in which Buddhism is being translated for the West (Batchelor, 1994). As a consequence, a Buddhist-inspired radical activism is also developing momentum in concert with other social movements, such as feminism (Dresser, 1996; Gross, 1993, 1998; Murcott, 1991), environmentalism (Jones, 1993; Kelly, 1994; Spretnak & Capra, 1984), antinuclear activism (Macy, 1983b, 1991), peace activism (Kraft, 1992), and those interested in critiques of global capitalism (Loy, 1997; Payutto, 1994; Watts & Loy, 1998; Whitmyer, 1994).

Socially-engaged Buddhism also offers a few suggestions for reconsiderations of critical pedagogy. Working from the socially-engaged Buddhist tradition we might begin to think in terms of pedagogies for universal responsibility. Taking from the Dalai Lama, this means cultivating concern for others as a basis for compassionate action. Pedagogies for universal responsibility would enable young people to develop their understanding of connectedness as a basis for thinking through ethics. The reality of our connectedness, or our interdependence, means that we have no choice but to take personal responsibility for the well-being of others. Thinking through connectedness also leads to the cultivation of contentment: that we are in this together can only mean that personal greed and acquisitiveness leads to harming others.

Thich Nhat Hanh's work pushes the idea of interconnectedness still further. That we "inter-are" means that we need to understand our coresponsibility for the present state of violence. Pedagogies of connectedness reject the illusion of our separateness and demand that we think through how implicated we are in everything that happens. For Nhat Hanh, struggling for peace involves both inner and outer work and that the inner work needs to precede the outer.

Working from Sulak Sivarksa, a pedagogy of universal responsibility would pursue forms of knowing/knowledge that build self and social awareness in equal measure. Such a pedagogy would provide opportunities to imagine ways of living that are nonexploitative, democratic, nonviolent and hence also opposed to forms of materialism that are obviously unsustainable and toxic to the environment, societies, and the psyche.

This is a big call, but then, do we have any other choice? As Foucault argues:

> Maybe the target nowadays is not to discover what we are, but to refuse what we are. We have to imagine and to build up what we could be to get rid of this kind of "double bind," which is the simultaneous individualization and totalization of modern power structures.

> The conclusion would be that the political, ethical, social, philosophical problem of our days is not to try to liberate the individual from the state, and from the state's institutions, but to liberate us both from the state and from the type of individualization which is linked to the state. We have to promote new forms of subjectivity through the refusal of this kind of individuality which has been imposed on us for several centuries. (Foucault, 1982, p. 216)

Acknowledgments

This paper is part of an Australian Research Council project (DP0451610), "Rethinking Reconciliation and Pedagogy in Unsettling Times." This project is a collaboration among Associate Professor Robert Hattam, Associate Professor Peter Bishop (University of South Australia), Dr. Stephen Atkinson (University of South Australia), Dr. Julie Matthews (University of the Sunshine Coast), Associate Professor Pam Christie (University of Queensland), and Professor Pal Ahluwalia (University of London). I would also like to thank Professor Basil Moore and Associate Professor Peter Bishop for their kindness during the process of drafting an earlier version of this chapter, and Khensur Losang Thubten Rinpoche for teaching me how to meditate.

References

Adhe, T. (1997). *Ama Adhe: The voice that remembers*. Boston: Wisdom.

Agger, B. (1989). *Fast capitalism: A critical theory of significance*. Urbana: University of Illinois Press.

Agger, B. (1998). *Critical social theories: An introduction*. Boulder, CO: Westview Press.

Aitken, R. (1993). Precepts and responsible practice. In T. Nhat Hanh (Ed.), *For a future to be possible: Commentaries on the five mindfulness trainings* (pp. 101–105). Berkeley, CA: Parallax Press.

Aung, S. S. K. (1991). *Freedom from fear and other writings*. London: Penguin.

Aung, S. S. K. (1997a). *Letters from Burma*. London: Penguin.

Aung, S. S. K. (1997b). *The voice of hope*. London: Penguin.

Batchelor, S. (1993). The future is in our hands. In T. Nhat Hanh (Ed.), *For a future to be possible: Commentaries on the five mindfulness trainings* (pp. 136–142). Berkeley, CA: Parallax Press.

Batchelor, S. (1994). *The awakening of the West: The encounter of Buddhism and Western Culture*. London: Aquarian.

Bauman, Z. (1998). *Work, consumerism and the new poor*. Buckingham, England: Open University Press.

Bauman, Z. (1999). *In search of politics*. Cambridge, England: Polity Press.

Beck, U. (1997). *The reinvention of politics: Rethinking modernity in the global social order*. Cambridge, England: Polity Press.

Benhabib, S. (1992). *Situating the self: Gender, community and postmodernism in contemporary ethics*. Cambridge, England: Polity Press.

Benhabib, S., Butler, J., Cornell, D., & Fraser, N. (1995). *Feminist contentions: A philosophical exchange*. London: Routledge.

Berrigan, D., & Nhat Hanh, T. (1975). *The raft is not the shore: Conversations toward a Buddhist/Christian awareness*. Boston: Beacon Press.

Best, S., & Kellner, D. (1991). *Postmodern theory: Critical interrogations*. New York: Guilford Press.

Bishop, P. (2000). Caught in the crossfire: Tibet, media and promotional culture. *Media, Culture and Society, 22*(5), 645–664.

Brennan, S., Behrendt, L., Strelein, L., & Williams, G. (2005). *Treaty*. Annandale, New South Wales, Australia: Federation Press.

Britzman, D., & Dippo, D. (2000). On the future of awful thoughts in teacher education. *Teacher education, 11*(1), 31–37.

Castells, M. (1996). *Information age: Economy, society, and culture*, vol. 1, *The rise of network society*. Cambridge, MA: Blackwell.

Castells, M. (1997). *Information age: Economy, society, and culture*, vol. 2, *The power of identity*. Cambridge, MA.: Blackwell.

Castells, M. (1998). *Information age: Economy, society, and culture*, vol. 3, *End of millenium*. Oxford, England: Blackwell.

Chân, K. (1993). *Learning true love: How I learned and practiced social change in Vietnam*. Berkeley, CA.: Parallax Press.

Chödrön, P. (1994). *Start where you are: A guide to compassionate living*. Boston: Shambala.

Clarke, J. (1997). *Oriental enlightenment: An encounter between Asian and Western thought*. London: Routledge.

Critchley, S. (1996). Prolegomena to any post-deconstructive subjectivity. In S. Critchley & P. Dews (Eds.), *Deconstructive subjectivities* (pp. 13–46). Albany: State University of New York.

Dalai Lama (1988). *The Dalai Lama at Harvard: Lectures on the Buddhist path to peace* (J. Hopkins, Trans. & Ed.). Ithaca, NY: Snow Lion.

Dalai Lama (1991). *Compassion and the individual*. Boston: Wisdom.

Dalai Lama (1992a). *Worlds in harmony: Dialogues on compassionate action*. Berkeley, CA: Parallax Press.

Dalai Lama (1992b). *The global community and the need for universal responsibility*. Boston: Wisdom.

Dalai Lama (1996). *Beyond dogma: Dialogues and discourses*. Berkeley, CA: North Atlantic Books.

Dalai Lama (1997). *My land and my people*. New York: Warner Books.

Dalai Lama (1999). *Ethics for the new millennium*. New York: Riverhead.

Dawa Norbu (1997). *Tibet: The road ahead*. London: Rider.

Derrida, J. (1996). Remarks on Deconstruction and Pragmatism. In C. Mouffe (Ed.), *Deconstruction and pragmatism* (pp. 77–88). London: Routledge.

Dresser, M. (Ed.). (1996). *Buddhist women on the edge: Contemporary perspectives from the Western frontier*. Berkeley, CA: North Atlantic Books.

Ekins, P. (1992). *A new world order: Grassroots movements for global change*. London: Routledge.

Eppsteiner, F. (Ed.). (1988). *The path of compassion: Writings on socially engaged Buddhism*. Berkeley, CA: Parallax Press.

Fine, M. (1994). Working the hyphens: reinventing self and other in qualitative research. In N. Denzin & Y. Lincoln (Eds.), *Handbook of Qualitative Research* (pp. 70–82). London: Sage.

Flax, J. (1990). *Thinking fragments: Psychoanalysis, feminism, and postmodernism in the contemporary West*. Berkeley and Los Angeles: University of California Press.

Foucault, M. (1982). The subject and power. In H. Dreyfus & P. Rabinow (Eds.), *Michel Foucault: Beyond structuralism and hermeneutics* (pp. 208–226). New York: Harvester Wheatsheaf.

Foucault, M. (1983). Structuralism and post-structuralism: An interview, by G. Raulet (G. Raulet, Trans.) *Telos, 55*, 195–211.

Fox, R. (1992). East of Said. In M. Sprinker (Ed.), *Edward Said: A critical reader* (pp. 144–156). Cambridge, MA: Blackwell.

Fraser, N. (1989). *Unruly practices: Power, discourse and gender in contemporary social theory*. Minneapolis: University of Minnesota Press.

Fraser, N. (1997). *Justice interruptus: Critical reflections on the "postsocialist" condition*. New York: Routledge.

Freire, P. (1972). *Pedagogy of the oppressed* (M. B. Ramos, Trans.). New York: Penguin.

Geshe, R. (1984). *The essential nectar: Meditations on the Buddhist path*. Boston: Wisdom.

Gilroy, P. (2000). *Against race: Imagining political culture beyond the color line*. Cambridge, MA: Belknap Press of Harvard University Press.

Gore, J. (1993). *The sruggle for pedagogies: Critical and feminist discourses as regimes of truth*. New York: Routledge.

Gottlieb, R. (Ed.). (1996). *This sacred earth: Religion, nature, environment*. New York: Routledge.

Gross, R. (1993). *Buddhism after patriarchy: A feminist history, analysis, and reconstruction of Buddhism*. Albany: State University of New York Press.

Gross, R. (1998). *Soaring and setting: Buddhist perspectives on contemporary social and religious issues*. New York: Continuum.

Gutman, A. (Ed.). (1994). *Multiculturalism: Examining the politics of recognition*. Princeton, NJ: Princeton University Press.

Harris, C. (1993). Desperately seeking the Dalai Lama. In S. Gupta (Ed.), *Disputed borders: An intervention in definitions of boundaries* (pp. 104–114). London: Rivers Oram Press.

Hattam, R. (2000, April). *Curriculum and Buddhism: critical pedagogy meets the Bodhisattva*. Paper presented at the annual conference of the American Educational Research Association, New Orleans, Louisiana.

Hattam, R. (2004). *Awakening-struggle: Towards a Buddhist critical social theory*. Flaxton, Queensland, Australia: PostPressed.

Iyer, R. (1990). *The essential writing of Mahatma Gandhi*. Delhi, India: Oxford University Press.

Jones, K. (1989). *The social face of Buddhism: An approach to political and social activism*. London: Wisdom.

Jones, K. (1993). *Beyond optimism: A Buddhist political ecology*. Oxford, England: Carpenter.

Kellner, D. (1988). Postmodernism as social theory: Some challenges and problems. *Theory, Culture and Society, 5*, 239–269.

Kellner, D. (1995). *Media culture: Cultural studies, identity, and politics between the modern and the postmodern*. London: Routledge.

Kellner, D. (2003). *From 9/11 to terror war: The dangers of the Bush legacy*. Lanham, MD: Rowman and Littlefield.

Kelly, P. (1994). *Thinking green! Essays on environmentalism, feminism, and non-violence*. Berkeley, CA: Parallax Press.

Kelly, P., Bastian, G., & Aiello, P. (Eds.). (1991). *The anguish of Tibet*. Berkeley, CA: Parallax Press.

Kotler, A. (Ed.). (1996). *Engaged Buddhist reader.* Berkeley, CA: Parallax Press.

Kovel, J. (1991). *History and spirit: An inquiry into the philosophy of liberation.* Boston: Beacon Press.

Kraft, K. (1992). Introduction. In K. Kraft (Ed.), *Inner peace, world peace: Essays on Buddhism and nonviolence* (pp. 1–9). Albany: State University of New York Press.

Kraft, K. (Ed.). (1992b). *Inner peace, world peace: Essays on Buddhism and nonviolence.* Albany: State University of New York Press.

Kraft, K. (1999). *The wheel of engaged Buddhism: A new map of the path.* New York & Tokyo: Weatherhill.

Lama Zopa Rinpoche. (1993). *Transforming problems into happiness.* Boston: Wisdom.

Lash, S., & Featherstone, M. (2002). *Recognition and difference: Politics, identity, Multiculture.* London: Sage.

Lati, R. (1980). *Mind in Tibetan Buddhism* (E. Napper, Trans.). Ithaca, NY: Snow Lion.

Liberman, K. (1986). The Tibetan cultural praxis: Bodhicitta thought training. *Humboldt Journal of Social Relations, 13*(1–2), 113–126.

Lobsang, G. (1997). *Bodhicitta: Cultivating the compassionate mind of enlightenment.* Ithaca, NY: Snow Lion.

Loy, D. (Ed.). (1996a). *Healing deconstruction: Postmodern thought in Buddhism and Christianity.* Atlanta: Scholars Press.

Loy, D. (1996b). *Lack and transcendence: The problem of death in psychotherapy, existentialism, and Buddhism.* Atlantic Highlands, NJ: Humanities Press.

Macy, J. (1983a). *Despair and personal power in the nuclear age.* Philadelphia: New Society.

Macy, J. (1983b). *Dharma and development: Religion as resource in the Sarvodaya self-help movement.* West Hartford, CT: Kumarian Press.

Macy, J. (1991). *World as lover, world as self.* Berkeley, CA: Parallax Press.

McCarthy, C., & Critchlow, W. (Eds.). (1993). *Race, identity, and repression in education.* New York: Routledge.

McDonald, K. (1984). *How to meditate: A practical guide.* Boston: Wisdom.

McLaren, P. (1997). *Revolutionary multiculturalism: Pedagogies of dissent for the new millennium.* Boulder, CO: Westview Press.

Moore, B. (1993, June 30–July 3). *Teaching for resistance.* Paper presented at the Curriculum in Profile Conference of the Australian Curriculum Studies Association, Brisbane, Queensland, Australia.

Murcott, S. (1991). *The first Buddhist women: Translations and commentary on the Therigatha.* Berkeley, CA: Parallax Press.

Nagarjuna. (1975). Precious Garland of Advice for the King. In Dalai Lama, *The Buddhism of Tibet* (J. Hopkins, Ed. and Trans.; pp. 107–206). Ithaca, NY: Snow Lion.

New London Group. (1996). A pedagogy of multiliteracies: Designing social futures. *Harvard Educational Review, 66*(1), 60–92.

Nhat Hanh, T. (1967). *Vietnam: Lotus in a sea of fire.* New York: Hill and Wang.

Nhat Hanh, T. (1987a). *Being peace.* Berkeley, CA: Parallax Press.

Nhat Hanh, T. (1987b). *Interbeing: Commentaries on the Tiep Hien precepts.* Berkeley, CA: Parallax Press.

Nhat Hanh, T. (Ed.). (1993a). *For a future to be possible: Commentaries on the five mindfulness trainings.* Berkeley, CA: Parallax Press.

Nhat Hanh, T. (1993b). *Love in action: Writings on nonviolent social change.* Berkeley, CA: Parallax Press.

Nhat Hanh, T. (1994). The art of living. In C. Whitmyer (Ed.), *Mindfulness and meaningful work: Explorations in right livelihood* (pp. 242–247). Berkeley, CA: Parallax Press.

Offe, C. (1987). Ungovernability: On the renaissance of conservative theories of crisis. In J. Habermas (Ed.), *Observation of the "spiritual situation of the age"* (pp. 67–68). Cambridge, MA: MIT Press.

Palden Gyatso. (1997). *Fire under the snow: Testimony of a Tibetan prisoner.* London: Harvill.

Payutto, P. (1994). *Buddhist economics: A middle way for the market.* Bangkok, Thailand: Buddhadharma Foundation.

Peters, M., Lankshear, C., & Olssen, M. (Eds.). (2003). *Critical theory and the human condition: Founders and Praxis.* New York: Lang.

Pinar, W. (2004). *What is curriculum theory?* Mahwah, NJ: Erlbaum. ←

Poster, M. (1989). *Critical theory and poststructuralism: In search of a context.* Ithaca, NY: Cornell University Press.

Pritchard, S. (1998). *Indigenous peoples, the United Nations and human rights.* Annandale, New South Wales, Australia: Federation Press.

Queen, C., & King, S. (Eds.). (1996). *Engaged Buddhism: Buddhist liberation movements in Asia.* Albany: State University of New York Press.

Rabtan, G., & Ngawang Dhargyey, G. (1997). *Advice from a spiritual friend.* New Delhi: Wisdom Culture.

Rahula, W. (1985). The social teachings of the Buddha. In F. Eppsteiner (Ed.), *The path of compassion: Writings on socially engaged Buddhism* (pp. 103–110). Berkeley, CA: Parallax Press.

Rigney, L. (2000, September 18). *A first nations perspective of Indigenous Australian participation in science: Framing indigenous research towards indigenous Australian intellectual sovereignty.* Paper presented at the Second National Indigenous Researchers Forum, Adelaide, South Australia.

Robertson, R. (1992a). Globality, global culture, and images of world order. In H. Haferkamp & N. J. Smelser (Eds.), *Social change and modernity* (pp. 395–412). Berkeley: University of California Press.

Robertson, R. (1992b). *Globalization: Social theory and global culture.* London: Sage.

Said, E. (1978). *Orientalism.* London: Penguin.

Saul, J. R. (1997). *The unconscious civilization.* Middlesex, England: Penguin.

Sedgwick, E. K. (1991). *The epistemology of the closet.* Berkeley: University of California Press.

Shor, I., & Freire, P. (1987). *A pedagogy for liberation: Dialogues on transforming education.* South Hadley, MA: Bergin and Garvey.

Sivaraska, S. (1992a). *Seeds of peace: A Buddhist vision for renewing society.* Berkeley, CA: Parallax Press.

Sivaraska, S. (1992b). Buddhism and contemporary international trends. In K. Kraft (Ed.), *Inner peace, world peace: Essays on Buddhism and nonviolence* (pp. 127–138). Albany: State University of New York Press.

Sivaraska, S. (1994). Making Buddhism radical: A conversation with Sulak Sivaraksa, by D. Rothberg. Retrieved 17 February 2007 from http://www.geocities.com/RainForest/7813/sul_turn.htm.

Sivaraska, S. (1998a). *Loyalty demands dissent: Autobiography of an engaged Buddhist.* Berkeley, CA: Parallax Press.

Sivaraska, S. (1998b, February). Revisioning "development": A Buddhist perspective. In *Paper given at a meeting with the World Bank and Religious Leaders.* Lambreth, UK.

Sivaraska, S. (2001, 12–15 July). *Culture and reconciliation.* Paper given at the Festival of Ideas, Adelaide, South Australia, Australia.

Spivak, G. (1987). *In other worlds: Essays in cultural politics.* London: Routledge.

Spretnak, C., & Capra, F. (1984). *Green politics: The global promise.* London: Paladin.

Stiglitz, J. (2002). *Globalization and its discontents.* London: Lane.

Swearer, D. (1996). Sulak Sivaraksa's Buddhist Vision for renewing society. In C. Queen & S. King (Eds.), *Engaged Buddhism: Buddhist liberation movements in Asia* (pp. 195–236). Albany: State University of New York Press.

Thurman, R. (1985). Nagarjuna's guidelines for Buddhist social activism. In F. Eppsteiner (Ed.), *The path of compassion: Writings on socially engaged Buddhism*. Berkeley, CA: Parallax Press.

Thurman, R. (1995). *Essential Tibetan Buddhism*. San Francisco: HarperCollins.

Torres, C. A. (1998). Democracy, education, and multiculturalism: Dilemmas of citizenship in a global world. *Comparative education review, 42*(4), 421–447.

Trifonas, P. (Ed.). (2000). *Revolutionary pedagogies: Cultural politics, instituting education, and the discourse of theory*. New York: RoutledgeFalmer.

Trifonas, P. (Ed.). (2003). *Pedagogies of difference: Rethinking education for social change*. New York: RoutledgeFalmer.

Trungpa, C. (1984). *Shambala: The sacred path of the warrior*. Boston: Shambala.

United Nations Development Project. (2003). *Human development report: Millennium development goals: A compact among nations to end human poverty*. New York: United Nations Development Programme.

Watts, J., & Loy, D. (1998). The religion of consumption: A Buddhist perspective. *Development, 41*(1), 61–66.

Watts, J., Senauke, A., & Bhikkhu, S. (Eds.). (1997). *Entering the realm of reality: Towards dhammic societies*. Bangkok, Thailand: International Network of Engaged Budddhists.

Welch, S. (1985). *Communities of resistance and solidarity*. Maryknoll, NY: Orbis.

Wexler, P. (2000). *Mystical society: An emerging social vision*. Boulder, CO: Westview Press.

Whitmyer, C. (Ed.). (1994). *Mindfulness and meaningful work: Explorations in right livelihood*. Berkeley, CA: Parallax Press.

Young, R. (1990). White mythologies: Writing history and the West. London: Routledge.

CHAPTER 5

The Gaze of the Teacher:
Eye-to-Eye with Lacan, Derrida, and the Zen of Dōgen and Nishitani

jan jagodzinski
University of Alberta

Is there such a phenomenon as the gaze of the teacher? And if so, can we bring together a number of philosophers from both the West and East who have written about the gaze with some passion and depth—Dōgen Zenji and Nishitani Keiji, Jacques Lacan, and Jacques Derrida—to help us think through it? That is the challenge of this particular chapter, which may present an odd mixture of voices. Here the Japanese Zen Buddhism of Dōgen and Nishitani, philosophers from the 13th and 20th centuries, respectively, are placed in relation to the Western philosophers Lacan and Derrida, who were contemporaries (as was Keiji), with Derrida having a love-hate relationship with psychoanalysis (perhaps because his wife was a practicing analyst). How could such an unlikely foursome be productively put to work for the question of the gaze? Only by asking questions of them might we find some common ground.

Seeing, like hearing, has a built-in paradox. Just as we aren't able, without the aid of a recording, to hear our own voices as others hear us (and thus the recorded voice often sounds alien), we are also unable to see ourselves seeing. The image in a mirror or a photograph often appears equally alienating; how often do we say, "That doesn't look like me!" as our imagined ideal ego clashes with some particular perspective caught by a camera lens? Western

Enlightenment thought bifurcated the inside and the outside, theorizing visual perception as an "either/or": it was either objectified—determining thresholds of physical perception, enhanced through various visual instruments (telescope, microscope, binoculars)—or it was subjectified. Vision was strictly an inner emotional experience best exemplified in the field of aesthetics: beauty was confined to the "eye of the beholder." A paradoxical logic of "both/and" is required as a way to theorize the gap, or space/time interval, of such a dichotomization.

If we go to Taoist or Zen thought, such a bifurcation is overcome by recognizing a "nonduality" between the perceiver and the perceived to grasp an ineffable, nondiscursive knowing when both aesthetics and ethics coalesce. Each of these four Eastern and Western philosophers have addressed this problem in his own unique way. To start, then, is first to theorize the so-called objectivity of the gaze, since the classroom is often imagined as a place of surveillance, with the teacher policing and reading student behavior. I hope to complicate Michel Foucault's (1995) view that this is best interpreted in terms of the apparatus of a panopticon—a view that has since become ironically infamous as to its effects given that Foucault no longer applied this metaphor to global capitalism characterized as a society of control where knowledge of the signifier barred entry to spaces. The idea was to keep people out, rather than in, by surveying/surveilling them.

Directions Not Taken: Seeing with the Cycloptic Single Eye

Seeing is both subjective and objective at once.[1] The phenomenology of Maurice Merleau-Ponty, especially in his book *The Visible and Invisible* (1968), identified this through the concept of *chiasmus*. The odd thing about seeing is that we are able to see ourselves only through a reflection in a mirror; this phenomenon raises complications that have been examined by Lacan in his *Seminar XI: Four Fundamentals of Psycho-Analysis* (1979) where the look and the gaze are differentiated. We see ourselves in reverse, for one thing, but the image that we see in the mirror is itself a specter, an alter ego. Lacan designates this as the look where the ego seems self-assured of its unity. Or, we see ourselves through the *Other*, which raises another complication, also exploited by Lacan. This Other is not only intersubjective—as a friend, a parent, a policeman or stranger would be—but also an amorphous and ephemeral Other. Lacan designates this as *the gaze*, which can make the ego anxious, because the way you are gazed at by a seemingly nebulous set of social "eyes" cannot be pinned down as to the direction from which they are looking at you. Here a story made paradigmatic by the anticolonial revolutionary philosopher Franz Fanon (1967) comes to mind. Fanon, an educated middle-class psychiatrist from the French colony of Martinique, tells of his experience while traveling in Paris in the 1950s. Upon seeing Fanon, a small boy responds to his mother, "Mama, see the Negro! I'm frightened!" (p. 112). Fanon reflects:

> My body was given back to me sprawled out, distorted, recolored, clad in mourning that white winter day. The Negro is an animal, the Negro is bad, the Negro is mean, the Negro is ugly; look a nigger, it's cold, the nigger is shivering, the nigger is shivering because he is cold, the little boy is trembling because he is afraid of the nigger, the nigger is shivering with cold, that cold that goes through your bones, the handsome little boy is trembling because he thinks that the nigger is quivering with rage, the little boy throws himself into his mother's arms: Mama, the nigger is going to *eat me up*. (pp. 113–114; emphasis added)

Fanon's response clearly illustrates the way such an amorphous gaze is materialized by the mistaken fright of the boy, which is preconditioned by a racial prejudice that his mother has transferred to him, either consciously or unconsciously.[2]

Such a gaze has the effect of making Fanon anxious, as if another image of his body has suddenly appeared, one he knows little of, an abjected body that carries all the racial markings that make him stand out from the Parisian crowd. He writes, in disbelief, "Frightened! Frightened! Now they were beginning to be afraid of me. I made up my mind to laugh myself to tears, but laughter had become impossible ..." (p. 112). Positioned under the racial gaze, Fanon is unable to shrug it off.

I start with this example because it illustrates the always already existing imaginary visual and symbolic discourses, forces of affect that subjectivate the body through a disciplinary hegemonic gaze possessed by those who claim ownership to it. In the above case, even a child can claim it. This gaze is not articulated in the positive—that is, representational—terms. In other words, it is not possible to specify all the characteristics that make an identifiable "French citizen" in the 1950s. Profiling (and more specifically, racial profiling) that follows distinct characteristics is precisely what raises problems with such categorizations and has caused such outcries of racism from African Americans, first, and now North Americans of Middle Eastern descent. Profiling the characteristics of students who are considered capable of shooting teachers and students in a school raises a similar issue. James McGee and Caren

DeBarnardo (1999) constructed a hypothetical profile after analyzing students who had committed serious shooting crimes in schools; they later had to add the assertion that such a profile was only a generalization, since it had led to teachers phoning in the names of many innocent students only because they looked like "geeks" and abjected kids. The gaze is much more subtle and slippery than such categorizations. It is precisely identifying characteristics that do not fit into an imaginary picture of being French (paradoxically, a non-definable, absent image that intuitively establishes "Frenchness") that enables the child in Fanon's story to be afraid of him. It is what the abjected body is *not* that defines for the child what the French body *should be*. Identification based on the dialectics of negativity—what is, what is not—presents the complicated phenomenon of nonrepresentability as informing representability; and this nonrepresentability is, for Lacan, unconscious and not easily articulated. The child *reacts* to Fanon; he doesn't think about it. Fanon's body immediately disturbs him. This is not a cognitive decision, but an affective one that is shaped by an imaginary aesthetics, as well as the force of *aisthetics* at the immediate bodily level—touch, smell, and taste that generate the ethics of tactfulness, flair, *sagacitas* (keenness of perception) and *sapientia* (contemplation). Fanon's body has somehow become "ugly," too close for comfort. It stinks, it is untouchable, it has to be spat out.

The objectification of sight is well established in sociological, anthropological, and geographical literature. Foucault's *panopticon* is perhaps the most cited exemplar of such a structuralist mechanism, but it also presents the narrowest of examples when it comes to the geopolitics of surveillance mechanisms. Lacan's notion of the gaze is much more subtle in the way anxiety and self-consciousness overwhelm a person because they are looked at as being "too" fat, or "too" black, or "ignorant" because of a spoken dialect or inability to speak the national language, and so on. Unfortunately, a great deal of educational research follows panoptic and profiling exemplars to determine difference as determined from a referential norm. A quick search on the Internet for "the teacher's gaze" brings up all sorts of educational research with an instrumental focus. In general, the gaze is one of the most thoroughly studied nonverbal gestures in psychology, since it is used to regulate conversation and provides clues for intimacy, agreement, and interest—all of which are of significant concern to educators.

The research team of Isabella Poggi and Catherine Pelachaud (2002a, 2002b) has turned the teacher's gaze into a variation of artificial intelligence, cast into the realms of "affective computerization." Through computer graphics a teacher's "gaze" is broken down into 175 items collected from classroom interactions, movies, and television fiction that display teachers' behaviors. Each item is then analyzed in terms of a taxonomy of nonverbal communicative meanings based on formational parameters like the movement of eyes, the raising of eyebrows, expressions of surprise and interest, head movements, and so on, to come up with a lexicon of signals that can then be mapped out on all possible and probable teaching behaviors. (It should be pointed out that already in 1734 Charles Le Brun, in his *Method to Learn to Design the Passions*, had developed a typology of emotions through a series of drawings that tried to capture the exact placement of the lips, eyes, eyelids, eyebrows, cheeks, and so on for each individual emotion.) From this, a profile of the teacher's gaze and its functions in classroom interaction is established, presumably to advance cognitive learning in the classroom. More amazingly, a "belief network" has been developed from this information through a sophisticated graphic computerization of the face. Depending on the facial communication and facial signals, certain meanings are conveyed. Raising or lowering the eyebrows provides a measure of certainty; a certain head direction gives a measure of dominance, and so on. The probability of expressions is then charted—for instance, the variety of expressions a teacher uses for "feeling sorry for" or for conflict resolution.

This type of research is only the tip of the iceberg when it comes to instrumentalizing the gaze. Further heights are reached by the research of Blascovich et al. (2001). Using immersive virtual environment technology, which tracks and displays a person's nonverbal behavior when interacting with another human being, it is possible to enhance or augment the visual image of such behavior without the subject being aware of such manipulation. The gaze can be reduced to face-to-face eye contact; head and eye movements can be augmented in interactions to enhance performance of information recall.

There is no need to further pursue this line of instrumentalizing the gaze, except to recognize its increasing importance in such computer-animated works as the Disney Pixar films *Toy Story* (1995), *Monsters, Inc.* (2001), *Finding Nemo* (2003), and *The Incredibles* (2004); Dreamworks' *Shrek* (2001); and so on. However, this is a controlled surfaced aesthetic. Each film takes many years to complete, with an enormous staff of animators and writers employed to ensure box-office success. No one can deny the incredible wizardry and uncanny ability of these films to convey effect through computerized graphics, but this raises a significant question for educators, a question that psychoanalytically informs the obsessive psyche: "Am I dead or alive?" What seems like an odd question to ask oneself makes sense when the anxiety that comes with this question concerns human beings and artificial intelligence. Research studies like that of Poggi and Pelachaud (2002a, 2002b) and Blascovich et al. (2001) raise the question, Is there any difference between human beings and machines? If the teacher's gaze can be instrumentalized and put into practice, where is the so-called human dimension to be found? To be dead is to be turned into a machine, but to be "alive" means to escape its machinations.

There is a danger here of falling into the worst sort of sentimental humanism when answering this question—a position that glorifies the self's ability to "feel" and express emotion through some sort of superior intuition. This direction can lead us to essentialist models of pedagogy based on sex/gender bifurcations: female teachers are more caring and nurturing, while male teachers are more distant and hard-line. More naively, this means male teachers have to find their "feminine" side. Another direction that should be questioned is the phenomenological turn, where the claim is made that subjective experience can be understood from a pretheoretical vantage point in order to see the world through the eyes of children/students as they become involved in school experiences. Phenomenology asks the question, "What is the teacher's gaze like?" or, more to the point, "What does it *feel* like?" The question of "being alive" (more commonly referred to as "being–in-the-world") is transcendentally and descriptively answered through the poetic work of language or art. In visual art, the abstract expressionism of the 1940s to 1960s claimed the same ground, as if, for instance, Mark Rothko's color-play paintings (*Blue, Green, and Brown*; *Red on Maroon*, and the like) were a direct translation of an emotional experience that somehow avoided the baggage of the signifier as well as the unconscious because color was a direct affective substance that moved the body universally despite cultural differences. For example, *Red on Maroon* was to be directly felt as "anger." Once a phenomenological description was completed, the claim was made that the teacher would understand school experience much better, and thus act accordingly.

Let's take as a paradigmatic example the elementary student who is afraid to stand in front of the class to face the gaze of his or her classmates during a period of "show and tell" (variously called "sharing period," "bring and brag," or "news time"; see Shapiro, 2002). Stage fright, a "universal" phenomenon, is precisely what is at issue. The anxiety of the objectified stare can be expressively described and pedagogically explored so that the teacher might become more sensitive to this ritualistic act in the class. *Might* is the operative word here, since having a more affective grasp of what it "feels" like and then pedagogically acting ethically on that feeling are worlds apart.

One of the major riddles that plagues phenomenology is how it is possible for someone with phenomenological "insight" to write sensitively about a phenomenon and yet act completely otherwise in everyday life. Surely, the case of playwright Jean Genet is a paradigmatic example. His plays explored the lives of gay men, prostitutes, and thieves. The outcasts of his plays are trapped in their own self-destructive circles, expressing the despair and loneliness of being caught in a maze of mirrors, trapped by an endless progression of images that are but a continuous series of distorted reflections. Genet's phenomenological insights enabled him to write grotesque and haunting plays that paradoxically brought stability into the otherwise unbearable existence of the protagonist by both cultivating and denouncing its living hell. Despite these phenomenological insights, Genet remained a thief and a gay prostitute, his plays providing a way to sublimate his own conflicted existence. One might say the same of Francis Bacon's personal, conflicted gay life and the grotesque expressionist paintings he produced that seemed to be phenomenological descriptions of tortured flesh.

There are equally strange contractions in literary history of white "racist" writers who seem to have been able to sensitively describe slave existence, yet acted (in)differently in their own "real" lives. Aphra Behn's short novel *Oroonoko* (1688) tells the story of a relationship between a middle-class white mistress and a royal black slave in which it appears that the author takes an antislavery point of view; and in the 18th and 19th centuries her novel was certainly read this way. Behn obviously had phenomenological insight as to what it was "like" to be a slave during her stay in the English colony in Surinam in 1664. Yet, her phenomenological intuitiveness does not escape her racism. Here we have a case of understanding the Other's "being-in-the-world" to act as a better exploitive racist unintentionally. The noble savage Oroonoko—as an object to be possessed and loved, as well as abjected—requires a psychoanalytic understanding, raising the difference between Lacan and Merleau-Ponty, who were close friends. To put it bluntly, Can a white person know what it is like to be black growing up in a racist society? For example, Steven Spielberg was criticized for his direction in the film *Amistad* (1997) for not portraying the story from the viewpoint of the rebellious slave Singbe Pieh (Joseph Cinque in the movie, as acted by Djimon Hounson). To put it even more bluntly, Can a man phenomenologically experience the birth of a child? Many feminists would say no. An irreducible difference emerges within such questions that draws the limit of phenomenological insight. When it comes to grasping the teacher's gaze, something is missing from its philosophical net.

A phenomenon such as "show-and-tell" illustrates quite dramatically the separation of the look from the gaze that distinguishes Lacan's critique of Jean-Paul Sarte's understanding of the look (1957, pp. 259–260) and Merleau-Ponty's phenomenology of visual perception. It is precisely the moment of exposure of the child's ego ideal as invested by the fantasy structure of the story or the object about to be shared (the child's own perspectival look as to who she or he is) that confronts the Ideal ego of the class, producing an amorphous aperspectival gaze. A "naked truth" emerges—*alēthia* in the anxiety that is experienced by the child. We have here another reenactment of Fanon's story, but now in the classroom. The question within the context of this essay is, How does the teacher confront the embarrassment and fear that the student experiences in the classroom as she or he confronts the very contradiction that emerges between ego ideal and Ideal ego? Show-and-tell risks the exposure of barring a child's "soul" by providing a glimpse of a part of the self that has been "covered over," repressed. Some teachers who are indeed savvy and sensitive to such an exposure become anxious themselves, unable to deal with the countertransference of a classroom exchange that often deals with "raw" truth. They institute mechanisms of control such as time, object, and theme restrictions to cover up such a performative potential. Show-and-tell thus falls under *their* rules, making it impossible for the children to present themselves and risk exposure. This can happen in any pedagogical endeavor—be it in creative writing or the visual or dramatic arts—in which self-exposure emerges as a transformative possibility. An enabling and "productive" gaze by the teacher is required. These are moments when the "object" that engages the child in show-and-tell "stares back" at both the child and the audience. An ethics of the look emerges, one that exposes the child's "true" self if it becomes pedagogically possible for the child to decenter her- or himself to grasp the objectivity of her or his own ego (*moi*); and to recognize her- or himself within those others (in this case, the classmates) to whom she or he would otherwise respond with revulsion or avoidance. The simple case of laughing at oneself might be one such indicator that such a displacement of the ego has indeed taken place.

Such thinking is consistent with Dōgen's authentication of the self "from thing advancing to the self," rather than the other way around, where "inauthentic selfhood results from the attempt of the self [ego] to authenticate experience, or to give it meaning, through its own agency" (Cook, 1985, p. 134). The gaze of the Zen Buddhist master teacher addresses the ethics that surround the "three poisons" that affect inauthenticity: delusion (of self), desire (as thirst), and hatred in the way these create suffering. Zen, as influenced by Mahayana Buddhism, incorporates the prominent ideal of compassion, which generally informs all forms of Buddhism. Dōgen takes this ideal seriously, outlining an ethics of commitment toward all beings and sympathy with their sufferings. In his discourses and essays, *Shōbōgenzō* (Dōgen 1975),[3] four volumes of which were written between 1231 and 1253 (the year of his death), there is a keen awareness of a deep-rooted anxiety that is expressed in the form of desire and hatred, both of which are rooted in the fear of impermanence (*anitya*) and death. In the teachings of Dōgen, the "inauthentic self" (ego) is obsessed with the fear of its own security and endurance, while the "authentic self" struggles to decenter itself from clinging to such an egocentric life and irrational fear of death. Cast in Lacanian-Freudian terms, this means facing one's own death, a confrontation with one's own mortality, which can lead to a transformation not only of the self but of the social order through an event that ruptures it.

Is this not what happened to Fanon? Even on the smallest of scales like show-and-tell, this can occur. The student faces her own mortality by exposing the ego. She or he can desperately cling to the self (as ego), or learn from its exposure, perhaps even let it go. The class, too, must face such an event, and is challenged to change its gaze. This is precisely what Dōgen says in "Shōbōgenzō Kajō" (The everyday life of the Buddhas and patriarchs, vol 1, pp. 107–110): that the everyday life of the seeker of enlightenment consists in the ordinary acts of everydayness (like eating plain boiled rice and drinking plain tea). In two other significant essays, "Hotsu Bodai-shin" (Awakening the Buddha-seeking mind, vol. 3, p. 71) and "Hotsu mujō-shi" (Developing the supreme mind, vol. 2, p. 55), Dōgen discusses what it means to commit oneself to the liberation of all beings, which also requires a radical de-anthropocentrism, extending the transcendence of egocentrism to include what today we would identify as a "green consciousness."[4] The gaze of compassion must include all sentient life. *Karunā* ("compassion") is the feeling of the pain and confusion that the teacher must have for the student. It also involves the desire to eliminate it. Prajñā is a seeing that moves past the distortions created by fear and insecurity. Both would characterize the gaze of the Zen master.[5]

So while a phenomenological direction is tempting for my question of the teacher's gaze (we will also encounter Emmanuel Lévinas later in the discussion), we have to look elsewhere given that Derrida (1989) has already deconstructed the Heideggerian foundations of this phenomenological enterprise, while Lacan's psychoanalytic postures in his *Four Fundamentals* against his friend Merleau-Ponty have shown where hermeneutical meaning and phenomenological intentionality fail. The Zen Buddhism of Dōgen and Nishitani answers, in general, to the objective instrumentality of looking and the subjective gestures of grasping the phenomenology of experience by claiming that "inauthentic selfhood" derives from the human tendency to superimpose patterns of thinking, categories, concepts onto an experience in order to manipulate it. This provides us with a meditation on the "Buddha Eye" that opens up further considerations for new pedagogical possibilities by the Buddhist injunction to "forget the self" (*jiko o wasururu*), where emptiness of the Self, or "no-self" (*anatman*), becomes a central consideration.

Can a Machine Laugh or Cry? Seeing with the (W)hole Eye (Between Laughing and Crying)

An obsessional's anxiety between a human being and a machine can be somewhat lessened when we review Derrida's remarkable meditation on visibility and invisibility (blindness) in his *Memoirs of the Blind: The Self-Portrait and Other Ruins* (1993), a response to an artistic exhibition of the same name held at the Louvre from October 26, 1990, to January 21, 1991. One might say that this is a further reworking of Merleau-Ponty's insight of the chiasm in his *The Visible and Invisible*. The subtitle of this section provides a clue as to what distinguishing features are to be considered if the student is to remain "alive" in the teacher's gaze rather than cast as a reified automaton where all risk of exposure has been lessened into the boredom of assignments. Both laughing and crying as iconically and allegorically represented by the two "bookend" masks of drama (as trauma itself)—the two words intimately connected when it comes to their unconscious expressions—reveal the life of the affective body. We live most of our life *between* the space of laughing and crying, but when we laugh and cry, both are spontaneous uncontrollable extremes of excessive life (*zoë*) that reveal our unconscious selves—our blindness to our own narcissism and to how vulnerable we truly are. A stain or blind spot always appears in the pool of water that reflects a mirrored image of how we see ourselves. I am always reminded of René Magritte's remarkable painting *Le Faux Miroir* (1928), which shows this dark spot to be the pupil itself. It floats in the middle of the iris, which is painted as a clear-blue cloudy sky.

The affinity of such a position sits well with the Buddhist notion of *anatman*, best translated as "self-is-not-an-essence-or-entity" rather than the usual "self-does-not-exist-at-all" (Galin, 2003, p. 108). The writings of Arya Nagarjuna, the apostle of the "middle way" (*Madhyamaka*), is helpful here.[6]

Nagarjuna presents a four-cornered logic (referred to in the Indian as *tetra-lemma* [*catuskoti*], which has similarities to the Derridean term *deconstruction*) to show that both "self" (*atman*) and "no-self" (*anatman*) are not to be understood as a structure of *either/or*, nor *both/and*, and not even *neither/nor*, but instead point to a void. Nagarjuna does not mean *void* as "nonexistence," but instead our inability to capture some final truth (see Mabbett, 1995). This points to the anxiety-ridden unrest or turmoil of the human condition (*duhkha*) of a divided subject, a subject who is "ignorant" about him- or herself. "Authenticity" (as enlightenment or "Buddha nature"[7]) restores this split—recognizing the moments when the objects look back at the subject, for the mind is constantly colored with love or hate. Any event is perceived as either beneficial or harmful to the self. The paradoxes of the in-between ground remain unexplored. It is this deep-seated insecurity that overinflates the importance of the ego, causing pathologies. A Zen teacher's gaze requires this vigilance within the pupil, to recognize moments that open up for him or her in order to grasp the authentic (I would say *unconscious*) self.

Such a Buddhist position is consonant with Lacan's recognition that "seeing" authentically (as *savoir* and not *connaissance*) takes place with the (w)hole eye. The term *(w)hole* accurately identifies a "hole" or an abyss in the center of a site/sight/cite,[8] which has many affinities with Dōgen and Nishitani's Zen of emptiness (*śūnyatā*).[9] This Sanskrit term *śūnyatā*, signifying "emptiness," is better translated as "boundless openness" or "luminosity" to avoid its negative connotations (Cook, 1985, 139). This "hole" is the unconscious, which is also unbounded. Transposed into Dōgen's terms, this is where "the myriad things come forth and experience themselves awakening."[10] This "suchness" is felt immediately on the body.[11] For Lacan, this is the psychic order of the *Real*, a dimension beyond symbolization and the imaginary. The Real is precisely where this "hole" is located. Within it the cause of desire to be "whole" is to be found since this is where fantasy provides us with a missing piece. Although our vision appears whole, it is framed by this Real, unconscious cause of desire. Vision subjected to the ego is always subject to *méconnaissance*—misrecognition, an "ignorance of ourselves" in Lacanian terms. But *méconnaissance* has a double meaning that is lost in English. It is both a "failure to recognize" and a "misconstruction." When an infant identifies with its reflection in a mirror or with the sight of its parents playfully mimicking its gestures, this results in a retrospective construction of a sense of identity that produces the illusion of recognition. So there is both a misconstruction as well as misrecognition of a self. This is consonant with the Buddhist notion of *anatman*, which shifts the notion of the Self elsewhere. The Self (*atman*) is not an entity, or a substance, or an essence, but a dynamic process characterized by a shifting web of relations among evanescent aspects of the person such as perceptions, ideas, and desires. The Self is only misperceived as a fixed entity because of the distortions of the human point of view. When the teacher and student meet eye-to-eye, *transference* of unconscious desire takes places. Whether this desire is that of the teacher, the student, or perhaps both, raises once more the responsibility of pedagogy. And so it is with the way to enlightenment. As Dōgen states in his first essay *Genjōkōan*, transformation of the self is confined to particular situations. Enlightenment is not a once-and-for-all event, but actualized repeatedly as each new event is experienced. It is an infinite process, or as Sigmund Freud has said of psychoanalysis, *interminable*. So dukkha, in this sense, cannot be once-and-for-all eliminated. Is this perhaps a difference (or is it sameness?) within Lacanian psychoanalysis? In one of his last works (*Seminar XXXIII: Le sinthome*; Lacan 1975–76), Lacan argued that one has to decide whether one wants to live with one's symptoms (*dukkha*). There is certain wisdom (*savoir*) in understanding what defines one's unconscious self (*je*). Such singularity forms our *sinthome* (rather than symptom). To transcend the fantasy of one's sinthome means fundamentally to change one's life, unraveling it—facing one's own death drive. This is not a dread of death; rather, it is a welcomed acceptance of it as to where it might lead—which makes suicide such a paradoxical act. If it is intentional, it becomes an object of conscious desire, paradoxically an evasion of death. But what if intentionality is marked by the limit of suicide, the point where intentionality is canceled out, where intentional and unintentional death come together as an ethical act?

Let us think of the emptiness of enlightenment as blindness in the Derridean sense, as the opposite of the Western idea of enlightenment, which has light at its center of vision. The decentering of dualisms happens just as easily in Buddhist thought as it does in Lacan and Derrida. In Taoism, everything is believed to come from *wu*, the zero of nonbeing.[12] I would call this *Zoë*, the raw energy of life itself, which has particular associations with Lacan's understanding of *jouissance* as forms of suffering (painful pleasure, pleasurable pain), which can in turn be equated to the Buddhist notion of suffering (*dukkha*). Zoë helps us to grasp why we, as teachers, try to light the "spark" inside a student. It seems to me this is very close to what Dōgen refers to as the Divine Light, as the whole universe in the dazzling light of self (*Shōbōgenzō*, vol. 1, p. 13; Kōmyō—Divine Light). At this point, paradoxically, Light and dark cancel each other in the zero of nonbeing (*wu*).

Before "the One," according to Lao Tzu, there was only the nameless *wu* (nothingness). Aren't this nameless nothing and the One simply another repeat of the universal (nothing) and the singular (One)? The universal concept of something is always defined by a particular instance of that concept. For Lacan the (w)hole is full and empty at the same time, the all and the not-all. The impossible (w)hole of something can only be realized by unbalancing that (w)hole with excess in it. One element of the (w)hole forms the ground for the rest of the whole by standing out from it and yet being a part of it. The Buddha (the element, the One) forms the ground for nothing—nirvana, emptiness. He is both inside and outside the system at once. In G. W. F. Hegel's terms, "the genus is always one of its species." For example, woman creates man. In the same paradoxical logic, blindness as an instance of seeing forms the fullness of sight as transcendentally attributed to blind men of the West, as Derrida points out: Oedipus; Samson; Tiresuias; and Eli, Issac, and Tobit, the blind men of the Old Testament. Blindness refers to a will that is beyond perception, a will that is beyond sight. This is the "other" meaning of blindness, the one counter to the one René Descartes provided. The figure of the blind man is the optical version of *res cogitans*, of the thing that thinks. He is but "a walking pair of eyeballs attached to the brain" (Zupancic, 1996, p. 33).

As Derrida (1993) has enigmatically put it, "We have yet to speak of the blind man's memory as the *experience of a mask*" (p. 44; emphasis in the original). What does the blind man "see" when he laughs or cries? Such a line of questioning directly addresses the teacher's gaze. If we go back to our querying the phenomenological description of show-and-tell, it is in the laughter of the class where the invisibility, blindness, and emptiness of the class's gaze lies—what they are laughing at veils their own anxieties, the frailty of their own egos, which can be diminished by the stare of the crowd. And it is the trauma of students telling (writing, acting, artistically rendering) intimate stories of their family life in front of the class—missing their moms and dads, being picked on by older siblings, being sexually abused, going to school hungry, the failure of love and trust, and so on—where tears flow, unveiling melancholia, suffering, and sadness in which, as Freud put it, "the ego itself becomes an object." The student becomes her own "abject object" when she talks about herself, as though she were talking about somebody else, often feeling worthless as the guilt attributed to the superego lashes and objectifies her ego. Recall in the passage from Fanon that he tried to laugh away the gaze of the child, but could not do so. Laughter, in Freud's and Lacan's terms, reverses the way the gaze of the symbolic order captures us; we laugh at the way we are caught in its web—through critical absurdities, ironies, and, of course, jokes as to how ridiculous we "truly" are. When we laugh at ourselves, it elevates and frees us; at the same time, the phenomenon is always there in its objectivized form—laughing at others, and others laughing at us. Fanon could not psychically reverse the superego. He could not treat himself as a child from an adult perspective, which is what laughing at oneself does. What then is the "laughter of the Buddha"? Are these simply moments of recognition of our "inauthentic" selves, and the follies of everyday life?

How, then, does a teacher respond to the inevitability of these lived excesses, this spillage of life? The loss of the teacher's control is immediately felt. To see eye-to-eye with a student in a state where something unexpected is being revealed, where a dimension of the student that was unexpected emerges, requires an emphatic, compassionate look, an attunement to the student that risks the failure of reaching out, lying somewhere between the iconic image of one hand holding another as a body dangles over a cliff, ready to fall, and the claim of transference of a priestly stigmata, actually wearing the wounds of Christ's crucifixion. The moment of the teacher's gaze is here faced with a death drive of a shattering ego that needs support as it balances over a cliff, but the teacher is unable to physically wear the wounds of sorrow. A student's self-esteem and the desire for recognition is but a fragile and shifting boundary held between the ego Ideal and the Ideal Ego, as mentioned earlier. Derrida tells us that "only man [sic] knows how to go beyond seeing and knowing [savoir], because only he [sic] knows how to weep" (1993, pp. 127). Yet, it is the "hole" within the eyes that enables us to weep: "It is impossible to weep with a single eye when one has two, or even, I imagine, when one has a thousand ..." (Derrida, 1993, pp. 127). Yet, as T. S. Eliot (1963, p. 55) writes, "I see the eyes but not the tears / This is my affliction." Despite the suffering there arises a limitation, an affliction that the teacher must own up to. Such an affliction is not disavowed, but acknowledged, still seeking to find compassion in the student.

To open up this question of the teacher's gaze we can continue to attune our theorizing to a dimension of (in)visibility that all four philosophers—Derrida, Lacan, Dōgen, and Nashitani—identify as that which "frames" sight in the first place: the Real in Lacan's case, the powerlessness of the eye when it comes to the trait or trace that gives the experience of the gaze over to blindness in Derrida's terms, and to Zen philosophers Dōgen and Nishitani the understanding of emptiness (śūnyatā) at the heart of vision of the Buddha's Eye. The trait—or trace—in Derrida's philosophy refers to paradoxical deconstructive logic, which simultaneously is both present and absent, confusing the boundary of the inside and outside. But such a paradoxical logic is not unlike Lacan's development of "extimacy," which obfuscates the inside and outside as well. Nor is it different from Nishitani's paradoxical logic of *soku/hi*, of "is and yet is not," and the "self-identity of absolute contradictions" (*zerroi mujunteki jiko dooitsu*; Dilworth, 1989, p. 66), both of which Nishitanti incorporates into his *Religion and Nothingness* (1982). The centeredness of the teacher's "look" is decentered by the "gaze" in Lacan's sense, which is absent but present in its effects, as the Fanon story shows. The gaze belongs to the psychic Real. Derrida decenters vision—which he calls the gaze (*le regard*), and which certainly confuses our discussion[13]—through the supplement of blindness. The centrality of sight is deconstructed by showing the aporia (a contradiction or irreconcilable paradox in the form of *is/is not*) of blindness that subverts seeing into indeterminacy, disseminating it into a chain of differential traces and floating signifiers (seemingly without end). But it is in this dissemination that questions emerge concerning the teacher's gaze in terms of faith and justice.

The Blindness of Vision and the Weeping Eye

Let us continue with Derrida and the question of his interesting insights into a draftsman's act of a representational drawing. We can substitute the teacher for the draftsman as someone who is also an artist who must "represent" or "sketch" an outline of each child in the classroom. To "represent" here takes on a doubled meaning, which perhaps is best captured in the German by the distinction between *Vorstellung* and *Darstellung*. First, as *Vorstellung*, it refers to the capture of a "portrait" of the student, to identify who she or he is; second, as *Darstellung*, it refers to the responsibility of "representing" the student like a lawyer must represent a client. The teacher must stand up for the student regardless of the "crime" she or he might have committed if a sense of justice and faith in the student are to be maintained. Within this doubled sense of representation is found the necessary blindness of the teacher's gaze, which makes justice and faith in the student possible in the first place. How so?

The clue is that the statue of justice wears a blindfold, and it is a she rather than a he. I am therefore purposefully fixing the law as historically masculine—patriarchal since it cannot be denied that history shows this, as so many feminists of various persuasions have argued. With this in mind, let us consider the first sense of representation (*Vorstellung*): the "portrait" of the student that the teacher must come to "see" as the teacher develops his or her emerging sense of the class and the actors that inhabit it. Let's do this by first considering such a task from the way of Zen of Dōgen and Nishitani, and then from Derrida's position, which has strong affinities.

In the Zen sense, looking is not "seeing." Seeing is more than cognitively registering percepts, and this something more has to do with the quality of attention. For Dōgen, such "seeing" is not a matter of learning but of unlearning: "Students cannot gain enlightenment simply because they retain their preconceptions" (1971, p. 65).[14] His advice to students:

> You should therefore cease from practice based on intellectual understanding, pursuing words and following after speech, and learn the backward step that turns your light inwardly to illuminate your self. Body and mind of themselves will drop away, and your original face will manifest. If you want to attain "suchness," you should practice "suchness" without delay. (Dōgen, 1973, p. 122; emphasis added)

Zen artistic vision not only requires an emptying of the self, but an ability of intuitive perception to attain *henzan*, a difficult notion that refers to learning the singularity of a Zen master and transferring over his inexplicable insights. "If we do not see ourselves, we are not capable of seeing others—both of these are insufficient. If we cannot see others we cannot see ourselves" (*Shōbōgenzō*, vol. II, p. 51, Henzan—Direct Study Under a Master, p. 96). Such vision no longer has anything to do with the physical eye; rather, Dōgen is referring to a "Buddha Eye" when it comes to "seeing" a student. We might ask, How is such an identity of the student to be maintained if it is not to be frozen, objectified, stilled, and controlled, nor constantly neglected, or—oppositionally—constantly attended to, cuddled "to death," as a mother might inadvertently psychically suffocate her child while thinking she is providing unconditional love? For Dōgen the necessary mode of seeing that is connected with the eye of the Buddha is a "not-seeing." This paradoxically involves seeing without a subject and without an object that is seen—a nondual seeing that is both subjectless and objectless.

Nishitani's Buddhist philosophy of the Kyoto School makes the same point concerning this not-seeing: "The eye is an eye through that essential not-seeing; and because of that essential not-seeing, seeing is possible" (1982, p. 152). Both Dōgen and Nishitani are referring to the art of Zen as resting or arresting the hyperactive intellect that would already judge and categorize the student, so as to be completely absorbed in what is perceived or experienced in relation to the student. Zen vision calls on an intensification of consciousness through a concentrated and sustained attention—once again, attunement. And this attunement is a synesthetic experience wherein the five senses undergo modification and become interchangeable.[15] It is an aisthetic (not aesthetic) experience at the bodily Real, in Lacan's terms. As a verse from Daito (1282–1337) puts it:

> When one sees with ears
> and hears with eyes
> one cherishes no doubts.
> How naturally the raindrops
> Fall from the leaves!

(as quoted in Suzuki, 1991, p. 19)

Dōgen said it earlier: "[W]e can hear the sound throughout our body in every part of our body" (*Shōbōgenzō*, vol. IV, p. 87; *Mujo Seppō*—The Proclamation of the Law by Inanimate Beings, p. 75). Dōgen uses the saying "listening to the sound through the eye" as a means of paying attention to the nature of things, while Nishitani (1982) puts it somewhat in circumlocutionary terms: "Emptiness here means that the eye does not see the eye, that seeing is seeing because it is not-seeing" (p. 153). In Nishitani's thought, śūnyatā is as much a program of reconstruction as it is deconstruction to reach the wellspring of "authentic interconnectedness" placing the person "in" the world as much as is possible. So to "reach" a student, to "touch" him or her in a place that "moves" him is a Zen of seeing eye-to-eye, a transference-like henzan.

Nishitani's Zen Buddhist emphasis on true emptiness (*ku*) or absolute nothingness (*zettai mu*), which is an infinite openness devoid of all fixed metaphysical centers, plunges East and West into the same place of the Real and Blindness through the same paradoxical differential logic of the signifier. Nishitani's search for a middle path between God-centered (theocentric) and human-centered (anthropocentric, egocentric) standpoints leads him to a multicentering of the reality continuum where each and every event is affirmed in its positive "suchness" (*aisthesis*) as a unique center in the field of absolute nothingness or emptiness (*śūnyatā*). Since this infinite openness is devoid of all absolute centers, all phenomena are affirmed as individual centers in the locus of absolute nothingness: "The field of śūnyatā is a field whose center is everywhere" (Nishitani, 1982, p. 164); "[t]he self in its is-ness, pure and simple, is compatible to a circle without circumference and, therefore, with its center nowhere—which is everywhere" (Suzuki, 1970, p. 2).

Taking our clues from Derrida, to avoid reifying the student, a certain skepticism has to be introduced into the teacher's authorial gaze, which has a moment of openness, uncertainty, and doubt in it that delays judgment about the pupil. Skepsis, as Derrida points out (1993, p. 2), has to do with the eyes. It refers to maintaining vigilance and attention during an examination. There is a delay in the conclusion as reflection takes place, and as a representation eventually forms itself. However, such a tension that avoids a definitive closing judgment has to be permanently in play in the teacher's gaze. What the student might become—his or her unique singularity—always confronts what the student *is*—that is, the general representation of the student that has necessarily been formed by the praxis and demands of education as always already embodied within the constraints of the educational ideology of schooling. It is in this singularity or invisible trait where the blindness of the teacher's gaze lies, for this is a place of unknowability, undecidability, and a potential "productive space" for justice and faith. Representation has to address its second meaning, as *Darstellung*:

> More precisely, the fidelity of faith [to the student] matters more than representation, whose movement this fidelity commands and thus precedes. And faith, in the moment proper to it, is blind. It sacrifices sight, even if does so with an eye to seeing at last. The performative [on the part of the teacher] that comes on the scene here is a "restoring of sight" rather than the visible object [i.e., the student], rather than a constatative [*sic*] [observed] description of what is or what one notices in front of oneself. (Derrida, 1993, p. 30)

In this passage Derrida is claiming a teacher's faith in the student requires a certain risk, which is itself a moment of blindness, required paradoxically to restore sight so that the student might "see."

While the singular and the collective will always cross paths as hypotheses, posits Derrida, they never confirm one another in absolute certainty. A gap or an abyss of blindness remains between them. The system never closes. In Lacan's sense, the singularity of the student's trait refers to *objet a*, the very cause of his desire; it is that which is "more" than the student him- or herself; unknowable and invisible, this trait frames the very generality of what the student "is"—his or her very being. The teacher "listens in watching" (Derrida, 1993, p. 2), always open to and addressing the student's singularity, the teacher's gaze formed in skeptical supposition as to the general portrait of the student, which is subject to change. In many respects Derrida is Zenlike by identifying the "nonseeing" in seeing.

The powerlessness of the eye, therefore, should not be understood as impotence or failure—on the contrary, this is precisely the very point where the power of the panoptic eye fails to see, where the object (the student) "looks back" at the teacher enabling the "seeing of seeing" to take place—the Zen phenomena of henzan. This is not a tautology; rather, the genitive indicates a doubling of vision where an exchange—eye-to-eye—takes place between the teacher and student in the place of blindness, the place of the abyss. Such impotency on the teacher's part is a necessity to open up what Lyotard (1971) has called a *figural space*, a space that can best be understood as marked by a tension between the singular and the collective. Consider the singularity of a line, a stroke, a mark, a smudge (all varieties of a trait for Derrida), which is open and free to form any possible shape it wants. The artist Paul Klee called this "taking a line for a walk." Such a line, free of determined meaning, comes in tension with an alphabetic letter, whose potential for the most part is already closed, already shaped by a former trait (a line) to produce meaning. It can only be opened up by manipulating the signifier itself (e.g., [w]hole, site/sight/cite). Through such a productive tension the teacher's gaze can maintain the temporality of a student's becoming, to remain open to the world.

It may not at first appear that a teacher "draws" the student, like a draftsman, with her gaze, but she or he does—or she or he *should*. The surprising thing about a closed representation—*Vorstellung*, the portrait of the student—is that it is formed by blindness: it is a drawing from memory. The teacher is always "writing" the student—through reports, corrections, exams, observations, and evaluations—and eventually forms a general representation that school ideology forces her or him to confine to a summative letter grade or a number, a generalization. The figural in the end is vanquished, as is singularity. A committed teacher who desires to further justice and faith in her or his students suffers as this lawful violent cut must be made, one might say, through a psychic branding and labeling on the ego's skin by the institution of schooling that demands categorization.

Yet, there is an aperspectival aspect of this graphic act (be it visual or written) that Derrida uncovers and plays with, which speaks directly to the ethical touch of the teacher's gaze. It once more speaks to *Darstellung*:

> Even if drawing [or writing] is, as they say, mimetic, that is, reproductive, figurative, representative, even if the model [student] is presently facing the artist [teacher], the *trait* must proceed in the night. It escapes the field of vision. Not only because *it is not yet* visible, but also because it does not belong to the

realm of spectacle, of spectacular objectivity—and so that which it makes happen or come cannot in itself be mimetic. The heterogeneity between the thing drawn [i.e., the student] and the drawing *trait* [the writing] remain abyssal, whether it be between a thing represented and its representation or between the model and image. (Derrida, 1993, p. 45; emphasis in the original)

Drawing portraits of students is therefore a blind groping consisting of an autoreflection, a re-trait or "retreat" or folding back, in Derrida's terms, on an object of scrutiny. Such self-searching is a blind monologue used to "know" each student. And, once more this is a very Zenlike way of understanding self-reflection as coming back to where you first started, to the "suchness" of the student.

As Derrida has puts it, the ocular is supplemented by the "abocular"—not from or by the eyes, but without the eyes. To unpack Derrida's insight in terms of the teacher's gaze, this unspectacular trait (Lacan's smudge, stain, trace, *objet a*) is precisely what forces the difficulty of evaluation. When having to grade students the obsessional anxiety once more rears its head: "Am I just a marking machine basing my evaluation on information, or am I more than that as a teacher, my evaluation also informed by the singular trait—the spark of life (*zoë*)—in each student that remains unknown to me but in terms of justice and faith I must somehow consider?" The double representation of the student once more emerges: a representation that is structured by the gaze of the institution (*Vorstellung*) comes into tension with the representation structured by the gaze of the teacher (*Darstellung*), which ethically should be "for" the student despite any "crimes" that have been committed; that is, within the schooling institution failing to make the grade.

The Singularity of a Trait: Between Seeing and Weeping

Educators speak of "drawing a student out," enabling them to risk and challenge themselves—to confront their own blindness. In a remarkable passage, Derrida captures what I believe the teacher's gaze should or could be about. Tears paradoxically "reveal" the sight while at the same time veiling it.

Now if tears come to the eyes …perhaps they reveal, in the very course of this experience, in this coursing of water, an essence of the eye…. Deep down, deep down inside, the eye would be destined not to see but to weep. For at the very moment they veil sight. Tears would unveil what is proper to the eye. And what they cause to surge up out of forgetfulness, there where the gaze or look looks after it, keeps it in reserve, would be nothing less than *alēthia*, the *truth* of the eyes, whose ultimate destination they would thereby reveal:

to have imploration rather than vision in sight, to address prayer, love, joy, or sadness rather than a look or gaze. Even before it illuminates, revelation is the moment of the "tears of joy." (1993, p. 126)

Derrida goes on to consider that the "night of this abyss"—the undecidablity caused by the productive tension of the doubled gaze and the doubled representation, what I take as the worrying anxiety at the heart of the teacher's gaze—can be interpreted in two ways. The first is as an anamnesic retrospective, as the "eve or the memory of the day" (Derrida, 1993, p. 43) in which the teacher's recall of the student in her memory faces the heterogeneity of the visible and invisible—as the lived history of the student in class as well as his or her future potential informed by the singular trait—does not appear to be problematic. In brief, the recollected memory forms the "picture" of the student unproblematically. The unary trait remains repressed and veiled.

The second is the singularity of a trait that can haunt the recollected memory; in other words, the teacher faces a nagging concern that a student's potential is not being reached, or that she or he as teacher is unable to pass judgment on the work with any sort of certainty, or that there is something about the student that will not rest. The "unbeseen" (like the unbeknownst) trait of the student comes front and center playing havoc with his or her recollected memory.

Here again, Lacan and Derrida come together. As in James Ivory's movie *The Remains of the Day* (1993), where the butler Stevens's memories of his relationship with Miss Kenton come to haunt him because they cannot be incorporated into his perfectionist construction of an obsessive lifestyle, the teacher's "days' residues"—in both the Freudian and Lacanian sense—come back to nag and pull at the teacher as well, raising an ethics that surround the Real of the student's singularity, of his or her difference. The Real is that psychic dimension that is beyond both language and image, and also a nonspectacular phenomenon, like Derrida's trait or trace. For Lacan, the Real is the "night of this abyss," which is encountered during the teaching day and returns at night in a teacher's dream, or perhaps as a recurring symptom, or a slip of the tongue in class—all moments that cannot be integrated in the framed representation of the teacher's job. But, this nagging of the day's remains also identifies Dōgen and Nishitani's call to step backward to the beginning, when one is on the road to enlightenment through *zazen* (seated meditation). To reach an encounter with the Real self (the *je*) in Lacan's terms, rather than the *moi* of the represented ego, seems remarkably similar to Nishitani's (1982) mediation on the classical doctrine of the "no-self." The appearance of nothingness (emptiness; *śūnyatā*) can be characterized thus: "the actualization of the true self equals the actualization of nothingness …" (70–71). Śūnyatā is "the point at which we become manifest in our own suchness as human beings" (90), and true emptiness is "what reaches awareness in us as one with our absolute self-nature" (106). I take this negation of the ego to have a direct infinity with Lacan's *je* and Derrida's trace. Nishitani's referral to the "suchness" of the "true self" is the "remains of the day" wherein the ego is negated. It enables the possibility of an ethical response to our students and to do them justice (*le droit*) if we have lapsed too easily into rules of strict conduct (*la loi*).

Is the Face of Lévinas Eye-to-Eye?

We are, of course, close to the phenomenologist Lévinas (1981) and his primacy of the ethical relationship, which acknowledges absolute alterity in the face-to-face relationship. Again, the difference here (with Lacan's ethics of the Real and Derrida's ethics of the trace) is Lévinas's stress on the absolute infinity of the exteriority of alterity; that is to say, the most radical sense of the Other is what he calls the infinite, the absolute Other, that must always be honored. Such a position accords a self-presence to the "otherness" of the Other; it often casts the ethical relationship as the difference between two presences in which the other is always encountered as alien. Lévinas's ethics slide between phenomenological descriptive and prescriptive accounts as to how to preserve this otherness of the Other at all costs. Breathing and caressing, as erotics of touch, are prescriptively preferred over devouring (eating) and grasping the Other. In my terms, the "crime" of the student would not be forgiven at *all* costs but pedagogically confronted by the teacher facing justice and faith that the student's alterity tests their very relationship. The teacher must risk defending the student against the law, but to do so by remaining skeptical—that is, siding and not siding with the student at once. This marks the difference between teachers who are caught by the morality of a student's conduct and those who are caught by an ethics of the student-teacher relationship. *Morality* refers to a closed system, a set of rules or codes for conduct. *Ethics*, on the other hand, confronts the teacher with how she or he is to encounter the other (the student) as "other" than her or his being—more specifically, how the teacher can live with what cannot be measured by the law, by the regulative force of morality. The student's "crime" must be suspended. In a school setting an asymmetry already exists; transference of authority is always already in place; and desire is always already continuously circulating through glances, looks, and gazes in the classroom. But, how far should the teacher go in recognizing a student's alterity? "To name others as 'the other' and as being characterized by otherness is, in a contradictory or paradoxical way, to contain the other within ontology. That is, the nature of being becomes alien being," notes Ahmed (2000, p. 142). Ahmed quotes Lévinas to bring her critique home: "'The other's entire being is constituted by its exteriority, or rather its *alterity*'" (Lévinas, 1987, p. 76, quoted in Ahmed, 2000, p. 142; emphasis added).[16]

There is a danger of the teacher reifying singularity (difference, particularity, alterity) as simply being characteristically present on the body, or on the face, or in the speech of the Other. The trait is "thingified"—made concrete, given the light of day and not covered by the night. To recall Fanon, although it is his blackness that frightens the child, his skin color is not what identifies his difference exclusively in the French gaze; rather, his skin acts like a lure, a container holding something more "frightening" inside that is liable to jump out and attack the child. It is the "uncertainty" of Fanon's difference that frightens the boy. The black skin of Behn's Oroonoko is not what exclusively appeals and at the same time repels his mistress. It, too, is a lure. Rather, it is his "primitiveness" that is alien. Oroonoko becomes a fetish assumed to contain an exotic otherness within the singularity of his form—his blackness. If the Other is radically other than me, and alterity is placed at the point of infinity, then the Other can, perhaps, never be reached—inverting Lévinas's claim to a solipsism. Derrida's critique is to state there are two alterities at play: one is infinite and transcendental and the other is finite. To love the Other is to love the irreducible difference. Here is where aesthetics (as lure) and ethics (the interrelation to the Other) coalesce in the Zen question of no-self. To what extent can one live with finite difference? The Zen of Dōgen and Nishitani does not tip toward the infinitely transcendental; rather, it is "realizational seeing," trying to live the paradoxes of difference that are irresolvable koans that illuminate the difficulty of lived life—its impossibilities where laughing and crying reveal the truth of *Dasein* as a being toward death.

When it comes to the gaze of the teacher, the phenomenology of Lévinas has much to offer. Yet the approach to the alterity of the Other (and here I have the student in mind) is always allusive and difficult, having no predetermined rules. In *Specters of Marx* (1994) Derrida pondered the depth of alterity as singularity, maintaining that a certain waiting is required, conditioned by generosity and hospitality before an event, before a change [in a student] takes place: "*[T]his condition of possibility* of the event is also its *condition of impossibility* ... without this experience of the impossible, one might as well give up on both justice and event" (p. 65; emphasis in the original). An individual is never "one with itself," never "present," but always caught up in relationships, always divided from within. The subject begins not in presence but in difference. Lacan's split subject or divided subject also rests on a similar premise. Unconscious desire is always desire of the Other. To have faith and justice in the student it is necessary for the teacher's gaze to always hold out for what the student is not, to wait patiently for the event—that is, his or her becoming, which belongs in the future anterior, the time of what will have been. While the teacher, in Lévinasian terms, is a "hostage" to the student's alterity, she or he need not become terrorized nor hysterized by the encounter.

Metaphorically, perhaps we should think of the student as being blind. Blind not to information and facts, but to things that a student cannot see in himself or herself; that allude his or her eye in the mirror; that constitute the area of ignorance (*méconnaissance*) as Lacan named it. Ignorance is unconscious; it is "knowledge which does not know itself" (Lacan, 1998, p. 88). In Zen Buddhism, ignorance forms part of the inauthentic self (*dharma*). The teacher must "touch" the student's eye (*je*), must lay a finger on it in order to let a student finally see or let "it" be seen. This may lead to tears or laughter. Yet, it is not all up to a teacher. A student can assert her own stubbornness and avoid owning her fantasies. Writes Derrida:

> A bad will—an unwillingness—would have driven man to close his eyes. The blind do not want to know, or rather, would like not to know: that is to say, not to see. *Idein, eidos, idea*: the whole history, the whole semantics of the European idea, in its Greek genealogy, as we know—as we see—relates seeing to knowing. (1993, p. 12)

There is a certain *jouissance*, a certain suffering and pleasure of the symptom in intentionally remaining blind. So the teacher must come to terms with the student's blindness, to become sensitive to the way a student implores, to grasp the suffering taking place that only tears can reveal. Derrida (1993) comments:

> The blindness that opens the eye is not one that darkens vision. The revelatory or apocalyptic blindness, the blindness that reveals the very truth of the eyes, would be the gaze veiled by tears. It neither sees nor does not see: it is indifferent to its blurred vision. It *implores*: first of all in order to know from where these tears stream down and from whose eyes they come to well up. From where and from whom this mourning or these tears of joy? This essence of the eye, this eye water? (pp. 126–127; emphasis added)

Thereby, Derrida can say "losing his sight man does not lose his eyes. On the contrary. Only then does man begin to *think* the eyes ... the tears see" (p. 128; emphasis in the original).

I interpret this as:

To touch
the student
with the teacher's gaze
is to make the eyes water.

The Emptiness of the Teacher as the Zen of Pedagogy: The Third Eye

To have introduced the Zen Buddhism of Dōgen and Nashitani has its hazards and worries. I am somewhat concerned that despite their compatibility with Lacan and Derrida in helping us understand the gaze of the teacher, their philosophy may fail to adequately address the horror of the gaze, that same horror that I presented with Fanon's story. Is zazen, the path to enlightenment, simply too contemplative, avoiding the sociopolitical struggles of everyday existence? Such a criticism has often been raised and countered, of course. Zen Buddhism is neither solipsistic nor individualistic. Self and Other are not separated entities. One must first find the way within one's self before the world of Others can change. Yet, the charge has serious consequences for the teaching gaze. So, let me map out the complaint of Western Buddhism that Žižek has brought to the table in the last few years: its link with global capitalism and a runaway technology.

As Žižek sardonically puts it, "If Max Weber were alive today, he would definitely write ... 'The Taoist Ethic and the Spirit of Global Capitalism'." What's behind such a brash statement? What he ironically calls Western Buddhism as exemplified by the followers of the Dalai Lama, as well as various forms of Tao, provides a fetishistic support to withdraw from social reality. On Žižek's account, it is an empty spirituality that doesn't call on the person to change anything. The most decadent Hollywood star can have this religion as a pure fetish; one thinks of Richard Gere in particular. Ideologically, as a fetishistic support, Western Buddhism enables its practitioner to participate in the frantic pace of the capitalist game while, at the same time, sustaining the perception that she or he is not really in it. The capitalist spectacle is disavowed so that what really matters can be forwarded—namely, the peace of the inner self to which the mediator can withdraw to find peace and harmony. Zen is a concentration on the present moment, with the practice of Soto Zen being one of earnest sitting (meditation). Indeed, to be unkind, the statue of Buddha is always a plump fellow with a big belly showing very little bodily activity; all of it is confined to the mind. Perhaps that is why he is smiling? "[I]t is no longer possible to oppose this Western Buddhism to its 'authentic' Oriental vision; the case of Japan provides conclusive evidence," notes Žižek (2003, p. 26). (Japanese managers practice "corporate Zen."[17])

More disturbing is Žižek's claim that in the last 150 years Japan's rapid industrialization and militarization can be quite easily legitimated through Buddhist teaching despite its emphasis on compassion and peace. Drawing on the work of Brian Victoria's *Zen at War* (1998), uncomfortable details emerge like D. T. Suzuki's support, in his youth in the Japan of the 1930s, the spirit of utter discipline and militaristic expansion. It seems that the Buddha's gaze can function to support the most ruthless killing machine. One can, of course, claim that this "warrior Zen" is a perversion of the "true" Zen message; but what if, Žižek asks, "Zen meditation is ultimately just that: a spiritual technique, an ethically neutral instrument which can be put to different sociopolitical uses, from the most peaceful to the most destructive?" (2003, p. 31). A recent rash of films, including Ang Lee's *Crouching Tiger, Hidden Dragon* (*Wo hu cang long*; 2000), Yimou Zhang's *Hero* (*Ying Xiong*; 2002), and *House of Flying Daggers* (*Shi mian mai fu*; 2004), all box offices successes, were Hong Kong productions, the city being a hotbed of Western-style Chinese capitalism with direct links to Japanese capitalism. For anyone who has seen these films the Zen quality of the human fight scenes is remarkable. The aesthetic stilling of the "presence" of the moment to its full potential through the use of special effects and slow motion is nothing short of remarkable. This is in marked contrast to the other filmic genre that has captured a global market—the dystopian narratives of Japanese *anime*. Has Zen Buddhism gone to a surface aesthetic in keeping with globalized designer capitalism via the eye of such directors as Yimou Zhang, or is there a call back to history to rethink East Asia's past?

Nishitani, when discussing the situation in Japan after World War II, already makes the claim that traditional philosophies like Buddhism and Confucianism that served as protective shields against nihilism have lost their power, "leaving a total void and vacuum in our spiritual ground" (1990, p. 175). He sees a state of contemporary atheism (see Maraldo, 1995; Tetsurō, 1995). For Nishitani it is a question of the will to the future and an engagement with the responsibility toward the ancestors. He comments, "For us Japanese now, the recovery of this primordial will represents our most fundamental task" (1990, p. 177). According to Tetsurō (1995), Nishitani saw Japan as presenting the new East Asia order "as the locus of this great encounter between the cultures of East and West. Even if the two worlds within Japan were still in a state of chaos, this chaos was 'a mark of superiority'" (p. 328). Buddhist emptiness, in Nishitani's terms, provides an absolute openness that enables a genuine self-realization that breaks free of egocentrism and anthropocentrism. By drawing on its own historical tradition, Japan was "to give birth to a cultural world within oneself and also to open up a cultural *horizon of globality* in one's innermost depths" (Nishitani, as quoted in Tetsurō, 1995, pp. 328–329; emphasis in the original). But can such a gesture of practicing śūnyatā sustain yet another critique?

The question of the Buddha's gaze as a benevolently peaceful, withdrawn gaze as represented by iconic statues points out a disturbing omission.[18] Such a gaze, in its inwardness, lets things be; it abandons any urge to control things. But as Darian Leader (2002) points out, there is an odd detail that throws doubt into this assertion of reaching the Buddha eye of nirvana. When painting the eyes of the statute, the ritual of their rendering requires that the artist not look at the statue in the face. No face-to-face (or better still, eye-to-eye) contact with the Buddha is allowed. Rather, the artist turns his back to the statue, painting sideways or else maneuvering a mirror over his shoulder so that he might then render the eyes. Once he has done so, he is said to have the dangerous gaze himself and must be led away blindfolded, and

> [t]he blindfold is removed only after his eyes can fall on something that he then symbolically destroys. … The fact that for the temperate and pacifying reality of the Buddhist universe to function, the horrifying, malevolent gaze has to be symbolically excluded. The evil eye has to be tamed. (Leader, 2002, pp. 38–39; emphasis added)

As Faure points out, the Buddha icon already presupposes cult status, an "inapproachability" however close it may be. This unrepresentable excess, Faure notes, "is the invisible *usnisa* [in Chan/Zen, in Chinese, *dingxiang*; and in Japanese, *chinzo*] or fleshy protuberance on top of the Buddha's head. We are told that this *usnisa* remains invisible because no one can look down on the Buddha" (1998, p. 789). So while there are, technically speaking, 32 signs that configure the Buddha's body, including the *usnisa*, this is the "spot" of his supramundaness, divinity, or transcendency, which is at odds with the "third meditating eye" that appears as a "dot" on the forehead, a mark that alludes to the tuft of white hair that apparently was nestled between the Buddha's eyebrows. But the point here to note is that the "dot" is again only a lure for the meditation. The gaze of the Buddha (an icon, in this case) emanates from the blind spot on top of his head.

For Žižek (2003), therefore, the Buddhist experience of the peace of nirvana "is not an ultimate fact," but something that "has to be excluded in order for us to attain this peace, namely, the Other's gaze" (pp. 20–21). The Lacaninan evil gaze that poses a threat to the subject is disavowed in Buddhism. A rather curious conclusion is reached if we follow the full implications of such a disavowal. Recall that the Other's gaze refers again to an amorphous "big" Other of the symbolic order discussed with the Fanon story. This amorphous gaze represents the effects of the superego—the unstated abjected and controlling values that psychically hold together a society, nation, group, and the like. All "patriotic" eyes were on Middle Eastern people living in the United States after 9/11. As it states in Genesis (3:5), "Then the eyes of both were opened, and they knew that they were naked." Adam's and Eve's bodies were exposed to the Other's gaze. Shame, guilt, and the emergence of an "original sin," a pathological stain at the heart of being human, emerges. But, as Derrida (1993), points out, the blind have no guilt:

> More naked than others, a blind man virtually becomes his own sex, he becomes indistinguishable from it because he does not see it, and not seeing himself exposed to the other's gaze, it is as if he had lost even his sense of modesty. The Blind man has no shame. (p. 106)

The bizarre logical consequence of this exchange among psychoanalysis, deconstruction, and the emptiness of śūnyatā as the horizon of the undifferentiated One is that only the blind can reach Nirvana. To recall the enigmatic sentence that Derrida does not return to, "We have yet to speak of the blind man's memory as the *experience of a mask*" (1993, p. 44; emphasis added). *Is this mask not the inner imagery of how one might appear to this amorphous Other?* Surely this is conveyed through the symbolism of language. Are the blind not capable of weeping and laughing? Even the blind do not escape the gaze of the Other.

How should this be taken when we consider the teacher's gaze in the context of what has been introduced herein? Žižek argues that Buddhist compassion reaches out to the Good when emptying desire and any attachment to things, but this fails to take into account the "original sin" of being human—that is, radical evil and a choice of an unconditional attachment to some specific object, person, or Idea that overwhelms the person in both joy and suffering, even until death. One need only think of a love affair that has gone bad or mad.

A fundamental contradiction seems to lie at the heart of Buddhism. Striving (or its opposite, compulsive craving) for enlightenment is already a desire that is disavowed, erased in the very act of meditative striving. In this sense a fundamental evil already preexists the striving for enlightenment (nirvana) itself. Yet, paradoxically the koan states, "If you meet the Buddha, kill him!" Emptiness or the void as the only true Good, the harmonizing of intersubjectivity and intrasubjectivity through attunements of the particular raise the question of an originary stain of pathology that is dismissed, or paradoxically always erased by the impossibility of answering a koan: "To seek Zen is already to fail to practice Zen." But then the pupil asks, "How will I realize Zen?" The master replies, "When you realize it is Zen, Zen is no longer there. But, when you don't realize it, you don't understand Zen at all." And so on as an elusive tautology of the striving desire for the Zen of life.[19]

Although Žižek, a talented Lacanian philosopher, is attempting to spear the blind spot of Zen Buddhism in the eye, there are many touchstones that might help salvage aspects that are fruitful for continuing this meditation on a teacher's gaze, and that is to (re)turn to the difficult question of śūnyatā. Žižek reads this emptiness as the Good without a pathological stain; it is, perhaps, a questionable reading: that stain, although disavowed, is nevertheless there. Siddhartha Gautama, of course, represents that original pathological stain before he became the Buddha. His proper name remains repressed, much like no one dwells on Jesus's family name, the one that belonged to Mary and Joseph. The earthly roots are there only to make note that this is transcendence made flesh, incarnate. An impossible gap exists between a saintly harmonized Good and an earthly pathological stain. To relinquish desire one would have first had to know what an addiction to desire was, to have suffered the *jouissance* of one's symptom in the first place. Siddhartha Gautama was no peasant, but a prince who was used to the royal high life. His father Suddhodana was a minor king, the head of the Sakyas, who protected his son from the peasant world outside the royal gates. Siddhartha was next in line to inherit his father's position as the head of the clan.

Psychoanalytically, Siddhartha's transformation can be read as a rebellion of the son against his father, and as a coming-of-age story. The prince, at the "tender" age of 29, married and with two children, was serendipitously exposed to four shocking sights that turned his life around: a decrepit old man, a sick person racked with disease, a human corpse, and a begging man with a shaved head but a tranquil and serene demeanor. Siddhartha left his family to seek enlightenment. To me, this indicates that the horror of the gaze played the same transformative role for Siddhartha as it did for Fanon. Of course, this brings up a contentious issue between Buddhism and Christianity when it comes to an "original" pathology. The Buddha was not interested in the question of origins per se, but only in the Way to end suffering. Whether one posits an originary pathological evil or a deeply repressed fear of one's own groundlessness of nonbeing—a lack (*manque*); that (w)hole that, in Lacan's sense, is both empty and full at once, its paradoxical nature exists "beyond good and evil," always in a state of "worse." Perhaps there is a difference here between the Buddhist conceptualization of "lack" and Lacan's notion of lack, which designates anxiety. Yet, in both cases no object is involved. The Way, be it psychoanalytic or Buddhist, remains interminable. To think otherwise is to be disingenuous, a fall into some sort of permanent state of transcendence. Put another way: a Buddhist perspective can be a form of psychoanalysis, but can psychoanalysis be a form of Buddhism? If so, can it be said that the stain is the One, the pathology that enters the void, and to face the One is to face the void of the self—as *je*, not *moi*? Whatever the differences, it seems that pedagogy as practiced by psychoanalysis, Derridean deconstruction, and the practice of Zen Buddhist śūnyatā come together as East–West dialogue when questioning the pathologies of everyday life—as Shōbōgenzō kajō. As educators, should we not confront the paradoxical nature of the gaze with our students, the horror of nature—its catastrophic events like hurricanes, earthquakes, and tsunamis—as well as its beauty? By examining the impact of such events within ourselves the transformation of the self (*je*) and the world must surely take place. But there are no guarantees.

Notes

1. One eye of the Cyclops, like Polyphemus in the Odyssey who is unable to "see" Homer, rests in the middle of his forehead while his other two eyes are blind. He is capable only of one-dimensional sight. To him, Homer is a nobody who has no name. This image becomes the very antithesis of the exteriorization of the Buddhist "third eye" in the middle of the forehead, appearing as a mark of transcendence, capable of insight and multiple perspectives.

2. See the important essay by Homi Bhabha, "Interrogating Identity" (1994), which is a long meditation on Fanon's book *Black Skin, White Masks*.

3. These essays that appear throughout the four volumes are numbered 1 through 92. Generally, they are referenced herein as "Shōbōgenzō," followed by the Japanese title and then the English translation. For example, the first essay in volume one would be Shōbōgenzō, 1:1. Genjōkōan—The Actualization of Enlightenment.

4. I wish to thank Claudia Eppert for mentioning the work of Yoshiharu Nakagawa (2000), one of the contributors in this book, and his explication of the way that Buddhism presents a challenge to holistic education, which has a particular ideology of "green consciousness."

5. These are the terms the translators of Dōgen use.
6. I wish to thank David Smith for pointing me to the writings of Arya Nagarjuna (ca. 150–250 C.E.).
7. Dōgen, in Shōbōgenzō, 4:91, Busshō, clarifies his understanding of "Buddha nature" by saying that this is not some sort of permanent state of enlightenment. Rather, as I understand it, it is a state of constant becoming, as "a man on the Way" (p. 121) to awakening. Authentic experience is a "watching" devoid of a specific moment, better understood as a gerund, to watch where it becomes a practice that incorporates within it a certain "active passivity," a waiting where there is no wait per se. The teacher must *wait*, and *watch* the student. This is what I mean by vigilance. And, here again we have a strange affinity with psychoanalysis, for the moment of enlightenment between analyst and analysand may never come, or "when the times comes," as Dōgen puts it, "time has already come" (p. 123). Nagarjuna is of the same mind. *Samsara* and *nirvana* are coterminous. There is no state or place that is separate from the world we know, with its chaos and inconsistencies. Nirvana is not a new state, but shows us the states of our selves as they really are. This is the meaning of *enlightenment*.
8. I am using this homonym to designate Lacan's three psychic registers: *site* for the Real, *sight* for the imaginary, and *cite* for the symbolic.
9. Emptiness is a key concept in the ontology of Mahayana Buddhism. The phrase "form is emptiness; emptiness is form" is a celebrated paradox, the supreme mantra that originates with the Heart sutra.
10. In this case I have used the translation of the Genjō Kōan by Robert Atiken and Kazuaki Tanahashi (1985). The Shōbōgenzō Genjōkōan in volume 1, translated by Kōsen Nishiyama and John Stevens, is slightly different: "It is an illusion to try to carry out our practice and enlightenment through ourselves, but to have practice and enlightenment *through phenomena*, that is enlightenment" (pg. 1; emphasis added). *Phenomena, myriad things,* and *suchness* are equivalent terms. These are moments when the object stares back at you.
11. *Suchness* (as a term essentially synonymous to *phenomena* and *myriad things*) is clarified by Thomas Cleary (1986) in his commentary on Dōgen's meditation on Such (Immo). Herein I use the term *aisthesis* (and its forms *aisthetic and aisthetics*) to convey the same affective feeling at the unconscious body level.
12. The One, or Tai Chi then follows Wu. I thank Hongyu Wang for helping me to clarify this point.
13. The French do not distinguish the look from the gaze. Both English words are translated as *le regard*, which has caused difficulties when translating Lacan's *Four Fundamentals*, where a distinction has been made between both.
14. Reihō Masunaga's *A Primer of Sōto Zen* (1971) is an excellent source of Dōgen's instructions to students in finding "the Way."
15. See Malcolm David Eckel's attempt to unravel the complexities of synesthesia in his "Buddhahood and the Language of the Senses" (1992).
16. Dussel (1978) makes the same case against Lévinas from the standpoint of liberation theology. Dussel accuses Lévinas of Eurocentrism, positing that Lévinas never thought that the other could be Indian, African, or Asian, and hence faults Lévinas for working at an abstract level without discussing concrete instances.
17. However, Jones (2003) has recently argued for an emerging "fourth eye" that implicates the new emerging Buddhism with social action and change. Further, the Buddha's plumpness may be attributed to the abundance obtained through enlightenment (Claudia Eppert).

18. As one reader of this chapter pointed out, the Buddha's gaze also contains a "knowing" smile as to, perhaps, what is going on, a smile as enigmatic as that of the Mona Lisa—namely, the very futility of completeness of such a withdrawal. Such "knowing" is a form of action in Taoist terms.

19. See, for example, http://www.darkzen.com/teachings/thekoanqa.htm.

References

Ahmed, S. (2000). *Strange encounters: Embodied others in post-coloniality*. London: Routledge.

Bhabha, H. (1994). Interrogating identity: Franz Fanon & the postcolonial prerogative. In *The location of culture* (pp. 40–65). London: Routledge.

Blascovich, J., Loomis, J., Beall, C., Swinth, H., Crystal, L., & Bailenson, J. N. (2001). Immersive virtual environment technology as a methodological tool for social psychology. Retrieved 4 September 2004 from http://citeseer.ist.psu.edu/blascovich01immersive.html.

Cleary, T. (1986). Such. In Dōgen, Shōbōgenzō: *Zen essays by Dōgen* (T. Cleary, Ed. & Trans.; pp. 47–56). Honolulu: University of Hawaii Press.

Cook, F. H. (1985). *Dōgen's view of authentic selfhood and its socio-ethical implications*. In William R. LaFleur (Ed.), *Dōgen studies* (pp. 131–149). Honolulu: University of Hawaii Press.

Derrida, J. (1989). *Of spirit: Heidegger and the question* (G. Bennington & R. Bowlby, Trans.). Chicago: University of Chicago Press.

Derrida, J. (1993). *Memoirs of the blind: The self-portrait and other ruins* (P. A. Brault & M. Naas, Trans.). Chicago: University of Chicago Press.

Derrida, J. (1994). *Specters of Marx: The state of the debt, the work of mourning, and the new international* (P. Kamuf, Trans.). New York: Routledge.

Dilworth, D. A. (1989). *Philosophy in world perspective: A comparative hermeneutic of the major theories*. New Haven, CT: Yale University Press.

Dōgen, Z. (1971). *A primer of Sōtō Zen: A translation of Dōgen's Shōbōgenzō* (R. Masunga, Trans.). Honolulu, HI: East-West Center Press.

Dōgen, Z. (1973). Dōgen's Fukanzazwngi and Shōbōgenzō Zazengi (N. Waddell & M. Abe, Trans.). *Eastern Buddhist*, 6(2), 115–128.

Dōgen, Z. (1975–1983). *The eye and treasury of the true law: A complete English translation of Dōgen Zenji's Shōbōgenzō* (Trans. K. Nishiyama and J. Stevens; 4 vols. Sendal, Japan/San Francisco: Dalhokkaikaku/Japan Publications Trading.

Dōgen, Z. (1985). Shōbōgenzō, Genjō Kōan—actualizing the fundamental point. In K. Tanahashi (Ed.) and R. Aitken & K. Tanahashi (Trans.), *Moon in a dewdrop: Writings of Zen master Dōgen* (pp. 69–73). San Francisco: North Point Press.

Dōgen, Z. (1986). *Shōbōgenzō: Zen essays by Dōgen* (T. Cleary, Ed. and Trans.). Honolulu: University of Hawaii Press.

Dussel, E. (1978). *Ethics and the theology of liberation* (B. F. McWilliams, Trans.). Maryknoll, NY: Orbis.

Eckel, M. D. (1992). Buddhahood and the language of the senses. In *To see the Buddha: A philosopher's quest for the meaning of emptiness* (pp. 131–152). Princeton, NJ: Princeton University Press.

Eliot, T. S. (1963). Eyes that last I saw in tears. In *T. S. Eliot's collected poems 1909–1962*. New York: Harcourt Brace Jovanovich.

Fanon, F. (1967). The fact of blackness. In *Black skin, White masks* (C. L. Markmann, Trans.; pp. 109–140) New York: Grove Press.

Faure, B. (1998). The Buddhist icon and the modern gaze. *Critical Inquiry*, 24(46), 768–813.

Foucault, M. (1995). *Discipline and punish: The birth of the prison* (A. Sheridan, Trans.). New York: Vintage.

Galin, D. (2003). The concepts 'self,' 'person,' and 'I' in Western psychology and in Buddhism. In B. Allan Wallace (Ed.), *Buddhism and science: Breaking the ground* (pp. 108–143). New York: Columbia University Press.

Jones, K. (2003). *The new social face of Buddhism: A call to action.* Essex, England: Wisdom.

Lacan, J. (1975–1976). *Seminar XXXIII. Le sinthome.* Unpublished manuscript.

Lacan, J. (1979). *Seminar XI: The four fundamental concepts of psycho-analysis* (A. Sheridan Trans., J. A. Miller, Ed.). Harmondsworth, England: Penguin.

Lacan, J. (1998). *Seminar II: The ego in Freud's theory and in the technique of psychoanalysis, 1954–1955* (S. Tomaselli, Trans., J. A. Miller, Ed.). New York: Norton.

Leader, D. (2002). *Stealing the Mona Lisa: What art stops us from seeing.* London: Faber and Faber.

Lévinas, E. (1981). *Otherwise than being: Or, beyond essence* (A. Lingis, Trans.). The Hague, Netherlands: Nijoff.

Lévinas, E. (1987). *Time and the other and additional essays* (R. A. Cohen, Trans.). Pittsburgh, PA: Duquesne University Press.

Lyotard, J. F. (1971). *Discours, figure.* Paris: Kilincksieck.

Mabbett, I. W. (1995). Nagarjuna and deconstruction. *Philosophy East and West, 45*(2), 203–225.

Maraldo, J. A. (1995). Questioning nationalism now and then: A critical approach to Zen and the Kyoto School. In J. W. Heisig and J. C. Maralso (Eds.), *Rude awakenings: Zen, the Kyoto school, and the question of nationalism* (pp. 333–362). Honolulu: University of Hawaii Press.

Merleau-Ponty, M. (1968). *The visible and invisible* (A. Lingis, Trans.; C. Lefort, Ed.). Evanston, IL: Northwestern University Press.

McGee, J. P., & DeBarnardo, C. (1999). The classroom avenger. *Forensic Examiner, 8,* 2–3.

Nakagawa, Y. (2000). *Education for awakening: An eastern approach to holistic education.* Brandon, VT: Great Ideas in Education.

Nitishani, K. (1982). *Religion and nothingness* (J. V. Bragt, Trans.). Berkeley and Los Angeles: University of California Press.

Nitishani, K. (1990). The self-overcoming of nihilism (G. Parks, Trans.). Albany: State University of New York Press.

Poggi, I., & Pelachaud, C. (2002a). Signals and meanings of gaze in animated faces. In P. McKevitt, S. Ó Nualláin, & C. Mulvihill (Eds.), *Language, Vision and Music* (pp. 133–144). Amsterdam: Benjamins.

Poggi, I., & Pelachaud, C. (2002b). Subtleties of facial expressions in embodied agents. *Journal of Visualization and Computer Animation,* 13(5), 301–312.

Sarte, J. P. (1957). *Being and nothingness* (H. E. Barnes, Trans.). London: Methuen.

Shapiro, A. (2002). *Show and tell: It's a Window on their Lives.* Retrieved 9 October 2004 from http://www.phenomenologyonline.com/articles/shapiro.html.

Suzuki, T. D. (1991). Self the unattainable. In F. Franck (Ed.), *The Buddha eye: An anthology of the Kyoto school* (pp. 15-21). New York: Crossroads.

Tetsurō, M. (1995). Nishitani Keiji and the question of nationalism. In J. W. Heisig and J. C. Maralso (Eds.), *Rude awakenings: Zen, the Kyoto School, and the question of nationalism* (pp. 316–332). Honolulu: University of Hawaii Press.

Victoria, B. (1998). *Zen at war.* New York: Weatherhill.

Žižek, S. (2003). *The puppet and the dwarf: The perverse core of Christianity.* Cambridge, MA: MIT Press.

Zupancic, A. (1996). Philosopher's blind man's buff. In R. Salecl & S. Zizek (Eds.), *Gaze and voice as love objects* (pp. 32–58). Durham, NC: Duke University Press.

CHAPTER 6

Shanti, Peacefulness of Mind

Takuya Kaneda

Otsuma Women's University

Some Westerners may regard Japan as the country of Zen philosophy. However, I knew very little about Zen Buddhism when I was a student there. As one of the generation born after World War II, since childhood I was more familiar with American pop culture than Japanese traditional culture. My first travels across Asia from Turkey to India during my college years revealed how much I didn't know about Eastern thought. Ever since, the profound nature of Eastern wisdom has attracted me. I began to research Eastern philosophies, mostly in India and Nepal, where Buddhism began before it spread to Japan nearly 1,500 years ago, influencing Japanese traditional culture so deeply. After my marriage to a Nepalese woman, the Hindu world became part of my life, providing many opportunities to see Hindu cultures from the inside.

The indiscriminating mass murder case of the Aum Shinrikyo cult in 1995 (in which members of the cult released the deadly nerve gas sarin into the Tokyo subway system) deeply shocked me because the cult first began as a group teaching yoga and meditation. They combined this with their misinterpretation of Buddhist and Hindu terminology. The cult captured a number of young people, especially those who felt alienated in a materialistic Japanese society. It was then that I realized that youth in Japan who are separated from traditional religious values have no power to resist the appeal of false spiritual groups, as compared to young people in India and Nepal, where spiritual tradition is still alive in all of daily life. I believe that my unique stance as a

Westernized Japanese who is searching the heart of Eastern thought will provide an interesting perspective in this chapter.

Since I worked as a volunteer in an Afghan refugee camp in 1980, peace and education for children has been my central concern. Even though it is in the beginning of the new century, we have to live in a world filled with terror and violence. Traditionally, the East has sought peace through compassion and tolerance rather than violence and aggressiveness. Peacefulness is one of the key concepts in Eastern philosophies—especially in India, where Buddhism and Hinduism were born.

Aum, shanti, shanti, shanti: the sacred words are written at the beginning of holy scriptures such as the Upanishads and are often chanted at the end of spiritual practices in India. *Aum* is a sound that represents the essential vibration of the universe, and *shanti* means "peace." In Sanskrit, *shanti* indicates a peaceful mental state as well as a peaceful world without any violence and war. Traditional Indian thought holds that the world cannot become peaceful unless each person is at peace, emphasizing interconnectedness between both body and mind and between the outer world and the inner world. From this point of view, various techniques of breathing and meditation were developed in India to attain a peaceful state of mind, which was regarded as essential for enlightenment. Those practices were a very important part of traditional education in India. In this chapter, I first examine the traditional idea of education and then focus on the educational practices of Ravindranath Tagore, Sri Aurobindo, Jiddu Krishnamurti, and Sri Sri Ravi Shankar as key Indian educators in the 20th century who attempted to bring traditional Hindu ideas of education into their experimental schools and emphasized nurturing peacefulness in education through the integration of body, mind, and spirit. Last, I explore the possibilities of cultivating peacefulness of mind for students in schools facing violence and conflict on a daily basis.

Indian Spiritual Tradition

India bears the roots of many religions such as Buddhism, Hinduism, Jainism, and Sikhism. It is easier to define Buddhism as a religion founded by Gautama Buddha in ancient India but rather difficult to define Hinduism in such a short phrase. Hinduism has its origin in Vedic religion in ancient times and developed into the present form of Hinduism that merges various beliefs and customs in India. In a broader sense, Hinduism can include Buddhism and Jainism. Actually, many Hindus regard Buddhism as one sect of their religion and worship Buddha as one god of their pantheon of deities. The term *polytheism* may not be the one to use to represent the nature of Hinduism because Hinduism claims that God is only one, but is made manifest in numerous forms. Although there are a number of colorful figures of gods and goddesses in Hindu temples, they are merely different forms of the one God, who is nameless and formless.

Historically, India has been very accepting of different thoughts and customs brought from outside; these have enriched the country's culture. This convergence of many belief systems created fertile soil for the growth of a high tolerance of different, even contradictory, matters, whether the new or the old, the beautiful or the ugly, the sacred or the secular. As the River Ganges flows, engulfing so many different things from a drip of melted glacier to ashes of cremation, India has become a country of diversity where a variety of ethnic groups live together in various natural environments from the tropical jungle to the frozen Himalayas. It could be said that Indian people developed their wisdom of inclusiveness and tolerance of different values in order to survive in such a land of cultural and geographical diversity. The tolerance of contradictory values is related to the worldview of the Indian traditional thought, which suggests that all the things coexist as complements in the world, as two sides of a coin that cannot be separated. In Hinduism people worship Shiva, the god of destruction, as well as Brahma, the god of creation, who has a complementary role to Shiva. In the Hindu iconography, the goddess Durga, or the Mother Divine, is depicted by a fierce image with many arms holding weapons. The powerful and peaceful are complementary in this image.

This chapter does not intend to survey the history of religions in India but to examine the common aspect of spirituality in the religions from the point of view of education for peace. Therefore, in this chapter, the term *Indian spiritual tradition* includes not only Hinduism but also Buddhism. It should be noted that Indian spiritual tradition is always greatly concerned with self, meaning that self that is beyond individual self or ego. This tradition claims that self-attachment causes possessiveness and aggressiveness. Whether in Hinduism or Buddhism, *peace* means to be free from all attachment and is the goal of spiritual fulfillment.

Dharma and Ahimsa

Dharma

The term *Dharma* in Sanskrit is similar to *religion* in English in a certain sense, but it is not exactly the same as the concept of religion in the West.

The meaning of *dharma* is beyond the Western meaning of religion. It means "righteousness," "duty," or "the right way of life" rather than a particular creed. Dharma is concerned with all aspects of life and there is no separation between religious and secular life in this concept. The term *Hindu* is derived from the name of the place beyond the River Sindhu, the Indus, as it was originally referred to by Persians outside. It also implies the religion of the people who live beyond the River Indus (Sen, 1961, p. 17). Some Hindus believe that their religion is not merely local but universal in nature, although the name of Hinduism itself indicates a religion of a particular place. This idea of the universal religion is called *sanatan dhaarma*, which is the essence of Hinduism and the matrix of Buddhism.

Ahimsa

The *Sandilya Upanishad* describes this word as one of the ten forbearances, and as such, *ahimsa* is an important doctrine in the Indian spiritual tradition, whether in Buddhism, Hinduism, or Jainism. *Ahimsa* literally means "noninjury" or "nonkilling," and implies the total avoidance of the harming of any kind of living creatures—not only by deeds, but also by words or thoughts. *Ahimsa* is also a moral and ethical principle. It is not a notion of passiveness, weakness, and cowardice but requires active, strong, and brave practices, such as those of Mahatma Gandhi (1869–1948) and his nonviolence movement in the resistance of British colonial rule. As Gandhi once stated,

> Nonviolence is the law of our species as violence is the law of the brute. The spirit lies dormant in the brute, and he knows no law but that of physical might. The dignity of man requires obedience to a higher law—to the strength of the spirit. (1920, August 11)

This philosophy of nonviolence is one of the five precepts in Buddhism. It is needless to say that *ahimsa*, nonviolence, is a key concept in achieving a peaceful world.

War and Peace in the Bhagavad Gita

The *Mahabharata* is a famous Hindu epic filled with stories of war and massacre. It seems a warlike epic, but its final message is of the vanity of war. According to its first book, titled *Adi Parva*, "Whatever is spoken about virtue, wealth, pleasure, and salvation may be seen elsewhere; but whatever is not contained in this is not to be found anywhere" (*Mahabharata*, 1896, p.

123). The *Mahabharata* describes greed, cruelty, and violence. Even today the world cannot stop the tragedy of war, which is depicted in the *Mahabharata*. One important chapter of the *Mahabharata*, the Bhagavad Gita, is known as an important, sacred scripture to Hindus. The Bhagavad Gita starts with a dialogue between Lord Krishna and the warrior-prince Arjuna in the midst of the battle field. Arjuna is hesitant about fighting his enemies and requests Krishna's advice. Krishna has tried many times and ways to find a peaceful solution to avoid war, but paradoxically, he teaches Arjuna to fulfill his duty as a warrior. Should we interpret this to mean the approval of warfare as a final solution? Gandhi suggests an answer to this question; he regards the Bhagavad Gita as a spiritual reference book that inspired his nonviolence movement. He writes,

> The author of the *Mahabharata* has not established the necessity of physical warfare; on the contrary he has proved its futility. He has made the victors shed tears of sorrow and repentance, and has left them nothing but a legacy of miseries. (Gandhi, 1946, p. ii)

Lord Krishna continued teaching Arjuna about the four different paths of *Yoga*. The first is *Raja Yoga, or* meditation; the second is *Bhakti Yoga,* or devotion; the third is *Karma Yoga,* or selfless action; and the last is *Jnana Yoga,* or knowledge. The word *Yoga* itself means a holistic philosophy of physical, mental, and spiritual practices. How are these paths for spiritual pursuit related to battle? Stephen Mitchell (2000) points out that the battle is a metaphor for the internal battle—war within ourselves. The Baghavad Gita gives us the profound insight necessary to ponder both inner, or spiritual, peace and outer, or worldly, peace. The following passages express Ghandi's ideas (1946) about shanti, or peace; and nirvana, or supreme liberation:

> He who finds peace and joy and radiance within himself—that man becomes one with God and vanishes into God's bliss. (p. 86)

> Constantly mastering his mind, the man of yoga grows peaceful, attains supreme liberation, and vanishes into my bliss. (p. 91)

Education in the Indian Spiritual Tradition

Traditionally, education was considered as a part of dharma in India. If education is defined as a learning process of how to live, then in a broader sense education could become synonymous with dharma or the right way of life.

However, one of the major differences between modern school education and education in dharma is the emphasis in the latter on spirituality. While modern education does not concern itself with spiritual matters, the main objective of traditional education in dharma is spiritual growth. This Indian tradition has an idea of four different stages of life: *brahmacharya*, "learning"; *grihastha*, "running the house"; *vanaprastha*, "living in the forest"; and *sanyasa*, spiritual life. The first stage is the period of discipline and learning. Completing this stage, one has a spouse and raises children to maintain family and social life. After fulfilling family and social duties, one concentrates on spiritual life in the forest. In the last period, one has to abandon material necessities and lead an austere life in order to pursue the spiritual.

In the first stage of brahmacharya, children are sent to a guru, a spiritual master, who lives in the forest far away from the town, to learn various things. This first stage is very important for building the physical, mental, and spiritual base for the following stages of life. This ancient residential school in nature is called a *gurukul*, where *sishya* (students) and the guru live together, usually in the same house. Students learn from the guru through his daily life. This custom of keeping a simple life and studying with the guru for learning was widely practiced in India before modern school education prevailed. The main purpose of gurukul education is to provide children a peaceful environment for their holistic development with the guru.

Key Indian Educators in the 20th Century

It might be appropriate to call Ravindranath Tagore, Sri Aurobindo, Jiddu Krishnamurti, and Shri Shri Ravishankar gurus or spiritual masters rather than educators in the modern sense, although Krishnamurti did not want to call himself a guru. In Sanskrit, the original meaning of the term *guru* is "dispeller of darkness." The educational practices of these great teachers provide us new ideas and new ways of thinking about contemporary education, and especially about how education can be made more responsive to today's conflicts.

Ravindranath Tagore

Ravindranath Tagore (1861–1941), a Nobel Prize laureate in literature, was the first person to establish an experimental school based on the traditional idea of gurukul in modern India. In 1901 he founded his own school, Santiniketan (*Shanti-niketan*), the Abode of Peace. As this name represents, he emphasized the importance of peacefulness in education. Tagore has written that "peace is in the inner harmony which dwells in truth and not in any outer adjustments" (1931, p. 67).

Advaita Philosophy

Tagore ardently claimed the necessity of world peace, especially the unity of the East and the West. Writing in 1921 (but formally publishing it in 1961), after World War I, he notes,

> We can hear men and women beyond the seas crying for peace, and we must tell them that there is peace when there is well-being, and well-being when there is unity. We must convey to them the ancient Indian message that the Advaita, the One and the Invisible, is peaceful and eternal. (1961, p. 250)

Most of Tagore's poems are devoted to the idea of oneness, his lyrical words bringing a deep feeling of peacefulness into the very depths of our hearts. His great concern about both inner and outer peace is manifest in his experimental education at Santiniketan as well as in his writing. For him, the purpose of education is spiritual fulfillment. His educational ideal is based on the philosophy of *advaita,* or nonduality. As his poetry is filled with mystic imagination, so also are most of his essays on education full of spiritual insight. He often referred to religious matters in his writings and lectures, but his concept of religion is not limited to orthodox Hinduism. He advocates the unification of different religions and repeatedly mentions oneness in terms of the idea of advaita, citing from the Upanishads: "He who sees all beings in his own self and his own self in all beings, he does not remain unrevealed" (1961, p. 244). The consciousness of oneness is the heart of Tagore's philosophy and is deemed essential in realizing a peaceful mind. He believes that peacefulness in children can be nurtured only through brahmacharya.

Brahmacharya Education at Santiniketan

Tagore was born to an aristocratic family in Calcutta, India. His bitter memory of school education during childhood compelled him to start his experimental school Santiniketan, which was entirely different from ordinary schools. He envisioned reviving the gurukul, or the traditional learning place utilized during the brahmacharya period at the beginning of the 20th century. As the gurukul had been located in a forest, Santiniketan was also located in a very peaceful environment far away from busy town life, approximately 180 kilometers north of Calcutta. He tried to create "a place where the truth of spiritual world is not obscured by a crowd of necessities assuming artificial importance; where life is simple, surrounded by fullness of leisure, by ample space and pure air and profound peace of nature" (Tagore, 1917, p. 135). The importance of a peaceful environment for education was realized in Santiniketan as the school was surrounded by a variety of trees such as mangoes and coconut palms, as well as colorful flowers. In such a peaceful environment, children could become aware of their own oneness with nature, which has been regarded as part of the divine from ancient times in India. He practiced giving children a period of meditation at this school: "I set aside fifteen minutes in the morning and fifteen minutes in the evening for that purpose" (p. 145), insisting that "they remain quiet; that they exert the power of self-control, even though instead of contemplating on God, they may be watching the squirrels running up the trees" (p. 146).

To nurture the child's spiritual nature, which forms the basis of a peaceful mind, he considered taking joy in beauty to play a very vital role in the flowering of the child's aesthetic sensibilities, writing, "Beauty carries an eternal assurance of our spiritual relationship to reality, which waits for its perfection in the response of our love" (1931, p. 67). Sensual perception was usually regarded as a hindrance to spiritual pursuit, but the perception of beauty through the five senses was not totally denied in the Indian tradition, which includes various visual images of the absolute and a variety of devotional songs and dances. While the physical world as perceived through the senses was not the ultimate object of spiritual pursuit, aesthetic sensibility nonetheless opened a door through which to access the spiritual world. Tagore stressed the necessity of aesthetic experiences through music and creative activities in education. He himself was very creative in music and the fine arts, as well as literature, and insisted on the significance of art in education: "The true principle of art is the principle of unity" (1917, p. 20). He compared art with science, noting, "The scientist seeks an impersonal principle of unification, which can be applied to all things" but "the artist finds out the unique, the individual, which is yet in the heart of the universal" (pp. 23–24). His idea of art was also based on the philosophy of advaita: "In Art the person in us is sending its answers to the Supreme Person, who reveals Himself to us in a world of endless beauty across the lightless world of facts" (p. 38). He encouraged various art activities among students at Santniketan, where school life was (and still is today) colored with creative artwork such as poetry, painting, music, dance, and drama.

At the beginning the school was very small, but later became much expanded into an educational institution that included education components such as Ananda Pathsala, a nursery school; Patha-Bhavana, an elementary and secondary school; and a university, Visva Bharati. During its hundred years, numerous students have studied there and had experiences that differed greatly from those of regular school life. The former Indian prime minister Indira Gandhi, world-famous film director Satyajit Ray (also a Nobel laureate), and Amartya Sen all studied at Santiniketan. Each made a great commitment for peace in the very different fields of politics, art, and economics, respectively.

Sri Aurobindo

Sri Aurobindo (1872–1950) was another one of those spiritual seekers in modern India who was concerned with peace and education. His concern for peace developed during and as a result of his political activities against colonialism.

The Fight Against British Colonial Rule

Sri Aurobindo was born in Calcutta, India, and sent to England for his education at the age of seven. After studying Western culture, including Latin and Greek at Cambridge University, he returned to India and became involved with the nationalist movement during British colonial rule. In the beginning, he was not entirely a pacifist, for he secretly participated in revolutionary activities to prepare for a national insurrection. His approach against the British government was different from Mahatma Gandhi's. Like Gandhi, Sri Aurobindo recognized nonviolence to be preferable as a rule; however, he considered dharma as relative, and admitted that violence could be permitted in certain situations. It is reminiscent of the dialogue between Lord Krishna and Arjuna in the battlefield in the Bhagavad Gita. Sri Aurobindo tried to translate the scripture into English, emphasizing the value of acting without desire for the results of the action, as Lord Krishna posited. In Baroda, he came across a yoga master whose influence gradually changed his political direction toward the Indian spiritual tradition. He continued his political activities and was charged and imprisoned by the British colonial government. After his release, he went to Pondicherry, a French colony, where he founded an ashram, an Indian traditional hermitage for spiritual seekers.

Integral Yoga

Sri Aurobindo, an aggressive freedom fighter, was changed radically into a peaceful spiritual seeker after practicing yoga and meditation. He claimed that peace was the very basis of yoga practice. In Pondicherry, he attempted to embody a new system of spiritual development called *integral yoga* with his French spiritual partner, Mira Alfassa (1878–1973), later to be known as The Mother. The reason why she was called The Mother may be related to the tradition of motherhood worship in India. Hindu people don't kill cows or eat beef, regarding the cow as the mother who nourishes us with milk. There are many episodes of reverence for motherhood in Hindu mythologies. The goddess Durga represents the Mother Divine. Durga, *devi*, or The Goddess, and *ma, mata, amma*, or mother, are almost synonymous for Hindus. As Sri Aurobindo has written about motherhood, "The Mother's love to her children is without limit and she bears patiently the defects of their nature. The imperfections of human nature do not count against that love" (1991, p. 72). In the Pondicherry ashram, Sri Aurobindo left his political activities and concentrated on his integral yoga with The Mother. He has remarked, "Peace is part of the highest ideal, but it must be spiritual or at the very least psychological in its basis; without a change in human nature it cannot come with any finality" (1972, p. 40); this clearly indicates his view on peace and that nurturing inner peace is an essential part of an integral education. This state of peace he has explained by noting, "When the mind is silent there is peace and in the peace all things that are divine can come" (1993, p. 120). Silence and stillness are very important to maintain a peaceful mind during meditation. Sri Aurobindo has admitted that anger, hatred, and violence are in human nature but has suggested that the growth of spiritual consciousness and of inner peace would help to purge them, emphasizing, "Peace is the first condition without which nothing else can be stable" (1993, p. 122).

Sri Aurobindo revealed his idea of integral education based on his fivefold classification of the human being as physical, vital, mental, psychic, and spiritual. The *physical education* portion concerns a perfection of the physical body; he considered a sound condition of the body as the first requirement for all spiritual fulfillments. According to Indian tradition, spiritual growth does not mean merely developing a mental state; it is attained holistically through both the body and mind. The *vital education* segment is for the building up of character, which is related to moral and ethical behavior. Sri Aurobindo regarded beauty as an expression of the spirit and stressed the importance of cultivating the aesthetic senses in education; the training of aesthetics was part of vital education. The *mental education* area deals with developing the faculties of judgment, imagination, memory, observation, comparison, reasoning, and so on. These mental activities are usually regarded as the faculties of the intellect. Sri Aurobindo added other layers of faculty such as discernment, intuitive perception, and inspiration, and insisted on the necessity to encourage those faculties in education (Pavitra, 1961, pp. 61–62). He warned that the intellect could be as great an obstacle for spiritual growth as the vital and the body, and has suggested that "[t]he thinking mind has to learn how to be entirely silent" (Aurobindo, 1993, p. 242). *Psychic and spiritual education* remains central to the idea of Sri Aurobindo's educational vision. According to The Mother, there is a distinction between psychic education and spiritual education; psychic education is "a higher realization upon earth" and spiritual education is "an escape from all earthly manifestation, even away from the whole universe" (cited in Pavitra, 1961, p. 70).

In 1943, The Mother started a school for children in the ashram. The school has since developed into the Sri Aurobindo International Centre of Education, which spans kindergarten to college levels. After Sri Aurobindo died in 1950, The Mother succeeded him and started building an experimental international city called Auroville to realize his teaching. The experiment is still proceeding in Auroville, which has some schools for children that implement his educational vision.

Jiddu Krishnamurti

Jiddu Krishnamurti (1895–1986) was also an Indian spiritual thinker who showed a great interest in education and peace. He was born in Madanapalle, a town in the south of India, and grew up within the Theosophical Society, which gave him an exceptional education that led to his becoming a spiritual leader of the society. In 1911, the Order of the Star in the East was founded to support him. He became head of the group, and in fact, was expected by many members to be a world teacher or messiah. In the same year he was sent to England to be educated and thereafter remained in Europe.

"Truth Is a Pathless Land"

In 1929 Krishnamurti dissolved the Order of the Star in the East in front of thousands of members at Ommen, Holland, where he declared, "Truth is a pathless land, and you cannot approach it by any path whatsoever, by any religion, by any sect. That is my point of view, and I adhere to that absolutely and unconditionally" (Lutyens, 1976, p. 293). This famous speech arose from his own experience of the limitations of the religious organization in which he had been so involved. After that, he traveled worldwide, giving lectures and writings on spiritual matters until his death in 1986. Having lived through the two world wars, he was greatly concerned about world peace and yet didn't show any interest in political solutions for peace. Instead, he emphasized the importance of the individual's inward transformation rather than social reformation. His book *Education and the Significance of Life* connects education and world peace:

> Peace is not achieved through any ideology, it does not depend on legislation; it comes only when we as individuals begin to understand our own psychological process. If we avoid the responsibility of acting individually and wait for some new system to establish peace, we shall merely become the slaves of that system. (Krishnamurti, 1953, p. 70)

Concerning the causes of conflict, Krishnamurti also severely criticized nationalism, organized religions, and class and race consciousness, all of which create division and egotism in our minds: "Beliefs, ideologies and organized religions are setting us against our neighbours; there is conflict, not only among different societies, but among groups within the same society" (1953, p. 71). He pointed out that "[t]here is the incredible brutality and extraordinary violence that human hearts carry—though outwardly educated and conditioned to repeat prayers of peace" (1972, p. 10), and examined violence with his students, noting, "There is a great deal of violence in the world. There is physical violence and also inward violence. . . . Inwardly, we are always quarrelling, battling, not only with others, but with ourselves," and "[i]n the world, as we grow up, we see a great deal of violence, at all levels of human existence" (Krishnamurti, 1974, p. 61). For Krishnamurti, the inner world is identified with the outer world: "When the individual is in conflict within himself he must inevitably create conflict without, and only he can bring about peace within himself and so in the world, for he is the world" (1995, p. 183). He spoke relentlessly about the necessity to be aware of violence within our minds, noting, on one occasion, "If one is capable of looking at violence and understanding it, then perhaps there is a possibility of resolving it totally" (1995, p. 187). While Krishnamurti was against any religious tradition, it is possible to find similarity between the core of his thought and the philosophy of the Upanishads.

Krishnamurti founded several schools in India, England, and the United States to implement his educational ideas stressing the importance of a sensitive body and a sensitive mind in awareness of ourselves. Speaking about sensitivity to students at one of his schools in India, he commented,

A human being who is aware of his environment, as well as aware of every moment of thought and feeling, who is a harmonious whole, is sensitive. How does that sensitivity come about? How can there be a complete development of the body, of the emotions, of the capacity to think deeply and widely. . . ? (Krishnamurti, 1974, p. 44)

Such questioning was one of the teaching methods he used to evoke self-examination among students.

Most of the schools that he founded are located in isolated, peaceful places away from busy city life, and are boarding schools where students learn by living with their teachers. His experimental schools seem to be a newer version of the ancient gurukul, where students learned much from their guru, or teacher.

Rishi Valley School

I once had an opportunity to teach students at one of Krishnamurti's schools in Rishi Valley in India for several months. Rishi Valley School is a boarding school of 350 students from the fourth grade to the 12th grade living with 50 teachers in a beautiful, natural surrounding. Every morning, students gather in an open-air assembly hall. When all of them sit down in the hall, they stop their lively chatting and briefly observe silence. This silence occurs very spontaneously, without any command. Then, after the moment of silence, they start chanting in Sanskrit; a very peaceful moment thus passes with the fresh air of every morning. Krishnamurti rejected any kind of religious rituals, but admitted the importance of the vibration of such chanting. Besides the morning chanting and optional yoga class, there is no special spiritual practice such as meditation in this school. Krishnamurti articulated the necessity of meditation but always warned against it as a mechanical habit. For him, "meditation implies the whole of life, not just the technical, monastic, or scholastic life, but total life and to apprehend and communicate this totality" (1974, p. 177).

Through my interaction with many students I found them to be very quiet and at peace. In my observation, no special curriculum or teaching methodologies were adopted in the school, but the peacefulness of the school environment seemed to play a significant role in developing students' peaceful natures. It is believed that a snake never bites people in a peaceful place; innumerable snakes live around Rishi Valley but I heard that serious snake bites had never happened to students in the school. Once I argued about the stereotypical violent image of snakes with students. They claimed that snakes were also part of nature and it was more important not to be exclusive but to coexist with nature in order to keep the environment peaceful. There is no doubt that the environment itself had a kind of educational influence, and that the students' simple lifestyle was also important. Television and computer games were not allowed; students woke up early in the morning before sunrise and went to bed early, rather than late, at night. This description may seem to present the image of very strict monastic life, but to the contrary, actual school life was quite vivid and joyful, with many interesting aspects such as dancing and walks under the full moon. There is no question that such a peaceful environment and simple lifestyle had influence upon the spiritual development of these students' bodies and minds.

Sri Sri Ravi Shankar

Sri Sri Ravi Shankar (1956–) is a contemporary spiritual master known as the "Guru of Joy" (Gautier, 2002). He was born in south India, and from his early childhood he showed a keen interest in the ancient spiritual tradition of India and could even recite the Bhagavad Gita at the age of four. He studied traditional spiritual scriptures and also obtained an advanced degree in modern science. In 1982 he developed his own style of breathing practice, *Sudarshan Kriya*, which is intended to release mental stress and negative emotion.

The Art of Living

Sri Sri Ravi Shankar established the Art of Living Foundation, a nonprofit educational and humanitarian organization for the promotion of self-development and health-related educational programs that included his breathing techniques and meditation. Basic courses to learn those techniques have been conducted in more than 140 countries, and his teachings have thus attracted a great number of people all over the world. Sri Sri Ravi Shankar teaches the spiritual wisdom of ancient India in a direct and quite contemporary manner. He shows a great concern about world peace. Just after the tragedy of 9/11, he talked about terrorism and suggested this list of remedies for terrorism:

> Inculcating a broader perspective of life.
> Valuing life more than race, religion and nationality.
> Providing education in human values—friendliness, compassion, cooperation and upliftment.
> Teaching methods to release stress and tension.
> Cultivating confidence in achieving noble aims by peaceful and nonviolent means. Weeding out destructive tendencies with spiritual upliftment. (Sri Sri Ravi Shankar, 2003, p. 44)

To achieve a peaceful world, he has conducted various educational endeavors such as ART Excel, or All Round Training for Excellence, which is a personal development and empowerment course for children and teens to help them effectively handle stress and negative emotions such as fear and anger and to live harmoniously with others. Care for Children is another program that provides all-round education to disadvantaged children in rural India by facilitating the growth of their minds, bodies, and spirits. Sri Sri Ravi Shankar also founded an educational trust to run more than 50 schools in India based on his educational idea, "Live what we teach," emphasizing the importance of educating children holistically:

> We have to see the needs for complete development because body and mind are linked. The body and mind are so linked that what we put in the body reflects in the mind and what is in the mind reflects in the body. Violence in the mind reflects in the body and in their actions. (Sri Sri Ravi Shankar, 1999, p. 67)

He has posited that "[t]he natural tendency of consciousness is to expand, to become bliss. Like the natural tendency of water is to flow downward and the natural tendency of air is not to be under pressure," and concludes that "the natural tendency of consciousness is to expand and to be at peace" (Sri Sri Ravi Shankar, 2002, p. 12). Thus, he repeatedly advocates practicing breathing techniques and meditation to expand our consciousness, whose natural tendency is essentially to be at peace.

Worshipfulness

Sri Sri Ravi Shankar believes firmly in the role of the teacher; about the need for the presence of teachers to create the human touch and human connection, he has stated, "Students used to take pride in their teachers. That sense of belongingness with the teacher and the teacher-student relationship would be established. If this was not important, they could just learn from the computer" (1999, p. 72). This "belongingness" is one of the key concepts of his teaching.

He also has an interesting view on the necessity of a worshipful feeling among children. In contrast to the West, he identifies worship as a means of seeking the ideal, with a feeling of respect and gratefulness:

> For many years in the West the idea of worship has been discouraged. This has been spreading to the East also. Instead of stopping worship, we need to increase

the worship. Because we have stopped adoring people and respecting people, it has led to more violence in our societies. (Sri Sri Ravi Shankar, 1999, p. 75)

He further explains that the feeling of worshipfulness is essential and necessary to arouse this feeling within people's hearts, and in a genuine way, and has suggested that this idea of worship should reflect the relationship between students and teachers (Sri Sri Ravi Shankar, 1999, p. 76). The traditional relationship between a guru and his disciples is based on respect, reverence, adoration, and worship. Westerners are very cautious about such worshipfulness because it may cause blind obedience and, notably, many problems have been caused by such blind obedience to leaders, as the example of the criminal case of the Aum Shinrikyo cult in Japan shows. It is quite interesting that there are very few cult problems in India compared with other countries, even though so many gurus exist there. One of the reasons may be simply that the polytheistic character of Indian cultural background works to prevent people from blind obedience to any one guru. Hindu mythologies have many gods and goddesses, but they never fight with each other. This is because it is believed that there is one supreme being, Vishnu, but that its manifestations come in many different figures and names. In India, individual family members are allowed to worship different deities, and, generally, Indians aren't prohibited from visiting gurus other than their own; in fact, any guru's devotees are allowed to learn what they may from any other guru. It is essential in the pursuit of peace that we develop this kind of tolerance toward different beliefs, especially in the many societies that have recently become more multicultural and multiethnic and consists of various religious groups.

Sri Sri Ravi Shankar emphasized the necessity of multicultural and multireligious education in his address at the United Nations 50th anniversary celebration:

A person learns to embrace all the religions of the world as his own and can choose to practice one without decrying the other. Members of a family can practice more than one religion. This should be the strategy for the 21st century. (Sri Sri Ravi Shankar, 1999, p. 10)

He stresses that the self and the absolute are one, and that different religions represent the truth in different ways, an idea that apparently is rooted in advaita philosophy. If worshipfulness and tolerance of beliefs are properly coencouraged, it is then possible to fully nurture a feeling of respect and gratefulness among students without bringing about blind obedience. In India, Sri

Sri Ravi Shankar's teaching is especially attractive to the educated urban middle class, including the younger generation, who have become very Westernized and alienated from their traditional culture.

Implications for Global Peace Education

An overview of Tagore, Sri Aurobindo, Krishnamurti, and Sri Sri Ravi Shankar's educational ideals and practices reveals that all of them are inspired by Indian spiritual tradition. As dharma includes religion, spiritual pursuit, and education, all these things are inseparable for these four spiritual leaders. Whether in religion, spiritual pursuit, or education, their final goal is *shanti*, or peace—both inwardly and outwardly. Therefore, it is not so easy to extract a particular element of peace education from these educational practices, as their whole educational ideas are integrated into the seeking of peace. They consider the main purpose of education to be the nurturing of our spirituality, with emphasis on the interconnectedness of body, mind, and spirit. They insist that peace in our minds is a very important state for spiritual growth, correlating the development of inner peace with outer peace. According to their educational ideals, learning is not limited to the school, but should also include the whole process of learning in life. They are especially concerned with education during the *Brahmacharya*, the learning period that builds children's physical, mental, and spiritual bases in preparation for the following stages of life. These four gurus are not only idealists but also practitioners in education, and each has established his own educational institution in order to crystallize his individual vision.

The educational practices of these spiritual leaders are exceptional in that most schools in India today follow Western educational methodologies. It is very difficult, however, to assess whether these gurus' educational practices have actually succeeded in creating peaceful children. Peacefulness in a child's mind cannot be measured outwardly in the same way that one cannot judge another's enlightenment. Perhaps the result of these gurus' educational attempts might best be evaluated by knowing whether or not their schools' alumni are spending their lives peacefully. These four gurus' educational ideals can be accepted as universal principles regardless of whether they do or do not follow Hindu traditions. How then, can we implement these very precious teachings from India in our own classes, potentially so filled with violence? As Vokey (2000) notes, it is true that we face many difficulties in the attempt to introduce spirituality into public schools.[1] In such a situation, I would like to propose several suggestions.

Different Paths

Although their goals hold a lot in common, it is important to notice the differences in methodology among these four gurus in order to implement their educational ideas in our classrooms. For instance, Krishnamurti rejects any kind of techniques and methods for spiritual fulfillment, but Sri Sri Ravi Shankar insists on the necessity of a regular practice of breathing techniques and meditation. He has remarked on the views of Krishnamurti, who "rebelled against technique or organized teachings," and once, while answering a question about Krishnamurti's views in a public speech, commented,

> There are many techniques, many methods, or nonmethods to be in meditation. It is okay from the level of Krishnamurti to say, drop all the methods and mantras, nothing is necessary, but be aware, that instruction is also another method. (1990, p. 160)

Such a difference in methodology sometimes makes us confused; yet, this is an important point we should learn from the Indian spiritual tradition. There are various paths for spiritual fulfillment even when the goal is the same, just as so many routes exist to reach the summit of a mountain. This inclusiveness and tolerance of different methodologies suggests paying more attention to individual differences and assures finding a way that is fitted to the individual. It can also prevent us from dogmatically clinging to a particular creed or a specific method even though it may sometimes cause inconsistence and contradiction. Concerning this point, Sri Aurobindo (1993) has articulated,

> The way that X takes is good for X, just as the way that you take is the right one for you, because it is in consonance with your nature. If there were not this plasticity and variety, if all had to be cut in the same pattern, yoga would be a rigid mental machinery, not a living power. (p. 97)

The scriptures of yoga present various systematic methodologies and instructions, but the application of each methodology differs from person to person. Tagore, Sri Aurobindo, Krishnamurti, and Sri Sri Ravi Shankar don't present systematic curriculum structures to embody their educational visions.

Regarding methodology, their educational ideals sharply contrast with Rudolf Steiner's (1861–1925) views on education. Steiner showed a great interest in Eastern spiritual philosophies and had once been a member of the Theosophical Society in Europe, which supported Krishnamurti. After leaving the society, Steiner also attempted to incorporate his own spiritual education in the Waldorf School. He presented a clear curriculum structure and a methodology of how to teach at his school, which the Indian thinkers had not. This indicates a distinction between Eastern and Western thought in terms of educational methodology. As a teacher at Krishnamurti's school once told me, "spirit can create methodology but methodology cannot create spirit."

Concern for the Outer World

In the beginning of this chapter I articulated that *shanti*, or peace, indicates peace from both within and without. The four gurus discussed herein focus on inner peace, but they never ignore the matters of the outer world; an important point for all four is seeing the interconnectedness of the inner world and the outer world, as mind is interconnected with body. All of them also show a great concern for social reform and have made commitments to social services—especially for people in rural areas. Tagore established a school called Siksha-Satra for the underprivileged children of the villages near Santiniketan, and his efforts toward rural development have been continued. Sri Aurobindo, who was once an aggressive political activist against British colonial rule, was also always concerned with social improvement. Even after Sri Aurobindo and The Mother passed away, various programs for social and economical development have been implemented in rural areas around Pondicherry. Krishnamurti's Rishi Valley School is running a rural development center for the neighboring villages that has an international reputation. Sri Sri Ravi Shankar is very active in facilitating various social service projects; combining spiritual pursuit through breathing techniques and meditation with social services, he emphasizes that service to others is the natural expression of spiritual fulfillment and encourages participants in his workshops to commit themselves to helping underprivileged people.

The Indian spiritual tradition repeatedly teaches the importance of *seva*, service to others. Enlightenment means that one sees oneself in all beings and sees all beings in oneself. An enlightened person perceives others' pain as the same as her own. This is the source of compassion, and it is an act of true seva. Mahatma Gandhi's devotion to the nonviolence movement is a good example of seva. It is needless to say that the encouragement of service to others is essential in educating for peace, and that we need to help students to understand the concept of seva in the context of their own lives.

Learning about Different Religions

It is also necessary to give students proper knowledge and information about different religions. Of course, accumulating knowledge of religion and spirituality is not related so much to individual spiritual development as it is to contributing to the cultivation of an atmosphere in which children's spiritual education for peace can be nurtured. As Sri Sri Ravi Shankar (1999) has stated,

> Due to lack of proper spiritual education and a total and comprehensive understanding of all religions of the world, religious fanaticism has taken root in many regions. Spirituality, without dogma, and with understanding which is all-encompassing, is the need of the 21st century. (p. 11)

Encouragement of Aesthetic Experiences

Another step we can take for the sake of our students is the encouragement of art and music in the classroom. The four gurus discussed herein have all strongly encouraged a variety of student activities in art, music, dance, and the like at their schools. This is the lesson we learn from the East, where art has always been regarded as part of life, and artistic expression as a way of connecting mind and body. Tagore stresses creative art activities in education, and Sri Aurobindo includes aesthetic experiences in his "vital education." Krishnamurti remarks on the development of the sensibility to appreciate beauty. Sri Sri Ravi Shankar himself sings and dances joyfully, and encourages people to do so to release their egos. It is surely possible to implement the study of different religions and to focus on aesthetic experiences within a current educational framework.

Teachers' Awareness

The following two recommendations are for teachers themselves. The first is that teachers provide themselves enough opportunities for self-inquiry. It is very important for teachers to be aware of holistic relationships between the body and mind; all four gurus discussed herein have suggested that it is more important for teachers to show *what they are* than it is to be concerned only with *what they teach*. Teachers must be encouraged to engage themselves in the pursuit of spirituality. It is emphasized that teachers can teach only to others what they themselves have realized. If teachers are not at peace with themselves, how can they teach the importance of peace to their students? Both teachers and students need to live a peaceful life, and if teachers themselves can find peace they will surely be able to find a way to bring peacefulness into their classrooms.

The second point about which teachers should be concerned is the lesson of inclusiveness and tolerance of differences that is evident in the Indian spiritual tradition. *Tolerance* means accepting something different; it leads to forgiveness and compassion. In contrast, recent terrors and conflicts in the world are caused by an intolerance that does not accept different creeds and ideas. It is obvious that tolerance is one of the important keys to realizing education for peace. If teachers have a sense of tolerance, their educational practices will be very flexible (perhaps similar to those used in the teaching of yoga), and this will change the atmosphere in their classrooms. This flexibility is at the core of the Indian spiritual tradition. If we cling to a fixed methodology or curriculum for spiritual development we will find ourselves to be farther and farther from our goal. The sense of tolerance in a guru is an appropriate guide in knowing whether the guru is genuine. In the seeking of spirituality, Indian tradition suggests the necessity of a genuine guru in leading disciples toward a true path. It is a fact that there exist some disreputable cults that abuse some Indian spiritual teachings; it is therefore very important to distinguish a genuine guru or spiritual group from a false one. To do that, it is worthwhile to keep in mind the tolerance of the Indian cultural character. Genuine gurus or spiritual groups always maintain their openness and inclusiveness and are never exclusive as cult figures or groups.

If we follow the ancient wisdom represented by these four modern gurus we must start by realizing our own spirituality before trying to teach it to our students. In other words, we need to stop discussing educational theories for a little while, breathe deeply, and contemplate our own consciousness. This is just the beginning of education for spiritual fulfillment. It does not mean a total rejection of rational thinking, but merely the relaxation of a stressful mind. If this can be attained, the rational mind will be more sharpened toward the attainment of truth. For educators and for everyone, this is the invaluable treasure of ancient Eastern thought.

Notes

The author wishes to thank Dr. Janet Montgomery for reading an earlier manuscript of this chapter.

1. In addition, in Japan it seems very difficult to introduce spirituality in school education, as many educators are very nervous about it especially after the criminal efforts of the Aum Shinrikyo cult. Nonetheless, some educators are seriously making efforts to introduce spiritual elements in education. The Japan Holistic Education Society has organized several workshops toward this goal.

References

Aurobindo, Sri. (1972). *On himself.* Pondicherry, India: Sri Aurobindo Ashram.

Aurobindo, Sri. (1991). *Gems from Sri Aurobindo: First series.* Wilmot, WI: Lotus Light.

Aurobindo, Sri. (1993). *The Integral Yoga: Sri Aurobindo's teaching and method of practice.* Pondicherry, India: Sri Aurobindo Ashram.

Forbes, S. H. (2002). Krishnamurti's approach to education. In J. P. Miller and Y. Nakagawa (Eds.), *Nurturing our wholeness: Perspectives on spirituality in education.* Brandon, VT: Foundation for Educational Renewal.

Gandhi, M. (1923). *Young India 1919–1922.* New York: B. W. Huebsch.

Gandhi, M. (1946). *The Bhagavad Gita according to Gandhi.* Ahmedabad, India: Navajivan.

Gautier, F. (2002). *The Guru of joy: Sri Sri Ravi Shankar and the art of living.* New Delhi: Books Today.

Krishnamurti, J. (1953). *Education and the significance of Life.* London: Gollancz.

Krishnamurti, J. (1974). *On education.* Madras, India: Krishnamurti Foundation India.

Krishnamurti, J. (1995). *The book of life.* New York: HarperCollins.

Lutyens, M. (1976). *Krishnamurti: The years of awakening.* New York: Avon.

The Mahabharata of Krishna-Dwaipayana Vyasa. (1896). (K. M. Ganguli, Trans.). Available online at http://www.sacred-texts.com/hin/maha.

Mitchell, S. (Trans.) (2000). *Bhagavad Gita: A new translation.* New York: Three Rivers Press.

Pavitra, Saint-Hilaire. (1961). *Education and the aim of human life.* Pondicherry, India: Sri Aurobindo International Centre of Education.

Ravi Shankar, Sri Sri (1999). *Wisdom for the new millennium.* Bangalore, India: Vyakti Vikas Kendra.

Ravi Shankar, Sri Sri (2002). *An intimate note to the sincere seeker* (vol. 4). Bangalore, India: Vyakti Vikas Kendra.

Ravi Shankar, Sri Sri (2003). *An intimate note to the sincere seeker* (vol. 7). Bangalore, India: Vyakti Vikas Kendra.

Sen, K. M. (1961). *Hinduism.* London: Penguin.

Tagore, R. (1917). *Personality.* London: Macmillan.

Tagore, R. (1931). *The religion of man.* Boston: Beacon Press.

Tagore, R. (1961). *Towards universal man.* New York: Asia Publishing House.

Vokey, D. (2000). Longing to connect: Spirituality in public schools, *Paideusis 13*(2), 23–41.

CHAPTER 7

My Lived Stories of Poetic Thinking and Taoist Knowing

Xin Li

California State University

This is a narrative inquiry
— "stories lived and told"[1]
about composing poems—the process of research report writing
by the poet—the researcher
in a poem—the representation.
It is a search for answers to how and why the poems were composed,
—an attempt to inquire into poetic thinking
in the self-reflexive direction
to release and enrich the forever partial self understanding
—the mystery that has been pondered over and over
by humans since their birth.

The first poem I wrote
was a love letter
in the classical Chinese form of *wu yan* (五言)
—five words in each line
—a verb in the middle of the line
—four lines in each stanza
—and the last words of first, second, and fourth lines rhyme,

after reading pages after pages of love letters from my admirer
  who was going to be a professional writer,
after being accused of writing too few words,
  and too little message,
after having struggled to articulate my feelings of "love."

I do not remember my poem anymore,
but recall my first innate drive to let poetry write me,
my primitive poetic thinking of love.
I do not remember my poem anymore,
but the strong feelings compressed
into the two stanzas of 40 words.
The love had faded away
because the admirer slipped his secret purpose of writing
those pages and pages of love letters to me
by counting the words
and displaying his pride in the amount of words he was capable of producing.
His linguistic production was realistic thinking,
to use Rieser's terms[2],
culminating in concept building and cognition
if not only pragmatic thinking;
Mine was poetic thinking
cleaving to the inner imaginary world, to a dreamlike content
riveted on configurations deviating from reality.

The second poem I wrote
was in English.
When I was asked to define poetry
in an English poetry class,
I wrote down a string of words,
a poem without a verb, without a definition, without a line of logic:
"a drop of water,
a petal of red rose,
a grain of sand,
a beam of sunshine through the leaves of a thick forest,
and a passenger train."

The strong feelings compressed in the first poem

were remote; so were the verbs,
the grammatical sentences, the rhythm and rhyme
as in poetic composition.
What's left was a direct visual abstraction of my understanding of poetry;
a hidden link verb to all the configurations deviating from reality;
a pattern of utilizing nouns
that creates dreamlike graphics in imagination;
and the aesthetics about the graphics
—the abstracted and conceptualized feelings toward
water, rose, sand, sunshine, and a passenger train.

Later, in the same English poetry class,
I wrote "A Passenger Train":
"on that passenger train,
some are given seats with respect;
some take their seats quietly;
some search for seats restlessly
some lose their seats violently;
some fight for seats feverishly;
some give their seats honorably;
some persevere in creating their seats,
and some ponder over and over
why passengers of life do such things to their seats."

Depicting life's picture,
I was wondering about its meanings,
lost and gained on life's journey,
the dialectics of *You* (有) and *Wu* (無)
                    Something and *Nothing*
in Taoist philosophy about the world.

I approach Taoism as a philosophy—the study of
   Lao Tzu and Chuang Tzu (老莊哲学),
not the history or literature—the study of different Taoist schools,
nor the rituals—as the study of the communal practice,
or the practices and techniques of alchemy, longevity, and divination.[3]

The train, in my poem, was a direct visual abstract of life
as it was of poetry in general,
of a drop of water,
a petal of rose,
a grain of sand,
a beam of sunshine through the leaves of a thick forest.
The water is water without a why,
it flows because it flows,
it cares not for itself, asks not if anyone sees it.
The rose is a rose is a rose,
it blooms because it blooms.
So is sand, sunshine, and a passenger train.
More important were my abstracted feelings of love for life
imbedded in the paralleled pattern of pictures.

After a long interval,
during which I was occupied with life's game
   with seats on the Passenger Train
I started to write poetry again.
This time, I was working within the autobiographical
   and biographical frames.

One day,
while struggling to summarize chapter two "To Live"[4]
which describes five Chinese immigrant women's lives in China,
as in the rapid torrents of danger,
                        of uncontrollable and capricious violence,
                        of invasion and rebellions,
                        of massacres, famine, flood, and starvation,
                        of the powerful oppressing powerless,
                        of feuds resulting in entire families
                        being murdered or destroyed, wives
                        and children seized and enslaved,
                        of hideous injustice surrounding
                        the Imperial throne,
                        of Ssu-ma Chien's (145–90 B.C.) castration,
                        for writing a more accurate but
                        unwelcome memorandum,

I wrote down lines as such:
"To live, we[5] hope;
to hope, we dream;
to dream, we imagine our improved future.
to imagine, we act;
we make constant effort to realize our dreams;
To realize our dreams, we improvise our realities.

We live, because we have been at the edges of life and death;
in desperation, we improvised to survive.
We improvised, because we knocked at the door of death;
in the reflection of the door of death,
we did not see the end of the world;
we admitted that we were limited;
we realized that horizons could be breached;
and the breach would take place in the midst of improvisation.

We learned that change is the law and the norm;
we struggled at the bottom of water;
we knew a time would come when we could surface.
We swam against the stream;
we were sure a time would come when we would swim with the stream.
Go in with a descending vortex;
come out with an ascending one.
In the Taoist web of time and change,[6]
we improvised the shapes of the currents.
Torrents among the rocks, rapids and waterfalls,
they all change in the moments of improvisation by the Taoist swimmers.

Taoist improvisation is ancient and modern;
it is arts;
it is philosophy;
it is life.
To live, we improvise."

At this point, I left the computer screen,
went to my second office—kitchen.

When I returned, my 12-year-old son was sitting
  in front of the screen, reading.
"Mom, are you writing a poem?"
"Oh, no!"

I grabbed the mouse, and changed the poetrylike page into a solid paragraph:
"To live, we hope; to hope, we dream; to dream, we imagine our improved future. To imagine, we act; we make constant effort to realize our dream. To realize our dream, we improvise our realities. We live, because we have been at the edges of life and death; in desperation, we improvised to survive. We improvised, because we knocked at the door of death; in the reflection of the door of death, we did not see the end of the world; we admitted that we were limited; we realized that horizons could be breached; and the breach would take place in the midst of improvisation. We learned that change is the law and the norm; we struggled at the bottom of water; we knew a time would come when we could surface. We swam against the stream; we were sure a time would come when we would swim with stream. Go in with a descending vortex; come out with an ascending one. In the Taoist web of time and change, we improvise the shapes of the currents. Torrents among the rocks, rapids and waterfalls, they all change in the moments of improvisation by the Taoist swimmers. Taoist improvisation is ancient and modern; it is arts; it is philosophy; it is life. To live, we improvise."

I was embarrassed being reminded that
I, a new immigrant with English as my second language,
was writing a poem for my Ph.D. dissertation.
I was more at ease to squeeze the passage back into its expected format;
now I fit.

After my son left the room,
I began to read the passage out loud to myself,
it did not sound right.
The right format did not fit the content,

It did not allow time or space for the reader to read,

                     to connect,
                     to savor,
                     to internalize,
                     to interact,
                     to understand.

Then I wrote the same message down in a more conventional way:

"In this chapter, titled as 'To Live', I described how five Chinese immigrant women lived our lives in China. Despite the difficulties we had, we not only survived, but lived. We kept hoping, imagining, and dreaming. When opportunity came, we worked for a better future. In fact, we realized our dreams. Therefore, we improvised our realities."

At this point, I stopped.
I felt betrayed by the format
emotionally, intellectually, and aesthetically.
For many years,
five of us Chinese immigrant women
had worked on our stories, our experiences in the past and at the present,
we grew together,
we were committed and bonded to one other.

For many years, five of us Chinese immigrant women
had created a collective identity
which acknowledges our emotion,
　　　empowers our dynamic multiple selves, and values aesthetics
　　　as one of the most important assets of life's giving.[7]

In addition,
Applying a Chinese standard of composition,
　which emphasizes succinctness,
I would be wasting so many words like:
"In this chapter titled as 'To Live,'"
"In fact," "Therefore"
I would be congesting readers' mind with predigested texts,
　　　manipulating readers' reasoning,
　　　imposing linear logic of cause and effect,[8]
　　　in order to defend a thesis.
My dissertation would drag over six hundred pages
with my logic only
so that I could pass the defense more easily.
I would lose my focus on the target
to the tools that were invented to assist shooting the target.

I would create readers,
    who would have fewer opportunities to think for themselves,
                to experience our cultural lives
                to see our perspectives.

Therefore, I let poetry write parts of my dissertation,
—life stories of five Chinese women immigrants including myself.

Recently, I was driven to understand poetry again,
by a friendly reminder that what I wrote was not a poem.
I wrote down a few sentences about what poetry is NOT:
not just neatly lined-up text with rhythm and rhyme,
not only a representation
"the process of transforming the contents of consciousness
into a public form so that they can be stabilized, inspected, edited,
  and shared with others"[9]

"Poetry owes its existence
not to an arbitrary act of the poet,"[10]
but to an innate drive;
that is not the result of a decision,
but that it is a natural phenomenon;
that something compulsive clings to it;
that it rises from an inner pressure,
even though it is true also
that it is not conceivable outside a social context.

In the social context,
in search of my cultural selves,
poetry wrote me,
while I was inquiring narratively,
while I was struggling to find a seat on my Passenger Train,
while I was searching feverishly for a place I would call home,
while I was composing and recreating my multiple selves.

Poetry wrote part of my autobiography;
poetry ordered my fragmented cultural selves;
poetry found me a way "out of the wasteland

in which the glare of scientism and one-eyed reason reduces
   even rock to dust, …"[11]

A poet creates affectionately.
She is not keen on clarity or sobriety,
but capable of recovering dust back into rock in Isaac Newton's science,
where emotions are muted,
unconscious backgrounds are quiescent.

A poet creates affectionately.
She connects intimately to the world revealed
with her own range of feelings;
she creates in the throes of excitement;
she creates rhythm
controlling ideas as their linguistic container, their outer shape,
forming order out of chaos,
holding in thrall ideas produced by emotions,
reflecting the temper of the poetic soul,
depicting the frame of the poetic mind.[12]

The poet's mind,
no, the human mind,
is equipped with a drive for order.
The ordering through the poetic creative process
engulfs the verbal material in its topographical position;
dominates the cognitive impulse of the psyche,
pushes it to cognition and awareness.
Ordering through the poetic creative process
is rooted in the will to appropriation, and
simultaneously, in the will to self-liberation.[13]
Ordering through the poetic creation awakes Newton's science
   of linear reasoning.

In poetic creation,
words pronounce with rhythm and rhyme.
In poetic creation in ideographic language,
words depict images, as well as pronounce rhythm and rhyme.
Each word creates an image,
the concentration on individual word is intensified.

Thinking in such languages
is "not about univocal concepts and their coherent connection,
but about images whose meanings are multi-
    dimensional and inexhaustible."[14]

Such images are seen through the ideographic language like Chinese,
Such multidimensional connections are found in Chinese syntax:
The intensified concentration on individual written word
the multidimensional combination of words
    and phrases, orally and in script,
nurtured my way of thinking—a Taoist reasoning.
The image of the word China is two words combined in Chinese:
中 and 國
中 means center by the image of a rectangular with a stroke in the middle;
國 means country by the image of territory with a border surround it.
The combination of the two-word 中國 taught me
China was in the center of the world,
like many other countries which may also believe they were in the
    middle of the world,
such as 希 腊國 Greece, 英國 England, 美國 US, and 印 度國, India.
I learned that 中 centers could create many worlds, large and small,

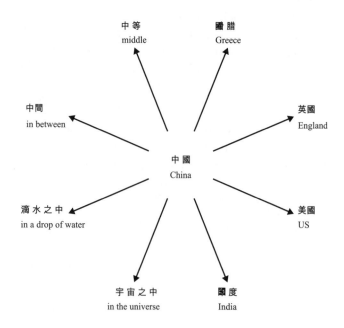

such as 宇 宙 之 中 in the center of the universe,
  and 滴 水 之 中, in a drop of water.
—a multidimensional logic.
"It is not the forms of language that generate meaning,
      but the use of such forms to think about something."[15]
"To think is to confine yourself to a single thought."[16]
"We never come to thoughts. They come to us."[17]

"Thirty spokes converge on a single hub, 輪
it is in the space where there is nothing
  lies the usefulness of the cart.
Clay is molded to make a pot, 罐
it is in the space where there is nothing
  lies the usefulness of the clay pot.
Doors and windows make a room, 房
it is in the spaces where there is nothing
  lies the usefulness of the room.

Benefit may come from something, 有
it is in nothing 無 that we find usefulness."[18]

Such Taoist reasoning focuses on images created by individual words,
          creates likely images unrelated in alphabetic languages,
          depicts a dialectic interplay between
          something and nothing,
          gives readers a space to interact
          to recreate their own
          multidimensional interplay.

The re-creation happens in the exchange of information
directly from the poem and the visual and emotional remembrances
triggered by the poem,
followed by choosing,
          comparing,
          filling up ambiguous areas of memory and comparison,
          and reorganizing thinking.[19]

Such re-creation produces novelty,

includes the reader's experience with the poem;

such re-creation relies on a direct abstraction of the visual and
  emotional image.

Such direct abstraction depicts

a very important characteristic of the poetic thinking in Chinese language,

"象 外 之 象,"

"境 外 之 境,"

"韵 外 之 致,"

"言 外 之 意,"

image beyond image,

scene beyond scene,

music beyond music,

meaning beyond words,[20]

Learning to think poetically in Chinese language,

I experienced Taoist reasoning,

and Taoist poetry writing.

My Taoist poetry writing is representation and content in one;

 poetry and thinking in one;

 public and intimate in one;

 rational and emotional in one;

 order and chaos in one;

 truth and method in one.

It is a simple and concrete "Being-there" in Heidegger's term[21]

My Taoist knowing is better articulated in poetry,

a direct "visual 'abstract' of the world," [22]

 an ideographic philosophy of life,

 a way of thinking,

 a direct experience of reasoning.

"Ontological and poetic experience are one."[23]

Notes

In order to maintain a balance between poetic writing and academic writing, I quote academic texts directly in the poem and give endnote sources that refer to the reference list that follows them.

1. Clandinin & Connelly, 2000, p. 20.
2. Rieser (1969) has found that scientific writing demonstrates realistic thinking, which culminates in concept building and cognition, while poetry writing shows poetic thinking that cleaves to the inner imaginary world, to a dreamlike content, riveted on configuration deviating from reality (pp. 15-20).
3. Kirkland, Barret, & Kohn, 2004, pp. xxx–xxxi.
4. This was chapter 2 of my Ph.D. dissertation, which was later published as a book (Li, 2002).
5. "We" here refers to all five of the Chinese immigrant women, including myself.
6. Rawson & Legeza, 1973/1995, p. 11.
7. I believe in one of the Taoist aesthetic principles: to appear simple but convey profoundly, to include few words but contain abundant messages, to talk little, but say a lot.
8. As an elementary school student in China, I was taught that in Chinese composition, it is considered better writing to use fewer structural words, such as *because, consequently, as a result,* and *and so on.* Good writing conveys its logic to readers without "wasting" these types of words.
9. Eisner, 1993, p. 6.
10. Rieser, 1969, pp. 15–16.
11. Diamond & Mullen, 1999, p. 17.
12. Rieser, 1969, pp. 30–38.
13. Rieser, 1969, pp. 20-21.
14. Poggeler, 1987, p. 68.
15. Geertz, 1995, p. 46.
16. Heidegger, 1971, p. 4.
17. Heidegger, 1971, p. 6.
18. *Tao Te Ching,* chapter 11; my translation.
19. Luo, 1994, pp. 17–18; my translation.
20. Luo, 1994, p. 21; my translation.
21. Rieser, 1969, p. 24.
22. Halliburton, 1981, p. 8.
23. Chang, 1963/1970, p. 46.

References

Chang, C. Y. (1970). *Creativity and Taoism: A study of Chinese philosophy, art, and poetry.* New York: Harper and Row. (Original work published 1963)

Clandinin, D. J., & Connelly, F. M. (2000). *Narrative inquiry: Experience and story in qualitative research.* San Francisco: Jossey-Bass.

Diamond, C. T. P., & Mullen, A. C. (Eds.). (1999). *The Postmodern educator: Arts-based inquires and teacher development.* New York: Lang.

Eisner, E. W. (1993). Forms of understanding and the future of educational research. *Educational research, 22*(7), 5–11.

Geertz, C. (1995). *After the fact.* Cambridge, MA: Harvard University Press.

Halliburton, D. (1981). *Poetic thinking: An approach to Heidegger.* Chicago: University of Chicago Press.

Heidegger, M. (1971). *Poetry, language, thought* (A. Hofstadter, Trans. & Ed.). New York: Harper and Row.

Kirkland, R., Barrett, R. H., & Kohn, L. (2004). Introduction. In L. Kohn (Ed.), *Daoism Handbook* (pp. xi–xxxviii). Leiden, Netherlands: Koninklijke Brill.

Li, X. (2002). *The Tao of life stories: Chinese language, poetry, and culture in education.* New York: Lang.

Luo, Z. Q. (1994). *On some classical Taoist works.* Taibei, China: Wenjin.

Poggeler, O. (1987). West-East dialogue: Heidegger and Lao-tzu. In G. Parkes (Ed.), *Heidegger and Asian thought.* Honolulu: University of Hawaii Press.

Rawson, P., & Legeza, L. (1995). *Tao: The Chinese philosophy of time and change.* London: Thames and Hudson. (Original work published 1973)

Rieser, M. (1969). *Analysis of poetic thinking.* Detroit, MI: Wayne State University Press.

CHAPTER 8

Engendering Wisdom
Listening to Kuan Yin and Julian of Norwich

Petra Munro Hendry
Louisiana State University

It has been argued that concerns of social justice and liberation could not properly belong to the mystics. Spirituality, it is held, is private. It has to do with the inner, subjective relation of the soul to God. Social justice, by contrast, is necessarily public, seeking to bring about at political and structural levels conditions which will foster the dignity of each individual and the welfare of the community. The spiritual and the social are therefore opposites: concentration on one means to that extent letting go of the other.

—Grace M. Jantzen, *Power, Gender and Christian Mysticism*

Some, like Jantzen, assert that to speak of the spiritual and social change in the same breath is to enter into paradox; to speak of mysticism and social change is to engage the absurd. Yet, my study of women mystics and embodied knowing has made it imperative to confront what in some circles had previously been inconceivable—a conversation between the political and the spiritual.[1] Rather than "let go" of either, this chapter seeks to bring the spiritual and the political into conversation as a means to address issues of social justice. This conversation will, I hope, be enriched by engaging both Eastern and Western mystics—specifically, Kuan Yin, a Buddhist goddess, and Julian of Norwich, a 14th-century English mystic. Kuan Yin, known as the bodhisattva of compassion, sacrifices her life to save those of others and provides comfort to those who suffer. Likewise, Julian of Norwich becomes an anchorite, literally "dead to the world" in order to meditate on the meanings of Christ's suffering and death as the embodiment of his compassion and love. While among the Chinese Kuan Yin is considered a goddess, and not an actual person, she, like Julian of Norwich, is considered part of the mystical tradition.

As women who either symbolize or embody a role for women as active agents, both Kuan Yin and Julian of Norwich stand outside the normative gender traditions of their time. In this sense, they were both exemplars of rebellion, in which they confronted injustice from a "passionate and compassionate concern for oneself and for others" (Bartlett, 1992, p. 84). *Splagchnoisomai*, the Greek word for compassion, means to "let one's innards embrace the feeling or situation of another" (Brueggemann, 2001, p. 89). Central to both Kuan Yin's and Julian's narratives is the experience of embracing the pain of others. It is this internalization of pain that leads to personal and social transformation. Compassion, according to Brueggemann (2001) constitutes a radical form of criticism, for it "announces that hurt is to be taken seriously, that the hurt is not to be accepted as normal and natural but is an abnormal and unacceptable condition for humanness" (p. 88). Compassion for others, by taking on the hurt of others (especially those traditionally marginalized), disrupts blind allegiance to the status quo of unequal social arrangements. Social justice is not necessarily the result of rebellion or revolution. For transformative social change both rebellion and compassion are necessary.[2]

The element of compassion in the narratives of both Kuan Yin and Julian is reminiscent of the current discourses of the "ethics of care." Until recently, Western philosophical discourse has largely ignored an ethics of care as significant to human morality. Care was a taken-for-granted function that was basic to human existence. In this regard, it was seen as natural and, most notably, the province of women. More recently, an ethics of care has been articulated by many, including Carol Gilligan (1982) and Nel Noddings (1984). Among other qualities, Gilligan's "care ethics" is a relational approach to morality that avoids generalization in favor of particularity and connection. She juxtaposes an ethic of care to an ethic of justice where morality is based on abstract universal principles. Noddings, in her book *Caring* (1984), maintains that caring is an ethic that arises out of women's experiences, primarily that of the mother-child relationship. However, she makes a distinction between "natural" caring as instinctual, and "moral" caring as based in choice.

Criticisms of "caring" have been grounded in arguments that they are essentialist (Tong, 1998; Groenhout, 1998). They maintain that an "ethics of care" is embedded in a dualistic view of gender that reifies a unitary subject. My concern is on deemphasizing the individual (whether male or female) in these theories and instead examining the social, communal, and relational dimensions of caring and compassion. Like Maurice Hamington (2004), my evolving understandings of caring also include an understanding of caring as embodied and imagined. Consequently, an ethics of caring or compassion is more than an abstract theory; it is a radical—lived—way of knowing that serves as a mode of critique and social transformation. I turn to the stories of Kuan Yin and Julian of Norwich to illuminate three central aspects of their narratives in relation to compassion: the role of suffering and interrelationality, the role of experience, and the role of an integrated body, mind, and spirit. First, I will give a brief introduction to mysticism.

Mysticism

The aim of every mystic is union with the divine or God. For the mystic, the divine is not merely an object of belief, but a living fact experientially known; it is a life based on a conscious communion with God (Underhill, 1925). The mystic way, with its three stages of purgation (purification and detachment from earthly interests), illumination (peaceful certitude of God), and union (self-forgetting harmony), is a formula that was first used by Neoplatonists and borrowed from them by Christian writers on the spiritual life (Underhill, 1925).[3] There are two theories as to the method for achieving union: transcendence or immanence. *Transcendence* is a journey upward and outward; *immanence* is the realization of something that is implicit in the self and in the universe, that earth is literally "crammed with heaven" (Underhill, 1911, p. 96).[4] Medieval Christian women mystics tended toward immanence. St. Teresa of Avila has described her union with God as one in which she saw "God in a point" (Flinders, 1993). This experience is one in which selfhood ceases to have meaning and the individual soul touches the life of all. German mystics (Hildegard of Bingen, Mechthild of Magdeberg) have described it as the attainment of the "still wilderness" or "lonely desert of the deity." British mystics like Richard Rolle have described it as the "Cloud of Unknowing."

Eastern mysticism as found in Buddhism offers "metaphysical enlightenment," while Christian mysticism offers theological salvation. However, as Thomas Merton (1968) points out, the two religions do have a psychic "limitlessness in common" (p. 8). The Christian "union with God" and the Buddhist "enlightenment" describe an emptiness or freedom that is central to the mystical experience. Only when we are empty can we be filled—in this case, with compassion. In the Christian mystic tradition we become our "true self" and in the Buddhist tradition we achieve "egolessness." While I honor differences between Buddhism and Christianity, they share similar epistemologies that provide a space to explore the concept of compassion as a way of knowing.

The Origins of the Chinese Kuan Yin

Similar to the veneration of the Virgin Mary (Mother of Jesus) by Catholics, or Iamanja of Brazil, Kuan Yin, who appears in her current form in 600 B.C.E., is one of the most popular devotional figures in China (Edwards, 1991). *Kuan-yin* in Chinese signifies "looking at the sounds of living beings" and "listening to the world's sounds." She is best known for her mercy and compassion; she protects, relieves, and comforts in sorrow. However, the story of Kuan Yin is a complex one;[5] it is full of transformations that blend Chinese folklore, Buddhism, and Hinduism and ultimately reflects a great deal of the historical, social, and cultural ideologies of the times. While I will focus on Kuan Yin's role in China, she is also a deity of veneration in Japan, Korea, and Tibet. Situating her story within a larger historical and social context is important to understanding the epistemological foundations of her image.

Kuan Yin's image may be derived from the pre-Buddhist goddess Nu Kwa (Stone, 1979). Nu Kwa, the great ocean-snail-snake-dragon woman, gave birth to all life and the patterns of the universe. In the texts of the Chou period (about 1000 B.C.E.) and the later Han period in China, it was written that Nu Kwa created all people, thus revealing her nature as the original parent or most ancient ancestress (Stone, 1979).[6] She was also described as the one who established harmony and the patterns of the universe, arranging the order of the seasons, and setting the stars and planets upon the proper paths. It is this complex and omnipotent view of the "The Mother"—not only as she who first gave birth to people, the creator of human life, but also as she who arranged the workings of the universe, the patterns of nature—that reveals that the image of the most ancient ancestress was that of nature herself (Stone, 1979).

Early Chinese texts record the mythic memories of this time as the "Era of Great Purity." In the *Chuang Tzu*, written in the third century B.C.E., the time of Great Purity is described as a time when all people lived in a state of innocence, being genuine and simple, spontaneous and direct in their conduct. They were in harmony with the seasons and with the ways of nature; animals and humans did no harm to one another. The Chinese texts then explain that this paradise was destroyed by mining minerals in the mountains, felling trees to build houses, hunting, fishing, and even by learning to make and control fire. The period of the obliteration of this perfect life, and the loss of touch with the patterns of nature was referred to as the "Great Cosmic Struggle." Nature had been defied and this was said to be the original cause of discord and problems (Stone, 1979).

This story parallels other creation stories in terms of its narrative structure, with a time of innocence and purity (harmony), a fall from grace (disharmony), and the resultant struggle for reunion. That China has a goddess whereas Christian, Islamic, and Judiac traditions have a god is of less interest to me than the similarity in the stories. When God, humankind, and nature are in harmony there is purity; it is good. What causes disharmony or lack of balance is humanity's estrangement from the cosmic divine through reliance on its own self-knowledge (symbolized by the apple or fire). When humans believe they can rely on themselves and control nature through knowledge, they have severed their relationship to the divine. In other words, they forget their interrelatedness and interconnectedness, that they are intricately bound to one another and nature. This false sense of knowledge (an epistemology of separation) results in disharmony (going it alone, without the divine).

A careful reading of the *Tao Te Ching* (the most basic book of Taoism), believed to have been written about 600 B.C.E. by Lao Tzu (which means "ancient teacher"), reveals that it is to some degree a mirror that reflects the ideas and beliefs that may once have been the theological and philosophical core of ancient goddess reverence in China. According to Stone (1979),

> In the *Tao Teh* [*sic*] *Ching*, we do not find prayers to a concept of the Goddess that is external to, or separated from, earth and ourselves, but rather the understanding of nature as the maternal spirit essence that is inherent in all that exists and occurs. It is a concept of Goddess that is also found in the texts of India, concerning the Goddess as Shakti or Devi, and in the texts of Egypt, concerning the Goddess of Maat. It is this gentle omnipotence of She who is the essence of the patterns of the universe, all that is actually implied when we speak of Mother Nature that appears to be the core of the wisdom and the way of *Tao Teh* [*sic*] *Ching*. (p. 25)

This feminine principle embodied by Nu Kwa can later be seen in Kuan Yin. Although not as all encompassing as Nu Kwa, Kuan Yin retains the idea of gentle but consistent, determined action. This is a form of agency that is characterized by learning from the ways of nature.

The image of Nu Kwa and what she embodied eventually intersected with Confucianism and Buddhism. Confucianism was adopted as a state ideology during the Han dynasty (220 B.C.E.–240 C.E.). The appropriation of Confucianism by the state took up the hierarchical nature of relations, while Confucius himself emphasized social hierarchy in relation to achieving harmony and balance. The Confucian self is one that exists in a communal and cosmic relatedness. Confucius (551–479 B.C.E.) did not formulate an abstract idea of the self or an essentialist view of human nature. He was much more concerned with how to bring out the best in humanity by education than he was with metaphysical speculations about human nature. According to Hongyu Wang (2004),

> in contrast to Western transcendental traditions which support a substance view of self, the Confucian self is based upon an ontology of events, not of substances. While transcendental principles define the Western nature of the self, the Confucian immanent view of the world situates the self within its concrete interactions in particular settings. As a result, the Confucian self is an interactive process, dependent upon specific events which both determine and are determined by contexts. In such a process, one's disposition, character, and behaviors are cultivated and transformed toward the full realization of humanity. (p. 56)

The appropriation of Confucianism as the official state ideology resulted in a more rigid embodiment of social relations in which women were positioned as submissive (see Wang, 2004). One consequence was the decline of the worship of Nu Kwa.

Buddhism reached China from India in the second century during the late Han dynasty. Buddhist storytellers said that Kuan Yin was actually a man who had reached a state of Buddha being and then decided to come to Earth as a *bodhisattva*, a spiritual teacher, in the form of a woman (Edwards, 1991).[7] In Hindu India, Kuan Yin was portrayed as a handsome young prince. *Kuan* (which means earth) and *yin* (the feminine balance to *yang*) means "she who hearkens to the cries of the world," and is a translation of the Sanskrit name of her chief male progenitor, Avalokitesvara. Among all the deities in Buddhism, Avalokitesvara is the most beloved bodhisattva in China (Blofeld, 1977). In Sanskrit, the word *avalokita* means "observes the sounds of the world" and *isvara* means "lord." The full name *Avalokitesvara* has been variously interpreted as "the lord who hears/looks in every direction" and "the lord of hearing the deepest." The great vow of the Avalokitesvara is to listen to the supplications from those in difficulty in the world and to postpone Buddhahood until every being on earth has achieved enlightenment (Yu, 2004). Kuan Yin has been popularly revered as a goddess in China for a thousand years or more, though she is not really a goddess but a celestial bodhisattva who formerly embodied the male form of Avalokitesvara.

During the Tang dynasty in China, in the seventh and early eighth centuries, a female figure became the dominant portrait of the bodhisattva. Jie Yu (2004) attributes four factors to the transformation: the goddess worship tradition in China, the decline of such goddess worship by Confucianism in the Han Dynasty (204 B.C.E.–220 C.E.), the attraction of Kuan Yin's quality of mercy and compassion to oppressed Chinese women and the particular character of the Tang Dynasty (under the Empress Wu Zetian). By 828 C.E. there was a statue of Kuan Yin in every monastery through China, numbering 44,000 statues in all (Paul, 1985).

The other element in the transformation of Kuan Yin came at the end of the Song dynasty (960–1279 C.E.). The wife of a well-known Confucian (and she herself was one) compiled a book, *Biography of Bodhisattva Kuan-yin*, telling a complete story of Kuan Yin's origin from the Chinese folktale of the princess Miao-shan. Miao-shan is thought of as a manifestation of the bodhisattva of compassion, the so-called goddess of mercy, Kuan Yin (Avalokitesvara). Indeed, her legend may, in part, be responsible for the feminization of Avalokitesvara as this deity's cult moved from India to China and he/she was transformed from a male bodhisattva into a female one.

Thus, Chinese folklore intersected with Buddhism at a particular political, social, and cultural moment in Chinese history when Confucianism had solidified itself as the state ideology. The image of Nu Kwa, who embodied interrelationality with nature and the divine, and the story of Miao-shan intersected with the Buddhist diety Avalokitesvara to transfigure into Kuan Yin.

Gender Bending: The Transformation of Kuan Yin

John Strong, in his book *The Experience of Buddhism* (2002), suggests that the story of Kuan Yin is significant for the intersection of several themes. According to Strong, the legendary Chinese princess Miao-shan, who later became Kuan Yin, defied her father's plans to marry her off and instead pursued a religious vocation. First, the story shows the situation of a young

Chinese woman dominated by her father and living in a context where filial piety is the norm. Second, it reflects a Buddhist solution to a classic dilemma: Miao-shan defies her father in order to become a nun, but because of this she is eventually able to save her father. Thus, despite her original apparent rejection of filial piety, in the end her sacrifice makes her a model of filial piety. The story of Miao-shan and her transformation to Kuan Yin is told below. Kuan Yin has just entered the monastery and rejected her father's command that she marry and take a husband:

Miao-shan says: "Empty things come to an end—I desire what is infinite."

The king, in a great rage ordered troops to surround the monastery, behead the nuns and burn down their quarters. But Miao-shan was taken off by a naga spirit to the foot of Hsiang-shan mountain, not a hair of hers injured.

Three years passed when the king, in return for his crimes of destroying the monastery and killing the religious, contracted jaundice and could find no rest.

Doctors could not cure him.

Then, a strange monk appeared saying "If you use the arms and eyes of one free of anger to blend into a medicine and take it, then you will be cured."

The king ordered an emissary to go the hills of Hsiang-shan where a holy one whose practice of religion had come to completion and was free of anger. The request was made for her arms and eyes in order to save the king's life. Hearing this the holy one gouged out her two eyes and severed both arms with a knife. At that moment the whole earth shook.

The king recovered from his sickness.

The king and his lady went to Hsiang-shan to offer humble thanks and veneration. They were moved by a painful thought that "The holy one looks very like our daughter."

The holy one said; "I am indeed Miao-shan. Your daughter has offered her arms and eyes to repay her father's love."

The king wept saying "I was so evil that I have made my daughter suffer terrible pain."

The holy one said: "I suffer no pain. Having yielded my mortal eyes I shall receive diamond eyes; having given up my human arms I shall receive golden-coloured arms. If my vow is true these results will certainly follow."

Heaven and earth then shook. And then the holy one was revealed as the All-merciful Bodhisattva Kuan-shih-yin of the Thousand Arms and Thousand Eyes, solemn and majestic in form, radiant with dazzling light, lofty and magnificent, like the moon amid the stars. The king and his lady, together with the entire population of the land, conceived goodness in their hearts and committed themselves to the Three Treasures. (Dudbridge, 1978, p. 71)

Wisdom as Compassion

My analysis focuses on the notion of compassion as the starting point for thinking about an epistemology of social action. Kuan Yin's story is compelling in many respects. Women need to follow their hearts, their desires, even if these do not at the outset conform to traditional notions of filial piety. Miao-shan is the rebellious, independent daughter who rejects the marriage plot (as well as becoming a princess) in order to pursue a celibate, religious life. Her rebellion is a form of social critique, a criticism of the dominant order and law, in this case Confucianism. Ironically, her rebellion results in her being the most filial of all, this is the paradox. Dudbridge (1978) has suggested that this story functions to resolve the inherent tension between Buddhism (which requires separation from family and retreat to monastic life) and Confucianism (which emphasizes the ethical practice of filial piety). Kuan Yin's rebellion narrative provides not only a cultural compromise at a specific historical moment but also provides an alternative consciousness by its focus on compassion and the corresponding themes of interrelationality, experience, and embodiment.

Kuan Yin's rejection of predetermined order and law (Confucianism) suggests an alternative epistemology, one predicated on intersubjectivity and interrelationality.[8] Instead of an absolute worldview, Kuan Yin's emphasis on oneness between heaven and earth, between the divine and the human, posits a self that is constructed in intersubjectivity. The self is not an object or subject, but one that is constituted in experience, context, relationality, and, ultimately, in acts of compassion. It is in being present to the injustices of the world and acting in the world that "beingness" occurs. Compassion is not grounded in a set of laws or moral ethics, as in Confucianism, but predicated on being present to suffering, attending to others, and witnessing and listening to the cries of others.

Kuan Yin's notion of compassion is an ontological and epistemological stance that guides actions/interactions. There is an interdependent relationship between self and society that contrasts with poststructural, especially Foucauldian, understandings of self against society (Wang, 2004). The mode of *with* versus *against* implies a different civilizational orientation toward subjectivity and society. Freedom is harmony with "the Way," not a rupture in society. Consequently, compassion becomes the way to maintain and deepen relations rather than sever them. Kuan Yin does not ultimately reject her father or sever relations with him, and her compassion in the form of the sacrifice of her arms and eyes is not seen as a personal sacrifice but one that in the end is done for maintaining harmony and balance in society. The Chinese—indeed Eastern—notion of harmony is contrary to, rather than compatible with, conformity. Harmony is not achieved by agreement; rather, criticism is necessary for reaching harmony.

Kuan Yin embodies both the human and the divine, and like other religious figures mediates between the human and the divine (Jesus, Mohammed, Moses). This state of both/and is dependent on Kuan Yin's experience of sacrifice/death and rebirth—in other words, engaging in the cycle of life and death. By suffering (through death) she experiences life/love and is transformed. Compassion is also something that is experienced in the body. In order to save her father, Kuan Yin loses her eyes and arms. Her compassion is embodied, deeply felt. This act of sacrifice brings body, mind, and spirit to the act of compassion. In this sense, compassion is an integrated, holistic way of knowing that transcends gender as well as purely rationalist ways of knowing.

This transfiguration narrative is common in other religions, including Christianity and the mystery cults of Greece and the Middle East. In this narrative, Kuan Yin separates from her family, performs acts of deliverance that require personal sacrifice, and is then transfigured and reintegrated. Yet, what is significant is that unlike other transfiguration narratives in which the individual "transcends" the earth, Kuan Yin remains on earth. The most striking element of the story is that the way to enlightenment is through acts of compassion—not just feeling compassion, but acting, and acting compassionately. The motivating force behind the actual practice of the bodhisvatta and the Buddha path is the element of compassion, the desire to help alleviate the sufferings of others, either by guiding them to enlightenment or by assisting in more material ways. Clearly, this image of the Buddhist sacred and divine suggests that the affective, emotional, maternal realm is necessary for both women and men in the fulfillment of religious goals and for the alleviation of suffering (Paul, 1985). Kuan Yin is the compassionate savior of the distressed world. According to the *Lotus Sutra* (chapter 25), Kuan Yin is the eyewitness to suffering who immediately relieves the sorrows of those who call out her name. She is "generally described as a mother who hears the suffering of her children, regardless of their earthly station" (Sangern, 1983, p. 16). Inclusivity is central to her compassion. She is a favorite among those traditionally marginalized, including prostitutes, social outcasts, childless women, and the mentally and physically disabled. What links these disparate groups according to Sangern (1983) is "the unity of humanity that arises under Kuan Yin's protection" (p. 20). Essential to enlightenment is compassion, not just transcendence, and rebellion as well as conformity.

Elizabeth Ann Bartlett (1992), drawing on the work of Albert Camus, suggests that justice is intertwined and arises out of compassionately witnessing the oppression of others. She maintains that

> acts of true compassion—voluntary and self-affirming choices to "suffer with" others—transcend individual concerns and build political community. Indeed, actions based on compassion may provide a more sound foundation for political obligation than do those obligations based on contract, which may be performed resentfully out of a sense of duty or fear of repercussion. (p. 85)

Kuan Yin's compassion for others is a recognition of people's basic human dignity, not merely a dispassionate calculation of rights.

What is highlighted in this tale is that to attain enlightenment, one needs vast stores of wisdom and compassion in perfect union. Wisdom includes full and direct perception of one's own egolessness and of the nonexistence of anything like the "ego self" in any object. Compassion is the prime means of destroying all clinging to selfhood, and thus a path to enlightenment (Blofeld, 1977, p. 22). In other words, enlightenment is awareness of foundational inter-relationality. The truly selfless person is one who realizes that by himself he is nobody, and that his real worth is to be found in relationships (for Kuan Yin, relationships include those with the self, other, nature, and the divine). According to Silvade (1979), this implies a "self-less commitment to the service of man, a collective life, and a socially oriented work-style" (p. 10).

According to Raymond Gawronski (1995), Buddhist compassion—*Karuna* or *maitri*—remains fundamentally different from that of the West. In the East, one must renounce being an "I" because the divine is egoless. In the West, most especially in the Christian understanding of agape, one loves God for His own sake and one's fellow humanity because her person is absolutely loved by God (Gawronski, 1995, p. 24). For the East, the way to end suffering is to achieve a state of egolessness. The extreme case is in Zen Buddhism, where enlightenment is the attainment of absolute nothingness. In other words, the divine, what in the West is called God, is annihilated to nothingness. The doctrine of ideas disappears in Zen. According to Gawronski (1995), Zen represents the most intense, the most extreme, human attempt to escape the limits of the human condition. In contrast to Zen, in Mahayana Buddhism, and in particular the story of Kuan Yin, the notion of enlightenment is predicated on attending to the salvation of all humans prior to reaching Nirvana. Enlightenment—in other words, the transcendence of the self and union with the divine—is not like the Zen notion of "nothingness," but a state of interrelationality and connectedness. Kuan Yin's compassion is thus not one of self-erasure through pouring oneself out to others, but an active attending to and listening to the cries of others who seek compassion.

Wisdom is in the act of being present to others, not the acquisition of knowledge. Compassion, not scientific reason, is the premise for an epistemology of social justice. Scientific reason has been focused on information accretion, whereas another kind of subjectivity, that of compassion remains focused on and aware of the depth, strength, intensity, clarity, and openness of the mind to others (Klein, 2004). As Anne Klein (1994) maintains, compassion deserves more contemporary philosophical respect in Western philosophy. I would also suggest that compassion should be considered as an epistemological underpinning for social action. Social action not grounded in traditional notions of revolution or even change, but on attending to and listening to others in ways that make us present to them. This "letting go" of our own preconceived notions of what is justice, liberation or social change through compassion provides a third way to theorize change.[9]

Julian of Norwich

The motif of mother and child is central to all the world's mystical traditions; even Buddhism, which Westerners tend to see as essentially cerebral in its emphasis on mental training, has as one of its central tenets the Buddha's own instruction, "Learn to love the whole world as a mother loves her only son" (Flinders, 1993, p. 94).

Love—unconditional love—was the path to enlightenment for many medieval Christian women mystics including Hadewijch of Antwerp, Julian of Norwich, Mechthild of Magdeburg, and Teresa of Avila, among others. They considered unconditional love as the path to understanding the divine. For these women, love was neither sentimental nor esoteric; it was embodied, and came from a union of body, mind, and spirit. To learn to love as a mother does a son circumscribes love within the maternal. This maternal understanding of love is one that is deeply inscribed in societal gender norms and historically contingent. Like Kuan Yin, whose story represents a more fluid notion of gender, medieval women mystics also disrupt gender in profound ways. One consequence of this rupture is the possibility of reexamining love and compassion as a way of knowing. In the same way that Kuan Yin brings compassion to our understanding of what knowing entails, medieval women mystics focused on the passion and suffering of Christ as a meditation on the meaning of a radical message of love. Like Kuan Yin's notion of compassion, Julian's epistemology of love provides a profound way of knowing.

Disrupting Gender through Love

Julian of Norwich (1342–1413) was a medieval English mystic and anchorite whose book, *The Divine Revelations of Love*, is considered to be the first book in English authored by a woman (Julian of Norwich, 1966). While there is little external evidence that she had any formal education, her writing indicates that she was well-read, knowing the Christian Neoplatonists, the Dominicans, the Franciscans, and Bernard of Clairvaux. The book was originally written in 1373, when Julian was age 31, after she had received a series of visions on her sickbed. *Revelations* is an intimate and loving recollection of her visions.[10] Upon her recovery, she chose to become an anchorite. *Anchorite* is derived from the Greek verb meaning to "retire." Anchorites were regularly referred to as dead to the world, shut up as with Christ in his tomb.[11] She lived the rest of her days in a cell attached to St. Julian's church (this is where her name derives), where she used her solitude to engage in a contemplative life.

Like Kuan Yin, Julian chose to separate herself from the material world and to undergo a trial of great suffering. In her youth Julian prayed for three things: for an understanding of the passion of Christ; for a physical illness so severe that she herself and everyone around her would think that she was dying; and for three wounds: true contrition, loving compassion, and the longing of the will of God. In her 31st year, Julian became violently ill. When her physical suffering ceased, a succession of 16 visions began, the first 15 lasting from early morning until mid-afternoon, the last seen late that night. Throughout her 16 visions there is a fine counterpoint between Julian's suffering of illness and the suffering of Jesus on the cross. Her first vision is of Christ's bodily experiences on the cross:

> Because of the pull of his nails and the weight of that blessed body it was a long time suffering. For I could see that the great, hard, hurtful nails in those dear and tender hands and feet caused the wounds to gape wide and the body to sag forward under its own weight, and because of the time that it hung there. His head was scarred and torn, and the crown was sticking to it, congealed with

blood; his dear hair and his withered flesh was entangled with the thorns, and they with it. (Julian of Norwich, 1966, p. 89)

According to Jantzen (1995), no medieval writer—not even Francis of Assissi—ever focused so lovingly or in anything like such detail on the physical body of Jesus on the cross. Julian revises the experience of being acted on by illness, of being a prisoner of the body that suffers. Her illness, like Kuan Yin's suffering through the loss of her arms and eyes, becomes a site for embodied knowing. For Julian the traditional association with illness as passivity turns into passion as her wounded body is conflated with Christ's. This union becomes the center of her autobiographical reflections in which she represents herself as an active agent in relation to the divine. Both Kuan Yin and Julian alternately embrace suffering and death as a means of transformation that results in a deeper understanding of the meaning of the divine and a directive to share that understanding. It is this embodied experience that results in oneness or union with the divine that becomes the experience of interrelationality and in which the self as an autonomous object is disrupted.

At the end of the first revelation, in which Julian is in union with Christ's bodily pain during the crucifixion, she states, "All this was shown to me in three ways, in actual vision (physical), in imaginative understanding (mind) and in spiritual sight (soul)" (Julian of Norwich, 1966, p. 76). For this medieval mystic, bodily experience is also a spiritual and imaginative experience. The body does not become a mere conduit for experience, but bodily experience *is* spiritual experience and imaginative experience. She writes:

> For just as the body is clothed in its garments, and the flesh in its skin, and the bones in their flesh, and the heart in its body, so too are we soul *and* body, clothed from head to foot in the goodness of God. (Julian of Norwich, 1966, p. 70)

Thus, in reading gender, the body, which is traditionally associated with female, is textualized not as either male or female but as *both* male and female. We are both body and soul, thereby disrupting gender. In this way, "mystical self-representation resists the duality and finality of gender" (Gilmore, 1994, p. 133). Julian is not privileging the body but on some level is suggesting an integrated theory of body, soul, and mind as an epistemological framework. This epistemology is in stark contrast to a Platonic or traditional Buddhist or

Christian understanding of the body in which the body must be transcended in order to achieve union with the divine.

What is ultimately shown Julian through these mediums is that souls, minds, and bodies are clothed in the goodness, the love of God. Jantzen (1995) maintains that "Julian's teaching concerning spiritual progress has everything to do with receiving and trusting the faithful love of God and nothing to do with standard themes of distrust of the body and especially sexuality" (p. 140). Julian reconceives the female body from the Christian notion of bodily sin and site of evil and temptation to one in which she has absolute conviction that the body is a site of goodness and the love of God. The body embodies goodness, and thus control and repression of the female body (the normative Christian reading) are absent in Julian's text. Like Kuan Yin, Julian rebels against the social and religious norms that seek to subjugate women. The body is essential for union with God, and not something to be suppressed. The fact that God chooses to manifest himself in a human body is evidence enough that the body is sacred and a profound site for knowing. For Julian, love is God's message. Like the compassion that Kuan Yin embodies through her suffering, Julian's illness and suffering teach her that love, not judgment, is a way of knowing.

Love

> Wouldst thou written thy Lord's meaning in this thing? Learn it well: love was his meaning. Who shewed it thee? Love. What shewed he thee? Love. Wherefore shewed it he? For love. (Julian of Norwich, 1966, p. 32)

According to Colish (1997), Julian's most distinctive contribution to Christian mysticism is her understanding of the affective bond between the mystic and God in terms of maternal love. Julian was by no means the first to articulate Jesus or God as mother. The idea of God as mother can be found in the Bible and in the monastic writing of Augustine and of Bernard of Clairvoux, as well as among other female mystics. Hildegard of Bingen writes, "God showed me his grace, again as … when a mother offers her weeping child milk …"; Hadewijch speaks of the soul being nursed with motherly care; Bridget explains that "this bird represents God, who brings forth every soul like a mother" (Spearing, 2002). This emphasis on God as mother coincided with a general shift in the Middle Ages toward an emphasis on Christ's humanity, with God inhabiting a suffering human body, culminating in the mutilation of that body in the Passion and Crucifixion (Spearing, 2002). Christ's bodily experiences of bleeding, feeding us with his blood and body were likened to those of what a mother does for her child. The maternal love of the Virgin as the universal mother of all Christians also contributed to an image of God as mother. Julian choses motherhood to describe God's love because she regards it as the purest, most selfless, most moving form of human love. Notably, Kuan Yin is seen as a compassionate mother who will bring relief for suffering, and specifically she is prayed to by women who desire children.

Julian has been attributed with the most developed concept of the reconceptualization of Christ as female through her theology of God as mother. However, a close reading of her text suggests that she is not simply substituting female for male. In fact, Julian subverts the gender dichotomy that this metaphor reinforces: "And so I saw that God rejoices that he is our father, and God rejoices that he is our mother, and God rejoices that he is our true husband, and our soul his beloved wife" (Julian of Norwich, 1966, p. 151). Julian speaks of creation as a maternal act because God, in taking on humanity in the Incarnation, gives himself to us as a mother gives herself the fetus she bears (Bynum, 1992, p. 206). God has made himself totally vulnerable by embodying himself as human in the life of Jesus through Mary.

Historically contextualized, the notion of Christ as female was quite accepted within medieval theological doctrine. Both male and female mystics called Jesus "mother" in his eucharistic feeding of Christians with liquid that exuded from his breast and in his bleeding on the cross, which gave birth to our hope of eternal life. Jesus took on female characteristics through the eucharist of nourishing with his body and blood. Both male and female mystics saw Christ as female. Male mystics (among them Bernard of Clairvaux, Francis of Assisi, Richard Rolle) whose religiosity was most experiential and visionary, often described themselves in feminine images and learned their pious practices from women. Yet, taking up the notion of Christ as female took on different meanings for religious men and women. For monks and church officials, this signification might have been an expression of a desire to "project a more loving, less authoritarian image of leadership" (Lerner, 1993, p. 89). This was not insignificant since it occured at the time when the church was under severe criticism and attack for its elitism. This symbolism of Christ as female also coincided simultaneously not with an increase in women's power in the church but the curtailment of women's power.

This image of God as mother is quite congruent with dominant medieval conceptions of gender as more fluid. Julian's appropriation of God as female is perhaps more complex. If we look at the quote above, Julian resists a unitary reading of God as female. God is both male and female. What Julian does is to reconceptualize the son of God as *both* male and female, thus disrupting the very notion of gender as binary. Julian writes:

> And thus in our Creation God almighty is our kindly father, and God who is all wisdom is our kindly Mother, with the love and the goodness of the Holy Ghost-all of Whom are one God and one Lord ... Thus in our Father God we have our being, and in our mother of mercy we have our reforming and our restoration, in Whom all parts are united and all made into perfect end, and by the yielding and giving grace of the Holy Ghost we are fulfilled ... for our nature is whole in each person of the Trinity which is one God. (Julian of Norwich, as quoted in Lerner, 1993, p. 90)

This disruption of gender as a binary functions on two levels. First, it disrupts traditional notions of women as evil and sinful. This functions for Julian as a form of rebellion to normative gender roles. Second, it suggests that dualisms such as male/female deter us from more holistic, integrated, and interrelational modes of being that are the basis for love and compassion. In fact, according to Thomas Long (1995), it is the union of binary opposites (like male/female, yin/yang, mind/body) that are required for enlightenment or wisdom.

Radical Compassion

Jantzen (1987) maintains that Julian's theology is one in which "the love of God that is manifested in the wounded Christ becomes the salvation of humankind" (p. 67). For Julian, her mediation of Christ on the cross results in such a profound and sensual experience that it goes beyond the senses and beyond words: "his suffering and self-abnegation so far surpasses anything we might experience that we shall never wholly understand it" (Julian of Norwich, 1966, p. 105). God's unconditional love is incomprehensible. Likewise, Kuan Yin's compassion has no boundaries or conditions. Both Kuan Yin and Julian experience suffering, not in order to "understand the other" but to be transformed by experiencing love. Merton (1968) maintains that "since ordinary everyday human existence is full of confusion and suffering, then obviously one will make good use of both of these in order to transform one's awareness and one's understanding, and to go beyond both to attain 'wisdom' in love" (p. 51). Both Kuan Yin and Julian emerge from suffering and illness with an embodied relationality. Kuan Yin is present to the suffering in the world and "hears the cries of the world." Julian is present to the suffering of Christ on the cross. It is the living experience of "being" in relation that transcends all conceptual formulations. Merton maintains that "being is not an abstract objective idea but a fundamental concrete intuition directly apprehended in personal experience that is incontrovertible and inexpressible" (p. 26). Compassion becomes a way of being and knowing in the world. It is an epistemology grounded in interrelatedness (thus disrupting notions of self/other and the binary of gender), in an integrated experience of body, mind and spirit; one that is deeply grounded in daily experience. Wisdom or knowledge is thus not about transcending the body, or emptying the self, but of being present to others, being in relation.

The emphasis on compassion and love in the narratives of Kuan Yin and Julian speak to a profound epistemological shift. Knowing begins when we empty ourselves through suffering and death. This emptying and death of the egocentric autonomous self enables compassionate engagement. The transfiguration trope in both the narratives of Kuan Yin and Julian are similar to traditional Buddhist and Christian enlightenment narratives. There is suffering, death, and rebirth. What is significant is that *rebirth* takes on new meaning in these two narratives. Rather than transcending (like Jesus or Buddha), both of these narratives suggest that transformation occurs through staying embodied—literally, in relation to others—in experience and in the body.

It is through acts of compassion that we know and become. While caring and compassion have traditionally been seen as "feminine ways of knowing" and thus targets of the criticism of essentialism, these narratives suggest an epistemology that is predicated on abandoning distinctions of sex and gender. Compassionate knowing is one that rejects binaries like male/female, king/peasant, self/other, black/white. Compassion necessitates that we must see beyond these worldly categories. The disruption of gender in both narratives—Kuan Yin's gender transformation from male to female and Julian's transgendered understanding of the divine and thus love—are radical disruptions of a binary concept of gender. In deessentializing gender, they provide a way to think of an epistemology of compassion that does not reproduce feminine or masculine ways of knowing. This third space provides a place in which to envision social justice from an epistemology of compassion where being present to others is a mode of acknowledging injustice in the world.

Notes

1. See Hendry 2005.
2. Rebellion is understood here as a form of disrupting or resisting dominant ideologies through the use of nonviolent forms.
3. These stages are also referred to as the three classic states of the fire of love, the spiritual marriage, and the inward light.
4. According to Underhill (1911), non-Christian mystics have made a forced choice between these two dogmatic expressions of their experiences. The two chief features of Christian schematic theology are the Trinity and Incarnation, and Christian mystics make room for both.
5. For a full account of the multiple myths and legends of Kuan Yin, see Palmer and Ramsay (1995).
6. According to Stone (1979), the most detailed accounts of Nu Kwa's creation of all people, and her repair of the universe, are from texts of the Han period (200 B.C.E.–200 C.E.). They appear in the writings known as the *Lieh Tzu*, the *Feng Su Tung Yi*, and the *Shan Hai Ching*. But according to Chinese tradition, the story of Nu Kwa repairing the universe dates to about 2500 B.C.E.
7. Edwards (1991) speculates that by masculinizing her origins that storytellers were trying to grapple with the reality of the Goddess in a patriarchal context.
8. While the Confucian self is predicated on intersubjectivity, this relational self is one that is the result of a predetermined set of rules and obligations that are to be followed and obeyed without question.
9. By *third way* I mean a space between the dualisms of activity/passivity, revolution/ acquiessence, revolt/conformity.
10. In fact, she wrote her experiences twice: once in a short text, written immediately after her revelations, and then again 20 years later, after she had received continuous inward instruction on their meaning.
11. Anchorite was one of several religious vocations taken up by women during the Middle Ages. They did not necessarily belong to a religious order, but did need the approval of the Bishop in order to be enclosed. While the symbolic notion of being dead was present, anchorites, while being physically enclosed, often provided counsel and guidance to others even though they never left their cells. Persons would speak to an anchorite through a black curtain that was hung in front of a small window in the cell. For more information on Julian's life as an anchorite, see P. Hendry (2005).

References

Bartlett, E. (1992). Beyond either/or: Justice and care in the ethics of Albert Camus. In E. B. Cole & S. Coultrap-McQuin (Eds.). *Explorations in Feminist ethics* (pp. 82–88). Bloomington: Indiana University Press.

Blofeld, J. (1977). *Bodhisattva of compassion*. Boston: Shambala.

Brueggemann, W. (2001). *The prophetic imagination*. Minneapolis, MN: Fortress Press.

Colish, M. (1997). *Medieval foundations of the Western intellectual tradition 400–1400*. New Haven, CT: Yale University Press.

Dudbridge, G. (1978). *The legend of Miao-shan*. London: Ithaca Press.

Edwards, C. M. (1991). *The storyteller's goddess*. San Francisco: HarperCollins.

Flinders, C. (1993). *Enduring grace: Living portraits of seven women mystics*. San Francisco: Harper and Row.

Gawronski, R. (1995). *Word and silence: Hans Urs von Balthasar and the spiritual encounter between East and West*. Grand Rapids, MI: Eerdsmans.

Gilligan, C. (1982). *In a different voice: Psychological theory and women's development*. Cambridge, MA: Harvard University Press.

Gilmore, L. (1994). *Autobiographics: A feminist theory of women's representation*. Ithaca, NY: Cornell University Press.

Groenhoot, R. (1998). Care theory and the ideal of neutrality in public moral discourse. *Journal of Medicine and Philosophy, 23*, 179–189.

Hendry, P. (2005). Disrupting the subject: Julian of Norwich and embodied knowing. *Journal of Curriculum Theorizing, 21*(1), 95–108.

Jantzen, G. (1987). *Julian of Norwich: Mystic and theologian*. Wiltshire, England: Cromwell Press.

Jantzen, G. M. (1995). *Power, gender and Christian mysticism*. Cambridge, England: Cambridge University Press.

Julian of Norwich. (1966). *Revelations of divine love* (Ed. and trans. C. Wolters). Harmondsworth, England: Penguin.

Klein, A. (1994). *Meeting the great bliss queen: Buddhists, feminists, and the art of self*. Boston: Beacon Press.

Klein, A. (2004). Buddhist understandings of subjectivity. In Tsomo, K. L. (Ed.), *Buddhist women and social justice* (pp. 23–34). Albany: State University of New York Press.

Kolbenschlag, M. (1996). *Eastward toward Eve*. New York: Crossroad.

Lerner, G. (1993). *The creation of feminist consciousness*. New York: Oxford University Press.

Long, T. (1995, March 18). *Julian of Norwich's 'Christ as Mother' and medieval construction of gender*. Paper presented at the Madison Conference on English Studies, James Madison University, Harrisonburg, Virginia.

Merton, T. (1968). *Zen and the birds of appetite*. New York: New Directions.

Noddings, N. (1984). *Caring: A feminine approach to ethics and moral education*. Berkeley and Los Angeles: University of California Press.

Palmer, M., & Ramsay, J. (with M. Kwok). (1995). *Kuan Yin: Myths and prophecies of the Chinese goddess of compassion*. San Francisco: HarperCollins.

Paul, D. (1985). *Women in Buddhism: Images of the feminine in Mayana tradition*. Berkeley and Los Angeles: University of California Press.

Sangern, P. (1983). Female gender in Chinese religious symbols: Kuan Yin, Ma Tsu, and the "Eternal Mother." *Signs, 9*(1), 4–25.

Silvade, L. A. (1979). *The problem of the self in Buddhism and Christianity*. London: Macmillan.

Spearing, E. (2002). *Medieval writings on female spirituality*. New York: Penguin.

Stone, M. (1979). *Ancient mirrors of womanhood*. Boston: Beacon Press.

Strong, J. S. (2002). *The experience of Buddhism*. Belmont, CA: Wadsworth.

Tong, R. (1998). The ethics of care: A feminist virtue ethics of care for healthcare practitioners. *Journal of Medicine and Philosophy, 23*, 131–152.

Underhill, E. (1911). *Mysticism: A study in the nature and development of man's spiritual consciousness*. London: Methuen.

Underhill, E. (1925). *The Mystics of the Church*. Cambridge, England: Clark.

Wang, H. (2004). *The call from the stranger on a journey home: Curriculum in a third space*. New York: Lang.

Yu, J. (2004). *The image of Kuan-Yin: An indicator of vicissitudes of women in the history of China*. Unpublished manuscript.

CHAPTER 9

Eastern Wisdom and Holistic Education
Multidimensional Reality and the Way of Awareness

Yoshiharu Nakagawa
Ritsumeikan University

When we approach traditions of Eastern thought, we can follow two different directions, and each would equally contribute to reaching greater understanding. One way involves examining each tradition and respecting the uniqueness of different perspectives. The other way entails investigating the basic structures underlying Buddhism, Confucianism, Hinduism, Sufism, Taoism, and other schools of thought and uncovering remarkable resonances. This chapter follows this second direction. I draw extensively on cross-cultural resources including classical scriptures, texts, and the sayings of sages in the domain of Eastern thought in order to show deep interconnections and reveal how different traditions share a path of increasing awareness.

Another aim of this chapter is to provide a philosophical basis for holistic education, which emerged in the late 1980s in North America and has achieved global prominence as a significant outgrowth of Western postmodernism (J. P. Miller, 1988/1996; R. Miller, 1990/1997). Holistic education has been particularly active in bringing the teachings of spiritual traditions into curriculum and pedagogy (Miller, 1994, 1999, 2006). Eastern philosophies have been playing increasingly important roles in this endeavor, and my own research has been directed toward elaborating the possibilities involved in this East–West conversation (see Miller & Nakagawa, 2002; Nakagawa, 2000). This chapter summarizes the basic points I have developed and introduces some further thoughts on this undertaking.

Multidimensional Views of Reality

What strikes me as particularly fascinating about Eastern thought is the multidimensional view of reality that it elucidates. As Toshihiko Izutsu, a distinguished scholar of Eastern philosophies, states in his *Sufism and Taoism* (1983/1984), "Existence or reality as 'experienced' on supra-sensible levels reveals itself as of a multistratified structure. The reality one observes in this kind of metaphysical intuition is not of a unistratum structure" (p. 479). In general terms, this multidimensional reality encompasses three phases: the surface dimension of separate things, various intermediate dimensions, and the deepest dimensions of Brahman, Sunyata, and Tao.

We can take Taoist scriptures as an example. Taoist philosophy regards *Tao*, or *wu* (nonbeing), as the deepest reality, out of which all the other dimensions of being emerge. Lao-Tzu (2001) writes, "The ten thousand things under heaven are born out of Being. Being is born out of Non-Being" (p. 104). Describing this in symbolic numbers, he adds, "The Way [Tao] begets one. One begets two. Two begets three. And three begets the ten thousand things" (p. 108). Another important Taoist philosopher, Chuang Tzu (1968), remarks in a similar way that "[i]n the Great Beginning, there was nonbeing; there was no being, no name. Out of it arose One; there was One, but it had no form. Things got hold of it and came to life, and it was called Virtue" (p. 131).

Tao as nonbeing is the groundless and "nameless" depth. Izutsu (1983/1984) regards it as "the absolute in its absoluteness, or existence at its ultimate stage, qua something unknown/unknowable, transcending all qualifications, determinations, and relations" (p. 486). Then, nonbeing evolves into "one." The "one" is located between nonbeing and being with a chaotic potency toward being. Izutsu (1983/1984) writes, "The one is ... the metaphysical unity of all things, the primordial unity in which all things lie hidden in a state of 'chaos' without being as yet actualized as the ten thousand things" (p. 400). Tao creates the universe by articulating the primordial one into "two," namely *yin* (the passive force) and *yang* (the active force), and interactions between these two forces give rise to all phenomenal things.

Likewise, according to the Neo-Confucian metaphysics, *wu-chi* (the ultimate of nonbeing) is the deepest dimension of reality, and *t'ai chi* (the great ultimate) is the primordial unity that generates yin and yang (Chan, 1963, p. 463; see also Izutsu, 1976). These views recognize the metaphysical source from which the whole universe emerges and takes its form. *The Secret of the Golden Flower* (Cleary, 1991), a classic of Taoist meditation, clearly describes the sequence of creation starting from the "original spirit" to the universe as follows:

> From the point of view of the universe, people are like mayflies; but from the point of view of the Way, even the universe is as an evanescent reflection. Only the true essence of the original spirit transcends the primal organization and is above it.
>
> Vitality and energy degenerate along with the universe, but the original spirit is still there; this is the infinite. The production of the universe all derives from this. If learners can just preserve the original spirit, they live transcendentally outside of *yin* and *yang*. (p. 13)

The following discussion outlines more fully a multidimensional structure of reality found in Eastern thought. I am largely guided by Izutsu's basic framework presented variously throughout his later works (Izutsu, 1979, 1980, 1983, 1985), although the materials specifically referred to in this chapter have been chosen from diverse sources.

The Phenomenal World of Things and Its Construction of the Mind

The surface plane of reality is the phenomenal and empirical world in which myriad things are perceived as objective, material, and separate substances. This objective reality is often marked by such qualities as diversification, differentiation, and fragmentation. Even though it looks objective enough, it is a specific view of reality produced by what Izutsu calls "subjective fabrication" or "semantic articulation" of the mind. This function of the mind molds the immediate, inarticulate state of sensory experience into an ordered world of things. As Izutsu (1979) describes it:

> The essential mechanism of the mind … is such that it immediately transforms this bewildering chaos of sense data into an ordered world by producing within itself sensory images having their structural basis in the semantic evocations of words. (p. 436)

The mind articulates immediate chaos into a meaningful world of things by forming "sense images" in accordance with the "semantic configuration" of language. Underlying the surface level of myriad things is a semantic construction of reality. An object is given meaning and identity by language.

It is very interesting to note that the function of the mind was fully recognized by ancient Eastern philosophers. For Lao-Tzu (2001), Tao is hidden and nameless, but "The Named is the mother of ten thousand things" (p. 28). The *Awakening of Faith* (Hakeda, 1967), a Mahayana Buddhist classic, claims that the appearance of different things comes from the "deluded mind," or conceptual thinking:

> Since all things are, without exception, developed from the mind and produced under the condition of deluded thoughts, all differentiations are no other than the differentiations of one's mind itself. [Yet] the mind cannot perceive the mind itself; the mind has no marks of its own [that can be ascertained as a substantial entity as such]. It should be understood that [the conception of] the entire world of objects can be held only on the basis of man's deluded mind of ignorance. (p. 48)

Philosophers in the East have recognized the constructive function of the mind to give rise to apparent separation among things, but they also underline that it is simultaneously the primary cause of our delusive perception of reality, for the true nature of reality is disclosed only when the function of the mind is suspended or ceases to be.

Sankara (1979/1992), the greatest philosopher of Advaita Vedanta, or the nondualistic thought in the Vedanta school in India, sees that *avidya* (ignorance or nescience) produces phenomenal differences: "Nescience is [defined as] the superimposition of the qualities of one [thing] upon another" (p. 235). That is to say, a quality that does not refer to *Atman* is superimposed upon Atman. Superimposition is the primary function of the mind (*manas*) to discriminate the one into the many. Indeed, the phenomenal world is a fabrication of superimposition, and it is in this sense that Advaita Vedanta regards this world as an illusion (*maya*). Sankara notes, "This whole [universe] is qualification, like a beautiful ornament, which is superimposed [upon *Atman*] through nescience. Therefore, when *Atman* has been known, the whole [universe] becomes non-existent" (p. 116).

Eastern philosophers understand that difficulties and suffering arise from our exclusive identification with the delusive function of the mind and with the apparent surface dimension of separate things thus produced. Therefore, their essential teachings are centered upon liberating people from the delusive perception created by the mind.

The Intermediate Realms of Imagination

Delving into deeper realms of reality, the world becomes more subtle, fluid, and chaotic. To use James Hillman's (1975) conception, the intermediate dimension is a vast imaginative world of the "soul." Underneath "sensory images" correlated to phenomenal things exist the archetypal, mythic, and symbolic images that produce imaginative pictures of reality—namely, images of deities, spirits, celestial beings, metaphysical lands and realms. Many Eastern traditions developed their own wondrous imaginative worlds: the mythic world of Hinduism, the celestial worlds of religious Taoism, the symbolism of the *I Ching*, the cosmic world of Abhidharma Buddhism, the cosmological worlds of buddhas and bodhisattvas in the celestial "buddha fields" described in Mahayana Buddhist scriptures, and the mandalas of Tantric Buddhism.

Izutsu specifically refers to *mundus imaginalis (alam al-mithal)*, the world of archetypal images developed in Sufism. With regard to this concept, Henry Corbin (1984/1995), a French philosopher of Islamic mysticism, recognizes threefold universes corresponding to threefold modes of perception; namely, the "physical sensory world," the "suprasensory world of the Soul," and the "universe of pure archangelic Intelligences" (p. 8). The corresponding organs of perception are the senses, the imagination, and the intellect. The mundus imaginalis is an intermediate world, "a world as ontologically real as the world of the senses and the world of the intellect" (p. 9). About the intermediate status of images, one of the greatest Sufi poets and masters, Jalaluddin Rumi (1994), has remarked in his discourse:

> In comparison with the world of concepts and sensibilities, the world of mental images is broader because all concepts are born of mental images; but the world of mental images is narrow in relation to the world where mental images are given being. (p. 203)

In addition, regarding Ibn Arabi's notion of "Creative Imagination," Corbin (1958/1969) notes that

> the world of Idea-Images, the world of apparitional forms and of bodies in the subtle state (*alam al-mithal*) to which our imaginative faculty specifically relates, is the intermediary between the world of pure spiritual realities, the world of Mystery, and the visible, sensible world. (p. 217)

The imaginative world is real in the sense of having its "immaterial materiality." Here the imagination is not attributed only to a human faculty but has its own presence in reality. It is an ontological organ of the creative manifestation of the divine, called "theophany." Corbin (1958/1969) writes, "As such, creation is an act of the divine imaginative power: this divine creative imagination is essentially a theophanic Imagination" (p. 182). The creative imagination articulates the archetypal images of many sorts as self-manifestations of the absolute mystery.

The archetypal images appearing in the imaginative world have, therefore, their own meanings, even though they appear to be absurd fantasies to our common-sense rational mind. Izutsu (1979) states that

> the symbolic images which make their appearance in the mythopoetic space of that psychic domain are extremely valuable in that the figures of the things looming up through the mist of these images do represent the primeval configurations of a reality which are psychically far more real and more relevant to the fate and existence of man than the sensory reality established at the surface level of consciousness. (p. 443)

The Deepest Reality and the Twofold Movement of Contemplation

Even the wondrous pictures of archetypal images, however, are not the deepest reality for Eastern thinkers, because reality is absolutely formless and infinite on the ultimate plane. The ultimate dimension of reality is diversely called *nirguna Brahman* (formless absolute) in Vedanta, *nirvana* (extinction) in early Buddhism, *sunyata* (emptiness) and *h'sin* (pure consciousness) in Mahayana Buddhism, *Tao* and *wu* (nonbeing) in Taoism, *wu-chi* (the ultimate principle of nonbeing) and *li* (principle) in Neo-Confucianism, *wu* or *mu* (nothingness) in Ch'an/Zen Buddhism, and *haqq* (truth) in Sufism. Izutsu himself calls it the "Zero Point of Consciousness and Existence," to mean "the absolute unarticulated."

Regarding these concepts, it is not necessary to prove whether they all signify the same single ultimate reality, for this kind of discussion might surely bring us bewildering questions with no exit and oppositions with no resolution. Rather, my approach agrees with Jorge Ferrer's (2002) recommendation of "a more relaxed spiritual universalism" that recognizes that "*the various traditions lead to the enactment of different spiritual ultimates and/or transconceptual disclosures of reality*" (p. 147; emphasis in the original). At this point, my emphasis is on the very simple fact that all those concepts mentioned above are identical in trying to describe something infinite beyond any qualifications. Following Huston Smith's (1976, pp. 54–55) reference to the "Infinite," this dimension may be called "infinite reality."

In the East, multidimensional ideas of reality have been inseparably united with the practice of contemplation or meditation. Eastern traditions of wisdom have developed a great variety of spiritual practices to attain infinite reality by transforming our consciousness and existence. The full realization of infinite reality is called *samadhi* (nondual ecstasy), *moksha* (perfect liberation), *turiya* (the highest awareness), *sambodhi* (authentic awakening), *satori* (enlightenment), *fana* (annihilation or passing away), *rig-pa* (the state of presence), and so forth. From the ancient times, Easterners have taken such inner transformations to be the ideal way of life.

However, a critical point is that many traditions do not regard just attaining infinite reality as the final phase of contemplation. This accomplishment actually covers only the first half of the way. If one sees infinite reality as the final destination, one will fall into false attachment to it, which will lead to serious dualism between realities. Contrary to much common Western perception, Eastern thought does not represent infinite reality as a transcendental realm clearly distinct from the ordinary world. This means that a spiritual seeker has to disidentify with attachment of *any* kind, even to infinite reality as such, in a ceaseless movement of disidentification.

The *prajna-paramita* (the perfection of wisdom) thought of Mahayana Buddhism mostly discusses this issue. For example, the *Diamond Sutra* (Price & Wong, 1990) says, "A bodhisattva should develop a mind that alights upon nothing whatsoever; and so should he establish it" (p. 28). There is no absolute abode where one can eternally dwell, even when she is fully enlightened. This point is elaborated by the concept of *sunyata* (emptiness). Sunyata does not indicate a transcendental realm separated from the other dimensions of being, but a dynamic ceaseless movement toward emptying any representations, including the very conception of sunyata. If it were viewed as a separate realm, it would have its own substance as opposed to the dimension of being. Therefore, as the modern Zen philosopher Keiji Nishitani (1961/1982) remarks, "Emptiness in the sense of sunyata is emptiness only when it empties itself even of the standpoint that represents it as some 'thing' that is emptiness" (p. 96).

In the ceaseless movement of "self-emptying," any dualism between nonbeing and being disappears, and sunyata becomes one with being. Nishitani (1961/1982) adds that "true emptiness is not to be posited as something outside of and other than 'being.' Rather, it is to be realized as something united to and self-identical with being" (pp. 96–97). Masao Abe (1985) is clear on this point: "True Emptiness and wondrous Being are completely non-dualistic: absolute Mu [Nothingness] and ultimate Reality are totally identical" (p. 130).

Here, *nirvana* becomes one with *samsara*, which originally means "cyclic existence" through rebirths and, in the Mahayana context, this phenomenal world of transition. Therefore, Nagarjuna (1995), the founder of the Madhyamika school of Mahayana Buddhism, remarks, "There is not the slightest difference / Between cyclic existence and nirvana" (p. 75). In one of the essential texts of Ch'an Buddhism, *On Trust in the Mind*, Seng-ts'an (1993), the third patriarch of Ch'an, or Chinese Zen, describes the nondualistic nature of reality as follows: "Being—this is nonbeing, nonbeing—this is being. Any view at variance with this must not be held!" (p. 152).

To put this in a different way, there is a turning point of contemplation from the seeking to the returning mode: once the seeker attains infinite reality, he has to return immediately to all the other levels without any attachment to it. The twofold movement of seeking and returning, which is traditionally called ascent and descent, marks a dynamic character found in many Eastern spiritual practices. Whereas the seeking path negates anything, the phenomenal and the imaginative on all levels, through and through to attain the infinite, the returning path reveals the positive and creative activities of the infinite that engender all beings on the other levels. As Izutsu (1977/1982) comments:

> The Oriental Nothingness is not a purely negative ontological state of there being nothing. On the contrary, it is a plenitude of Being. It is so full that it cannot as such be identified as anything determined, anything special. But it is, on the other hand, so full that it can manifest itself as anything in the empirical dimension of our experience, as a crystallization of the whole spiritual energy contained therein. (p. 82)

In the returning mode, both phenomenal and imaginative beings reappear as the self-manifestations of infinite reality. Izutsu (1983/1984) states, "In the eye of those who have experienced this spiritual awakening, all things, each in its own form and on its own level, manifest the presence of 'something beyond'" (p. 481). In this resurrection the infinite permeates all levels, tracing no division between them. Izutsu notes, "The only 'reality' (in the true sense of the term) is the Absolute, revealing itself as it really is in the sensible forms which are nothing but the loci of its self-manifestation" (p. 480). Here, each finite being in this world comes to appear as an absolute wondrous being. Even a tiny thing in this world reveals the infinite as it actually is. For instance, *The Flower Ornament Scripture* (Cleary, 1984/1993), the principal sutra of Huayen Buddhism (see also Izutsu, 1980), conveys this phase in many beautiful descriptions, one of which says as follows: "In the atoms of all lands / Are seen

Buddhas existing there" (p. 215). By way of twofold contemplation of seeking and returning, the Eastern approach recovers the wholeness of multidimensional reality as actualized in each existence.

Ordinary Life as the Ultimate Reality

Viewed from Eastern perspectives, it is *this* world disclosed in great awakening or full enlightenment that is truly the ultimate reality. The ultimate reality thus realized is called *tathata* (suchness) in Mahayana Buddhism, *baqa* (abiding in God) in Sufism, and *saguna Brahman* in Advaita Vedanta. As D. T. Suzuki (1956/1996) notes:

> *Tathata* is the viewing of things as they are: it is an affirmation through and through. I see a tree, and I state that it is a tree; I hear a bird sing and I say that a bird sings; a spade is a spade, and a mountain is a mountain; the fowls of the air fly and the flowers of the field bloom: these are statements of *tathata*. (p. 263)

As Suzuki describes here, tathata is the absolute affirmation of things as they are, but it is fundamentally different from the ordinary state of perception that objectifies things. It is made possible in the returning phase of contemplation, after one attains wisdom (*prajna*) of sunyata, or the true empty nature of things.

Sufism maintains that *fana* (annihilation) leads to *baqa* by way of *fana al-fana*. Like sunyata, fana finally annihilates the consciousness of fana as such. R. A. Nicholson (1914/1989) remarks, "The highest stage of *fana* is reached when even the consciousness of having attained *fana* disappears. This is what the Sufis call 'the passing-away of passing-away' (*fana al-fana*). The mystic is now rapt in contemplation of the divine essence" (pp. 60–61). In the state of baqa, one returns to this world and reexperiences it as the sheer manifestation of the divine. Nicholson writes:

> To abide in God (*baqa*) after having passed-away from selfhood (*fana*) is the mark of the Perfect Man, who not only journeys to God, i.e. passes from plurality to unity, but *in* and *with* God, i.e. continuing in the unitive state, he returns with God to the phenomenal world from which he set out, and manifests unity in plurality. (p. 163)

Whereas the seeking path of contemplation deconstructs all beings in order to attain infinite reality, the returning path reconstructs them all as they are. With regard to this point, Advaita Vedanta discerns the two faces of

Brahman: *nirguna* and *saguna*. While *nirguna Brahman* means infinite reality transcending any qualifications, *saguna Brahman* means the aspect of Brahman that has reappeared through human consciousness. According to Eliot Deutsch (1969), "*Saguna Brahman—Brahman* with qualities—is *Brahman* as interpreted and affirmed by the mind from its necessarily limited standpoint" (p. 12). Saguna Brahman is the phenomenal appearance of *nirguna* Brahman through human conditions. Brahman is now known in the fullness of beings in the cosmos as saguna Brahman. S. Radhakrishnan (1953/1994), a representative Indian philosopher, explains:

> *Brahman* is not merely a featureless Absolute. It is all this world. ... *Brahman* sustains the cosmos and is the self of each individual. Supra-cosmic transcendence and cosmic universality are both real phases of the one Supreme. In the former aspect the Spirit is in no way dependent on the cosmic manifold; in the latter the Spirit functions as the principle of the cosmic manifold. The supra-cosmic silence and the cosmic integration are both real. The two, *nirguna* and *saguna Brahman*, Absolute and God, are not different. (p. 64)

As these concepts clearly show, the Eastern approach to human life is not nihilistic in the sense of just escaping from this world, but it is fundamentally positive in that it promotes full engagement with everyday life; it is a way to awaken us to the profound richness of our ordinary life thus realized.

This is why Ch'an/Zen masters have always emphasized everydayness. Lin Chi (1993), one of the greatest masters, states:

> Followers of the Way, the Dharma of the buddhas calls for no special understandings. Just act ordinary, without trying to do anything particular. Move your bowels, piss, get dressed, eat your rice, and if you get tired, then lie down. Fools may laugh at me, but wise men will know what I mean. (p. 31)

Needless to say, everyday ordinariness such as this is realized as tathata in one's enlightenment. This is related to a further remarkable quality of those who have attained enlightenment, which is commonly described in the scriptures of Eastern wisdom. Here are a few examples from different traditions. The *Bhagavad Gita* (Radhakrishnan, 1948/1973), the most beloved scripture in India, celebrates a sage who has attained Atman as follows: "He whose mind is untroubled in the midst of sorrows and is free from eager desire amid pleasures, he from whom passion, fear, and rage have passed away, he is called a sage of settled intelligence" (p. 123). One of the most well-known Buddhist classics, the *Dhammapada* (Radhakrishnan, 1950), says: "Those whose minds are well grounded in the (seven) elements of enlightenment, who without clinging to anything rejoice in freedom from attachment, whose appetites have been conquered, who are full of light, attain *nirvana* in this world" (p. 87). And Chuang Tzu (1968) addresses the "true man" in the Taoist sense: "The True Man of ancient times knew nothing of loving life, knew nothing of hating death. He emerged without delight; he went back in without a fuss. He came briskly, he went briskly, and that was all" (p. 78). These descriptions eloquently refer to a total liberation from attachment of any kind to the positive as well as to the negative in everyday life. This quality comes from selfless stillness opened up in one's enlightenment.

Furthermore, true compassion flows out through such liberated persons, for compassion is essentially the self-manifestation of the infinite into this world through their selfless activities in taking care of things in wholehearted ways. They can really commit to actual issues in everyday life more intensely without self-interested attachment and with boundless compassion and creativity. Mahayana Buddhism highlights *karuna*, or compassion, in this sense, and, in recent years, engaged Buddhism has focused on critical and transformative orientations in the social actions of compassion.

Disidentification in the Art of Awareness

The truth of Eastern wisdom is not authorized without one's spiritual cultivation and inner transformation, because it is essentially a practical teaching to be explored by each. For example, Dōgen (1985), the distinguished Zen thinker of medieval Japan, values *zazen* (sitting meditation) as the true gate to the Buddhist teachings:

> All buddha tathagatas, who directly transmit inconceivable dharma and actualize supreme, perfect enlightenment, have a wondrous way, unsurpassed and unconditioned. Only buddhas transmit it to buddhas without veering off; self-fulfilling samadhi is its standard. Sitting upright, practicing Zen, is the authentic gate to the unconfined realm of this samadhi. (p. 143)

In terms of multidimensional reality, the primary task of spiritual cultivation is to help us do away with the surface level and explore the deeper levels of reality. This is why Eastern teachers celebrate disidentification through and through. Advaita Vedanta is very clear on this process, developing the method of negation called *neti neti*, or "not-this, not-this." Sankara (1979/1992) claims that only *vidya*, or the true knowledge of Atman, removes primordial ignorance caused by superimposition. He used to ask his students: "Who are you, my dear?" If they answered the question with reference to qualifications such as social position, family class, bodily existence, and so on, he immediately disclosed that those qualifications were not Atman. Any identification with them must be negated: "One attains [Atman] in some such way as 'I am not this. I am not this'" (p. 108).

Sri Ramana Maharshi (1959), one of India's greatest modern mystics, recommends that people ask "Who am I?" to see where the path of negation will take them:

> Who Am I? I am not this physical body, nor am I the five organs of sense perception; I am not the five organs of external activity, nor am I the five vital forces, nor am I even the thinking mind. ... (pp. 39–40)

Walking throughout the path of negation, that which ultimately remains is what truly I am. Maharshi goes on to note:

> Therefore, summarily rejecting all the above-mentioned physical adjuncts and their functions, saying "I am not this; no, nor am I this, nor this"—that which then remains separate and alone by itself, that pure Awareness is what I am. This Awareness is by its very nature Sat-Chit-Ananda (Existence-Consciousness-Bliss). (p. 40)

This brief statement clearly describes the seeking path of contemplation, and I will now discuss it further in terms of awareness.

Among various significant paths of spiritual development, the art of awareness is an essential method of disidentification that enhances the level of awareness and eventually leads to a great awakening. In an excellent guidebook for this method, Charles Tart (1994) states, "I can summarize the essence of the higher spiritual paths simply by saying, be openly aware of everything, all the time" (p. 25). The art of awareness is a simple method of carefully noticing what is actually going on in the present moment as it is, without any interference or distortion. Awareness in this sense is alternately called *attention*, *mindfulness*, *witness*, *observation*, or *presence* in meditative traditions such as early Buddhism, Sufism, Zen, and Dzogchen. And teachers like Ram Dass, G. I. Gurdjieff, and Jiddu Krishnamurti have always emphasized the central importance of awareness in our spiritual development.

The ordinary state of our consciousness is almost always occupied with predominant forces of the mind, body, and emotions. It is unconsciously and automatically identified with physical, emotional, and/or mental responses.

Therefore, ordinary consciousness is often metaphorically called a "dreaming" process in "sleep" without awareness. This is why "awakening" has a special meaning in this context. As Chuang Tzu (1968) writes, "Only after he wakes does he know it was a dream. And someday there will be a great awakening when we know that this is all a great dream" (p. 47). The word *awakening* has been used as a common metaphor among spiritual traditions to describe a radical transformation of consciousness. In Buddhism, for instance, "the Buddha" means "the awakened one," and the whole effort of Buddhist practice is dedicated to attain *bodhi,* or awakening.

The continual practice of awareness could eventually bring us to the point where no identification remains and in this great awakening even the observing self is finally dissolved into the boundless ocean of pure awareness. As the *Ashtavakra Gita* (Byron, 1990), a classic belonging to the lineage of Advaita Vedanta, repeatedly makes the point, the true nature of reality is "pure awareness." Having realized this by himself, another modern Indian mystic, Sri Nisargadatta Maharaj (1973/1982), states: "Awareness is primordial; it is the original state, beginningless, endless, uncaused, unsupported, without parts, without change" (p. 29). The art of awareness can bring us to a realization that there is only the infinite reality of pure awareness.

The Art of Awareness in Holistic Curriculum

The art of awareness contributes to educational practice in significant ways. Here I would like to take first Aldous Huxley's idea of awareness, for he presents a pioneering model of education using both Eastern and Western methods of awareness. Huxley (1978), in his article on the Alexander Technique (the original work appeared in the *Saturday Review of Literature*, October 25, 1941), combines this somatic method to highlight conscious direction to the body with "the mystic's technique of transcending personality in a progressive awareness of ultimate reality" (p. 150), conceiving "a totally new type of education." The following statement is still of great importance for the education of awareness:

> Be that as it may, the fact remains that Alexander's technique for the conscious mastery of the primary control is now available, and that it can be combined in the most fruitful way with the technique of the mystics for transcending personality through increasing awareness of ultimate reality. It is now possible to conceive of a totally new type of education affecting the entire range of human

activity, from the physiological, through the intellectual, moral, and practical, to the spiritual—an education which, by teaching them the proper use of the self, would preserve children and adults from most of the diseases and evil habits that now afflict them; an education whose training in inhibition and conscious control would provide men and women with the psychophysical means for behaving rationally and morally; an education which in its upper reaches, would make possible the experience of ultimate reality. (p. 152)

Finding an essential connection between psychosomatic and spiritual methods, Huxley presents a comprehensive model of the education of awareness from the elemental to the highest levels. The somatic methods such as the Alexander Technique and sensory awareness can cultivate what Huxley (1969) calls "elementary awareness." They are "somatic meditation," as it were, to increase elementary awareness by paying attention to immediate experiences of the bodily movements and senses, serving as a basis for further evolution of awareness.

Huxley (1956) also provides the idea of the "nonverbal humanities" (p. 19) that include both psychosomatic and contemplative trainings from East and West such as the Alexander Technique, Zen, and the approaches of Meister Eckhart and Krishnamurti (for a comprehensive account of Huxley's ideas on education, see Nakagawa, 2002). Huxley acknowledges the central importance of the art of awareness not only in educational curriculum but also in everyday human life. In his last novel, *Island*, Huxley (1962) calls for "the yoga of everyday living": "Be fully aware of what you're doing, and work becomes the yoga of work, play becomes the yoga of play, everyday living becomes the yoga of everyday living" (p. 149). For Huxley, awareness is the key to enlightenment. He writes, in the same novel, "Everybody's job—enlightenment. Which means, here and now, the preliminary job of practising all the yogas of increased awareness" (p. 236).

Education with a spiritual orientation is defined as an attempt for awakening or enlightenment through a continual practice of enhancing awareness. This definition follows the traditional view of contemplation that highlights the seeking path, and it is indeed an authentic view of education resulting from Eastern perspectives on spiritual cultivation.

I think, however, that the art of awareness can provide another possibility of education with regard to the returning path of contemplation, and this aspect is far less emphasized in the education of awareness. As I discussed earlier, everything resurges in the returning path as a creative manifestation of infinite reality, and this happens in pure awareness that has been cultivated in the seeking path. Nisargadatta Maharaj (1973/1982) describes, "I saw that in the ocean of pure awareness … the numberless waves of the phenomenal worlds arise and subside beginninglessly and endlessly" (p. 30). Here, the art of awareness is to witness, with compassionate eyes, what comes up from the primordial process of life. When Namkhai Norbu (1989), a Tibetan master of Dzogchen, refers to "presence," it means this function of awareness. Norbu remarks that

> the practice of Dzogchen means that one learns to relax whilst all the time maintaining one's presence in whatever circumstances one finds oneself in. Thus, in a state of total completeness, one remains relaxed and present in relation to all the infinite manifestations of energy that may arise. (p. 55)

From the depths of everyday life, a subtle event always emerges, caused contingently by inner and outer conditions, and unfolds itself into a particular form of experience such as sensation, perception, movement, imagination, feeling, emotion, or thinking. Here awareness attends to every detail of the birth, growth, decay, and passing away of each particular experience with no attachment.

The following is an instruction for meditation given by Krishnamurti (1974) in his talk to students, which is also relevant to our discussion:

> First of all, sit very quietly; do not force yourself to sit quietly, but sit or lie down quietly without force of any kind. Do you understand? Then watch your thinking. Watch what you are thinking about. You find you are thinking about your shoes, your saris, what you are going to say, the bird outside to which you listen; follow such thoughts and enquire why each thought arises. Do not try to change your thinking. See why certain thoughts arise in your mind so that you begin to understand the meaning of every thought and every feeling without any enforcement. And when a thought arises, do not condemn it, do not say it is right, it is wrong, it is good, it is bad. Just watch it, so that you begin to have a perception, a consciousness which is active in seeing every kind of thought, every kind of feeling. (p. 59)

Admittedly, Krishnamurti talks about how meditation, or what he calls "choiceless awareness," works to go beyond thinking, and it is of primal importance to see that the true nature of thought is empty and transient. However, this saying simultaneously refers to how one observes a generation of a thought in a very careful way. In the meditative state of awareness, one is fully present to what spontaneously emerges from the depth of life, then to the subsequent articulation of a form of thought, and finally to its passing away. In this way, awareness can create a space for allowing a thought to follow its course and fulfill its intrinsic meaning.

Likewise, something is always arising from the primordial depth of life and evolves into a different form of experience such as sensation, movement, imagination, feeling, emotion, intuition, or thinking. The art of awareness is to witness in a choiceless and compassionate way how a subtle event happens, and takes a definite form of experience, and then decays and passes away, leaving no desire to preserve it. Whether one is enlightened or not, or even if one is still in the initial stage of spiritual development, the art of awareness in this returning mode of contemplation becomes another significant task of spiritual practice, for the wholeness of life is definitely composed of a ceaseless flow of diverse experiences.

As we are always unconsciously caught by predominant habitual reactions that are conditioned and automatically activated, we tend to ignore subtle experiencing processes in the deeper levels of life and have only surface experiences presupposed by our belief system. However, awareness inhibits habitual reactions and attends to what is actually taking place in each moment on the deeper levels, and it creates a space for a real experience to evolve and fulfill its meaning. In doing so, it makes us possible to live our everyday lives with the full richness of real experiences.

In this way, choiceless, compassionate awareness becomes an essential component of a holistic curriculum that helps us actualize what is potent in our deep experiencing processes. In educational settings, the art of awareness—in combination with methods such as somatic techniques, visualization, creative arts, poetry, creative writing, and other expressive activities—helps students express their potentialities in sensing, moving, feeling, imaging, and thinking.

Education must affirm the multiplicity of lived experiences, because every real experience has some meaning to fulfill in our life. However, diverse experiences that happen moment by moment tend to bring fragmentation unless they are integrated. Awareness can lay a foundation for the flow of multiple experiences; with the continuous presence of awareness, even very different forms of experience flow, one after another, in a streaming manner. Herein lies what is really "holistic." If holistic education only artificially assembles different methods, it is not necessarily called holistic but still remains fragmentary approach. The integrity of holistic curriculum consists in the art of awareness that makes possible both the multiplicity and the flow of real experiences.

To sum up, the art of awareness has a twofold function; it is an essential path with which to go beyond any forms and to awaken to infinite reality, and it is also a basis for realizing every kind of real experience. These two directions must be unified; otherwise two different dangers will arise. In the first place, there is the danger of disregarding rich forms of experience when seeking something infinite and thus falling into a false, life-negating attitude. Spiritual cultivation is not intended to negate life but to realize the infinite in the midst of everyday life. The other direction brings the danger that we may forget our potentiality of enlightenment to realize the infinite nature of reality. This forgetfulness causes us to identify with each finite form of experience without insight into the fact that any form is essentially impermanent and empty. In avoiding both dangers, the art of awareness walks the middle, a way where two directions reflect each other and eventually become one process in a nondual manner.

References

Abe, M. (1985). *Zen and Western thought* (W. R. LaFleur, Ed.). Honolulu: University of Hawaii Press.

Byron, T. (Trans.). (1990). *The heart of awareness: A translation of* Ashtavakra Gita. Boston: Shambhala.

Chan, W-T. (Trans.). (1963). *A source book in Chinese philosophy.* Princeton, NJ: Princeton University Press.

Chuang Tzu. (1968). *The complete works of Chuang Tzu* (B. Watson, Trans.). New York: Columbia University Press.

Cleary, T. (Trans.). (1991). *The secret of the golden flower.* San Francisco: HarperCollins.

Cleary, T. (Trans.). (1993). *The flower ornament scripture: A translation of the* Avatamsaka Sutra. Boston: Shambhala. (Original work published 1984)

Corbin, H. (1969). *Creative imagination in the Sufism of Ibn Arabi* (R. Manheim, Trans.). Princeton, NJ: Princeton University Press. (Original work published 1958)

Corbin, H. (1995). *Swedenborg and esoteric Islam* (L. Fox, Trans.). West Chester, PA: Swedenborg Foundation. (Original work published 1984)

Deutsch, E. (1969). *Advaita Vedanta: A philosophical reconstruction.* Honolulu: University of Hawaii Press.

Dōgen (1985). *Moon in a dewdrop: Writings of Zen master Dōgen* (K. Tanahashi, Ed. & Trans.). New York: Farrar, Straus and Giroux.

Ferrer, J. N. (2002). *Revisioning transpersonal theory: A participatory vision of human spirituality.* Albany: State University of New York Press.

Hakeda, Y. (Trans.). (1967). *The awakening of faith: Attributed to Asvaghosha.* New York: Columbia University Press.

Hillman, J. (1975). *Re-visioning psychology.* New York: Harper and Row.

Huxley, A. (1956). *Adonis and the alphabet.* London: Chatto and Windus.

Huxley, A. (1962). *Island.* London: Chatto and Windus.

Huxley, A. (1969). Education on the nonverbal level. In H. Chiang & A. H. Maslow (Eds.), *The healthy personality: Readings* (pp. 150–165). New York: Van Nostrand Reinhold.

Huxley, A. (1978). End-gaining and means-whereby. In W. Barlow (Ed.), *More talk of Alexander* (pp. 149–153). London: Victor Gollancz.

Izutsu, T. (1976). The I Ching mandala and Confucian metaphysics. *Eranos Yearbook 1976, 45,* 363–404.

Izutsu, T. (1979). Between image and no-image: Far Eastern ways of thinking. *Eranos Yearbook 1979, 48,* 427–461.

Izutsu, T. (1980). The nexus of ontological events: A Buddhist view of reality. *Eranos Yearbook 1980, 49,* 357–392.

Izutsu, T. (1982). *Toward a philosophy of Zen Buddhism.* Boulder, CO: Prajna Press. (Original work published 1977)

Izutsu, T. (1983). *Ishiki to honshitsu: Seishinteki toyo o motomete* [Consciousness and essence: A seeking after the Eastern spirit]. Tokyo: Iwanami Shoten.

Izutsu, T. (1984). *Sufism and Taoism: A comparative study of key philosophical concepts.* Berkeley, CA: University of California Press. (Original work published 1983)

Izutsu, T. (1985). *Imi no fukamie: Toyo-tetsugaku no suii* [Into the deeper dimensions of meaning: The levels of Eastern philosophy]. Tokyo: Iwanami Shoten.

Krishnamurti, J. (1974). *Krishnamurti on education.* New York: Harper and Row.

Lao-tzu. (2001). *The way and its virtue* (T. Izutsu, Trans.). Tokyo: Keio University Press.

Lin-chi (1993). *The Zen teachings of master Lin-chi* (B. Watson, Trans.). Boston: Shambhala.

Maharshi, R. (1959). *The collected works of Ramana Maharshi* (A. Osborne, Ed.). London: Rider.

Miller, J. P. (1994). *The contemplative practitioner: Meditation in education and the professions.* Toronto: OISE Press.

Miller, J. P. (1996). *The holistic curriculum* (2nd ed.). Toronto: OISE Press. (Original work published 1988)

Miller, J. P. (1999). *Education and the soul: Toward a spiritual curriculum.* Albany: State University of New York Press.

Miller, J. P. (2006). *Educating for wisdom and compassion: Creating conditions for timeless learning.* Thousand Oaks, CA: Corwin Press.

Miller, J. P., & Nakagawa, Y. (2002). *Nurturing our wholeness: Perspectives on spirituality in education.* Brandon, VT: Foundation for Educational Renewal.

Miller, R. (1997). *What are schools for? Holistic education in American culture* (3rd rev. ed.). Brandon, VT: Holistic Education Press. (Original work published 1990)

Nagarjuna (1995). *The fundamental wisdom of the middle way: Nagarjuna's* Mulamadhyamakakarika (J. L. Garfield, Trans.). New York: Oxford University Press.

Nakagawa, Y. (2000). *Education for awakening: An Eastern approach to holistic education.* Brandon, VT: Foundation for Educational Renewal.

Nakagawa, Y. (2002). Aldous Huxley: A quest for the perennial education. In J. Miller & Y. Nakagawa (Eds.), *Nurturing our wholeness: Perspectives on spirituality in education* (pp. 140–163). Brandon, VT: Foundation for Educational Renewal.

Nicholson, R. A. (1989). *The mystics of Islam.* London: Penguin. (Original work published 1914)

Nisargadatta, M. (1982). *I am that: Talks with Sri Nisargadatta Maharaj* (Rev. Ed.; S. S. Dikshit, Ed., M. Frydman, Trans.). Durham, NC: Acorn Press. (Original work published 1973)

Nishitani, K. (1982). *Religion and nothingness* (J. V. Bragt, Trans.). Berkeley and Los Angeles: University of California Press. (Original work published 1961)

Norbu, N. (1989). *Dzogchen: The self-perfected state* (A. Clemente, Ed., J. Shane, Trans.). London: Penguin.

Price, A. F., & Wong, M-L. (Trans.). (1990). *The Diamond Sutra and the Sutra of Hui-Neng.* Boston: Shambhala.

Radhakrishnan, S. (Ed. & Trans.). (1950). *The Dhammapada*. Delhi, India: Oxford University Press.

Radhakrishnan, S. (Ed. & Trans.). (1973). *The Bhagavadgita*. New York: Harper and Row. (Original work published 1948)

Radhakrishnan, S. (Ed. & Trans.). (1994). *The principal Upanishads*. New Delhi, India: HarperCollins India. (Original work published 1953)

Rumi, J. (1994). *Signs of the unseen: The discourses of Jalaluddin Rumi* (W. M. Thackston Jr., Trans.). Putney, VT: Threshold Books.

Sankara (1992). *A thousand teachings: The* Upadesasahasri *of Sankara* (S. Mayeda, Ed. & Trans.). Albany: State University of New York Press. (Original work published 1979)

Seng-Ts'an (1993). On trust in the mind (B. Watson, Trans.). In S. Bercholz & S. C. Kohn (Eds.), *Entering the stream: An introduction to the Buddha and his teachings* (pp. 147–152). Boston: Shambhala.

Smith, H. (1976). *Forgotten truth: The common vision of the world's religions*. San Francisco: HarperCollins.

Suzuki, D. T. (1996). *Zen Buddhism: Selected writings of D. T. Suzuki* (W. Barrett, Ed.). New York: Doubleday. (Original work published 1956)

Tart, C. T. (1994). *Living the mindful life*. Boston: Shambhala.

CHAPTER 10

Krishnamurti and Me
Meditations on His Philosophy of Curriculum and on India

Jane Piirto
Ashland University

Jiddu Krishnamurti always began his meditations with an observation of nature or his surroundings, and so the day after I met him through his school in Chennai (formerly Madras), on the east coast of India, in December of 1998, I wrote a meditation after his example:

To See The Beauty in The Filth of The Streets of Chennai

Three puppies, one blonde, two dark, with tails that curlicue, cavort on the lawn behind the hotel, hastily running into the bushes when people approach. They doze in the sun and nip each other, fighting and tussling. As I look out the window on this morning city, the blonde one squats on the green of the lawn, relieves herself, and nuzzles her flank where some fleas have taken up residence.

Are they wild dogs? Few of the dogs that roam the streets here seem to have a home. Many are mangy. They all have short hair, and are medium-sized. Some have spots and some are plain black or tan. Whose dogs are they? If they are wild, why are they so calm? Do they have disease? Would they bite me if I petted them? They range over the garbage dumps and pick at the plastic debris, along with the rag pickers and the cows. In a vegetarian society are the dogs vegetarian also? No cats. Many dogs. What do we learn from the lives of wild dogs in the cities of India? Why must we learn anything? Is it not enough that they exist here in harmony with the noise and pollution?

I saw several of these Indian dogs a few minutes ago, while walking the road over the bridge through shit and spit. Huge gobs of spit, some white mucous, some red betel-stained, dot the pavement where I walk.

Shit also has its place here, out in the open air. Voluminous orbs of buffalo shit, rounded piles of goat shit, long tubes of dog shit, dried straw in the old animal shit forms the soil of the street, mingling with the dust, and the dirt, swept aside by the morning sweepers, bent with their brooms moving the dirt into piles of shit, leaves, dirt, stones, left in spaced intervals for whom to pick up? Or do the day sweepers just spread it out again so they can, Sisyphian, sweep it into piles again tomorrow morning? I scrape the shit off my shoes at least once a day.

The substance has a constructive place in India. I remember last week sitting at a roadside stand near Pune with a feminist activist organizer, Shobha Shrikant Pafsalkar, the head woman of a village, drinking coke, her treat, her stand, talking about her trip on a bus with village women to Dehli. Here we were, three women: Shobah, a social activist who ran her own business and kept a bank for the women of the village at lower interest rates than commercial banks; the woman showing me around, Suvarna, graduate of Jnana Prabhodini school, and committed social activist, my guide, who runs programs for women; and me, Jane, the visiting educator from the west. But there was a fourth woman—the nameless woman in a bright pink sari nearby, stooping to pick up, with both hands, steaming buffalo dung near the noisy, truck-filled highway to put in the basket on her hips and head. I see many huts shingled with flattened buffalo dung-shaped tiles.

Out at the pool, the sweeper, a barefooted brown woman, most likely of lower caste, in a red and yellow print sari, her black hair in a bun at the nape of her neck, bends with a soft flowing brush, sweeping the deck of the pool. In graceful swaths, the small detritus tumbles to the small wind caused by the broom's motion. Much of it blows into the grass lining the pool deck.

Weaving in and out of children playing among the tin-roofed shacks down back roads, among flapping clothes strung on jerry-rigged lines, I take the autorickshaw hailed outside of the hotel, to my various destinations in this large city. The smells of spicy cooking from open-air small grills blend with the odor of rotten fruit tossed into piles for the cows to eat, as I am glad to be near the street and not in the leased car with driver, that my colleagues commandeer each morning. I feel nearer to what Chennai is all about, the "madam" professor in her straw hat and long leather purse with sketchbook, camera, tape recorder, pencils, and enough rupees to be considered disgustingly rich here. In the open bouncing one-stroke gas oil three-wheeled polluter, I am near to the shit, spit, ownerless dogs, no cats, many cows, cows all over the place. The animal life of the city assaults, and here I feel my animalness too.

In his writings, after the description, Krishnamurti would then launch into a discussion of some sort. As I write this, I have spent a year reading his meditations, books, and letters to schools. The voyage began one day, in Chennai, formerly Madras, India, in December 1998, when I and three colleagues at my university were on a month-long study trip. I was visiting schools. The head of the Jnana Prabodhini School in Pune, where I had spent a week, listed for me schools throughout southern India at the cities we were to visit, which had as part of their philosophy and *raison d'etre* to encourage their bright students to help the world, beginning at home, rather than to pursue their own aggrandizement and social mobility. "You will find these schools interesting," he said. One of the schools was the Krishnamurti Foundation of India School in Chennai, based on the educational philosophy of Krishnamurti.

Krishnamurti's electric presence, some thought, was so intense that a normal person could not face him directly. George Bernard Shaw called Krishnamurti "a religious figure of the greatest distinction" and added, "He is the most beautiful being I have ever seen." Henry Miller wrote, "There is no man I would consider it a greater privilege to meet." Aldous Huxley, after attending one of Krishnamurti's lectures, wrote, "It was like listening to a discourse of the Buddha—such power, such intrinsic authority." Kahlil Gibran wrote, "When he entered my room I said to myself, 'Surely the Lord of Love has come'" (Krishnamurti Foundation of America, www.kfa.org.).

That morning I went to Adyar, an elegant region across the bridge and near the sea, to The Krishnamurti Foundation of India School at Damodar Gardens/Besant Avenue/Adayar, Madras 600 020. School officials do not permit vehicles to drive onto the property, and I walked down a tree-lined greenery-lit lane to the large, yellow pillared colonial style building set back in a cleared grove lined with flowering bushes. The lack of motorized sounds pervaded, after the dense noise of the city. A feeling of peace fell over me, and as I walked slowly down the shaded lane into the sunny lawn at the end, I even heard insects. The polluted potpourris of the smells of the streets of Chennai faded.

I climbed the steps to the veranda, where a sign warned me to remove my shoes before entering. I did so, and entered a bare room, with a bare desk and a few empty chairs. As I copied down the material on a bulletin board, I was greeted by a middle-aged man in a tan cotton shirt and pants. I asked for Mr. G. Gautama, the principal. A poster read:

> Guru—someone whose proximity can ingrain the essentials of fulfillment into a student. Someone who can help the growth of the mind, intellect, and soul. Someone who through dedication, diligence, and discipline has arrived, after years of struggle, at self-knowledge and self-realization. A visionary. An enlightened being. A guru. The SPICMAY Gurukul Scheme offers students an opportunity to spend one month with such a person. Living in close proximity ...

Guru? This school encouraged their children to seek out gurus. Later I read Krishnamurti, in his *Letters to the Schools,* written on 17 November 1983:

> You learn from a guru if he is at all the right kind, a sane guru, not the money-making guru, not one of those who want to be famous and trot off to different countries to gather a fortune through their rather unbalanced theories. Find out what it is to learn.

The headmaster/principal came and greeted me. Mr. Gautama, a slim, austere man, balding, with gray hair, focused with intensity as he shook my hand. He beckoned me to sit down in one of the four cane chairs in his bare office, and he told me that this Krishnamurti School is one of seven such schools in India. It is a K–12 school, with a postschool program as well. Other Krishnamurti schools are the Rishi Valley School, the Madanapalle School, the Sholai School, the Rajghat Besant School, the Bal-Anand School, the Valley School, the Bhagirathi Valley School, the Sahyadri School, the Riverside School in Thailand, the Brockwood Park School in England, and the Oak Grove School in Ojai, California.

As we sat in his office, Mr. Gautama's piercing eyes and intensity, his calm and his vegetarian-induced slimness somehow made me take notice, and I scrawled these quotes in my thought log:

> Education is one whole part of human endeavor. It is the gathering of knowledge one needs. It is possible not to gather with prejudice? What separates man

from man? Is there a way that man [sic] cannot gather the other knowledge which provides prejudice? No learning happens without the other knowledge. Fear makes learning of any kind learning with a motive. The action is not revealed when there is fear. Is there some way out of the nature of the need that is always describing?

Many children take naturally to philosophy. They are capable of deep and marvelous conversation if the atmosphere is created where such conversation can begin in a matter that is noncoercive, and noncompulsive, nondogmatic and nonindoctrinating, not moralistic. Today there is a death of conversation between old and young, between adults and children. There is an absence of soul talk with children. If you don't have soul talk with adults by your teen years, you're stuck.

The strength of this school is conversation. We are learning about conversation with children. We try to create as many problems as possible where teacher and students are equal without letting go of the responsibility of the teacher.

We take them out to a farm we have. Students need to know how little they really need in life—if they can learn that they will not forestall opportunities to learn. We are engaged in a rich environmental debate. Plurality and multi-nationalism mean an appreciation of the diversity of the nation. Our students make acquaintance with the environment through positive work. You can't wish away the fact that we have environmental problems. They need a space where they can discover how little they need. We try to strip them of the television, the comforts, the radio. They sleep on mats in huts.

In a sense what we're attempting is a joyful shift in the conversation with the young. We accept the engagement.

You must listen not only with your ears. You listen with your whole being. We have been doing this.

He said, "It's a pity you can't stay longer. It would take 15 days to see what this school is about." He told me that the parents are also very involved in the school. "We ask them whether they would really like [their] children to observe the world without competition."

I was dazed, giddy. I felt as if I were in the presence of a life-changing force, almost as if I were praying, or taking Holy Communion. Gautama's words and his intensity about education hit me, and I sat back, stunned, looking behind him out the sunny window, listening to a bird that took this moment to sing. I rose with effort, breathless, as if I had just run a long distance, my head spinning. I had never heard a principal whose school I was going to tour talk like this.

We walked through several buildings with classrooms open to the air, somewhat dark and sandy classrooms, the children on mats, no desks. Each room had blackboards and chalk. Some student work was pinned to the walls, but it seemed haphazard, as if those who hung the work were in a hurry or as if display of one's work didn't matter except in the art room. The art room seemed a sanctuary, and indeed, two teachers on break or grading papers sat there in its peace and calm, near the open-air, sun shining on the vegetation outside.

Tarit Bhattacharya, the art teacher, has written a book called *The Child, Art, and Everyday Material*. The room filled the eyes with such. Much student work was up: works of clay, straw, poster paint, drawings, collages. A bush with bright orange flowers shone in the sun through the open window. Two girls, in a special tutorial for the national art exam, quietly murmured. The humanities teacher was there, and the music teacher, Ranarajam, entered. Bhattacharya explained that he thinks creativity is inherent in all children: "Many children are very creative even if they are not so good at [math]. Something can be started for them. Art education has a role to play." I agreed, and left him my book on creativity.

When we came to the dining room, Gautama said, "We cut off the legs of the tables and we got rid of the chairs. Children sit on mats and have conversation. It got rid of the noise and it's much cleaner. It's an acquaintance with their culture not to always sit on chairs. They might as well do what they probably do at home. Chairs and tables are not Indian custom." He explained that he had become headmaster after a lot of thought and exploration. His training was in engineering. He said he thought that engineers make good school administrators because they are interested in how things work.

I repeated what the tourist agent who had met us said, "The KFI. School? Those students get a one-way ticket to the United States." Mr. Gautama said, "The school is well respected. About 20% are affluent. It asks a very small tuition—about 10,000 rupees a year—$240." He showed me the assembly hall, again a room without chairs, and brought me back to the art room, where my orientation was taken over by teachers. His parting comment was memorable and seemed a response to the public perception of the school: "Krishnamurti said, 'If five people turn their back on money and power, then your school has done its job.'"

It was 10 A.M. and time for the tea break. I sat on a wall ledge in the center of the clearing, sipping sweetened tea. Three sleeping dogs lay in the sun, oblivious to the whole school, its children, its teachers, its visitor, drinking tea around them. Did they belong to any person, or to the whole school? Gautama came over to me, and he said that the government was requiring the teachers in the school to be certified. They all have expertise in their subject matter, but not in the pedagogical training that leads to government pensions after many years of teaching. He then flew off to a meeting somewhere else.

Ranarajam, the music teacher, resumed guiding my tour and showed me the corridor where the high school students studied. I peeked into a mathematics room, where the students seemed to be doing trigonometry. Krishnamurti has written on how to teach mathematics. He believes that the teacher must be able to perceive order and disorder in the universe through thought:

> Let us say I am a teacher of mathematics. Mathematics is order, infinite order. … Thought is capable of seeing the order of mathematics but this order is not the product of thought. … I myself must study this order and disorder before I can convey it to my pupils. (1985, p. 42)

Krishnamurti often disparages book learning, saying that it is only necessary for getting a technical job, but that learning from books is not true learning. In *Education and the Significance of Life* (1953), he writes, "To be the right kind of educator, a teacher must constantly be freeing himself from books and laboratories; he must be ever watchful to see that the students do not make of him an example, an ideal, an authority."

He feels strongly that a student should gain self-knowledge, and not necessarily book knowledge: In the second volume of his *Letters to the Schools* he writes, "Learning has been the ancient tradition of man, not only from books, but about the nature and structure of the psychology of a human being." In *Education and the Significance of Life* (1953) he writes, "The ignorant man is not the unlearned, but he who does not know himself, and the learned man is stupid when he relies on books, on knowledge, and on authority to give him understanding." Reading books is often escapism, and "Such education offers a subtle form of escape from ourselves and, like all escapes, it inevitably creates increasing misery."

In fact, in my reading of Krishnamurti, I find him giving no other human beings credence or reference as having had thoughts that are valuable to him. But Krishnamurti himself communicated with the world through the word, both spoken and written. Among others, I read several books by Krishnamurti on education: *Education and the Significance of Life*, *Krishnamurti on Education*, both volumes of *Letters to the Schools*. Perhaps he disparaged book learning out of a concern that students would take book authoi themselves, as authorities.

Krishnamurti writes, "We have been taught to conform to of a teacher, of a book, of a party, because it is profitable to d

Krishnamurti does not think the sacred books of various religions are to be trusted, viewing organized religion as a means of forcing conformity and of preserving the status quo: "Each religion has its own sacred book, its mediator, its priests and its ways of threatening and holding people," he writes in *Education and the Significance of Life*. True religious education is "to encourage the child to understand his own relationship to people, to things and to nature."

One could say that Krishnamurti should know: his family were Brahmins, the high caste from which religious leaders are drawn, and Krishnamurti took on the sacred thread at the proper age, six, in typical Indian ceremonial ritual, his Upanyanam. Krishnamurti's father was a Theosophist. Helena Petrovna Blavatsky, the cofounder of Theosophy, along with Colonel Henry Steele Olcott, an American Civil War veteran, had moved the headquarters to India in 1882, with an opinion that India was a country that paid more attention to spiritual matters than any other country. A compound of colonial-style stucco houses had grown up along the Adyar River, behind high stone walls. Blavatsky died in 1890, at the age of 60.

After Krishnamurti's father retired on a very small pension, he begged the world head of the Theosophists, Annie Besant, an educated social reformer who had converted to Theosophy after reading the controversial works of Madame Blavatsky, and C. W. Leadbeater, a former Catholic priest who had converted also, to let him be a secretary to one of them; they refused. Krishnamurti's father finally moved himself and his three surviving sons to the gates of the Theosophical Society, where they took up residence in a shabby hut outside the gates. Besant and Leadbeater finally relented.

Krishnamurti and his brother Nitya would go down the river to watch the white folks bathe. Leadbeater, a clairvoyant, saw the scrawny, malarial young Krishnamurti, and noticed his aura. Saying that the boy had no selfishness in him, Leadbeater picked out Krishnamurti and began to groom him to be an orator and spiritual teacher. After Krishnamurti was brutally caned by his schoolmaster to the extent that his psychic presence was damaged, Leadbeater persuaded the father to let the two boys live with him in the main house of the Theosophical Society compound. The year was 1909, and Krishnamurti was 13 years old.

Krishnmurti's father was honored to have this attention from the Theosophical Society leaders paid to his sons at first, but then, when the scandal over Leadbeater's relationships with young boys threatened the whole worldwide theosophical movement, he sued—and sued and sued—for something resembling "alienation of affections." Leadbeater was always surrounded by boys who were his accolades, altar boys, and students. Lewd headlines accused Leadbeater of all manner of improper conduct.

Biographer Mary Lutyens has noted, however, that all those boys seem to have married happily, and that Leadbeater shrugged off the accusations. Leadbeater defended himself by saying he was only trying to teach them the value of masturbation as a way of letting off steam, and of bathing the full body, naked, and not with a loin cloth on. After long court battles Besant won guardianship of the boys. Ironically, Besant herself had deserted her own children when she began to follow Theosophical teachings.

Krishnamurti never attended formal classes in an upper school, though he did attend as a young child, just before and after his family moved to Madras, where the schoolmasters were of the kind that beat children, especially dreamy children like Krishnamurti, who seemed to be often gazing out the open windows. He was often caned and sent outside. After Leadbeater took over, Krishnamurti had some tutors from among the young men who followed Theosophy. Several considered him dim-witted. The main tutor was Leadbeater, but the Theosophists seemed to care most about his spiritual development, and Krishnamurti and his brother Nitya often "flew" with Leadbeater to the astral plane in their sleep to visit the masters of Theosophy. Mostly, Krishnamurti seems to have just studied on his own. The brothers were sent to England to prepare for taking the entrance examinations for Oxford University.

Nitya passed and entered law school, but Krishnamurti failed the examination twice. He also failed the entrance examinations for Cambridge University. Krishnamurti then sat for examinations at London University, but failed the mathematics tests. He then attended lectures. He wrote many letters vowing to study more "philosophy, languages, and maths." He also spent time in France learning French and taking elocution lessons in order to be able to speak many languages to those they anticipated he would speak to as the chosen one. Facility in languages was among his strengths, and he studied Sanskrit. He often wrote to Besant and Leadbeater saying that he felt his education had been neglected.

While he was in France he wrote a letter saying that he enjoyed Friedrich Nietzsche's *Thus Spake Zarathustra* and Fyodor Dostoevsky's *The Idiot*, and one summer when he was at a cabin on donated land in Ojai, California (which later became his home), his spiritual masters, during an evening visitation, told Krishnamurti that he was ignoring his education, so he and the group began to memorize one of William Shakespeare's sonnets each day.

Krishnamurti was a published poet, but he seems to value poetry as a means of personal meditation, writing about it, "To depend on a person, a poem, or what you will, as a means of release from our worries and anxieties, though momentarily enriching, only creates further conflict and contradiction in our lives" and "When one really wants to write a poem, one writes it, and if one has the technique, so much the better; but why stress what is but a means of communication if one has nothing to say?" Even without formal education he was very literate, serving as editor of several publications of the Theosophical Society and carrying on a voluminous correspondence with friends and supplicants. In one of his letters he seemed to be surprised to recapture his gift of healing, saying that many student friends in London were visiting him with their aches and pains.

Krishnamurti and Nitya were shuttled as guests from Theosophist to Theosophist, with never a place to live or call their own, and only a small allowance from the Theosophical Society, though they did have exclusive use of some digs in London, Austria, Germany, and Holland from time to time. They learned from some of these hosts how to eat well and how to dress expensively, with tailor-made clothes, but when they made the long ocean voyages back and forth to India, and then to Australia, they were shunned and ridiculed as being "black" and for having such well-tailored clothes and well-polished shoes. Many young women thought that Krishnamurti was quite attractive—as did some older women (as witnessed by the attentions of Besant and Lady Emily Lutyens). In fact, it appears that he was always surrounded by admiring women. His eyes seem to have been the feature that attracted them. This was a good thing for a future leader of a spiritual society that was made up of mostly women, quite a few of them wealthy. Krishnamurti fell in love with a woman of his own age only once; this was with Helen Knothe, a 17-year-old American violin student whom he met in Holland.

In August of 1920, Krishnamurti began to undergo a "process," as he called it, of spiritual transformation that lasted, off and on, an intense four years, focusing on a painful spiritual awakening through his spine. It began with a lump at the nape of his neck, and the pain threw him about the room for several hours each night, after which he would recover, only to have it happen at 6 P.M. the next night. The only people who could comfort him were his brother Nitya and two young women, both unmarried. When one of the married women who was in his entourage tried to be with him during the evening "process," she was cast out as being too impure.

Both Krishnamurti and his retinue thought that this process was the *kundalini* energy arising, although they were not yoga masters, nor did they practice yoga except for exercise. Krishnamurti did not see a doctor during these periods, which took place for many days at Ojai, and later in Austria and in India. Seeing a doctor would have made the process stop, he felt, and he believed that the process was another step in his spiritual growth path. He would leave his body to the pain, and depart to another plane, to talk with the masters, the Buddha, Jesus, and Maitreya. The process was witnessed by several people, but by no medical doctors or psychiatrists.

At the time, Krishnamurti was on the path to be the next world leader of the Theosophists, and the next great world spiritual leader in the path of the great spiritual teachers of the world. Krishnamurti would write to Leadbeater and to Besant about the process, asking them for explanations. Besant confirmed that Krishnamurti was indeed undergoing one of the last initiations to be world teacher. Here is an account of what would happen to him during the daily process, from eyewitness Lady Emily Lutyens:

> Krishnaji went away as usual at 7 and was off till 8:40. He suffered a very great deal and his body groaned and wept. … Helen was very tired and not very well and the physical elemental [they believed that he left his body to visit with the master's] seemed conscious of this and tried to control his groans—but at one time they were so bad that Krishna came back and asked what was happening. They said nothing and when he had gone again the physical elemental or whatever is in charge of the body was dreadfully distressed at having brought Krishna back and said Krishna had told him to control himself and he had done his best and could not help it. The Church bells begin to ring always about 8 o'clock and their noise causes him agony. Last night he fainted twice while they were ringing.[1] (1975, pp. 176–177)

During the long years when this process was occurring, Krishnamurti wrote poems every day. He also wrote letters to confidants about hating to speak to the mammoth crowds who came to hear him. Nitya was diagnosed with tuberculosis in both lungs. He died at age 27, in 1925, and Krishnamurti was alone, without family members near, for the rest of his long life. He never married, though he was always surrounded by *gopis*, young women who compared themselves with the milkmaids who surrounded the Hindu god Krishna.

On August 3, 1929, at Ommen Camp in Holland, Krishnamurti dissolved the group and refused to be considered the new world teacher. Among the comments he made are:

"I say again that I have no disciples."

"Everyone of you is a disciple of the Truth if you understand the Truth and do not follow individuals."

"Do not quote me afterwards as an authority. I refuse to be your crutch. I am not going to be brought into a cage for your worship."

He was 32 years old. What he said then seems to have become a keystone of his educational ideas.

In 1926, Krishnamurti had sought to acquire land for a school in the Rishi Valley, close to where he was born. The land was finally acquired in 1928, and the school is still in existence, along with the school I visited in Chennai. He visited the schools as often as he could, and talked with the children and teachers. He was determined to change the face of mass education to that of a more humane system, and small schools with small classes were among the essentials.

At the KFI School, teachers either leave in the first two years or stay for a long time. Once they find themselves in agreement, they stay. Teachers find the school is very demanding in terms of its commitment of time and energy, one reason being the many dialogues and discussions among teachers. A series of parent meetings where they discuss "career versus calling," "leisure and knowledge," or "the role of television" is held. Once a month a voluntary study group for parents discusses the works of Krishnamurti.

Gautama gave me some yearly reports with regard to how the philosophy is made practical. One student wrote about the untouchables, the scavengers and sweepers omnipresent but almost invisible. Here is an echo of my own thoughts as I watched the sweeper at the pool:

They Have a Right to Dream

Scavengers. The word brings to mind animals or birds feeding on carrion. But, sadly, there are human scavengers, too. They are the Bhangis, or the scavenger race. A video was shown to us by parents of the school, on the Bhangis of Gujarat. The Bhangis are the lowest among the low in the social strata and widely considered to be pollutants. Recently a 12-year-old Bhangi boy, while watching the world cup matches on TV at a paan [bread] shop, accidentally touched the paan platter.

The error cost him his sight. The paanwalla, infuriated at his wares being polluted, threw a bowl of lime at the boy's face. He is now blinded for life. The Bhangis of Gujarat are so badly treated because of their profession. It is their job to collect human waste from illegal dry bathrooms.

With only a metal piece they must scrape excreta into their tin cans, carry it out on their heads and deposit it at the dump. The sight of them cleaning excreta was revolting to us and it left us shaken and stirred.

However, as we were reminded, we were only seeing it; the smell worsened it a hundredfold. It must be added that though laws do exist banning dry toilets, in actual fact the government does little about them ... such practices exist even today. The aim is to start a nationwide campaign abolishing their very existence. It is time to allow Bhangis to lead respectable lives. It is time to allow them to dream and to fulfill their dreams. Scavenging has to be abolished.

KFI school students are expected to do community service and to have knowledge of the social problems of the area. At the rural education center, students make charts of diseases that affect the region, help people learn to count money and to make measurements, conduct surveys on villagers' marital status, income, and health conditions. Environmental education is also encouraged at Krishnamurti schools. Students take part in debates on the building of a new hydroelectric dam, and protest its building on grounds that it will destroy indigenous wildlife. Students also do building work, gardening, beach cleaning, and tree planting as well as bird-watching.

Multigrade grouping of students was being experimented with in the lower grades at the KFI School. Much discussion with parents, teachers, and students about this means of grouping children took place before they tried it. There is now a proposal to adopt the methodology in some 2,000 schools spread over 20 mandals in 7 districts of the state.

Students in Krishnamurti schools have discussions about their place in the world vis-à-vis their talents, privilege, accomplishments, caste of birth, and such. One topic was, What does it mean to be accomplished? A student wrote,

To understand the full implications of this, one needs to reflect on the flip side of this attitude. What happens to the human being who is not greatly accomplished? Does one have no regard for him? In fact this is exactly what one sees the world over. Is a different approach not possible? Is it not possible to respect a person simply as a human being? Implied in this is the act of listening: listening completely, without any censor coming in, listening without any barrier at all, with a mind that is naturally quiet, like the deep waters of a lake. Krishnamurti once told his audience, "Listening is one of the most important things in life. ..."(He used to refer to listening, looking and learning as the three great arts of life. What an extraordinary statement!) Perhaps here lies the key to our question: in listening lies respect; listening is respect. Can we listen to one another in this manner, with a complete absence of all barriers? And can we work towards bringing about a culture of listening in our schools?

Students at Krishnamurti schools are encouraged to discuss, to meet, and to discuss again. Principal Gautama said that every change, every decision, takes a long long time, as nothing can be done authoritatively, and all people involved in the decision must have input. Again and again, the writings of Krishnamurti are consulted.

I made my way out of the KFI school compound to the street, where I entered a moderate bustle; walking on the street and not on the sidewalk, among cattle, bicycles, strollers, a muttering madman, and stalls open in front selling tea, fruit, bread, and services, I passed several other schools of other persuasions: a Christian school, a Catholic girls' school, a private primary school. When I tried to enter the grounds of the Theosophical Society, about a block down, I was turned away because it was closed. Even in December, it was very hot. I walked on the streets among the schoolgirls buying figs for a rupee in the dust and dirt, amid car horns and other noise, spit and feces. My soul was lonely here, during this holiday season, far away from family holiday traditions. Annie Besant spent every winter here, and Krishnamurti was in residence over Christmas and New Year's as well, almost every year of his life.

The next day I found respite from my homesickness when I went back to the Theosophical Society, the gated, walled compound founded in the late 1800s by the Theosophists. Here I discovered a miraculous haven of tranquility in the melée. Near the library of this esoteric society I sat doing a watercolor of a magnificent old tree, its branches spreading widely, shading the dappled green lawn beneath it. As I sat, the tree became an individual to me—a special tree, not a tree among trees, but its own tree. As my eyes framed it and my pen and brush tried to be its rendered mirror, I reflected on all trees. The grounds contain, interspersed and labeled, in the international spirit of Theosophy, donated native trees from many countries, now mature and thriving. I felt a Krishnamurti-like meditation coming on, and in fact, after this day, I began my daily journals for the next few weeks in India with such meditations.

I entered the library, took off my shoes on the cool marble floor, and climbed to the reading room, which contains ancient religious texts from many religions. I didn't have the special researcher permission to peruse these texts, but I was led into the small display room, where I saw several ancient holy manuscripts from various religions. Staring at these and watching people in African robes, Indian dhotis, and western dress enter the library gave me some idea of the research that this library supports.

Bemused, I began to walk down the shady, lush lane. Autorickshaw and car traffic has been banned or curtailed here, and I walked gratefully, enjoying the mightiness of world species grown up to shade the path. I paused on a bench next to a grove of palms and focused on the orange blossoms blooming by the side of the road, through which I could admire the palms. I sat for a long time beneath the famous ancient banyan tree, the second largest one in India, that has been the site of many legendary Theosophist Society gatherings.

As I walked, the crows took up a huge cry, and about 20 or 30 of them lighted on a few palm trees right next to my walk. In India, crows are always in the sound waves. I thought of legends of crows and ravens, the tricksters, the messengers, the Hermes of the natural world. This flock—which flew into the banyan grove near the road where I was walking, loudly cawed at me for about 10 minutes, and then flew off—continued to engage my thought throughout 1999.

In October, 1999, my undergraduate interdisciplinary studies creativity class went to our hometown Ohio cemetery, meditating on the "dark side," and a raven did the same to one of my students, who was peacefully writing in her thought log in long grass. The raven sat above her and scolded her. I told her about Raven, the trickster, and can't help but think there are means and ways within the animal world that we can't understand but to which we must pay attention. Why did those crows in the Theosophical Society compound pause to speak near me, and why so many?

Two small birds hopped on a log and an animal like a chipmunk scurried among them. The place was inhabited by a few workers busy with brushes, brooms, carts, and bicycles, with messages being delivered, food being hauled, clearing being done. Few others appeared, except for an occasional Indian couple walking as if in romance, and a few elder gentlemen with pens stuck in the pockets of their flowing cotton shirts gliding by me with serious faces intent on their thoughts, striding purposefully in their leather sandals. Four workers chatted with each other up on a bamboo scaffold, the women on top, thatching or fastening with cane leaves, the men below giving orders and pointing. I discovered that the place has its own post office, a cool, quiet building with no customers: Besant Station.

The bookstore stands at the other side of the compound. In it were many works by the original Theosophists, as well as other works by Indian religious thinkers of Hindu and Buddhist persuasion. Theosophy itself purports to sponsor no specific beliefs. I bought several books by Krishnamurti, to begin a study of his philosophies of education, as well as his other thoughts. The books are lovely, with soft, handmade paper covers, fitting comfortably into a purse or pocket, printed on tan paper. They cost about 45 rupees, a little more than one U.S. dollar.

Off and on all year I studied my lovely small beautiful Krishnamurti books, using the meditations and journals as spiritual texts, as the intensity of the principal of the KFI school would not leave my mind.

Figuring out the educational philosophy of Krishnamurti was either too simple or too complex. I would start reading, and then get waylaid by thought. Sometimes one sentence was enough to start me off in cogitating, meditating about what associations came to me from the sentence, but then, my unquiet mind would begin to think about everything but the sentences my eyes were reading. I was unable to finish any of the books, as everything seemed circular, and soon Krishnamurti's sentences started sounding the same, ponderous and prescriptive in the manner of Indian philosophy. I am an avid reader, often reading a book a day. Why couldn't I put together what Krishnamurti was saying? Why couldn't I synthesize this? I read sentence by sentence, plodding, slowly.

In order to summarize what he says about education, I designed myself a textual analysis study. I copied every fourth sentence of *Education and the Significance of Life* (1953), and the first 363 sentences of the second volume of *Letters to the Schools* (1985), his first and last books about education. The reason I took every four sentences is that the first book is more comprehensive and, as I said, Krishnamurti seemed to repeat himself in different form, many times in each chapter. Then, in order to analyze an unbroken text, I copied an almost equal number of sentences, in the order written, from the second volume of *Letters to the Schools*. I then did searches in both texts for certain key words that kept seeming to pop up repeatedly. In my search, I found the following frequencies:

Frequency of Key Words in Chosen Sentences By Krishnamurti	
educate or educator	appears in 103 of 676 sentences (15%)
teacher or teach	appears in 60 of 676 sentences (8%)
self	appears in 43 sentences
mind	appears in 42 of 676 sentences (6%)
knowledge	appears in 40 sentences (5%)
freedom	appears in 40 sentences (5%)

conditioning	appears in 37 of 676 sentences (5%)
intellect or intelligence	appears in 32 sentences (4%)
fear	appears in 32 sentences (4%)
create or creative	appears in 32 sentences (4%)
relationship	appears in 23 of 676 sentences (3%)
love	appears in 22 sentences (3%)
attention or inattention	appears in 22 sentences (3%)
learning	appears in 19 sentences (2%)
integration or disintegration	appears in 17 sentences (2%)
true or truth	appears in 15 sentences
right	appears in 12 sentences
desire	appears in 12 sentences
nationalism	appears in 6 sentences
flowering	appears in 4 sentences

In this manner I was able to conduct an exegesis, to analyze the words and their associated concepts and Krishnamurti's use of them in company with other sentences containing the same words. I was able to decipher, by placing the sentences in proximity, what he meant when he wrote a word. For example, the adjective *right* was used in the phrases *right kind of education*, *right thinking*, and *right kind of educator*.

In studying the sentences and words in their various combinations, I was able to choose 13 sentences that seem to most reflect Krishnamurti's philosophy of education. Several of these had many of the key words in them. (Note: emphasis added in the examples that follow.)

Thirteen Sentences: Krishnamurti on Education

1. The *right* kind of *educator*, seeing the inward nature of *freedom*, helps each individual student to observe and understand his own *self*-projected values and impositions; he helps him to become aware of the *conditioning* influences about him, and of his own *desires*, both of which limit his *mind* and breed *fear*; he helps him, as he grows to manhood, to observe and understand himself in *relation* to all things, for it is the craving for *self*-fulfillment that brings endless conflict and sorrow (1953, p. 29).
2. The function of *education* is to *create* human beings who are *integrated* and therefore *intelligent* (1953, p. 14).
3. *Education* then is *freedom* from *conditioning*, from its vast accumulated *knowledge* as tradition (1985, p. 23).

4. *Fear* perverts *intelligence* and is one of the causes of *self*-centered action (1953, p. 35).

5. If in their hearts the *teachers* have put away all *fear* and all *desire* for domination, then they can help the student towards *creative* understanding and *freedom*; but if there is a conscious or unconscious *desire* to guide him towards a particular goal, then obviously they are hindering his development (1953, p. 95).

6. Because he is devoted solely to *the freedom* and *integration* of the individual, the *right* kind of *educator* is deeply and truly religious; he does not belong to any sect, to any organized religion; he is *free* of beliefs and rituals, for he knows they are only illusions, fancies, superstitions projected by the *desire* of those who *create* them (1953, p. 111).

7. *Intelligence* is much greater than *intellect*; for it is the *integration* of reason and love; but there can be *intelligence* only when there is *self-knowledge*, the deep understanding of the total process of oneself (1953, p. 67).

8. One *teaches* because one sees that *self-knowledge* alone, and not the dogmas and rituals of organized religion, can bring about a tranquil *mind*; and that *creation, truth*, God, comes into being only when the "me" and the "mine" are transcended (1953, p. 116).

9. To be *creative* is not merely to produce poems, or statues, or children; it is to be in that state in which *truth* can come into being (1953, p. 128).

10. *Truth* comes into being when there is a complete cessation of thought; and thought ceases only when the *self* is absent, when the *mind* has ceased to create, that is, when it is no longer caught in its own pursuits (1953, p. 128).

11. The *true teacher* is inwardly rich and therefore asks nothing for himself; he is not ambitious and seeks no power in any form; he does not use *teaching* as a means of acquiring position or authority, and therefore he is *free* from the compulsion of society and the control of governments (1953, p. 99).

12. In thus helping the student towards *freedom*, the *educator* is changing his own values also; he too is beginning to be rid of the "me" and the "mine," he too is *flowering* in love and goodness (1953, p. 41).

13. There [in a certain type of small school] the *teacher* can establish this *relationship* and there he is deeply involved with the *flowering* of human beings (1953, p. 94).

Krishnamurti, in his books and letters, talks about schools where students understand that they are conditioned by society, that they approach ideas with a view toward realizing that there are differences among knowledge, intelligence, and creativity. *Knowledge* is what is needed to do a job in order to make a living; *intelligence* is what one does with the knowledge; *creativity* is the process of doing something new.

The right kind of education, Krishnamurti posits, is an education that goes beyond the cultivation of technique. The right kind of education integrates the personality and frees the child. This takes a change of heart, and not a somewhat mechanistic acquisition of facts and techniques.

Does this sound a little platitudinous? Or too simple? Too much like the fabled progressivists? I read and reread these ideas repeated in various forms with various elaborations and explanations: Fear produces people who both have courage and who are cowardly. The best education takes place in small schools with very close relationships between the students and the teacher. The teacher learns with the student and is not the authority. Students are to be taught with love and with care, so that they can flower. Krishnamurti's notions about education have to do with the metaphor of the flower in the garden, the school as a fertile place for children to grow, along with dedicated educators who will tutor them and bring them along at their own speed, without coercion.

In looking at Krishnamurti's own educational history, one can see that this, indeed, was how he was educated by the Theosophists, and, ironically, when he refused the mantle of being their world teacher, he became a world teacher to all who would listen. He died February 17, 1986, in Ojai, California, at the age of 91—the age at which he had predicted he would die back when he was experiencing the awakening "process" that turned him into a prophet and a seer for the 20th century. His views on education are worth study and consideration by those of us in the West. Perhaps this essay has given an introduction.

When I got back to the hotel later that momentous afternoon in Chennai, I went over the bridge, past a bare-torsoed beggar with no arm setting up his station right at the edge of the single-lane path so as to be able to solicit all comers, threading through the crowds who swarmed among the autos, motorbikes, and autorickshaws. The bridge overlooks a spillway with muddy water spurting through. On its bank I stopped to look at a small settlement of cane huts for people of low caste, just beneath the bridge. A barefoot boy and his friend played by pulling debris from the water. A plastic bag. A plastic bottle. No school for them today.

Notes

This chapter was originally published in 2000, in slightly different form, in the *Journal of Curriculum Theorizing, 16*(2), 109–124. The author would like to thank the Faculty Development Program at Ashland University, especially Dr. Katharine Flanagan and Provost Mary Ellen Drushal, for putting into place the interdisciplinary studies global awareness grant through which this research was undertaken.

1.　All biographical information taken is taken from Lutyens, 1975.

References

Krishnamurti, J. (1953). *Education and the significance of life*. Chennai, India: Krishnamurti Foundation of India.

Krishnamurti, J. (1985). *Letters to the schools* (Vol. II). Chennai, India: Krishnamurti Foundation of India.

Lutyens, M. (1975). *Krishnamurti: The years of awakening*. Boston: Shambhala.

CHAPTER 11

Radical Times
Perspectives on the Qualitative Character of Duration

Kaustuv Roy
Louisiana State University

What then is time? I know well enough what it is, provided that nobody asks me; but if I am asked what it is and try to explain, I am baffled.

—St. Augustine, *Confessions*

Time is what hinders everything from being given all at once. It is retardation. … It must therefore be elaboration. Would it not then be a vehicle of creation and of … indetermination?

—Henri Bergson, *The Creative Mind*

Futurism

This chapter addresses some issues concerning our naturalized attitudes toward time that make its qualitative aspect invisible in the construction of experience. I will explore the nature of this qualitative dimension and show that such invisibility results in the domestication of experience, taming the rich variability within the moment, contributing to the listlessness born of repetition. Let me clarify that in using the term *invisibility* with regard to time I am not being unmindful of the clocks, watches, and myriad other devices and temporal structures that constantly remind us of the passage of time. *Metric time is all too visible.* By time's *invisibility* I refer to the phenomenological experience of duration that all but disappears in the obsession with time as external measure.

In examining the dominion of time as external measure, I will also address alternative ways of thinking about and experiencing time that hold out the possibility of experiencing in ways other than through the rigid metric temporalization with which we are so familiar. But at the outset I will warn that my account here will be necessarily impressionistic owing to the fact that the history of time is vast and difficult; consequently, I will also ask the reader's indulgence for the high degree of selectivity in this presentation, where the main attempt will be to breach the implacable face of time.

Obviously, the first question that arises is, Why time, and what about it? Has not the anatomy of time been mapped adequately through history by some of the ablest of minds—Kant, Hegel, Einstein, and others? Is there any substance to time besides the scientific view of it as a purely abstract, iterative measure? Aren't we all in agreement about what constitutes a precise time interval? Is not the mechanical repetition of time reassuring and stabilizing? What more is there to be said? Plenty, as will be argued here; our agreements and assumptions have only succeeded in suppressing the rebellious nature of time, and have resulted in the thinning of our ways of experiencing. Theologically, scientifically, philosophically, and economically, the qualitative experience of time has been obliterated, put out of sight, silenced in different ways.

One consequence of this wide-ranging silence on the qualitative aspect of time has been a hollowing out of the present. It is not far-fetched to say that if time is a mere linear succession as in the scientific model, then the arrow of time drawn through successive moments—that is, the psychological consequences of linear progression—is a strengthening in the direction of anticipation, the movement of that arrow promising a significant disclosure to come. This is commonly understood as hope, a forward-facing sentiment on the slippery slope of time. But such a promise of a future, of the "not yet," is mostly not an openness to an as-yet-unthought alterity, but a more-or-less shallow hope that leaps over the immediacy of the present, compromising responsibility for the present.

We have to understand that this futurism is no isolated phenomenon; a firm belief in the future was built into the axiomatics of modernity that included a profound investment in the ideology of the market that was ever forward looking. In the hierarchy of societies that was to emerge out of Western colonialism, peoples that were not future oriented were automatically considered backward, stuck in time, their lives not worth living. Within the capitalist market system, futurism performed two complementary functions: it absorbed the momentum of desire that had been isolated in modernity's division of labor, guiding it toward a psychological future—the belief in a better tomorrow; and it promoted the commodification process within which desire could dissipate itself. The proliferation of objects in modern social life was a useful diversion for the thwarted being of doing. The more desire spent itself on the proliferation of objects, the more entrenched and vital became the promise of tomorrow, a cycle that was indispensable to the self-valorization of capital. *The externalization of time as measure was at the same time a domestication of desire.* The capitalist colonization of desire could not be wholly successful without a corresponding control of the grid of time on which experience was projected and within which it was validated. In other words, the domestication of desire was also in many ways the colonization of time.[1]

It requires no great leap of thought, then, to see why education within capitalist axiomatics must inevitably be future oriented. The preparing of students to be future workers—and even more important, to be good consumers—must be of the greatest priority that will aid each cycle of the circulation of capital to acquire newer "visions" of the future.[2] The terrain is, not surprisingly, strewn with future-oriented phrases: *preparing students to be future citizens, curriculum for a new century, tomorrow's teachers, classrooms of the future,* and so on. The discourse is saturated with such terms as *prospect, outlook, potential, expectations, opportunities,* and the like, each an indication, a measure, or a promise of a time to come, of a "not now." The inquiry into the present takes the path mainly of progress, or "betterment" for the future. It does not primarily reveal the content of the present—say, the actual nature of the educational experience of a child. The discourse of tomorrow is a deflection of the present, resting upon the invisibility of what is actually going on; it is another patina that maintains the invisibility of time's quality.

My attempt here will be to disturb this silence a little and bring to the foreground what has been relegated to the background—namely, the phenomenological experience of time. In order to do that, I will discuss two revolts against the commonsense understanding of time—first, the intuitionist perspective of Henri Bergson that lies at the fringe of Western philosophical tradition, and a second account from a radical Eastern tantric tradition. The two approaches disrupt in their own ways the linear modernist socialization that puts the immediate present out of sight, bringing back an indefinite time into the present.

First, Bergson's intuition brings sensation and affect back into the perception of time in order to regain contact with a lived and embodied time. Next, this affective and experiential nature of time is radicalized here by bringing on stage the tantric powers of the body that displace the centrality of time as measure as it appears in the modern consciousness. Such a rupture might disturb the existing blandness and the process of normalization through which we have been chained to a future. Let us begin with a brief introduction to the historical representations of time.

The Time of History

From very early on in civilization, perhaps even prehistorically, humans have been concerned with time. Awareness of the passage of time may even be one of the defining characteristics of self-consciousness. Ancient texts like the Vedas of the East often refer to time as a force unto itself and not just an inert background (Aurobindo, 1995). But conceptually, time remained elusive and questions about its essential nature continued to bother philosophers. Among the Greeks, the Stoics, in particular, suspected that there was more to time than mere events repeating themselves (Martinez, 2003). Stoic thought shows that two readings of time are possible, and demonstrates their reciprocal exclusion. The two readings of time are *aion* and *chronos,* respectively. *Chronos* represents the present that contracts into itself the past and the future, and moves from contraction to contraction, repeating, giving us a perceptual hold on the event. *Aion* represents the continual breakdown or decomposition of time as measure into infinite divergent pathways that can never repeat. The former is time as measure, whereas the latter is not amenable to measure. The order of chronos does not intersect the order of aion (Deleuze, 1990). Thus we witness a complex apprehension of time among some ancients.

Among the early moderns, Immanuel Kant (1990) makes the most systematic effort to comprehend time. In Kant we find a very geometric understanding of time thought along the lines of the Euclidean postulates. Time, for Kant, could not be derived from sensory observation, for neither simultaneity nor succession would be perceptually present unless preceded by some representation of time. Kant provides several characteristics pertaining to time as an ideal form. First of all, time exists as a "subjective condition" of perception, not for itself nor as an objective quality in things. Time is to be seen as the formal a priori condition for all appearance. To conceive of time as something objective would require its presence in things that are not objects of perception. Instead time, like space, is only knowable as an a priori form of intuition, and any other assumption about it cannot be substantiated. Time is also the form of our inner sense, of our intuition of ourselves and of our "own inner situation," and because this "inner intuition" as such assumes no shape, it has to be imagined. Kant denies to time, as well as to space, an absolute reality, maintaining that outside of its cognitive function "time is nothing." Unlike things in themselves that might exist independently of humankind's apparatus of perception, both time and space can be evoked only "in relation to appearance"—that is, only in relation to the world as it appears to our senses.

Kant thus sees time as a formal mathematical intuition that ordered experience, science, mathematics, and of course common sense settled on time as an extrinsic and uniformly divisible construct, a succession of ordered intervals much like space. And although scientists have acknowledged the possibility of a nonhomogeneous time, such a possibility was visualized only in the very early stages of the universe's evolutionary cycle (Hawking, 1988). In general— as the well-known scientist Ilya Prigogine, in differing from the established view, has observed—scientific, measurable, clock time was uniformly divisible and, in theory, reversible, and therefore posed no theoretical problem leading to its being relegated to the background (Prigogine & Stengers, 1997). That is, time, apparently, was not worth discussing further.

The Revolt of Henri Bergson

Perhaps the most important challenge to the modernist view of time as inert background imaginary comes from the work of the philosopher Henri Bergson, who draws our attention back to time by overturning Kant's apriority. Where Kant sees a given starting point for ordering experience, Bergson (2001) sees the possibility of decomposing further:

> Kant's great mistake was to take time as a homogeneous medium. He did not notice that real duration is made up of moments inside one another, and that when it seems to assume the form of a homogeneous whole, it is because it gets expressed in space. (p. 232)

Kantian time is a close correlate of space, and both appear as homogeneous and given in Kant's schema and not subject to further analysis. But, for

Bergson, space and time represent very different aspects of experience, and to understand the difference between the two is key to the operation of intuition that allows us to look at phenomena differently. Space represents quantitative differences or discrete multiplicity and can be broken up into equal and repetitive intervals, whereas time represents qualitative differences or continuous multiplicities. Bergson's intuition consists in disentangling the qualitative side from the quantitative, and thereby in deriving a different understanding of phenomena that is not based on discrete behavior or measurement.

This is a singular contribution to philosophy as it freed phenomena from the yoke of a determinate time. Acknowledging this, the philosopher Emmanuel Lévinas (1985) has observed that "the credit goes to Bergson for having liberated philosophy from the prestigious model of scientific time" (p. 27). Lévinas further observes that "this affirmation of the somehow 'ontological' and not merely psychological priority of duration irreducible to homogenous time" is a remarkable development that is to significantly affect continental thought (p. 27).

Bergson notes in his investigations that, to begin with, the homogeneous and metric perception of time is at odds with our lived lives, in which time is experienced qualitatively. In terms of the everyday, who has not experienced time stretching or contracting under differing circumstances? For Bergson, this is not merely psychological; sensation has being and a complex ontology, and therefore these differential experiences are not to be dismissed as illusions or overwritten quickly with the metrical. Instead, they are to be seen as the preliminary bearing of a fact that there are other flows besides uniformly measurable time. This qualitative time has little to do with marking off equal intervals but instead is the arising of sensations differently folded in each other—plastic, capable of infinite contortions producing heterogeneous and continuous multiplicities and, consequently, different realities. The regular contractions that repeat occlude the other reading of time for Bergson. Real duration, instead, comes out of infinite *decomposition* rather than composition of successive, external moments that follow each other.[3] It is thus our expression, our representation that makes time appear what it is rather than any essence.

With this bold theoretical move, Bergson sets off down a different path that leads him to systematically posit a time that is qualitative and nonhomogeneous, which he calls *duration*. Real duration is not to be found on a time line but folded onto itself, and the unfolding of duration is not predetermined but always a becoming, its quality dependent on the nature of each interaction.

Time appears as homogenous only due to our being socialized into a pattern that projects social reality onto an external, fixed grid, which is then internalized. But for Bergson (2001),

> duration [is that] which gnaws on things, and leaves on them the mark of its tooth. If everything is in time, everything changes inwardly, and the same concrete reality never recurs. Repetition is therefore possible only in the abstract: what is repeated is some aspect that our senses, and especially our intellect, have singled out from reality, just because our action, upon which all the effort of our intellect is directed, can move only among repetitions. Thus, concentrated on that which repeats, solely preoccupied in welding the same to the same, intellect turns away from the vision of time. It dislikes what is fluid, and solidifies everything it touches. We do not think real time. But we live it. … (p. 106)

Duration "gnaws" on things—that is, it directly acts on the body, expressing itself through qualitative change, making each instant elastic and a nonrepeatable event. But, socially programmed to selectively focus on those aspects of phenomena that ostensibly repeat, we fail to observe that incessant change never allows for reality to recur. Therefore, no two instants, no two occurrences are the same. Consequently, two moments, even when measured by the controlled recurrence of an event such as the oscillations of a pendulum, are never really the same, although we are accustomed to thinking of them as such. Pure repetition is impossible, for at the heart of every repetition is a difference, a displacement, or a witness to the repetition who also undergoes qualitative change in the time between repetitions.

But metric time is based on pure repetition, and if pure repetition is impossible then time as a succession of equal measures becomes questionable. This is to say that conventional time, as the homogeneous and externalized experience of simultaneity and succession, is more a habit and a product of *lack of observation* than anything intrinsic or a priori. A superior relation to phenomena would be possible through duration, which is internal to the event, being a nonmetric, heterogeneous density that is a more accurate descriptor of experience. Putting it differently, duration makes things qualitatively differ from one another in experience and is an inherent part of it.

Yet, while it is possible to grant this at the level of abstraction, the reader might object that duration appears to be in an extrasensory realm remote from any practical significance. Even if conceptually interesting, it seems out of reach for the purpose of any useful intervention. Not so, says Bergson; one does not have to go beyond the senses to arrive at this, nor is it irrelevant for practical considerations. Our daily experience is benumbed by the external and mechanical conception of time, and developing intuition means, in part, shaking off the social conditioning of clock time and becoming alerted to the qualitative nature of duration.

In other words, fresh thinking for Bergson is coming face-to-face with the unfolding of change, and that moment of contact cannot be contained within metric time. How is this achieved? For Bergson (1946, p. 15), it means breaking down "immobilities" and "fixities" and being forced to deal with qualitative transitions in phenomena, something that the intellect is generally averse to doing as it seeks resting points and moorings, operating in habit. This takes a different kind of effort and susceptibility without taking away anything from our functionality within metric time. We are able to enjoy a dual capacity—of chronos and aion, as it were.

Thus, it is that the revolt against time as pure extension is frequently encountered in the creative process and the attitude that resists time as measure—subverts it, even—is to be found in art, poetry, and literature.[4] These creative processes rework time as differential flows, opening up unseen intervals and pushing thought to its limits. To put it in Bergson's terminology, the "creative impulse" or the will is reactivated with the perception of duration, which is not succession or iteration. The decomposition of the moment brings to us the awareness of a seething pretemporal quality out of which the event makes its appearance, stitching together time as it were. The creative process selects the significant perceptual strands that lead to the description of the event. Therefore, creativity for Bergson is anterior to time as measure, and not the other way around. Such revisioning of time flies in the face of Kantian metaphysics and a priori time, but the modernist project based on the control of a nuanceless, externalized time brings about not a liberation of the spirit but a new bondage and impoverishment of the soul.

Supporting Bergson's view, the philosopher Jean-François Lyotard (1998) maintains that one of the defining characteristics of modernity is the obsession with controlling time. The problem of slippage of time has been the bane of modernity, and out of that fear has emerged a rather fixed notion of "progress" that is in part the control and shaping of time. And this obsession has led to an extreme and unhelpful objectification of temporality that interferes with our relationship to phenomena and to the event. This does not mean time by the clock can be disregarded, which is impossible anyway, but neither is it possible to live a thoughtful life without a critique of it, wherein lies the educational imperative. Lyotard adds that "if thinking indeed consists in receiving the event, it follows that no-one can claim to think without being *ipso facto* in a position of resistance to the procedures for controlling time" (p. 74). If to think afresh means to open oneself up to phenomena and to the event, it must require a change in our relationship to time through which we define the event, a deliberate resistance to the structures of controlling time and therefore of defining the event. And although there may be psychological security in being able to control time as a uniform measure and organize life around it, it also precludes the vulnerability that is essential if we are to experience phenomena as something that is always coming to be and not already determined.

It is important for educators to note this, for all too often education is seen as the communication and accretion of finished ideas and rarely the cultivation of sensitivity to transition and continuous change. We tend to approach learning as composition over time—that is, as an event in the frame of extensionality only—and seldom also as an unraveling of the moment by exploring how sense experience gets delimited in expression. Educators equipped with such perception would be well positioned to enrich their students' understandings by straddling both worlds—experience as bounded and limited and experience as flow—and moving between these frames as necessary, allowing into the conversation new ways of visualizing.

To summarize the Bergsonian position, then, sensation has being and ontology; systematic awareness of the transitions and differences in sensation unfolds in us the qualitative dimension of time. Bergson (2001) writes that when we have our first impression of, say, a town we visit, the environment produces on us "two impressions at the same time, one of which is destined to last while the other will constantly change." The latter is a concatenation of fleeting feelings and emotions, whereas the former is more lasting on account of the "solidifying influence of external objects and language on our constantly changing feelings" (p. 129). This lasting impression resists change although the objects themselves change and grow old. Yet, "this difference escapes the attention of most of us; we shall hardly perceive it, unless we are warned of it and then carefully look ..." (p. 130). Here, then, is the pedagogical moment that attempts to expand our field of attention. When we pay less attention to the fleeting feelings and instead rely on language to solidify the image, "we confuse the feeling itself, which is in a perpetual state of becoming, with its permanent external object, and especially the word which expresses this object" (p. 130), thereby objectifying reality. In teaching us how to look,

Bergson says that if we look carelessly, in an uninformed way, we will miss the nuances and the result will be the sacrifice of the becoming nature of the feelings to the hard impression of the external object. The upshot also would be an imperceptible hardening of time as measure.

In other words, rather than an irruption of so many passages of sensations that cannot be confined to chronos, the tendency to order in succession the measure of experience will get stronger. Further, the influence of language in giving fixed form to sensations is greater than we imagine, covering over the "delicate and fugitive impressions" of our actual experience. The pressure and the attempt to be a successful social being thus appropriates the word to impose a stability on the inherently unstable, but

> [t]he feeling itself is a being which lives and develops and is therefore constantly changing ... it lives because the duration in which it develops is a duration whose moments permeate one another. By separating these moments from each other, by spreading out time in space, we have caused this feeling to lose its life and color. (pp. 132–133)

By bringing back affect and sensation into the question of time Bergson takes a huge step in disrupting the project of modernity, which heads inexorably into a bland and hollowed-out present with an eye mainly on the future. Making a direct appeal to affect and lived experience, Bergson uncovers duration. This is the first step in the embodiment of time.

This is a good place to make a leap into a rather unfamiliar realm and see elements of a tradition that singularly disrupts time as measure through a deepening awareness of the body. This is the Eastern tradition of tantra, an extensive and polymorphous set of transformative practices that vigorously rejects any tendency toward a split in body and mind, that illusory hiatus in which time appears. To the superficially acquainted, the term *tantra* might evoke an impossibly esoteric doctrine, and it is indeed cloaked in one, but the central assumptions and tenets are quite straightforward and accessible to those willing to experiment and interested in intensifying their experience of the living moment. Below I discuss a few major threads that run through the various schools of tantra to give us a glimpse of another plane that has little or no use for time as chronos. The attempt is to open up the body and mind to a cosmic alterity that is always already present but rarely felt or taken into account in daily life. I will begin with an introductory note that takes us to the heart of an ancient corporeal doctrine whose opening insight is that we inhabit the body but rarely know or understand what it is and what it is capable of. Spinoza knew this very well, as did Nietzsche, who would say that we stand amazed before consciousness, but the truly surprising thing is the body. Not knowing the body, or knowing it only from an external perspective, we tend to experience ourselves as spectators and consequently become trapped in time.

Tantra, or the "Loom" of Time

Among the Vedic scriptures of India, the spiritual teachings and practices called the *tantra* (one meaning of which is "loom") occupies a preeminent place. In fact, tantra, as John Woodroffe (1969) points out, may be thought of as a reference to this *yuga* or age in which we live, something that most commentators have failed to bring out. In other words, tantra is not only the spiritual practice appropriate for these times but is itself a vital understanding of the age. Additionally, it is intriguing to note that this age, our times, in the Vedas, is referred to as the *kali yuga*; *kali* comes from *kāla*, which means "time." In kali, kāla or time as a physical force becomes the source of heterogeneous experience as well as the destroyer. We can think of it in this way: kali is the age when time as an exteriority becomes prominent, and therefore tantra as spiritual practice is a way of navigating reality in this age. Discussing the emergence of tantra as a major spiritual movement, Mircea Eliade (1970) notes:

> We do not know why and under what circumstances it came to designate a great philosophical and religious movement, which, appearing as early as the fourth century, assumed the form of a pan-Indian vogue. ... In a comparatively short time, Indian philosophy, mysticism, ritual, ethics, iconography, and even literature are influenced by tantrism. ... (p. 200)

Tantrism has affected virtually every spiritual school in India. There is, for instance, a Buddhist tantrism and a Hindu tantrism, among others, with similarities and differences in practice. Here it is possible only to touch upon some general and oft-occurring themes without going into the specificities of the widely varying practices. It is important to note that no specific practice is absolutely essential to tantra; it is the transformations or the realizations that are important, and many are the gateways to it. For instance, popular conceptions equate tantra with the awakening of the *kundalini* or a psychic power associated with the spine and genitalia through yoga and meditation. While this conception is not entirely misplaced and some schools do lay emphasis on this technique, tantra is a heterogeneous multiplicity, marked mainly by spiritual rebellion against all forms of asceticism and puritanical tendencies.

In general, tantra can be understood as a set of liberatory practices that breaks the bonds of time and duality by means of an infinitely careful exploration of the body and its powers. But it is also full of difficult and esoteric knowledge that is easily misunderstood and widely misused. According to tradition, neither the Vedas nor the tantra have any authorship. They are merely remembered from a timeless past. Woodroffe (1969) notes, "The Tantra claims not only to be practical and to contain provisions for all without distinction of [race] or sex, but also to be fundamentally rational" (p. 80). Careful thought and reasoning are emphasized, which is one of the reasons why we can extract some useful signs for our purposes despite the obscure terminology and intentionally vague language that is typical of these texts. And although the *Tantra Sastra* (the tantric scriptures) are awash with intricate mythological allusions, symbols, and iconography of various personified natural powers, it is possible to uncover some basic philosophical attitudes and proceed without worrying about these symbolisms, navigating by means of an aesthetic reason and the gradual unfolding of a deeper intuition.

Now we will see why here we have a radicalization of the Bergsonian position that asserts the embodied nature of duration. In tantra we find the ultimate celebration of the body. It is a complete inversion of idealism and neoplatonic and Cartesian notions that isolate and privilege the mind. Here *corporeality is foundational*. In the *Hevajra Tantra* it is written, "I have not seen a place of pilgrimage and an abode of bliss like my body" (Dasgupta, 1946, p. 103). In this important passage the body is seen as a shrine for pilgrimage, in sharp contrast to religions like Christianity, where the body is perceived as "fallen flesh" and a source of liability for the onward journey of the soul. This is materialist thought at its height of excitement and, as we shall see, this exhilaration comes out of a knowledge of the body that is totally and absolutely physical. Eliade (1970) writes, "In tantrism, the human body acquires an importance it had never before attained in the spiritual history of India ... the body is no longer the source of pain, but the most reliable and effective instrument at man's disposal" (p. 227).

Consequently, there is a great deal of emphasis on the health and preservation of the body. But this must not be seen as health fetishism, as it is not about hygiene or fitness; it is, rather, an understanding of the body as sacred and therefore the treatment of it as such. Eliade further notes:

> We can distinguish at least two orientations, different, yet convergent, in this emphatic valuation of the human body and its possibilities: (1) there is the

emphasis accorded to the *total experience of life* as constituting an integral part of *sādhana*, and this is the general position of all tantric schools; (2) there is, in addition, the will to master the body in order to transmute it into a divine body. (p. 228)

What does this mean in relation to the conversation on time? If we pay attention to this embodied *total experience* of life, we will see that it would involve a slowing down and eventual irrelevance of time as measure. But we must be careful. What is experienced in tantra is not the mind's experience or knowledge of the body but the body's rising awareness of itself or the body's proprioception and constitution of itself. This total experience is a form of immanence and cannot project time outside of it as measure. In other words, time, which is an abstraction from total experience, lapses in duration. To put it differently, ceaseless attendance on the minutest detail of physical existence brings about singularities or one-pointedness that escapes the capture of time. By sinking the mind into the body from which it has arisen, there is born a deep inward intuition that makes us aware of the dimensions and workings of the body as never before. We begin to experience the body as a cosmic body, as a flux and interplay of forces and energies in which time as regular intervals of measure has little meaning.

Note also Eliade's reference to a "divine body," which reduces all notions capable of describing modal reality such as measure and time to an inferior level of being, to nothingness. There is not the gradual dissolution of the body over time but a reabsorption of time into a corporeal duration, a divine body. Implicitly and by definition, there is nothing outside the divine body that can measure it. We are no longer frightened of the slippage of time, which has been the bane of modernity, but it is from us, instead, that time proceeds. We have turned the tables and therefore no longer have the need to react fearfully further enmesh us in time.

How can one be acquainted with this process of corporeal awareness? First, there has to be a deep acknowledgment of the primacy of the existence of the body through various practices that might include meditation on the body and a careful attention to bodily actions and passions. This has nothing to do with indulgences or physical deprivations, but the acquiring of a fine internal balance that is not subservient to the mind or its categories. In order to achieve this, tantra practices are often directed at various dormant psychic centers or plexuses in the body that are to be awakened in order to interrupt the linear progression of time and thought. No longer are we in awe of or do we live in a disembodied mind, but the mind itself becomes one more action of the body. This disruption places the *sādhaka* or the practitioner *inside* duration rather than outside time. Eliade (1970) discusses the *Kalacakra-tantra*, one of the many esoteric books of tantra, in which it is written that the *Bodhisattva* or great teacher taught the king "to control the temporal rhythms by disciplining respiration—thus he could escape from the domination of time" (p. 204).[5] This is a reference to a practice called *kumbhaka*, or the sudden arrest of breath. Kumbhaka may occur through control of respiration, yoga, an aesthetic experience, a sexual performance, meditation, reflection, or deep absorption in work or study, again showing a fascinating pluralism in thought and practice within this philosophy. It must be understood that the arrest of physical breath is only an outer symptom of a deeper arrest of *Prāna* or the psychic breath that feeds consciousness or the endless progression of thought that is also time. What is realized in this sudden cessation is that all categories, including time, are empty and that this liberates us from the fear of passage of time. This notion of the emptiness of categories, found mostly in the Buddhist schools of tantra, is often mistranslated and misrepresented as the "void" or "nothingness." On the contrary, in that flash that is atemporal, we come in contact with the richness and the renewal of life in the present that is normally edited out of consciousness through the oppositions and binaries in which we are socialized.

Yet, a cautionary note may be appropriate here: in the attempt to provide a simple account we must not oversimplify; it must be understood that according to tradition, a great deal of preliminary work involving the stimulation of bodily imagination, understanding of the perceptions, and strengthening of the nervous system is necessary before we can hope to come to this intuition (see Woodroffe, 1969). This intuition is, to reiterate, a reversal of the process of time. Ordinarily time *eats into* the body or there is degeneration of the physical over time, but in tantra the body *eats* time, as it were, by elaborating or retarding physical processes like breathing and expanding the awareness of the different centers or plexuses and bringing the body in line with cosmic pulses. To the body and mind that are reciprocally related in this manner, there is nothing that stands outside the flow of experience to measure it. This sense of immanence also emanates, as we saw earlier, from Bergson's duration.

Educational Implications: The Slowing of Time

Let us next ask what could be some educational implications of the present discussion. If it appears to the reader that I am suggesting students or teachers undertake esoteric practices, such is not the case, for that would not only be unreasonable but patently alien to the context. All the same, immersing ourselves in a discussion on time has pedagogical value in terms of reeducating the sensibilities. To understand the relevance of time as quality in education, let us start from the intuitionist perspective and find out how it can enrich learning.

All along we have been discussing an epistemology and aesthetics that makes room within experience for novelty and the reopening of settled realities. In technological society, where everything seems to be geared toward the clock, the worship of clockwork efficiency sees things largely settled in advance of us—a closure applied irrespective of who we are and how we want our lives to be. This undoubtedly affects education wherein metric time is the measure of the school day, the distribution of curriculum, testing times, and so on. The question that must be asked is whether we can, through all that is thrust upon us as the consequence of settled realities, enter into a durational relationship with the event. We have seen that the Bergsonian praxis attempts to address not secondhand knowledge but perception itself, the way in which we order the event. It is not concerned with a mere rearrangement, or a progressive knowledge of things—which science, incidentally, does quite adequately. It is instead concerned with the sense of the new, itself, independent of its manifestations, that comes with the calling to mind of qualitative difference. Qualitative difference is durational time. Reorienting our inner dialogue along the lines of the epistemological stance offered here brings its reward for the educator, for it takes away "the fear of being in a world without novel possibilities, where everything is regulated in advance" (Lévinas, 1985, p. 28). The novelty made possible in Bergson's work breaks the hegemony of settled realities.

At the same time, it is not the valorization of the novel for its own sake that is witnessed here, but a "spirituality of the new" that comes with the attention to time and sensations that Bergson demands. Understanding time as immanent in the body is a move away from the obsession with the mind and a shift into corporeality that results in *slowing down time,* making possible a new relationship with the event. This is not some kind of mental exercise but a perception that breaks habitual ways of defining the event, a touch of which opens up the possibility of a deeply "absorptive" learning (James, 1983, p. 16). A sense of duration helps us escape the oppression of bounded time, breathing into everyday learning experience a sense of qualitative difference rather than the clinical sanitization of measurement.

Second, let us consider the issue of fragmentariness of the curriculum. Progressive educators such as John Dewey (1916/1944), who, referring to it as

the "parceling out of instruction," have despaired about the disjointed manner
in which school subjects are often taught. Efforts to integrate school subjects
have not worked very well because these attempts have typically been on the
plane on which the problem itself exists—that is, on the plane of fragmentary
experience. Recall Bergson's analysis, which showed us that experience in general is projected onto the quantified and measurable plane that is space. On
this plane no real integration is possible because the finitude, the boundaries
and limits, are the very characteristics of this plane. An educator who seeks to
truly integrate the curriculum cannot hope to do so merely by making some
superficial connections here and there, but must make an appeal to another
stratum. This stratum is the body-mind continuum. Then the very nature of
the problem changes, and we are no longer concerned with how to connect
math to history, or science to social studies, but learn to see how both math
and history are different expressions of the continuum of the body, mind, and
socius. The tantra shows us how a different presence of the body can be made
central. It is through the body that connections are made. The wisdom tradition helps us to reconsider the body's role in knowing, and eliminates the
fragmentation. We have to find ways by which to "sink" the mind back into
the body from which it has disassociated itself.

This corporeal knowledge is active in the body and not stored as information in the mind. A careful distinction must thus be made between the two
orientations. Obviously, no exhaustive list can be provided here of the means
of forming such organic connections, nor are there any "how to's" for raising
the meditative spirit, but a growing sensibility in the direction of the body and
awareness of the danger of leaving it at the margins, which feminist pedagogies have recognized, opens the door to endless possibilities of experimentation that can provide glimpses of duration.

Next, such a discussion as this one provides a counterpoint to the future-
orientedness of education that ends up oppressing and sacrificing the present.[6]
The future as a bureaucratic and totalizing concept is a projection of the iterative model of time and diverts our attention from qualitative differences and
divergences within individual moments that do not repeat. We become aware
of the vacuity of such orientations only through careful observation of sensations that reveal their heterogeneous multiplicity as discussed in the section
above on praxis. Duration is an awakening to the heterogeneity of the present
and therefore of creative anticipation rather than projection.

What then appears before us is well explained by what William James has
called "a sense of limitless significance" in the ordinary and the immediate,

endowing the ordinary moment with a moral quality. To elaborate on this notion James employs Robert Louis Stevenson's evocative prose: "'All life that is not mechanical is spun out of two strands: seeking for the time-devouring nightingale and hearing him'" (Stevenson, as quoted in James, 1983, pp. 136–137). This "hearing" retards or elaborates time, and helps us intuit a new meaning of the known that is lined with "authentic tidings" of the unknown, even if briefly. The point here is that it is the "hearkening" of this "birdsong" that is educationally important, making it clear that the creative or even moral life cannot be understood without listening very carefully to the present. But this present is nowhere if not in the body. The task of the educator is not to justify present undertakings by positing a future but to open up the present itself through embodied intuition. This is not to suggest that the future is unimportant, but that the quality of that projection will depend on our ability to listen to the present, otherwise what is to come will be mostly conditioned by the present.

The task of listening to the present is taken up in a powerful and bodily sentient way in the teachings of the tantra. Through ceaseless attention to breath, thought, posture, action, and the totality of experience, the tantra helps us to understand fear. The attention to the present frees us of the fear of the future which can be crippling and therefore frees up inner resources for truly absorptive learning. For the knower of the tantra, the future is in the ever-widening and deepening awareness of the now, and the pedagogic moment can be deepened by attending to all that is left out as unimportant in the immediate. Freedom from the fear of the future is in itself an unburdening that leads to an enrichment and a more meaningful present.

Conclusion

We have seen how time is a formal, a priori condition of appearance in the Kantian idealist rationalism that paved the way for modernity's reduction of time to uniform measure. This has brought about a deep schism between time as lived experience and time as pure extension, prompting Henri Bergson to assert a qualitative dimension of time as duration that could heal the split. This passage is made possible by means of a phenomenological attention to body, sensation, and affect. Next, a system of practice was examined that brought a bodily perception to center stage that does not require time as an a priori condition of perception. In other words, time as an external grid of measure, which holds center stage in modernist modes of perception, loses its meaning for the practitioner of the tantra. This is not the Kantian reduction of time as empty, mathematical formalism, but a nonengagement with simultaneity and succession through atemporal bodily rhythms.

In probing into the two different movements that run counter to time as external measure I have tried to avoid any kind of mysticism and provide openings through which we can perceive new ways of thinking about experience. In Bergson we see a sense of novelty that irrupts or is made possible by reclaiming the qualitative dimension of time. Beyond that, tantra opens up the radical possibility of crossing the temporal dimension by turning to the body-mind continuum or, to put it differently, by eliminating, through various practices, the superstition of the body-mind break. Whether elements of these two visions or practices can be combined in a single phenomenological inquiry is a moot point, but certainly the disruption to the usual modes of metricized thought that these two encounters provide is of praxeological value. For the educator, ways of observing and thinking about experience, time, and sensation along the lines suggested here contain the possibility that there may arise in our sensibilities a deepening, a fresh burst of attention that may lead to moments of incandescence within daily acts of learning. But one must be cautious here at the same time, for one must not see in these encounters apparatuses that can serve utilitarian or modernist ends. Rather, these notions bring to our attention a dense and rich preconceptual reality that is always bordering on the unknown, disturbing the hegemony of settled perceptions.

Notes

1. Even critical pedagogists seem to have ignored the temporal dimension in examining assessment procedures. For instance, what does mastery of time prove in test taking, and what might be at the root of the impulse?
2. Even the most insightful critique of capital—historical materialism—had internalized the scientific notion of time as linear progression and paid no more attention to it. Simultaneously, it had dismissed desire as an appendage of bourgeois individualism. This indeed was no mere coincidence.
3. *Decomposition* here refers to a shift in frame in which the measured instant reenters the flow and loses its fixed contours. More acute sensibilities causes usual temporal calibration to lose its fierce hold on experience.
4. Works of such diverse authors as Lewis Carroll, Jorge Luis Borges, William Faulkner, and Virginia Woolf are examples of this challenge to time.
5. *Disciplining respiration* refers to a set of practices that regulates the prāna or the breath. Details of this can be found in any work on Hatha Yoga.
6. The justification for curricula is often provided in terms of their usefulness in the future—the making of a citizen or a worker—and not in terms of *doing*, as Dewey (1944) has emphasized.

References

Augustine, St. (1986). *Confessions* (R. S. Pine-Coffin, Trans.). London: Penguin.

Aurobindo, S. (1995). *Secret of the Veda*. Twin Lakes, WI: Lotus Press.

Bergson, H. (1946). *The creative mind*. New York: Philosophical Library.

Bergson, H. (2001). *Time and free will: An essay on the immediate data of consciousness*. New York: Dover.

Dasgupta, S. B. (1946). *Obscure religious cults*. Calcutta: Firma KLM.

Deleuze, G. (1990). *The logic of sense* (M. Lester, Trans.). Minneapolis: University of Minnesota Press.

Dewey, J. (1944). *Democracy and education: An introduction to the philosophy of education.* New York: Free Press. (Original work published 1916)

Eliade, M. (1970). *Yoga: Immortality and freedom*. (Willard R. Trask, Trans.). Princeton, NJ: Princeton University Press.

Hawking, S. (1988). *A brief history of time: From the big bang to black holes*. New York: Bantam.

James, W. (1983). *Talks to teachers on psychology*. Cambridge, MA: Harvard University Press.

Kant, I. (1990). *The critique of pure reason* (N. Kemp Smith, Trans.). London: Macmillan.

Lévinas, E. (1985). *Ethics and infinity*. (R. A. Cohen, Trans.). Pittsburgh: Duquesne University Press.

Lyotard, J. F. (1988). *The inhuman: Reflections on time* (G. Bennington & R. Bowlby, Trans.). Stanford, CA: Stanford University Press.

Martinez, M. (2003). *The Revolt against time: A philosophical approach to the prose and poetry of Quevedo and Bocaangel*. Lanham, MD: University Press of America.

Prigogine, I., & Stengers, I. (1997). *The end of certainty: Time, chaos, and the new laws of nature*. New York: Free Press.

Spinoza, B. de (1994). *The ethics and other works* (E. Curley, Trans.). Princeton, NJ: Princeton University Press.

Woodroffe, J. (1969). *Introduction to Tantra Sâastra*. Madras, India: Ganesh.

CHAPTER 12

Hearing, Contemplating, and Meditating
In Search of the Transformative Integration of Heart and Mind

Daniel Vokey

University of British Columbia

"Do you think that it will be a poor life that a man leads who has his gaze fixed on that direction, who contemplates absolute beauty with the appropriate faculty and is in constant union with it? Do you not see that in that region alone where he sees beauty with the faculty capable of seeing it, will he be able to bring forth not mere reflected images of goodness but true goodness, because he will be in contact not with a reflection but with the truth? And having brought forth and nurtured true goodness he will have the privilege of being beloved of God, and becoming, if ever a man can, immortal himself."

This, Phaedrus and my other friends, is what Diotima said and what I believe; and because I believe it I try to persuade others that in the acquisition of this blessing human nature can find no better helper than Love. I declare that it is the duty of every man to honour Love, and I honour and practice the mysteries of Love in an especial degree myself, and recommend the same to others, and I praise the power and valour of Love to the best of my ability both now and always.

—Plato, *Symposium*

Transformative Learning

A growing number of authors representing many forms of education—including adult education, moral education, citizenship education, character education, holistic education, religious education, environmental education, and antiracist education—include among their aims the transformation of how we perceive the world and act within it. As O'Sullivan, Morrell, and O'Connor (2002) note, "Transformative learning involves experiencing a deep, structural shift in the basic premises of thought, feelings, and actions. It is a shift in consciousness that dramatically and permanently alters our way of being in the world" (p. xvii). This desire for transformative learning very often reflects a belief that, individually and collectively, we need a radical change of heart and mind to respond adequately to the social, political, economic, environmental, moral, and/or spiritual crises that (depending upon location/perspective) are seen to be either looming on the horizon or already unravelling the fabric of life.[1]

As an instructor both in the Outward Bound tradition of experiential education and in the philosophical traditions of Aristotle, Plato, and Socrates (among others), I have long sought to understand, for my own benefit as well as that of others, what kinds of educational initiatives can foster the wise and compassionate being and action so urgently needed in our troubled world. My intent in what follows is to indicate why I have come to believe that studying and practicing Mahāyāna Buddhism is one way to engage in, and support others in undertaking, a transformative integration of heart and mind. While my reflections are offered to anyone interested in progressive personal and social change, they are intended in particular for those who, like myself, work as faculty in institutions of higher education: teaching and supervising students, developing curricula, conducting research, administering programs, and assuming various service/leadership roles in academic and professional communities.

The Limitations of Intellectual Knowledge

I begin with the observation that the forms of education and learning that lead only to intellectual understanding are typically insufficient by themselves to effect the transformations of perception, feeling, and action that we desire. Very simply, this is because there is often a gap between what we know intellectually and what we actually feel and do. For example, I might have learned enough about cholesterol to know that the double chocolate doughnut on the plate before me is bad for my health, but still crave and consume it just the same. I might understand that exhaust emissions cause global warming and other harms to the environment in which I live and breathe, but still care so much about my short-term comfort that I leave my bike in its rack and drive my car to the supermarket instead. I might have some appreciation of how global capitalism results in unjust and unsustainable economic activity, afflicting great suffering on disadvantaged and oppressed people at home and abroad in a way that eventually harms us all, but still select mutual funds with a mind only to those that offer the most favorable rate of return.

My actions in such cases brings to mind Paul's lament in his First Epistle to the Romans (New English Bible, 7:19–20): "The good which I want to do, I fail to do; but what I do is the wrong which is against my will." Paul locates the source of the recurring gap between our espoused beliefs on the one hand and our actual desires and decisions on the other in a weakness of will traceable to Adam's original sin. He enjoins us to receive the Spirit of God in order to free our conduct from "the control of our lower nature" (Romans 8:3–4), advising, "Those who live on the level of our lower nature have their outlook formed by it, and that spells death; but those who live on the level of the spirit have the spiritual outlook, and that is life and peace" (Romans 8:5–6). I cite Paul to illustrate that how we understand the root cause of our failure to match lofty ideals with feeling, commitment, and action will determine the kind of transformation we will seek in order to bring word and deed into alignment.[2] The desire for a radically new and better way of being in the world thus leads naturally to the question, "What kinds of learning do we need in addition to intellectual insight in order consistently to know *and do* what is good?"

One answer to this question is found in Plato's understanding of the relation of knowledge to virtue, where *virtue* is short for human excellence in perception, feeling, thought, and action. The interpretation of Plato's position I have in mind is that provided by Kenneth Dorter (1997). Interpretation is required because we can find in Plato's texts at least two possible answers to the question of whether reason, where virtuous action is concerned, is able to stand on its own two feet. Plato sometimes appears to believe that we act virtuously only when our knowledge of what is wholesome and good is combined with self-control. For example, drawing upon a tripartite account of the soul, Socrates entertains the possibility that "vice occurs when either the spirited part of us, or the part of us that seeks pleasure and avoids pain and fear, dominates the knowledge-loving part" (Dorter, 1997, p. 315). Other times, however, Plato appears to hold that virtue results from knowledge alone, for in *Pythagoras* Socrates objects to the notion that the lower parts of the soul could overpower reason and "drag it around like a slave." It is not immediately clear, then, in what sense (if any) Plato believes the Socratic dictum that "virtue is knowledge."

To solve this puzzle, Dorter (1997, p. 323) takes a closer look at references by Plato to a distinct form of knowledge, *wisdom* or *sophia*, "a species of knowledge that cannot be taught, at least not in the straightforward way that other kinds of knowledge can be taught." Dorter (1997, p. 333) then draws from the doctrines of the great Neo-Confucian philosopher Wang Yang-ming (1472–1529) to argue that this wisdom arises from directly apprehending the true nature of virtuous feeling, thought, and action and thereby appreciating its true value. In this interpretation of Plato's final view, a love of virtue for its own sake that is strong enough to resist the attractions of lesser goods such as comfort, wealth, and fame comes only from the wisdom that is born of immediate and profound personal experience. In Dorter's (1997) words:

> For Socrates, as for Wang, we know something only to the extent that we have experienced it and have been able to taste its pleasure. Knowledge is virtue, then, not when it is only abstract and conceptual, or even when it is the know-how of a skill, but only when it is complete knowledge by acquaintance, the full experiencing of a certain condition. (p. 336)

To illustrate this kind of knowledge, Dorter cites the transformation experienced by slave trader John Newton, immortalized in the line, "I was blind … but now I see." Dorter (1997, p. 340) submits that the dramatic change in Newton's feeling, thinking, and acting did not arise from greater self-control, but from a sudden appreciation of the true moral significance of his actions—an appreciation that, in Newton's account, was made possible by God's gift of grace. Dorter then shows how understanding the difference between wisdom and less complete forms of knowledge as analogous to the difference between blindness and sight resonates with Plato's allegory of the cave: moving from *opinions* to *direct experience* about the intrinsic value of the virtuous life is like moving from glimpses of vague shadows thrown by flickering firelight to a clear view of real objects illuminated by the sun's rays. And "if we see clearly how virtue consummates our lives, and how trivial are the rewards of the activities that are counterproductive of virtue, then the latter lose their hold over us" (Dorter, 1997, p. 341). "To say that virtue is knowledge," notes Dorter, "would then mean that once we know *from experience* what it is to be virtuous, our convictions will become too firmly established to be dragged around slavishly by our appetites and passions" (pp. 336–337; emphasis added).

On Dorter's interpretation of Plato, instruction is of limited use in producing this kind of transformative learning that leads to genuine virtue precisely because wisdom arises from an experiential form of knowing that is analogous to direct perception and cannot be adequately communicated in words. Dorter cites a passage in Plato's Seventh Letter that refers to knowledge of this kind: "'It cannot be expressed in speech like other kinds of knowledge, but after a long attendance upon the matter itself, and communion with it, then suddenly—as a blaze is kindled from a leaping spark—it is born in the soul and at once becomes self-nourishing'" (Dorter, 1997, p. 342). At the same time, Plato's dialogues do assign teaching a role in supporting our educational ascent to the vision of the good and the wisdom its illumination affords. While instruction cannot substitute for the insight born of direct experience, it can offer ways of thinking that keep our mind open and properly attuned:

> Partly this is done in a negative way, such as by the Socratic technique of provoking *aporia*, an impasse of thought that shows us the darkness of what previously seemed to us to be most visible. Partly it is done in a positive way, by providing us with doctrines that we can accept as true opinions which, if put into practice, can lead to an experience of knowledge that converts us to virtue. (Dorter, 1997, p. 342)

Plato also asserts that educational initiatives supporting the emergence of wisdom work with a capacity or faculty that all humans *already possess*. Using the analogy to perception once again, Socrates maintains that education does not give us the power of sight, but guides and encourages us to look in the right direction:

> It looks, then, as though wisdom were different from those ordinary virtues, as they are called, which are not far removed from bodily qualities, in that they can be produced by habituation and exercise in a soul which has not possessed them from the first. *Wisdom, it seems, is certainly the virtue of some diviner faculty, which never loses its power, though its use for good or harm depends on the direction towards which it is turned.* (*The Republic*, 7:518–519; emphasis added)

I have argued elsewhere that Aristotle also holds that virtuous perception, feeling, judgment, and action result when intellectual inquiry is complemented by personal experiences that yield a love of virtue for its own sake, which renders self-control unnecessary (Vokey, 2001; see, e.g., pp. 211–213). If these classical philosophers are right, then educators seeking to experience transformative learning and to promote it in others need to know how one might gain such direct perception and appreciation of "the good." To reinforce this point, I want next to argue—taking work by Jerry Coombs (1998) as a point of departure—that understanding how intellectual inquiry might be joined with personal experience of the good is also crucially important to instructors of programs in professional ethics for educators.

Professional Ethics for Educators[3]

Citing research by James Wallace, Coombs reports that there are two kinds of practical ethical problems that educators and other professionals find particular vexatious: problems of relevance and problems of conflict:

> In a relevance problem, there is reason to think that the case at hand might fall under one of our ethical principles, and reason to think that it might not. In other words, the problem arises precisely because we are unsure whether or how our ethical principles apply to the problematic case. A conflict problem arises when two or more of our ethical principles apply to a case, but they recommend differing ethical judgments of the case or differing courses of action. (Coombs, 1998, p. 556)

Do contemporary courses in applied ethics succeed in helping teachers and administrators make sound judgments in such difficult cases? With this question in mind, Coombs reviews four texts published between 1988 and 1995, each of which exemplifies one of two standard approaches to teaching professional ethics for educators. The "applying ethical theories" approach starts from the assumption that "acting ethically means acting in accordance with well-justified ethical principles," and so "sets forth an ethical theory or set of ethical principles for educators to follow and instructs them on how these principles are to be applied" (Coombs, 1998, p. 556). The second, or "developing moral reasoning," approach undertakes to improve the process of deliberation through which teachers and administrators arrive at moral judgments. In this kind of course, participants are encouraged to develop their own ethical theories by formulating general ethical principles that achieve reflective equilibrium with their considered moral intuitions (Coombs, 1998, p. 555).

The fundamental problem that Coombs identifies with these two ways of teaching professional ethics is that moral philosophy has yet to provide compelling reasons to prefer one among the many competing ethical and political theories, each of which highlights different aspects of ethically problematic cases as most important to consider in deciding what to do. I would add that moral philosophy has produced no agreement whether, and if so how, one ethical perspective could in principle be identified as superior to alternatives. This leaves instructors of professional ethics courses with a choice between teaching the theoretical perspectives to which they subscribe or leaving it up to participants to choose one or more according to their own lights. Coombs finds neither option satisfactory. He observes that, in the latter case, course participants are likely to embrace those theories and principles that match their preexisting tacit moral commitments. However, he is skeptical that simply making their commitments explicit in the form of general principles will enable teachers and administrators to improve their ability to solve problems of relevance and of conflict. For one thing, it is not necessary to make tacit commitments explicit in order to use them to identify considerations relevant to ethical decision making in particular contexts of practice. For another thing, general principles are always open to interpretation because it is not possible "to identify all of the various kinds of actions that will and will not count as instances of acting on that principle" (Coombs, 1998, p. 557). Neither is it possible to determine in advance which principle or principles should take priority in ethical decision making, for often the same principle is given different weight in different contexts of practice.

Having discussed the limitations of the two standard approaches he finds in the literature, Coombs presents his own ideas about how courses in professional ethics for educators might help them reach satisfactory decisions in challenging ethical situations. He draws an analogy to legal studies to argue that the best resources for reasoning about problems of relevance are particular cases of practical judgment that are widely recognized to model the proper application of the ethical principle in question. He proposes that, when uncertain about whether or not the principle applies to a particular situation, one should "consider the extent to which the present case is similar to and different from the settled cases with regard to morally relevant features, and attempt to determine whether or not one has essentially the same reasons for applying the principle in the present case as in the settled cases" (Coombs, 1998, p. 567). With regard to problems of conflict, Coombs argues that one should attempt to preserve as much as possible of the values underlying the competing principles on a case by case basis rather than try to establish a hierarchy of principles to be applied independently of context.

At the end of his study Coombs considers the Aristotelian *aretaic* tradition of ethical instruction in which teachers "tend to be less concerned with developing deliberative abilities and more concerned with developing such things as relevant virtues, sensitivities, and powers of moral perception." He underlines the importance of these objectives by observing that "without moral perception and sensitivity, moral reasoning cannot get started."[5] To professional ethics instructors who decide to adopt these objectives, Coombs recommends that they give course participants opportunities both to increase the "depth and richness" of the ethical concepts they bring with them to class and to develop new ones. Coombs further recommends that sensitivity to the ethical dimensions of educational practice be enhanced by inviting teachers and administrators to consider how, in cases drawn from their own actual experience, their personal moral commitments are properly adapted to the particular forms of authority and responsibility that accompany their professional roles.

In my view, these recommendations are very good as far as they go, but they appear not to go far enough in addressing Coombs's own concern about ethical pluralism—namely, the unresolved tension among the incompatible priorities in ethical decision making that rival ethical theories provide. Coombs does not explain how, without presupposing the validity of one among rival ethical perspectives, participants in professional ethics courses would assess the reasons for—or otherwise judge the appropriateness of—either the new moral concepts to which they are introduced or the new applications of their current conceptual repertoire. Analyzing case studies from a range of perspectives might present teachers and administrators with opportunities to enrich and expand their moral vocabulary. However, if such discussion is to foster learning rather than simply exchanging viewpoints, there must be some way to identify which ways of responding to particular moral challenges are correct and which are not. Improving ethical decision making through case study analysis would thus appear to presuppose that participants will possess and exercise the very capacity for sound practical judgment that Coombs believes courses in professional ethics should undertake to improve.[6]

To respond to my concern, Coombs might turn to the one variation on the "developing moral reasoning" approach to ethical instruction to which he gives his (qualified) approval, and that is Ken Strike's (1995) goal of helping educational professionals become competent speakers of a public moral language. A public moral language is heuristically defined as "the language that members of a pluralistic society with different moralities can agree to use to discuss public issues" (Coombs, 1998, p. 564). Coombs agrees with Strike that to learn a moral language is to learn "a set of concepts and argument strategies" that provide "a shared way of thinking through ethical issues" (Strike, 1995, p. 33). Strike uses the game of tennis to illustrate how acquiring a language is acquiring perceptual and appraisal categories: One comes to make sense of what is happening on the court and to appreciate brilliant play by learning the proper application of such concepts as *ace, volley,* and *base line return.* As Strike (1995, p. 33) puts it, "The vocabulary constitutes the game. Learning to play requires learning to talk in a certain way. So it is also with ethics."

What is the connection between Strike's proposal and the problem of ethical pluralism? Strike recommends that educational professionals learn to use a public moral language in arriving at and defending ethical decisions precisely because a shared set of moral concepts would enable communication across the differences that exist within a morally pluralistic society. He argues that, to fulfill this function, a public language should (1) "have sufficient richness and sophistication to allow us to discuss educational issues cogently," (2) "be a language the vast majority of competent moral speakers in a society can speak conscientiously, despite disagreements about fundamental convictions," and (3) be widely shared (1995, p. 31). According to Strike (1995, p. 31), a public language meeting these three conditions would be composed of the following three "sublanguages": a language of *rights* that attends to due process, equal opportunity, fairness, and justice; a language of *caring* that celebrates kindness, compassion, and nurturance; and a language of *rational integrity* that enshrines respect for evidence, argument, and the pursuit of truth. By becoming competent speakers of this "tri-part public moral language" teachers and administrators would learn a comprehensive set of criteria for ethical decision making in educational practice.

I am very sympathetic to the project of identifying and extending common ground among speakers of different moral languages rooted in particular religious, philosophical, political, and/or cultural traditions. However, as Strike (1995, p. 32) himself recognizes, gaining competence in using a public moral language *requires*, rather than substitutes for, the exercise of sound practical judgment informed by intellectual virtues such as wisdom and moral virtues such as "sensitivity to context and individual need." For one thing, educational professionals need practical judgment to integrate the distinct perspectives afforded by the sublanguages of rights, caring, and rational integrity. Strike uses the task of assigning grades to show how each language points up different dimensions of an issue in a way that may yield conflicting recommendations. In such cases, practical judgment is required so impartiality can be balanced with sensitivity to differences in individual abilities and circumstances. Strike also shows how teachers and administrators need practical judgment to balance fidelity to the core values of their primary moral communities with commitment to the moral standards internal to the public moral language they speak as professionals. He observes that "often the motivation to follow the precepts of the public ethic comes from attachments and values formed in primary moral communities and then transferred to the public domain," concluding that a public moral language should not be seen as "either a competitor with or replacement for these various forms of moral speech" (Strike, 1995, pp. 34–35). Thus, even if we agree with Strike and Coombs that it is both possible and desirable for educational professionals to learn to speak a public moral language, we are still left with the question of how teachers and administrators can cultivate the wisdom that sound ethical decision making requires.

Since Coombs's review was published, a third way of conceiving and teaching courses in professional ethics for educators has emerged, in response (I suspect) to the limitations of its predecessors. This third way is the "multiple ethical languages" approach, represented by the courses Joan Shapiro and Jacqueline Stefkovich describe in their book *Ethical Leadership and Decision-Making in Education: Applying Theoretical Perspectives to Complex Dilemmas.*[7] (They refer to multiple ethical *paradigms* rather than *languages*, but in this context the two terms are essentially synonymous.) The courses they describe have three main components: the discussion of assigned readings, the construction of personal and professional codes of ethics, and the analysis and discussion of case studies.

To begin, lectures on and discussions of assigned readings introduce four distinct ethical paradigms in order to raise the widest possible range of questions during the ethical decision-making process.

The *ethic of justice* asks questions

> related to the rule of law and the more abstract concepts of fairness, equity, and justice. These may include, but are certainly not limited to, questions related to issues of equity and equality; the fairness of rules, laws, and policies; whether laws are absolute, and if exceptions are to be made, under what circumstances; and the rights of individuals versus the greater good of the community. (Shapiro and Stefkovich, 2001, p. 13)

The *ethic of critique* starts from critical social theory's and other sociological analyses of how unequal relationships of power and privilege are maintained among different social groups. In the process of becoming familiar with this perspective, participants learn the use of such concepts as oppression, power, privilege, authority, voice, language, and empowerment. This ethic asks "the hard questions regarding social class, race, gender, and other areas of difference, such as 'Who makes the laws? Who benefits from the law, rule, or policy? Who has the power? Who are the silenced voices?'" (Shapiro and Stefkovich, 2001, p. 15).

The *ethic of care*, represented by the work of such authors as Carol Gilligan, Jane Roland Martin, and Nel Noddings, emphasizes building and maintaining relationships and requires course participants to consider "multiple voices in the decision-making process." This in turn entails an appreciation of diversity, manifest in part by a commitment to learning how to listen to, understand, and respond to others. The questions corresponding to this perspective include:

> Who will benefit from what I decide? Who will be hurt by my actions? What are the long-term effects of a decision I make today? And if I am helped by someone now, what should I do in the future about giving back to this individual or to society in general? (Shapiro and Stefkovich, 2001, p. 17)

Shapiro and Stefkovich understand the ethics of justice, critique, and care as complementary perspectives on the ethical issues faced by administrators and other leaders in schools. At the same time, they believe that a fourth paradigm, the *ethic of the profession*, is needed to raise questions and concerns that might be overlooked by the other three. The ethic of the profession insists that every decision on moral matters made by a teacher or administrator must take their professional roles and responsibilities into account. What does this entail?

This question brings us to the second main component of courses designed according to this version of the multiple ethical languages approach. Shapiro and Stefkovich maintain that, although educational professionals must consult their associations' codes of ethics and other legal frameworks when making ethical decisions, these are usually too general to serve to identify "the right thing to do" in particular situations. To fill this gap, Shapiro and Stefkovich encourage participants in their courses to formulate their own, more substantial personal and professional codes of ethics by reflecting upon "what they perceive to be right or wrong and good or bad, who they are as professionals and as human beings, how they make decisions, and why they make the decisions they do" (2001, p. 21). These codes incorporate both the moral commitments at which participants have arrived through their own personal and professional experience and the moral standards of the professional and social communities in which they work. Furthermore, according to Shapiro and Stefkovich, those applying these codes in ethical decision making in educational contexts should be guided by one overriding principle in order to honor the professional's responsibility to their clients: Do what is in the best interests of the students, "taking into account the fact that they may represent highly diverse populations" (2001, p. 25).

How is this done? The third main component of the courses Shapiro and Stefkovich recommend is analysis and discussion of case studies, which are intended to enable participants do three things: (1) to see how the four perspectives bring different considerations to bear in decision making in particular educational contexts; (2) to test and refine their individual codes of ethics through comparison with their moral intuitions in particular cases; and (3) to come to appreciate how their classmates see, feel, and think differently about moral matters according to their particular points of view. Shapiro and Stefkovich believe that, in combination with the other two course components, practice in working through the complex ethical issues they face from each of these different ethical perspectives will improve the ability of teachers and administrators to resolve them in a satisfactory way.

There are obvious similarities between this multiple-paradigm approach to professional ethics for educators and the coaching of teachers and administrators in the tripartite public moral language that Strike and Coombs recommend. The additional paradigms or languages that Shapiro and Stefkovich include represent two improvements (in my eyes, at least) to Strike's proposals. First, the *ethic of critique* invites educators to uncover the histories of conflict through which certain ethical languages have come to dominate public moral discourse. I think this is important because I believe that to suggest without qualification that a widely shared public moral language exists either in Canada or the United States is to ignore the legacy and ongoing effects of colonization. Second, introducing the *ethic of the profession* foregrounds the kind of contractual and other responsibilities to students that educational professionals have a duty to fulfill.

My approval of these points notwithstanding, I find that the benefits the authors anticipate will result from teaching multiple ethical paradigms and corresponding languages goes well beyond what can be supported by the reasoning and evidence they provide. For one thing, they appear to assume that complex traditions of ethical thought can be translated into lists of questions without misrepresenting their internal tensions and disagreements, which I find implausible. Most significant, they provide no grounds for believing that simply raising a wide variety of questions will help educational professionals generate more satisfactory answers in "real-life, complex dilemmas." I think we have reason to doubt what they again appear to assume: that the different concerns represented by the ethics of justice, critique, care, and the profession will be always and only complementary.

In this connection, I find it highly significant that none of the many case studies that Shapiro and Stefkovich include illustrate how adopting these four distinct ethical perspectives enables educators to evaluate possible courses of action as morally better and worse. Rather, the authors' own observations suggest that their approach to professional ethics is likely to create as many ethical dilemmas as it resolves—for individuals no less than for groups. The section describing how course participants can develop individual codes of ethics surfaces no less than five kinds of possible conflict among their moral commitments. There were potential clashes between

1. personal and professional codes of ethics held by one individual;
2. two different professional codes of ethics held by one individual;
3. two or more professional codes of ethics held by different individuals;
4. the personal and professional codes of ethics of an individual teacher or administrator on the one hand and the moral beliefs of the majority of the members of the community surrounding the school on the other;
5. the moral beliefs held by different members of that larger community.

If the experiences that Shapiro and Stefkovich report (2001, pp. 105–106) are any indication, learning the key concepts and questions of the ethics of justice, critique, care, and the profession is likely to help teachers and administrators appreciate the range both of considerations relevant to an ethical decision and of moral perspectives within a group. However, it is unlikely to promote consensus among educational professionals on the right thing to do, or even the right way to decide. The challenge of ethical pluralism and the spectre of ethical relativism remain, and we are no closer than before to understanding what should complement ethical theory in order to develop sound practical judgment.

I have argued above that if either individual reflection or group discussion is to improve ethical decision making, then there must be some way to identify morally better and worse ways of responding to particular moral challenges. In other words, enhancing practical judgment requires a process within moral education that fulfills a function analogous to experimentation in scientific inquiry and problem solving. One such process is testing the theories and the general principles we advance in ethics on their ability to achieve reflective equilibrium with our considered convictions about what is morally right and wrong in particular cases—convictions at which we arrive through moral intuition. On this view, the possibility of progress in ethical inquiry depends upon the possibility of reliable intuition to generate the particular convictions to which we can appeal in testing ethical theories. This holds even if intuition is understood, not as infallible, but as open to correction in light of further experience and reflection.

The implication of the foregoing is that if our courses are to help teachers and administrators make better ethical decisions, then we must understand how to develop our capacity for moral intuition so that our convictions in particular cases might become more trustworthy rather than less. Plato's "divine faculty" that yields experiential knowledge of the good could represent one form of such intuition. Unfortunately, however, both Aristotle and Plato leave only incomplete accounts of how we actualize our potential to become, and support others in becoming, the kind of virtuous souls who consistently apprehend, take pleasure in, and enact what is intrinsically "noble and fine" without being unduly attracted to comfort, wealth, and prestige. In contrast, Mahāyāna Buddhist traditions of transformative learning, while rooted in ancient soil, are still very much alive today. Over the past 2,500 years Buddhism has been developing teachings and practices on how to actualize our best potentials as human beings through *hearing*, *contemplating*, and *meditating*. Within the scope of a chapter it is not possible to do justice to the rich detail in which these processes are described within even one of Buddhism's many traditions. In what follows, I undertake to summarize enough of the basics of the Mahāyāna path (according to the tradition in which I have been taught[8]) to draw some implications for the academic "lived curriculum."

Transformative Learning via Hearing, Contemplating, and Meditating

According to Mahāyāna Buddhism, the gaps that typically exist between our noble ideals and our actual actions can be attributed—at least in part—to ego. In Buddhist terms, *ego* refers to a collection of deeply ingrained habitual processes of perceiving, feeling, judging, and acting that continually reproduce self-attachment, and thereby limit our usual desires and behaviors to variations upon the themes of ignorance, possessiveness, and aggression. In other words, Buddhism observes that what arises in our experience tends to be automatically assessed in relation to our more or less subtle projects of enjoying what is pleasurable and avoiding what is painful or uncomfortable. Thus, what seems irrelevant we tend to ignore, what seems advantageous we seek to attract, what seems threatening we endeavor to attack or push away. Buddhism concludes that so long as we continue to experience the world dualistically in terms of a fundamental distinction between *self* (me) and *other* (everyone and everything else *but* me), we remain vulnerable to more and less subtle forms of greed, selfishness, envy, and similar vices.

This is not to say that unvirtuous behavior is simply a matter of misplaced motivation. If Buddhism is correct, our habitual tendencies to self-centeredness interfere with knowing as well as doing "the right thing." The explanation is that, to the extent we experience the world dualistically, our actions are ineffective because they are based upon projections rather than upon accurate perceptions of the ways things actually are. In Western psychology, *projection* is typically understood as the tendency to attribute to others what we reject in ourselves. The Buddhist analysis would agree that we are often more quick to blame others than to accept personal responsibility for the conflict and misfortune that we ourselves create. However, Mahāyāna Buddhism goes further in asserting that the separate existence of self and other is nothing more than ego's fabrication: a perceptual, emotional, and conceptual framework that we "project" upon experience. On this view, genuinely virtuous action eludes us because we spend most of our time in a kind of dream state, preoccupied with hopes and fears of our own construction (Loy, 1988, p. 279).

According to this Buddhist analysis, the path to virtue involves unlearning habits of perceiving, feeling, thinking, and acting rooted in dualistic assumptions; and such unlearning is possible because our basic nature is unconditioned awareness. This awareness is unconditioned in the sense that it is not created or manufactured but is always already there. It is thus unconditioned also in the sense that it is before thought, and as such is free from all conceptual reference points, including most particularly the basic duality of self and other. Unconditioned awareness makes unlearning possible because it is inseparable from the qualities of wakefulness, clarity, and compassion (Kongtrül, 1992). Mahāyāna Buddhism thus reports, in a manner reminiscent of the Platonic view, that an innate capacity for virtue is present in every person— indeed, in all sentient beings. In one traditional analogy, as the sun continues to radiate light and warmth even when hidden behind clouds, so the inherent wisdom and compassion of unconditioned awareness remain undimmed even when obscured by dualistic thoughts and emotions. Unconditioned awareness itself is like the sky: vast, unfathomable, without boundary or limit.

Philosophically speaking, that unconditioned awareness is distinct from and prior to dualistic experience provides for the *possibility* of unlearning our conditioning (Tolle, 1999). The educational question remains, "How can

one actually unlearn self-centred perception, feeling, thought, and action?"
Mahāyāna Buddhism recommends two complementary processes—each
process involving hearing, contemplating, and meditating—in order to address
the two fundamental features of the dualism that obscures wisdom and compassion: *confused thoughts* and *conflicting emotions.*[9]

Dispelling Confused Thoughts: Realizing the "Emptiness" of Self and Other

In the Mahāyāna Buddhist view introduced above, the basic confusion that
clouds our thinking is *dualism*, the taken-for-granted belief that subjects
(including, most particularly, the *me* that is the central character in our daily
dramas) and objects exist independently. Against this naive belief Mahāyāna
Buddhism argues that subjects and objects only exist *interdependently* and so
are "empty of self-nature." Since Buddhism originated at a time when teachings were passed on largely by word of mouth, becoming acquainted with
these related doctrines of "dependent origination" and "emptiness" is referred
to as *hearing* or *listening*.[10] Educationally speaking, what is particularly important at this initial stage of dispelling confusion is that we listen attentively and
accurately, so that what we hear and work with subsequently is as complete and
as undistorted as possible. Traditional reminders about how *not* to listen use
the analogies of overturned, leaky, and poisoned cups to warn against closed-
mindedness, forgetfulness, and arrogance: common obstacles to understanding views that challenge habitual ways of self-centered thinking.

Through the Mahāyāna path, hearing is properly followed by *contemplating*—in this case, critically investigating both accounts of and arguments for
nonduality through one or more of (1) individual study and reflection, (2)
group discussion and debate, and (3) question-and-answer sessions with a
trustworthy teacher. The task of contemplation is to examine what we have
heard thoroughly until we are confident both that we understand "the view"
of interdependence-emptiness correctly *and* that it holds up under dialectical cross-examination. In other words, this process is not complete until we
can explain and defend to our own complete satisfaction the arguments that
undermine naive belief in the independent existence of self and other.

Mahāyāna Buddhism has long recognized the limitations of purely intellectual insight, holding that it must be combined with direct experience to produce realization of the truth of nonduality. Acquiring such direct perception
is the third step in the process of dispelling confusion, and it is accomplished
through meditating on the understanding of emptiness reached through dis-

cursive reasoning.[11] As I have been taught, the path of formal meditation begins with *shamatha* practice, in which two inherent capabilities of the mind are strengthened: mindfulness and awareness.[12] *Mindfulness* is the ability to place attention on an object; *awareness* is the more environmental sense of where our attention is placed.[13] Typically, in shamatha, the first object upon which we meditate is our breathing, and the practice consists mainly of (1) maintaining a wakeful posture and (2) returning one's attention to one's breathing as often as one has noticed that one's attention has strayed. On occasion, we suddenly become aware during shamatha meditation that we had become so engrossed in remembering past events and/or imagining future scenarios that we had completely forgotten our intention to be mindful. The instruction for such occasions is to gently and patiently label the whole excursion into discursiveness as "thinking" and simply come back to the breath.

The intent to stay attentive to breathing highlights the fickleness and wildness of the discursive mind: One typical effect of shamatha practice is an enhanced awareness of the wide variety of sensations, feelings, and thoughts that arise and pass away in our experience, even when we are sitting quietly in places where there are few extraneous distractions. This awareness often contrasts with our day-to-day state of consciousness, during which we may be so immersed in our ongoing internal dialogues that we fail to recognize them as our own interpretive commentary. Remembering the past and imagining the future without awareness are like being so caught up in a storyline that we temporarily forget that we are simply watching a movie or reading a book. In shamatha, the intention and practice of gently returning attention to breathing creates a "space" of relaxation in which we can witness internal dialogues without being captive to them. In other words, we gain perspective on our habitual patterns by learning to disidentify with our thinking.

A related benefit of mindfulness/awareness meditation practice is a certain degree of success in "taming the mind": gaining the ability to hold attention on the object of one's choice, whether that object be a sequence of physical sensations (breathing), an artifact such as a candle flame or picture, an image produced by our imagination, or an idea held in thought. Shamatha practice thus provides the stability and clarity of mind for subsequent stages on the path of inquiry into emptiness through the recursive process of hearing, contemplating, and meditating. In his descriptions of these further stages, Gyamtso (1988) describes how our initial experiential glimpses of the absence of a separate, substantial self enable us to understand more subtle and profound teachings on nonduality, which in turn have their corresponding meditations. At each stage, then, particular practices serve to test against direct experience "the view" arrived at through study and contemplation of arguments for nonduality. It is one thing to hear and assent intellectually to the position that I do not exist as a single, separate, permanent subject of "my" experience; it is quite another to see, even for a moment, the absence of any *experiencer* in *experiencing*.

The ultimate fruition of this path—unfortunately, something beyond my own personal experience—is enlightenment. The experience of enlightenment is traditionally compared to waking up from a dream because, in both cases, what we took to be real is seen to be a product of the mind. Thus, Mahāyāna Buddhism teaches that we really "wake up" to the way things actually are only when the mind is sufficiently trained to look directly at itself, thereby realizing the true nature both of the mind and the phenomenal world:

> Whether the mind is aware or unaware of its own nature, that nature does not change. ... [However,] as long as the nonconceptual, nonarising Wisdom Mind is not recognized, the dependent nature seems to arise, creating the dream manifestations that the confused mind imagines to comprise an outer world interacting with inner minds. From this confusion the idea of self and other, attachment and aversion, and all the other concepts and emotional disturbances arise. It is like getting totally confused and involved in a dream. Once the awakened consciousness returns, however, one quickly sees the dreams as merely manifestations of the play of the mind, and whether they subside immediately or not they do not disturb the mind at all. (Gyamatso, 1988, p. 87)

Pacifying Conflicting Emotions: Cultivating Unconditioned Compassion

We have seen how, in order to dispel the confusions of dualistic thinking, the process of hearing, contemplating, and meditating seeks to join intellectual understanding of the doctrines of dependent origination and emptiness on the one hand with insight born of direct experience on the other. On the Mahāyāna path, working with conflicting emotions is a parallel, complementary, and ultimately inseparable process. As confused thinking begins with taking the independent existence of self and other for granted, conflicting emotions spring from our habitual tendency to place ourselves at the center of the universe, holding our own well-being to be more important than that of anyone else. The alternative emotional position Mahāyāna Buddhism recommends is equally radical to the ontological claim that neither subjects nor objects have any separate existence, for it proposes that (to paraphrase

Shantideva) all suffering arises from desiring one's own happiness; all true happiness and fulfillment comes from desiring the happiness of others.

This is not a new thought, nor one unique to Buddhism. However, the first step in pacifying conflicting emotions is taken when we go beyond just listening to this or similar teachings to really hearing them, where the difference between listening and hearing is the difference between simply understanding words and being personally touched or moved by their meaning. It is the difference between being told many times of how women and visible minorities experience discrimination in the workplace and finally "getting it"—realizing something of what these words mean in terms of lived experience. Similarly, it is the difference between listening to reports of the harmful environmental effects of oil spills and actually being moved by the sight of seabirds struggling to survive; or—even closer to home— the difference between intellectual assent to the proposition that all humans are mortal and feeling in the pit of our stomachs that we really *are* going to die.[14] Thus, while intellectually we might agree that openhearted concern for others is an "enlightened" form of self-interest and an ideal to which we should aspire, we may need frequent reminders—Scrooge's transformation each December comes to mind—of why this is so in terms of how it actually feels.

As we have seen, Mahāyāna Buddhism acknowledges the power as well as the limitations of the intellect. The contemplation that follows hearing these teachings uses discursive reasoning to reinforce our first glimpses of the source of suffering on the one hand (habitual preoccupation with oneself) and the root of happiness and fulfillment on the other (unbiased concern for others). Like many other traditions, Mahāyāna Buddhism presents a variety of arguments that cultivating universal compassion is the best antidote to the ego's eternal dissatisfactions. Some traditional contemplations presuppose a Mahāyāna Buddhist cosmology and so might have little effect upon people with a different worldview. For example, although it follows from a Buddhist understanding of rebirth that all sentient beings have, at one time or another, been our mothers, those for whom rebirth is a foreign idea may not find rehearsing this chain of reasoning an effective way of extending to all beings the gratitude and love that a mother's care evokes. Other contemplations are more accessible, such as the reasoning that concludes from the interdependence of every living creature on this planet that there is no "enemy" we can defeat without simultaneously harming ourselves.[15] Another traditional contemplation to help deconstruct the dichotomy of us/them thinking is to recall specific cases in which people we had considered bitter antagonists became respected allies, and vice versa. Recently, the arguments in support of unbiased compassion that are available as objects for contemplation include those based upon the growing body of empirical research on the benefits of unlearning destructive emotions.[16]

Once *hearing* has provided the spark and *contemplating* the fuel, *meditating* enlists the power of the imagination to fan the initial flickers of other-oriented concern into a steady blaze of *bodhicitta* ("the heart of the awakened mind"). One traditional practice for arousing and expanding bodhicitta is to meditate on the "Four Limitless Ones": loving kindness, compassion, joy, and equanimity.[17] Another is the visualization practice of "giving and taking," or *tonglen* (Trungpa, 1993, pp. 46ff), in which the object of meditation is an image or thought that evokes feelings of sympathy for immediate others. These feelings are gradually extended so that we get used to including strangers and even enemies in the circle of our concern.[18]

In such practices, reversing our usual tendency to put our own well-being before that of others appears to be dualistic in a way that is inconsistent with recognizing the inextricably independent existence of self and other. However, this is one example of how Mahāyāna Buddhist practitioners can use familiar frames of reference in order eventually to go beyond them. Thus, while the ultimate truth of nonduality is not the conclusion of an argument grasped by the intellect, discursive reasoning can be used to help us gain enough confidence in the case against duality that we eventually can relax our attachment to conceptualization (no easy task for academics trained to think their way through any problem). Similarly, although there are no traces of duality in the boundless compassion of unconditioned awareness, Mahāyāna practices of putting others before oneself can be used to dismantle our habitual struggles to make our experiences live up to our expectations. Over time this fundamental kindness to oneself leads naturally to concern for others, for becoming less preoccupied with ourselves allows us to see that the suffering of sentient beings, and their desire for happiness, is no different, and no less important, than our own. Through this view, universal compassion is not something that we have to manufacture, for as a dimension of unconditioned awareness it is always already there—a traditional image is the full moon that is naturally reflected in every available pool of water. Tuning into this heart of the enlightened mind is very much a matter of where our (in)attention is focused; both contemplation and meditation serve to increase the chances it will be turned in the right direction.

In sum, for Plato and Aristotle, virtue requires that we combine knowledge with self-control until intellectual understanding has been enriched (and, to some degree, supplanted) by the wisdom that arises when we experience directly why virtue is its own reward. Similarly, Mahāyāna Buddhism offers a graduated path of teachings and mediation techniques to help us progressively cultivate ways of seeing, feeling, thinking, and acting that are more and more in tune with the truth of interdependence. As the fictitious nature of self and other is seen more and more clearly, compassionate and skilful action arises naturally in the absence of *ego's* confused thoughts and conflicting emotions.

The Lived Curriculum: Mahāyāna Teachings in the Academic World

I hope that this very abbreviated introduction to the Mahāyāna path provides some indication of what Buddhist traditions have to offer the theory and practice of transformative education. As much as I value the philosophical sophistication and power of its conceptual resources,[19] I believe that it is from Buddhism's emphasis upon joining intellectual understanding with direct personal experience that academics can learn most about facilitating transformative learning in ourselves and in those with whom we work. Because, as Parker Palmer (1998) reminds us, "we teach who we are," our first responsibility as educators is the cultivation of our own capacity for virtuous perception, feeling, judgment, and action. One way that educational initiatives support learning is by creating contexts in which key connections are easier to grasp; becoming familiar with relationships in simplified environments makes it possible to recognize similar dynamics in the more complex contexts of home and work. Shamatha practice can help us do just this: Through learning to observe precisely and sympathetically the play of the mind while sitting on our meditation cushions we become more able to see in everyday life the links between intention/thought and action reported by Gautama Siddhartha, the Buddha, over 2,500 years ago:

> We are what we think.
> All that we are arises with our thoughts.
> With our thoughts we make the world.
> Speak or act with an impure mind
> And trouble will follow you
> As the wheel follows the ox that draws the cart.
> We are what we think.
> All that we are arises with our thoughts.
> With our thoughts we create the world.
> Speak or act with a pure mind
> And happiness will follow you
> As your shadow, unshakable.

(BYRON, 1976, P. 3)

In part by helping us disidentify with our thoughts, the practice of mind-fulness/awareness enables us to see in a very immediate way how we *really do* reap what we sow.[20] This kind of direct insight naturally translates into action: The more clearly I see *why* I am compulsively reaching for the doughnut the more likely I am to leave it on the plate. Interrupting such habitual patterns may not seem like a significant success in light of larger social issues, but I believe that even just bringing mindfulness of intention to all of the conversations we have inside and outside academia would have genuinely revolutionary results.[21]

What about more direct initiatives to support others seeking positive change? In light of my remarks above, it will be no surprise that I expect that introducing meditation into classrooms would be an excellent way to join academic theorizing on transformative learning with direct experience. Doing so in a recent graduate course had encouraging results: beginning each class with shamatha practice provided a point of departure for analyzing readings on spirituality and education as well as an open, nonjudgmental environment for such creative activities as collective art making and collaborative poetry composition. Accordingly, I would encourage more and more educators to follow the lead of those who have introduced meditation practices in various fields of physical and mental health care and have carefully studied the results.[22]

As many have realized, mindfulness/awareness meditation practices can be introduced in our pluralistic social contexts because they need not be presented in association with particular religious or spiritual teachings. This advantage can also be a significant limitation. In Mahāyāna Buddhist traditions, sha-matha and other meditation practices are integrated with and complemented by many other elements of a complex pedagogical process. The rich variety of teachings and practices involved in hearing, contemplating, meditating are part of an even larger curriculum that includes working with the physical, emotional, intellectual, imaginative, intuitive, and transcendent elements of our experience. Perhaps most important, walking the Mahāyāna path properly involves undertaking to observe ethical precepts governing body, speech, and mind. It might also involve some or all of painting *thankhas*, executing calligraphies, memorizing slogans, visualizing mandalas, repeating mantras, engaging in dialectical debate, composing spontaneous songs of realization, or simply resting in the clear light of unconditioned awareness. To enjoy their full benefit, the different elements of the Mahāyāna path must be understood and practiced within their larger proper context.

From this I draw two recommendations. Although my focus here has been on Buddhism, I appreciate that there are many other living traditions with time-tested methods of integrating intellectual understanding with direct experience. To those who wish to explore the potential contributions of meditation to transformative learning I recommend that they remain within or find such a "wisdom tradition" with which they resonate personally so that the experiential dimension of their journey will receive proper direction and support. I also highly recommend taking advantage of one or more of the growing opportunities for dialogue among practitioners of different wisdom traditions seeking to understand their significant similarities and differences. My hope is that, by participating in such encounters and conversations, we will bring insights both into our personal paths and into how mainstream educational institutions and cultures can be inspired by principles of nonaggression, sustainability, and cooperation rooted in an appreciation of the sacredness of life. My wish is that a more and more complete and critical appropriation of Buddhist teachings by Western students will be part of a collective exploration of both old and new pathways to the transformative integration of heart and mind.

Notes

1. A case in point: the day after writing this sentence I received a copy of *Educating for Humanity: Rethinking the Purposes of Education*. Editor Mike Seymour begins his introduction with the statement,

    > By all accounts, humankind finds itself at a life-and-death turning point in the twenty-first century. We are on a course of unprecedented environmental destruction in terms of species extinction, global warming, and natural resource depletion. Population and consumption trends predict that humans will overshoot the earth's carrying capacity in many areas within the next century.

    He goes on to observe that "Einstein said, basically, the mind that got us into this mess is not the mind that will get us out of it. Humanity needs a change of mind fostered by a change of heart" (2004, p. 1). For an account of the current resurgence of interest in transformation in light of development in the sciences, see Karpiak (2000).

2. This is well illustrated by Kollmuss and Agyeman's (2002) survey of the "numerous theoretical frameworks" that "have been developed to explain the gap between the possession of environmental knowledge and environmental awareness, and displaying pro-environmental behaviour" (p. 239).

3. This section contains material from the paper "Teaching Professional Ethics to Educators: Assessing the 'Multiple-Ethical Languages' Approach," which was presented at the 61st Annual Meeting of the Philosophy of Education Society, San Francisco, 18–21 March 2005, and subsequently published (see Vokey, 2005).

4. See Coombs (1998, p. 556); similar advice is offered in Kidder (1995, p. 167).

5. See Coombs (1998, pp. 568–569) for this and subsequent quotes on moral perception and sensitivity.

6. According to Coombs (1998, p. 565), participants in professional ethics courses can acquire competence in an ethical language when their reasoning about real life ethical issues in discussions with colleagues is guided by a proficient speaker of the ethical language in question, who "knows what good moral reasoning requires." To avoid an infinite regress this point raises essential the same question in a different form: Through what process did such course instructors gain their proficiency and learn what good moral reasoning entails?

7. Shapiro and Stefkovich (2001). Kidder (1995) is another example of this "multiple ethical languages" approach, although he refers to three "resolution principles" associated with long-standing moral traditions rather than moral language. It is some testimony to the popularity of this approach that the British Columbia School Superintendents' Association invited Kidder to conduct seminars for administrators based upon his conception of "ethical fitness."

8. For a brief orientation to Buddhism and the place of Mahāyāna Buddhist traditions within it, see Vokey (2001, pp. 213–214). Since 1985 I have been fortunate to participate in many programs offered by Buddhist teachers; in particular those within the living tradition that has come to be known as Shambhala Buddhism. Even so, of course, my words are not an authoritative presentation of this or any other Buddhist tradition. To those who wish to know more about the history and distinguishing features of Shambhala Buddhism, a form of Mahāyāna-Vajrayāna Buddhism rooted in the traditions of Tibet, I recommend the material provided by Shambhala International at http://www.shambhala.org and http://www.shambhala.org/about_shambhala.html.

9. For one summary of this view, see Thrangu (2001, e.g., p. 69).

10. In modern times, of course, teachings can be transmitted in many different ways. However, it is significant that two of the main texts I draw upon for this chapter (Gyamtso, 1988 and Mukpo, 2002) are published transcripts of oral teachings.

11. I expect the practices of study and reflection involved in hearing and contemplating will be quite familiar to the readers of this text, since those disciplines are integral to education in the Western philosophical tradition. However, both in spite and because of the growing popularity of various forms of meditation in North America, I suspect a few additional words are advisable to clarify what, in this context, mediation is understood to add to intellectual comprehension.

12. For an excellent introduction to shamatha practice in the Shambhala Buddhist tradition, see Mukpo (2003).

13. Note that there are no universally agreed definitions of such general terms as *mindfulness* and *awareness*. For example, in his very clear and useful account from a psychotherapeutic perspective of the nature and cultivation of mindfulness, Germer (2005, pp. 5ff) cites the use of the term *attention* to refer to what I have called mindfulness, and the term *mindfulness* to refer to a combination of attention, awareness, and memory. The short definition of mindfulness he prefers is "(1) *awareness*, (2) *of present experience*, (3) *with acceptance*" (p. 7; emphasis in the original).

14. For this understanding of the distinction between listening and hearing I am grateful to Sakyong Mipham Rinpoche (Mukpo, 2002).

15. Examples of such arguments are provided by Tenzin Gyatso, His Holiness the Dalai Lama (1999, 2000), whose case for secular ethics rests on examples of how "negative actions always bring pain and sorrow, but constructive action brings us pleasure and joy" (1990, p. 140).
16. The research undertaken at the Mind and Life Institute is a case in point. For an overview, see http://www.mindandlife.org/initiatives_section.html.
17. Pema Chödrön (e.g., http://innerself.com/Spirituality/chodron_12054.htm) provides very popular contemporary teachings on this and other bodhicitta practices.
18. For a description of a complementary bodhicitta practice designed for when we are off our meditation cushions, see Trungpa (1993) on slogan practice in the "training the mind" tradition of Indian Buddhist teacher Atisha Dipankara Shriknana.
19. Elsewhere I have shown how a nondualistic metaethics drawing upon the conceptual resources of Mahāyāna Buddhism provides for progress on key problems in moral philosophy and moral education that modern Western intellectual traditions have so far been unable to resolve (Vokey, 2001). As this chapter indicates, I am currently extending this work to address the question of how courses in professional ethics can help teachers and administrators enhance their capacity for sound practical judgment. An important link I see to citizenship education is that gaining warranted confidence in one's ability to make ethical judgments is a form of autonomy crucial to responsible participation in pluralistic democratic societies. I hope eventually to show how gaining this form of autonomy, so far from reinforcing individualism, would necessarily involve an appreciation of the role of community and tradition in education for virtue. An additional work in progress is developing the implications for both the philosophy and practice of educational research of a Mahāyāna Buddhism account of language, meaning, and truth in the light of nonduality, which I believe anticipates post-modernism's rejection of absolutism without entailing "anything goes" relativism. On this view, modernist construction and postmodern deconstruction can be complementary moments within a critical and emancipatory pedagogy.
20. In affirming that the nature of our intentions affects the quality of our experience I am not proposing that those who suffer misfortune or oppression are getting what they deserve.
21. The practice of nonviolent communication (Rosenberg, 2003) gives good indication of this potential.
22. For a review of such work and list of resources see Boyce (2005).

References

Boyce, B. (2005, May). The man who prescribes the medicine of the moment. *Shambhala Sun*, 28–34, 72–75.

Byron, T. (Ed.). (1976). *The Dhammapada: The sayings of the Buddha*. New York: Random House.

Coombs, J. (1998). Educational ethics: Are we on the right track? *Educational Theory, 48*(4), 555–569.

Dorter, K. (1997). Virtue, knowledge, and wisdom: Bypassing self-control. *Review of Metaphysics, 51*, 313–343.

Germer, C. K. (2005). Mindfulness: What is it? Does it matter? In C. K. Germer, R. D. Siegel, & P. R. Fulton (Eds.), *Mindfulness and psychotherapy* (pp. 3–27). New York: Guilford Press.

Gyamtso, T. (1988). *Progressive stages of meditation on emptiness* (2nd ed.). Oxford, England: Longchen Foundation.

Gyatso, T. (1999). *Ancient wisdom, modern world: Ethics for a new millennium*. London: Little, Brown.

Gyatso, T. (2000). *Transforming the mind: Teachings on generating compassion*. London: HarperCollins.

Howe, K. (Ed.). (2005). *Philosophy of Education 2005*. Urbana, IL: Philosophy of Education Society.

Karpiak, I. E. (2000). Evolutionary theory and the "new sciences": Rekindling our imagination for transformation. *Studies in Continuing Education, 22*(1), 29–44.

Kidder, R. (1995). *How good people make tough choices: Resolving the dilemmas of ethical living*. New York: Simon and Schuster.

Kollmuss, A., & Agyeman, J. (2002). Mind the gap: Why do people act environmentally and what are the barriers to pro-environmental behaviour? *Environmental Education Research, 8*(3), 239–260.

Kongtrül, J. (1992). *Cloudless sky: The mahamudra path of the Tibetan Buddhist Kagyu School* (R. Gravel, Trans.). Boston: Shambhala.

Loy, D. (1988). *Nonduality: A study in comparative philosophy*. New Haven, CT: Yale University Press.

Mukpo, M. J. (2002). *Taming the mind and walking the bodhisattva path*. Halifax, Nova Scotia, Canada: Vajradhatu.

Mukpo, M. J. (2003). *Turning the mind into an ally*. New York: Riverhead Books.

New English Bible. (1970). Oxford, England: Oxford University Press.

O'Sullivan, E. V., Morrell, A., & O'Connor, M. A. (2002). *Expanding the boundaries of transformative learning*. New York: Palgrave.

Palmer, P. (1998). *The courage to teach: Exploring the inner landscape of the teacher's life*. San Francisco: Jossey-Bass.

Rosenberg, M. B. (2003). *Life-enriching education*. Encinitas, CA: PuddleDancer Press.

Seymour, M. (Ed.). (2004). *Educating for humanity: Rethinking the purposes of education*. Boulder, CO: Paradigm.

Shapiro, J., & Stefkovich, J. (2001). *Ethical leadership and decision-making in education: Applying theoretical perspectives to complex dilemmas*. Mahwah, NJ: Erlbaum.

Strike, K. A. (1995). Professional ethics and the education of professionals. *Educational Horizons, 74*(1), 29–36.

Thrangu, R. (2001). *Transcending ego: Distinguishing consciousness from wisdom*. Crestone, CO: Namo Buddha.

Tolle, E. (1999). *The power of now: A guide to spiritual enlightenment*. Vancouver, British Columbia: Namaste.

Trungpa, C. (1993). *Training the mind and cultivating loving-kindness*. Boston: Shambhala.

Vokey, D. (2001). *Moral discourse in a pluralistic world*. Notre Dame, IN: University of Notre Dame Press.

Vokey, D. (2005). Teaching professional ethics to educators: Assessing the "multiple-ethical languages" approach. In K. Howe (Ed.), *Philosophy of education 2005* (pp. 125–133). Urbana, IL: Philosophy of Education Society.

CHAPTER 13

The Strength of the Feminine, the Lyrics of the Chinese Woman's Self, and the Power of Education

Hongyu Wang

Oklahoma State University

It may well be that as we try to bridge two cultures—East and West, Male and Female—it is these [no-name Chinese] women who will lead the way.

—William E. Doll, Jr., Preface to Hongyu Wang, *The Call from the Stranger on a Journey Home*

In the current educational-reform rhetoric of pursuing excellence through masculine control in the United States, speaking about the strength of the feminine is out of place. But precisely in this "out-of-placeness" are sung the lyrics of another kind of subjectivity, a waterway construction of selfhood, constantly eroding the harsh edge of stone to sustain life and renew meanings. The power of the feminine does not lie in dominance or containment but resides in its movement, its constant flow for regeneration, and its flexible yielding to new shapes. Refusing "the logic of dominance" (Fleener, 2002, p. 43), the power of education is released by dwelling in this flowing space of self-cultivation.

This chapter focuses on the Chinese woman as an exemplar of this power (but without equating *the feminine* with *woman*) to not only deconstruct the Euro-American myth of her in "submission, oppression, and the bound foot" (Mann, 2000, p. 836) but also reposition women's thought as a source of inspiration and creativity. Foregrounding Chinese women's subjectivity in their complicated negotiations with Confucianism and Taoism in traditional China, I intend to listen to the teachings of the lower stream that point to new directions of human potential subsumed by the mainstream. In reimaging Chinese womanhood, the strength of the feminine becomes a powerful site for articulating the notion of the self, nurturing educational wisdom, and envisaging curriculum differently.

Understanding how Chinese women construct their own sense of the self, meandering through the inner contradictions of the dominant ideology to yield creative ways of womanhood, I will argue, is essential for renewing our understanding of subjectivity and education. Such an effort is not intended, however, to romanticize Chinese women; how the Chinese emphasis on the maternal and *yin* can be implicated in patriarchy will also be discussed. Neither is this effort an attempt to affirm so-called Asian values to serve the needs of conservative politics. Rather, this affirmation of the Chinese feminine is claimed through not only questioning patriarchal discourses that grant strength to the masculine and weakness to the feminine but through also following women's own paths to open alternative landscapes of sustainable human possibilities. Furthermore, this chapter does not intend to essentialize Chinese womanhood to produce a universal image applicable to different historical times and social contexts. While women's paths are each unique, their journeys intersect with each other, creating a mosaic of multiple shapes and producing a polyphonic symphony. Through this complicated understanding we may be able to enrich our ongoing conversations about gender, culture, and education as we reach toward new horizons in curriculum. As a final note, this chapter intends to speak to the Western audience and provoke a dramatic turning around to see the landscape of subjectivity and curriculum differently.

Confucianism, Taoism, and Gender

The conventional notion of traditional Chinese women as passive victims of patriarchy has already been forcefully contested by many scholars (Ebrey, 1993; Ko, 1994; Mann, 2004; Mou, 1999; Wang, 2003; Widmer & Chang, 1997). Studying how ancient Chinese women historically presented themselves and slipped through the hierarchical system to create their own spaces, these scholars argue, yields inspiring stories about women's transformation, not merely reinforcements, of Chinese culture. Their efforts have paved new paths beyond the stereotypical notion that pictures China as the other of the (progressive) West and Chinese women as the other of the (feminist) Western women.

Despite their differences, Confucianism and Taoism in Chinese thought generally share a nondualist conception of personhood, a nondichotomous view of body and mind, and an aspiration for the unity of universe and person, in contrast to Western philosophy. Western feminism has attempted to disrupt the Western philosophical dualism that serves patriarchal interests. While "traditional Chinese women" were depicted as victims by and large in the West, strangely, there has been a historical romance with the refinement of the Chinese female elite (Teng, 1996). Because Taoism and Confucianism emphasize interdependence, body, and ecology of selfhood, in the contemporary setting there are also efforts to look for commonality between feminist projects and these philosophies—dramatized, for instance, in the claim of Confucius as feminist (Wawrytko, 2000). In general, though, as Confucianism is criticized as patriarchal while Taoism is pardoned due to its valorizing of femininity, Taoism and feminism are more frequently linked. These are decontextualized readings, imposing Western conceptual frameworks upon Chinese situations. Chinese holism and relationship, precisely because it does not carve out a necessary space for differentiation, is implicated in Chinese patriarchy (Wang, 2004), and it is women's own effort to find "a room of one's own" that sings another lyric of selfhood.

Jinhua Emma Teng's (1996) analyses of both the victim and romance plots about the "traditional Chinese woman" in the Western academy is particularly illuminating. For her, both myths are the result of objectifying Chinese women to serve as a mirror for the West. The former lies in asserting the progressive image of both the West and Western feminism while the latter lies in alluding to what is suppressed in the West but is important to Western feminism. In such an objectification, I believe, the Chinese woman herself retreats behind the screen. As a Chinese woman working in the American academia, my primary concern in this chapter is to trace the historical construction of selfhood through Chinese women's eyes and voices, although this often means reading behind the official records written by men.

As a background for my effort to reposition Chinese women at center stage, I will provide a brief sketch of the relationship between gender and the philosophical discourses of Confucianism and Taoism, especially regarding the notion of the self and personhood.[1]

Confucianism and Gender

One of the central concepts in Confucianism is personal cultivation, a process that extends from the person outward to the family, the state, and the world. While a more detailed gender analysis of the Confucian self and the historical evolution of patriarchal codes can be found elsewhere (Wang, 2004), here it is sufficient to note that, although debatable if Confucian personal cultivation is fully inclusive of women, it is generally acknowledged that the Confucian self blurs the boundary between the inner and the outer, and the private and the public. Even though the separation of gender spheres is an orthodox Confucian principle, this separation cannot be complete since an ideal Confucian society is modeled upon an ideal harmonious family. Within this ambiguous space between the inner and outer, women played their roles in influencing the public world.

This ambiguity allowed the appearance of powerful women figures, including the female emperor Wu (and empresses who governed different dynasties through their sons or grandsons) as well as diplomats, warriors, officials, and generals. The importance of motherhood due to the mother's major role in regulating the family and her direct influences over her sons cannot be overlooked. While political power was only available to elites, the maternal influence was open to many ordinary women. In women's involvement with the public world, the role of motherhood is historically a powerful source for questioning (and sustaining) the Chinese gender hierarchy.

Moreover, women's multiple roles as daughter, wife, and mother under the official Confucian ideology presented contradictions within the paternal order by which one duty could be used against another duty. For instance, the loyalty of the wife could be reappropriated to disobey the father, the filiality of the daughter could be used against marriage, and the chastity of the widow could be excused for intellectual and artistic devotion. This offers a certain flexibility that women can use to assert their own choices in pushing the boundary of Confucian ethics.

Taoism and Gender

Two important Taoist resources for asserting women's power are the Taoist challenge of the conventional rituals/ethics that are the soil for gender inequality and the explicit valuing of yin and the feminine, especially in *Tao Te Ching*. Both open up more spaces for constructing creative womanhood.

The Taoist notion of personhood is ecological, a seeking to become one with nature to achieve personal freedom. Lao Tzu's, and especially Zhuang Tzu's, ridicule of the Confucian virtues including *ren*, rituals, and righteousness is well known (see *Tao Te Ching*, chapters 19, 38; *Zhuang Tzu*, chapters 1, 2, and 6). Their call for dissolving the attachments to moral codes and abandoning the impositions of ethics in order to achieve independent personhood poses a powerful challenge to Confucian gendered virtues.

More important, the conception of the feminine occupies a favorable position in Taoism. As the founder of Taoism, Lao Tzu was exceptional in emphasizing the sustaining strength of the feminine (see *Tao Te Ching*, chapters 6, 8, 28, 36, 40, 43, 52, 61, and 76). For Lao Tzu, the feminine is more powerful and life-affirming than its counterpart, the masculine. He tells us that when humans and plants are born, they are soft and supple; but when they die, they become stiff and hard. Strength, in its truest sense, comes from holding on to what is soft and preserving the vitality of life.

The Taoist notion of the feminine and the contemporary notion of gender is not the same, however. Gender as a concept emerged in the 1980s, emphasizing the social, historical, and cultural construction of (wo)man in contrast to the biological conception of (fe)male. In Taoism, however, yin/femininity and yang/masculinity are cosmic polarities and the correspondence between yin and femininity is not a literal but a metaphorical link. The Taoist preference of the feminine is not necessarily a prowoman position. In Taoist thought and in Chinese thought in general, both man and woman have both yin and yang, or femininity and masculinity, within the self. In *Tao Te Ching* and *Zhuang Tzu*, women as persons seldom appear, and the majority of people referred to in *Zhuang Tzu* are male figures. Lao Tzu's reference to *mu* (mother) and femaleness is an analogy. His reversal of the Confucian hierarchy of male over female is not complete, either. His emphasis on the power of the feminine is compatible with his dynamic view about Tao in interplay between yin and yang, and with his dialectic approach in which opposite forces are mutually changeable. For Lao Tzu, holding on to yin is the way to prevent losing yang, since yin can lead to yang and yang can lead to yin when each is pushed to the extreme.

While being cautious about reading Western feminist frameworks into Taoism, undoubtedly Taoism does offer more possibilities for women's (and men's) struggles historically and does provide inspiration for contemporary feminist projects. The title of this chapter implies the link between the feminine and woman; my intent here is to keep this tension between the metaphorical and the literal—after all, a metaphor has an important relationship to its original source—to play with a different sense of womanhood.

In foregrounding Chinese women's thought, my focus is not on feminist critiques of Chinese philosophy, but on how the "traditional Chinese woman" negotiates with the Confucian maternal and with the Taoist yin and on women writers' tradition that is constructed by and constructs Chinese discourses.

Dancing with the Power of the Confucian Maternal

In general, the Confucian maternal supports the Confucian vision of the ideal society, while the Taoist maternal is the creative source of the universe. In this section, I discuss Confucian motherhood.

In Confucian scholar Liu Xiang's (79–8 B.C.E.) book *Biographies of Exemplar Women,* the first section is devoted to exemplary mothers in 14 stories (see Wang, 2003). These stories were composed of the selections from the earlier texts. The important role of mother in the Confucian world is made clear here. The primary purpose of Confucian motherhood is to channel sons (and daughters) into the Confucian way. The celebrated mothers were usually widows with a relatively secure position in the family. They demonstrated their power through their sons' achievements. As Mou (1999) points out in her studies of two biographies of women in the Tang dynasty (written by male authors), the ideal picture of motherhood is "a widowed mother strictly disciplining her sons in preparation for a distinguished career that will bring honor to both the family and to herself" (p. 130). Thus, women's virtues are primarily defined through their relationships (with sons) rather than through themselves. Such an imposition of the relational intends to serve the Confucian hierarchy. However, this maternal power as a guardian of the family has been reappropriated by women throughout history in expanding and enlarging their own world.

Interpreting their understandings of Confucian doctrines in a flexible and creative way, mothers could utilize the inner contradictions of those principles to challenge the orthodoxy. The exemplar education of Mencius by his mother (Mother Meng, ca. 400–350 B.C.E.) is a household story for the Chinese. But less known is her reinterpretation of the Confucian ritual to save her daughter-in-law from the disgrace of being dismissed. According to Liu's record, when Mencius saw his wife half dressed in her room, he was displeased and left the room. His wife reported this to his mother and asked to leave. Mother Meng taught Mencius that he needed to practice respectfulness by looking down when entering a room, saying, "'Now you have not examined your own practice of decorum, but instead censor the decorum of others. Are you not indeed far from practicing proper decorum?" (as quoted in Wang, 2003, p. 154). Mother Meng's wisdom mediates the conventional relationship between husband and wife, at once making wifely obedience to the husband problematic.

From Mother Meng's story we also can discern the conflicting messages about a woman's position in the family due to multiple roles. In this story, the maternal power is wisely used by Mother Meng in her flexible reappropriation of the official code to help her daughter-in-law to achieve a certain sense of mutuality between husband and wife. Notably, this archaic image of alliance between mother-in-law and daughter-in-law has been suppressed by the image of the mutual bitterness between them. Susan Mann (2000), through comparing different versions of the Mulan story, also points out that the archaic image of sisterhood has been replaced by female jealousy. In mythologizing women's competition for men's affection, official discourses downplay the potential of female alliance and friendship. If these stories about women had been written by women themselves instead of male historians, the storylines could have been quite different.

The position of the mother resides on a powerful site as she expects the filiality of both sons and daughters (although her sons' filial loyalty to her is compromised by his privileged male status). Because of the permeable boundary between the inner and outer worlds, the widowed mother or grandmother as a "matriarch" running the family and indirectly influencing public affairs is not an uncommon image, both in fiction and in reality.

The importance of the maternal was also instrumental for advocating women's education, which not only included moral education but also literary education. Prominent sons often praised their mothers, who were well versed in the Confucian classics, and honored their mothers as their first teachers. Motherhood became an effective means for women to argue for the need of educating girls. Many literate mothers also taught their daughters the arts of poetry, calligraphy, and painting as well as the Confucian classics. The first female historian in Chinese history, Ban Zhao (45–114 C.E.) adopted the tone of the maternal in writing *Women's Lessons*. When women's poetry clubs became popular in the late imperial China, mothers (or grandmothers) were among the organizers, which was instrumental in building women's communities through literary networks.

The mother's special role in educating children led to the emergence of professional women as "teachers of the inner chambers" (Ko, 1994). The focus of

Dorothy Ko's book is about the 17th century, but it follows the long tradition of mother's teachings. To a degree, these teachers of the inner chambers substituted for or aided mothers in educating daughters, mostly in the specialized realms of art or literacy. Though not breaking away from the Confucian code, these women were granted the opportunity to travel outside of their own families, and many times to travel alone, and as a result the boundary of the inner and the outer was renegotiated. They were often accomplished poets or professional artists. Combining domesticity with a career, the blending of literary and artistic talents with feminine virtue created a new paradigm of womanhood, as Ko phrases it, in "talent, virtue, and beauty" (1994, p. 143). This expansion of the maternal role enlarged the range of possibilities for cultivating woman's own independence, including economic and cultural independence.

However, the valuing of motherhood did not in itself glorify women. In a patriarchal family, the lineage bears the father's name and passes along the line of the paternal. The primary fulfillment—both private and public—for mothers or mothers-to-be was through their sons. This reinforced the authoritarian position of the paternal in a multigenerational family. Women had little institutional power to enforce equal relationships with their male peers. An emphasis on the maternal did not lead to women's equality, but women's creative usage of it expanded women's space.

In the contemporary context, the elevation of motherhood can be utilized as a backlash at feminist efforts to achieve gender equality and equity in society (Tamney & Chiang, 2002). However, the danger of serving conservative politics, I argue, should not lead us to neglect motherhood's subversive potential for counteracting patriarchal discourses and practices. Creative motherhood is still a part of many women's experience, and should not be devalued. It was precisely in ancient Chinese women's improvised play with the dominant code of the maternal that meanings were reinvented. Their achievements were performed on the site of the margin, and it is on the border that new creations of women's identity can be inspired.

The Way of Water, the Movement of the Feminine

If the Confucian maternal has a sense of preserving order, then the Taoist maternal is the source of creativity. Lao Tzu states that Tao is the mother of heaven and earth (*Tao Te Ching,* chapter 25). The origin of vital energy for producing all things lies in the mystic female that endures and moves eternally: "That from which the universe sprang may be looked upon as its Mother"

(*Tao Te Ching*, chapter 52). The notion of the creative maternal is connected with Lao Tzu's overall positive views about femininity. Lao Tzu's statement that "knowing the masculine, maintaining the feminine, and being a ravine for all under heaven" (*Tao Te Ching*, chapter 28) is quoted by Zhuang Tzu as the heart of Taoism.

The Taoist Waterway Worldview

"Nothing is softer than water, but nothing is stronger than water in attacking what is hard, since nothing can change it," reads *Tao Te Ching* (chapter 78). Lao Tzu's teachings that the yielding prevails over the strong and the soft prevails over the hard affirm the power of the feminine through the metaphor of water. Lao Tzu also links this flowing power with his cosmic and political ideal of *wu-wei* (chapter 43).

Sarah Allan (1997) uses water as the root metaphor of Chinese philosophical ideas. Particularly, she points out that the term *Tao* has both noun and verb forms, and as a result, Tao is a moving force as well as an ideal. Qualities of water are linked to the feminine, as Lao Tzu often alludes. Water flows toward a lower level but it embraces the valley and the mountain and moistens 10 thousand things; the lowly position of the female here becomes a center that accumulates the strength of the world. Water adapts its shape to the surroundings but cannot be destroyed; an invincible force flows from the preserving and flexible movement of the feminine. Water does not occupy or possess but in the end transforms what it passes by; the creative energy of the feminine does not lie in the aggression of domination but resides in its dynamic interplay with what is different from itself. Water also can signify the unknown and the mysterious as, analogous to the mystery of female procreative power, its source is self-generative and its depth is difficult to tell.

Lao Tzu's valorizing of femininity does not necessarily make masculinity inferior. His view, in the context of challenging the conventional notion of strength, directs our attention to what is usually invisible and devalued so that the harmony of yin and yang can be achieved. Water needs a companion in order to play. If we read the *Tai-ji* symbol carefully, we can see a light dot in yin and a dark dot in yang, signifying that yin and yang also are embedded within each other. Water itself is powerful because of its inner strength, even though this strength is constructed differently from the formation of stone. By the same token, there is a built-in vulnerability in masculine hardness. In this sense, the critique of Taoist yin as submissive can be dissolved.

The Taoist waterway worldview has had a profound influence on Chinese poetry, painting, calligraphy, music, literature, religion, and way of life. It has permeated every aspect of Chinese culture and has historically undermined orthodox morality. It brings natural imageries of purity, harmony, and quietude to Chinese literature and art, nurtures aesthetic tastes in a spirit of carefree elegance, and cultivates an artistic thinking rich in inner experiencing.

I believe that the flowing strength of the feminine, embodied in both women's negotiation with the world and men's poetic thinking about the world, has sustained Chinese civilization for thousands of years despite all forms of horrifying aggression against women. It is not an exaggeration to say that Chinese culture as a whole in its unique forms of art, philosophy, literature, and lifestyle is founded upon this feminine power and maternal creativity. To discern such generative force underneath the surface of the paternal order, we can connect with the most vital part of humanity.

Waterway Movements and Women's Voices

Taoism is a poetic thinking, as Xin Li demonstrates in her chapter in the present volume. The classical Chinese writings, including prose and essay, are highly condensed with poetic rhythms. Moreover, the close relationships among poetry, calligraphy, and painting show an intimacy between language and aesthetics. In this sense, poetry and thought, poet and scholar, artist and intellectual have never been separated as they often are in the Western world. To talk about Chinese thought without understanding Chinese poetry misses important insights. Within the limits of this chapter, I will focus on one woman poet whose lyrical voice, trenchant pen, and creative thought demonstrate the power of the feminine.

Li Qingzhao (Li Ch'ing-chao, c. 1081–1151 c.e.), celebrated as one of China's greatest poets, was also a scholar, a critic, an art collector, a musician, a painter, a calligrapher, and a political commentator. Although she was hardly regarded as a Taoist, her unique ability to create an original form of art on the site of the feminine is amazing. Not only did her passion for nature, art, and life permeate her poetic imagination but her sorrow, loneliness, and suffering also found creative expression in her lyrics. One poetic style of *ci* was named after her.

Lyric poetry, or *ci,* is different from traditional poetry (*shi*) in that *ci* is written to popular tunes for singing, more suitable for expressing complicated and ambiguous sentiments. "Rich in sensitivity, pure in nature, tender in heart, and free in spirit" (Hu, 1966, p. 26), Li transformed both the content and form of *ci*. She centered the female artistic sensibility and created distinct female images in Chinese literature. Female voices and images in poetry were not heretofore uncommon, but they were usually written by male writers. Displacing the dominant male gaze, Li emerged on the central stage and saw the world and the self through her own eyes. Her form of *ci* has original imagery, musical rhythm, and linguistic beauty.

Femininity not only became a site for her literary originality, but supported a profound sense of "woman being" in a patriarchal society. Li went through personal loss and political turbulence but was never subsumed by them. The feminine delicacy, brilliance, and elegance in her poems were enabled by her free spirit. She was free to drink, to write, to wander, to sail, and to study, enjoying an equal relationship with her husband and neglecting housework. Her voices were not only lyrical but also assertive. *Ci* as a feminine writing was regarded as the other of *Shi*, but in her *Discourse on Ci*, Li strongly advocated *ci* as a distinct genre and sharply criticized male poets for their failure to capture the essence of *ci*. Her daring spirit was also conveyed well in her *Shi* poetry voicing her social criticism and political opinions. Chung Ling (1985) read one of her famous poems as a satire on the cowardice of Emperor Gao Zong.

According to Hu (1966), three major Chinese traditions that highly influenced Chinese poetry—Confucianism, Taoism, and Buddhism—did not make any defining mark on Li's poetic thinking. Neglecting Confucian moral and social concerns, Li's profound love for nature never reached the degree of dissolving the self as Taoism and Buddhism preached. Hu (1966) uses the term *egocentric* to describe Li, who placed herself in the center in her relationships. I would rather celebrate this as *self-centeredness* as it disrupts the myth of female sacrifice, and see it as the yang assertive spot in the yielding of yin. Flowing but located, Li invented her own subjectivity beyond the constraints of the conventional.

The Confucian maternal and the Taoist feminine, especially under women's reappropriation, have demonstrated the potential to counteract paternal control. They can, however, be implicated in patriarchal control, especially under institutional manipulations. The Confucian maternal is expected to transmit the Confucian values, while the Taoist yin does not pose fatal challenge to the paternal structure. The Chinese gender system preserved its patriarchal order by subsuming the Confucian maternal and pushing away the Taoist yin. Li's originality lies in her refusal to work *within* any male tradition and her creation of a strong authorial and subjective position. Following *and encountering* the way of water, Li created a womanhood which was both fluid and grounded. She conveyed a different formation of strength, a sustainable strength in laughter and in tears, a tender strength attentive to the fragility of human life but never giving in. She made a great contribution to the tradition of women writers, to whom I turn next.

Women Writers Reinventing Self

Female wisdom transforming the public world through words has a long tradition. *The Biographies of Exemplary Women* recorded a story about Tirong, who not only saved her father from corporal punishment but also changed the legal regulation of the time. Tirong submitted a letter to the emperor Han Wudi (140–85 B.C.E.) to plead for her father, who had committed a crime and would suffer harsh bodily punishment. She wrote,

> '[T]hose who are punished cannot once again be rejoined with society. Although they desire to change their wayward ways and start anew, there is no path for them to do so. I desire to offer myself to be a palace servant in order to redeem my father's crime and enable him to start anew.' (As quoted in Wang, 2003, p. 156)

Moved by her plea, Han Wudi abolished corporal punishment. The eulogy praised this young girl's words as echoing "the thoughts of sages" (p. 156). Here Tirong courageously and successfully used the Confucian daughter's filial role to challenge a country's legal code.

In contrast to the Western image of submissive, foot-bound, illiterate Chinese women, there were an exceptional number of women writers throughout history: from the ancient *Book of Odes* (probably 1000–600 B.C.E.), in which a dozen poems were attributed to women authors, through the high point of women's writings in the Tang dynasty (618–907), until the Ming and Qing dynasties (1368–1911), when women's anthologies of poetry and prose were published, women have left an indelible mark in Chinese literary and artistic history.

Xie Daoyun (fl. 399) appeared long before Li Qingzhao, but she also demonstrated intellectual brilliance and spiritual independence. She lived in a period when Taoism enjoyed a more prominent role and women had more freedom. Well-versed in Confucianism, Taoism, and poetics, she engaged in philosophical debates, literary criticism, and poetry competitions with her male counterparts in the public (Lee, 1994). More of a Taoist but blending two philosophies into her own style, she showed a disregard for convention, criticized openly her husband's talents, and remained calm in the face of the danger. Lily Xiao Hong Lee (1994) commends her for her independent thinking and courageous deeds that brought heroic themes into women writers' tradition. Grace S. Fong's (1994) analysis of the women lyric poets in the Song dynasty also points out how women writers inserted their self-assertion into the lyrics, which defied the confinement of the feminine.

Women's writerly tradition was better recorded in the Ming and Qing dynasties, including that of both high-level courtesans and women of the gentry (Widmer & Chang, 1997). Women of the gentry followed the lead of Ban Zhao and Li Qingzhao in the literati tradition. Courtesans usually came from lowly backgrounds, but they were accomplished artists and writers. Both groups of women reappropriated words and symbolism to affirm their authorial positions and thus redefine themselves. These women's voices opened a window through which we can view the negotiation of female subjectivity both with and beyond the traditional boundary.

According to Victoria Cass (1999), courtesans influenced and transformed the intellectual life of the time. Both the public literati world and the private domestic world were marked by these courtesans' influences. Trained for public performance, they mingled with male literary figures to discuss art and poetry, traveled among mountains and on rivers, and signed their names on their works. What was socially unaccepted for women at that time, they were able to accomplish at the margin.

A legendary figure among courtesans, Liu Rushi (Liu Shi, 1618–1664) was well known for her poetry, painting, and calligraphy and her woman warrior style. She associated with different literary groups, experimented with different poetic styles, and published her collections of works. The courtesan was an outcast in a Confucian society, but Liu pursued independence and self-creation on this site of exile. The boat became a symbol of freedom for her as she could undertake boat excursions to wander and to travel. The exile status of boat in its drifting image offered a possibility for detaching from (patriarchal) society and for imagining a different world. The metaphor of drifting as a way of asserting the self is ironic but powerful because it releases the strength of the feminine beyond the border to sustain the capacity for renewal. Following the flow of water evokes Lao Tzu's metaphor, yet Liu also affirmed her position as the one who was in charge of the boat's direction. Here elasticity, fragility, and strength are demonstrated all at the same time, and it is this simultaneity of different faces that breathes vitality into the lyrics of Chinese women's subjectivity.

As a courtesan, Liu had more freedom than domestic women to attend public events, and her poetry brought private sensuality and artistic flow to the public intellectual life. Such a blurring between two separate realms to reinscribe the feminine space with creativity was also echoed by the women of the gentry, albeit in different forms. They refigured the domestic sphere as a study room where women could choose to read and write.

Emptying out the gendered codes to reclaim a space for her own, Lu Qingzi claims, "'Closing the gate / I am free to do as I please'" (as quoted in Robertson, p. 206). Her ease with the darkness and depth of the private space behind the gate breaks the assumed tie between the feminine and the communal. But this inward journey provoked sharpened perceptions, enriched imageries, and deepened insights for her creative works. The private realm of reading and writing, on the other hand, connected to great minds of all historical ages. This investment in endowing the domestic with the literary and the artistic, as the efforts of many women of the literary family show, was successful in expanding women's intellectual, aesthetic, and spiritual worlds. The joining of solitude and femininity led to a wisdom reaching deeply inside and traveling expansively outside.

Other women of the gentry affirmed their sense of the self through connecting with other women within the limit of the domestic through writing letters to each other, providing commentaries and critiques of each other's works, or engaging literary activities in women's gatherings such as poetry clubs. Not often, but sometimes, women's friendship was extended between women of the gentry and courtesans. It is interesting to notice here that these two different female groups made efforts in different directions, as Kang-I Sun Chang (1994) acknowledges, with courtesans more publicly daring by directly engaging the male culture while women of the gentry were more daring in their writings, which challenged the male tradition. While Chang reads such differences as women of the gentry being more "feminist" than courtesan women, I valorize both efforts as multiple ways of transforming whatever space was available to them in order to invent their own sense of the self.

Such multiplicity is also demonstrated in women's own writings. Maureen Robertson (1997) has studied women writers' prefaces to their own works and their lyric poetry and found that there was a shift of authorial position between the two. Not surprisingly, these women were much more self-effacing in their prefaces, but they were more assertive in their composed poetry through assuming a variety of subject positions. With shifting positions, women used the strategy of multiple selves to negotiate with the gender system and create new meanings. The tale of the unitary self is a fiction, not just in this so-called postmodern age.

With an unbreakable flow, the site of the feminine cultivates the creativity of the human spirit. It is in the spirit of those ancient Chinese women that I speak about feminine strength. The maternal wisdom of Mother Meng, the soul-stirring poetic voice of Li Qingzhao, the historical accounts of Ban Zhao, the courageous protest of Tirong, the independent boating of Liu Rushi, and the solitary studies of Lu Qingzi exemplify such strength. These women left their names as they transgressed the domination of the paternal in various ways. They were mothers, poets, scholars, historians, knight-courtesans, artists, and lovers who did not obey the order. Their influences over the public world cannot be overemphasized. And they created new literary forms, new ways of writing history, new styles of artistic expression.

Not only did these outstanding women show courage and creative spirit, but ordinary women also resisted patriarchal control and expanded their horizons of life through seeking passages (Ebrey, 1993). As a matter of fact, the lowest class of Chinese women created a new language, "women's script," which was different from the traditional Chinese language in both spoken and written forms (Zhao, 1992). This language is particularly suitable for singing but linguistically more abstract than "men's" language. Women's script was learned and passed on exclusively within women's communities, building exceptional connections among themselves for expressing their own thoughts and feelings in lyrics, narratives, and letters free from men's surveillance. These women maintained their friendship within and across families, and the education of young women followed the maternal instead of the paternal line. This is a recent "discovery," and we are not clear about its origin: some trace it to centuries ago while others claim its existence thousands of years ago, but it was widely used by peasant women in Hunan province until the early 20th century. Isn't it amazing that a group of women formed their own exclusive communities through exchanging their literary products in women's script? These no-name women built a space of their own within "the patriarchal wilderness" (Pagano, 1990), and they were women writers in its truest sense. The courage, aliveness, and creativity of the feminine amid sorrow, despair, and suffocation gracefully invite us to rethink and reinvent the meanings of personhood, subjectivity, and education.

The Strength of the Feminine, the Power of Education

The thoughts, the works, and the lives of these Chinese women, ordinary or extraordinary, have demonstrated the strength of the feminine. It is a strength shining through the mask of female weakness. It is a strength capable of enduring suffering to dissolve violence and of transforming pain to create new words, images, and symbols. It is a strength that has shown a light through the darkness, including the darkness of our age, "the nightmare that is the present" (Pinar, 2004, p. 13). In rethinking our educational present, this feminine strength inspires us to travel into, with, and through the darkness.

Educational Reform and Feminine Power

Education in the United States has currently been captured by the speed of the Internet, the demand of standards, and the fantasy of maintaining (inter)national superiority through masculine control. Such a push is not necessarily educative, as our educational insights are brushed aside by conservative political initiatives. While shutting one's eyes, blind to the vibrant trembling of life, and covering one's ears, deaf to the inner voices of wonder, will the test scores, staying on top in the world, mean anything? Will the current drive for standardization and assessment bring us more intimacy with both ourselves and others? Precisely at such a moment when paternal order is reinforced, what we need is the movement of the feminine to erode the rigid structure, to flood over the border, to flow education into students' inner worlds. The stories of these Chinese women, ancient tales about silent breakthroughs even at the peak of overwhelming tyranny, have a particular significance for our efforts to challenge the current rhetoric of educational reform.

While the lyrics of Chinese women's subjectivity have a specific gendered construction situated in a different history and culture, their uniqueness is linked with what is shared by various groups at the margins across different cultures. What is so inspiring about these stories, similar to all inspiring stories about human courage and achievement, is a creative spirit that can never be crushed, a spirit that never gives in to any codified official rule, a spirit cultivated by what is weak and what is lowly, a spirit that sustains the flow of life. Such a spirit is what we need to nurture in education. This flow is where the power of education lies. As Mary Doll (2000) poetically articulates, "To know is to feel the coursing inside our living stream that flows into the wider cosmic ocean. To run the course of the inner coursing is curriculum's most urgent call" (p. 217).

Such an emphasis on the power of flow, on the other hand, by no means negates the necessity of claiming the feminist pursuit of self-assertiveness. To combat the hardness of the paternal structure, the firmness of a feminist stance is necessary. The Chinese woman's wisdom of strength in fluidity cannot be misread as an effort to mystify feminine meekness since such fluidity is enabled by the spirit of freedom as pointed out earlier. The intention here is to question the cultural and gendered obsession with toughness in the West. This reliance on competitive aggression can hardly be undone by resorting to more toughness. By embracing another way of constructing subjectivity—on the border, in the flow—women can refuse to be assimilated into the masculine architecture of selfhood. In deconstructing the cultural myth of the ultimately weaker sex—obedient, crippled Chinese women—we in the West are challenged to turn around, to relook at this fantasized image fabricated by a collective psychic projection, and to see in it what we are afraid to see in ourselves. When the inner vulnerability of tough guise is exposed, one is ready to be touched by the movement of the feminine. This movement follows alternative paths, affirming women's difference in their creativity and singularity, to lead toward a world where the violence of toughness gives way to the transformative power of water. Such a turning around is what I attempt to provoke, to displace the dominant hard core of masculinity, without intending to reify one particular mode of femininity.

More than a decade ago, curriculum theorists such as Madeleine R. Grumet (1988) and Jo A. Pagano (1990) already pointed out that what our schooling accomplishes is to deliver our children from the maternal nourishment to the paternal order. Such a delivery is not only reinforced but also hurried in federal educational reform initiatives such as the No Child Left Behind Act of 2001. Shutting out the imaginative, the spiritual, and the fuller meanings of life, such a delivery is dangerous. As Julia Kristeva (2002) tells us, without the movement of the feminine, our psychic space becomes flat, we are less capable of working through traumas, and our ability to deal with both external and internal turbulence is weakened. In such an era, our willingness and ability to hold onto "the running waters inside us, inside language, inside the cosmos" (Doll, 2000, p. 148) becomes crucial to releasing the power of education. Such is a strength in its most sustainable capacity and its most forceful mode.

Women Teachers and Pedagogical Interactions

To a certain degree, the role of today's women teachers is not so far from the position of those ancient Chinese women, as both are subject to the control of a hierarchical social and educational system. Women teachers' ability to move between spaces, to navigate through openings, and to improvise their own subjectivity, as what Miss O accomplishes under Ted Aoki's (2005) depiction, has kept the field of education alive, even under the massive attacks from politicians, businessmen, and the conservative public. Journeying along "polyphonic lines of movement" (Aoki, 2005, p. 209) rather than following preset technical procedures, the teacher situates her pedagogical wisdom within concrete teaching contexts in which all unique encounters require creative responses that cater to the needs of students. Such a mode of teaching is fluid and even messy, but also life-affirming. The sounds of such movements resonate in the lively cacophony of nature with the singings of birds, the chiming of wind, and the splashing of water. Feminine fluidity has a cosmic force that brings vitality to education. What administrators and politicians demand for teachers to comply with—in the name of reform for the sake of children—may be neat and orderly, but it is lifeless.

Confronting an officially prescribed curriculum, like those Chinese mothers who dove into the inner contradictions of the official code and came out with new possibilities, thoughtful teachers, attuning to the ebb and flow of a lived curriculum, dwell in the interstices of two curricula and reconstitute new pedagogies. This fluid negotiation between different spaces, this improvised moving through various channels to reach new open spaces, leads us onto alternative paths that cannot be defined by the paternal.

The strength of the feminine lies in its ability to transform the world through both adaptation and creativity. The movement of the feminine seldom follows a straight line, but with jumps, detours, falls, and meanderings, it shifts as what it encounters changes. Tactful interaction becomes a key here. To counteract a force with its opposite is a feminine wisdom rich with pedagogical insights. To deflect aggression with thoughtful questioning, to inspire self-affirmation with a gentle push, to let anger pass with a pedagogical waiting: all bring surprising turns to our everyday teaching and plant seeds for change.

Fluidity and movement are not only important to interactions between teacher and pedagogical situations (involving text, context, student, and other relevant persons), but they are also an essential part of language. Bringing fluidity into language itself is an educational task that holds the potential for transforming our intellectual landscape at large. When language is treated only as a rigid structure, the medium of our life becomes hardened. In order to keep our close connection with the feminine space, we must lovingly attend to the softness, rhythm, tone, and flux of words—those aspects of language repressed by the official curriculum.

Li Qingzhao's poetic creativity lies in her ability to keep language alive, to bring extraordinary brilliance to ordinary words through creating exceptional rhythms in her masterful arrangement of sounds. The musical effects of her poetry come not from its grammatical structure but from its feminine lyrics. If we do not want to deliver our children from the maternal lyrics to the paternal structure, we need to transform the convention of language and vitalize our curriculum. As Wendy Atwell-Vasey (1998) notes, we need to bring "nourishing words," rather than the language of standards, back to schools. When desires, passions, and bodily experiences in language are reincorporated into curriculum, the movement of *currere* (Pinar & Grumet, 1976) floods through the tough guise of masculinity to pave new paths of personhood. If the social no longer shuts out the maternal, if school embodies the polyphonic movement of the feminine, the interaction between femininity and masculinity will find creative and compassionate expressions of both, leading to the invention of new meanings of life, new meanings of educating and becoming educated.

Inspired by Chinese woman's lyrics of selfhood, acknowledging what is neglected within us, we envisage education and curriculum differently. Through the power of the feminine, the militant impulse of taking control is replaced by a generative engagement with life. Such an engagement is what education is about: our genuine concerns with cultivating children's intellectual, emotional, spiritual, and psychic strength in cocreating a more sustainable living and pedagogical space. As William Ayers (1993) teaches us, "There is a particularly powerful satisfaction in caring in a time of carelessness, and of thinking for yourself in a time of thoughtlessness" (p. 24). In a time besieged by the demand of standards, we must hold onto the power of fluidity and movement.

Following the flow of water, the playful dance of the feminine, listening to the melody of our foremothers' lyrics, the powerful rhythms of the creative spirit, we release the power of education in a perpetual circle, moving inward and outward simultaneously. The horizon of the East comes near to us as we step forward to meet a calling, distant in space and distant in time, yet this calling is also from the depths of our own inner lives. The horizon of the West unfolds and expands as we approach the other, stretching hands across different continents. The flow of water connects differences, blurs boundaries, leading us to new vistas of life, subjectivity, and education. Let us follow the flow.

Note

1. This chapter focuses on Confucianism and Taoism as philosophy rather than religion. Especially regarding Taoism, Western literature sometimes does not differentiate between Taoism as a philosophy and Taoism as a religion, but they are two different phrases in

Chinese language and refer to different bodies of literature and practice (although they are related). Taoism as a philosophy is attributed to Lao Tzu's and Zhuang Tzu's worldviews while Taoism as a religion emerged in the Han dynasty, centuries after Lao-Zhuang's time, which worshipped Lao Tzu as a god and searched for spiritual perfection and alchemy techniques for immorality. Taoist religion also incorporates Confucian rituals and Buddhist meditations.

References

Allan, S. (1997). *The way of water and sprouts of virtue.* New York: State University of New York Press.

Aoki, T. T. (2005). *Curriculum in a new key: The collected works of Ted T. Aoki* (William F. Pinar & Rita L. Irwin, Eds.) Mahwah, NJ: Erlbaum.

Atwell-Vasey, W. (1998). *Nourishing words: Bridging private reading and public teaching.* New York: State University of New York Press.

Ayers, W. (1993). *To teach: The journey of a teacher.* New York: Teacher's College Press.

Cass, V. (1999). *Dangerous women: Warriors, grannies, and geishas of the Ming.* Lanham, MD: Rowman and Littlefield.

Chang, K. S. (1994). Liu Shih and Hsu Ts'an. In Pauline Yu (Ed.), *Voices of the song lyric in China* (pp. 169–187). Berkeley and Los Angeles: University of California Press.

Chung, L. (1985). Li Qingzhao. In A. Gerstlacher, R. Keen, W. Kubin, M. Miosga, & J. Schon (Eds.), *Woman and literature in China* (pp. 141–164). Germany: Bochum.

Doll, M. A. (2000). *Like letters in running water: A mythopoetics of curriculum.* Mahwah, NJ: Erlbaum.

Doll, W. E., Jr. (2004). Preface. In H. Wang, *The call from the stranger on a journey home: Curriculum in a third space* (pp. ix–xi). New York: Lang.

Ebrey, P. B. (1993). *The inner quarters: Marriage and the lives of Chinese women in the Sung period.* Berkeley and Los Angeles: University of California Press.

Fleener, J. (2002). *Curriculum dynamics: Recreating heart.* New York: Lang.

Fong, G. S. (1994). Engendering the lyric. In P. Yu (Ed.), *Voices of the song lyric in China* (pp. 107–144). Berkeley and Los Angeles: University of California Press.

Grumet, M. R. (1988). *Bitter milk: Women and teaching.* Amherst: University of Massachusetts Press.

Hu, P. (1966). *Li Ch'ing-Chao.* New York: Twayne.

Ko, D. (1994). *Teachers of the inner chamber: Women and culture in seventeenth-century China.* Stanford, CA: Stanford University Press.

Kristeva, J. (2002). *Intimate revolt: The power and limits of psychoanalysis* (Vol. 2; J. Herman, Trans.). New York: Columbia University Press.

Lee, L. X. H. (1994). *The virtue of yin.* Canberra, Australia: Wild Peony.

Mann, S. (2000). Myths of Asian womanhood. *The Journal of Asian Studies, 59* (4), 835-862.

Mou, Sherry J. (1999). *Presence and presentation: Women in the Chinese literati tradition.* New York: St. Martin's Press.

Pagano, J. A. (1990). *Exiles and communities: Teaching in the patriarchal wilderness.* Albany: State University of New York Press.

Pinar, W. F. (2004). *What is curriculum theory?* Mahwah, NJ: Erlbaum.

Pinar, W. F., & Grumet, M. R. (1976). *Toward a poor curriculum.* Dubuque, IA: Kendall/Hunt.

Robertson, M. (1997). Changing the subject. In E. Widmer & K. S. Chang (Eds.), *Writing women in late imperial China* (pp. 171–217). Stanford, CA: Stanford University Press.

Temney, J. B., & Chiang, L. H.-L. (2002). *Modernization, globalization, and Confucianism in Chinese societies.* Westport, CT: Praeger.

Teng, J. E. (1996). The construction of the "traditional Chinese woman" in the Western academy. *Signs, 22*(1), 115–151.

Wang, H. (2004). *The call from the stranger on a journey home: Curriculum in a third space.* New York: Lang.

Wang, R. R. (2003). *Images of women in Chinese thought and culture: Writings from the pre-Qin period through the Song dynasty.* Indianapolis: Hackett.

Wawrytko, S. A. (2000). Kongzi as feminist. *Journal of Chinese philosophy 27*(2), 171–186.

Widmer, E., & Chang, K. S. (1997). *Writing women in late imperial China.* Stanford, CA: Stanford University Press.

Zhao, L. (Ed.). (1992). *Zhongguo nushu jicheng* [Nushu—women's script in China]. Beijing: Qihua University Press.

CHAPTER 14

Toward a Confucian Vision of Curriculum

Hua Zhang
East China Normal University

Introduction

Today's China is experiencing two intertwined crises: a loss of cultural identity resulting from the nation being fused into the global market, and environmental and social problems that are the great cost of compressed growth and modernization. While the former has given rise to a spiritual crisis, the latter has produced a physical crisis.

From the mid-19th century on, impacted by Western colonial powers, China embarked on a long path of losing its cultural identity. During the 20th century this path stretched farther because modernization became confused with Westernization. During the first half of the 20th century, China yearned for mainstream Westernization, and tried to use America's social system and culture. During the second part of the 20th century, China experienced "anti-Western Westernization" and copied the ideology of the Soviet Union.[1] In the cultural sphere, the Imperial Examination used to select government officials from (Confucian) scholars beginning in the Sui dynasty (581–618 C.E.) was banned in 1905. This signaled the end of the institutionalization of Confucianism, China's main cultural tradition. From 1949 to the most recent years, communist ideology has furthered the clearing away of Confucianism. So, for the past 100 years, Confucianism has become a "wandering ghost" in China, and the Chinese have lost much of their spiritual home. The fate of the Chinese curriculum field is reflected in this gradual transformation of Chinese society and culture (Zhang & Zhong, 2003).

This chapter suggests that decolonization is the prerequisite for the development of a productive and meaningful contemporary Chinese curriculum. Chinese scholars must recognize, recover, and rebuild their cultural traditions while also staying open to international possibilities. Intercultural curriculum research is necessary, and, as the dominant Chinese cultural tradition, Confucianism and the spirit of Confucius must be regenerated. In what follows, I will briefly outline the main principles of Confucianism, and then discuss their implications for curriculum theory and practice.

Confucius and Confucianism

Confucius (551–479 B.C.E.), for whom Confucianism is named, lived during the Spring and Autumn period (770–476 B.C.E.) of the Eastern Zhou Dynasty (770–256 B.C.E.). Confucius is widely considered to be the most important thinker in China because he created what Karl Jaspers has defined as the "axial period" of China's history.[2] Confucius brought to China a new spirit and tradition, from which the complicated school of thought known as Confucianism has been evolving for the past 2,500 years.

Confucian (the corresponding Chinese character is *ru*) means a person with a gentle disposition; it is the general name of a learned man (Xu, 2002, p. 1067). Confucianism, as the mainstream Chinese cultural tradition, is a thought system that involves "studying the phenomena of nature, acquiring knowledge, making one's will sincere, and correcting one's mind; cultivating oneself, putting one's family in order, running one's country well, and making all-under-the-heaven peaceful" (Zhu, 1983, p. 3). As one of the most complicated fields of Chinese culture, Confucianism is multifaceted. As a life philosophy, Confucianism is a continuous learning process in which a person persists in raising his life vision by self-cultivation. As a social ideology, Confucianism advocates a harmony-based social arrangement that upholds a system of rites and music. As a way of life, Confucianism permeates everyday life and forms a whole package of social customs and norms that emphasizes family relationships, filial piety, morality, and education.

The core of the Confucian spirit is moral inquiry—the study and practice of how to bring out the best in humanity and engage in personal and social transformation. One of the most important classics in China—the

Analects (which are generally acknowledged as a record of Confucius's and his disciples' teachings) reveal how Confucius and his students engaged in such inquiry. As will be explained, closely related to Confucius's doctrine of moral inquiry is that of moral creativity, which provides the transcendental ground for Confucians to understand the universe and their role(s) within it. This chapter thus maintains that if we are to understand curriculum as a Confucian text, we need to uncover the essence of curriculum based on moral creativity. From this we can generate new possibilities for curriculum research.

Moral Creativity as the Essence of a Confucian Curriculum

As a philosophy, Confucianism generally encompasses a moral metaphysics (Mu, 1997), and recognizes "moral creativity" to be the noumenon of the world—that which encompasses and governs the universe. To explain further, let's refer to chapter 26 of *The Doctrine of the Mean*—another Confucian classic:

> It is said in *Book of Songs* [in Chinese: *Shi Jing*, a collection of 305 poems, which appeared in the Zhou Dynasty (more than 2,500 years ago), and which some scholars claimed edited by Confucius]: "The way of the Heaven is perfect and endless." That explains the way the Heaven is. It is said again: "How glorious the pure morality of King Wen is!"[3] That explains why he was conferred the posthumous title of "Wen" which means refinement. King Wen's morality is as pure and endless as the way of the Heaven.
>
> The way of the universe can be completely described in a single sentence: as it is constant in taking honesty as the only proper course, its way of bringing up all things is extremely subtle because it creates one thing as the only thing, and it creates things unpredictably.

The above two paragraphs answer three vital questions. First, what is morality? For Confucius, morality is the creator and the ultimate ground for humans and heaven: cosmic order is moral order, and vice versa. Morality is that which centrally unites human beings and heaven. Second, how does morality create the world? The answer above maintains that the "way of bringing up all things is extremely subtle." In other words, the way of the universe is organic, nuanced, and unpredictable—in a word, creative. Hence, Confucius conjoins morality and creativity: morality is creative, and creativity is moral. Third, why is the way of heaven (or the universe) moral? Because heaven is intrinsically honest. Chapter 26 of the *Doctrine of the Mean* states:

Honesty [*cheng*; also translated as "sincerity"] underlies everything, from its beginning to its end. Without honesty, there can exist nothing. Therefore, the gentleman values honesty the most. ... Honesty is the way by which he can consummate himself. ... Honesty is the way of the Heaven, to be honest is the way of man.[4]

According to Confucius, to be honest is to be true. So, in Chinese, truth and honesty always go together. As heaven is perfect, endless, and honest, so the gentleman should follow the way of heaven and make unremitting efforts to be honest.[3]

Individuals benefit from following the way of heaven by acquiring "moral wisdom," another key concept in Confucianism and traditional Chinese philosophy. Wisdom is the natural outcome of creative morality. Contemporary Chinese philosopher Feng Qi sheds additional light on the meaning of moral wisdom:

Moral wisdom is the embodiment of Tao (the way of the Heaven, the way of human beings, the way of cognition) in self-justification of morality ... In a sense, it is the unity of truth, goodness, and beauty. It is free morality. If someone has free morality, he will realize that "I and the way of the Heaven are one," that "I have a feeling of fullness," that "I am self-sufficient and independent from the outside," and that I can experience absoluteness and infiniteness through relativeness and finiteness. (Feng, 1994, p. 639)

Moral wisdom as the outcome of moral creativity justifies the way of heaven and human beings. Both wisdom and creativity embody free morality, as morality is intrinsically free, intrinsically creative. Because moral creativity/wisdom is the unity of truth, goodness, and beauty as well as the unity of heaven and human beings, it is a life vision—an ethics. Unity is the overriding and guiding concept in Confucian philosophy. Unity between heaven and human beings is what Confucianism centrally aspires toward. In the Confucian vision, when unity is attained, the world is in harmony, and this harmony brings peace to both the self and the world.

An Etymological Study of Curriculum (*Ke Cheng*)

In China, the word *curriculum* (*ke cheng*) first appeared in the context of Confucianism. Several years ago, I conducted a primary study of the etymological origins of *ke cheng*, based on the book *Exploring the Etymology of Chinese Words* (in Chinese, *Shuo wen jie zi*). This is the most authoritative text on the etymology of Chinese characters and was authored by Xu Shen (about 58–147

C.E.), a famous Confucian in the Eastern Han dynasty (Zhang & Zhong, 2003). Xu Shen spent 22 years writing this book (from 100 to 121 C.E.). I would now like to expand my etymological research by addressing the question of the original and changing meanings of *ke cheng* in China.

Before the Tang dynasty (618–907), the two syllables *ke* and *cheng* appeared independently. According to *Exploring the Etymology of Chinese Words*, *ke* means "to examine, or make use of something" or "to enable something to function" (Xu, 1963, p. 52); *cheng* means "many persons gathering in one room and sharing" (Xu, 1963, p. 146). It also means a unit of measurement: "Ten hairs form one *cheng*; ten *cheng* form one *fen*; ten *fen* form one *cun*" (Xu, 1963, p. 146). When we combine the meaning of *ke* with that of *cheng*, we get the earliest Confucian interpretation of curriculum: "to enable sharing to work," or the standard to measure how sharing works—in other words, curriculum as sharing. So, in China, the word *curriculum* from the very beginning is accompanied with the meaning of relationship, with people coming together and sharing.

It is said that the first person to put *ke* and *cheng* together as one word was Kong Yingda (574–648 C.E.), one of the most important Confucian scholars in Chinese history. Born during the period of the Northern dynasties (386–581 C.E.), Kong Yingda lived during the Sui dynasty, and reached the peak of his career during the Tang dynasty. Kong Yingda's most important work was *Interpreting the Five Confucian Classics* (in Chinese: *Wu jing zheng yi*). Tang Taizong (599–649 C.E.), one of the most famous emperors in ancient China, ordered Kong Yingda to edit this book, which was also the curriculum standard for the Imperial Examinations in the Tang dynasty. When Kong Yingda interpreted the *Book of Songs*, he created the word *ke cheng* (curriculum). Note that in the original *Book of Songs*, the part "The Lesser Odes—Slanderous Talks," chapter 4, reads,

> Magnificent indeed is the temple,
> Which has been constructed by the moral person.
> Great indeed is the Tao (the Way),
> Which has been formulated by men of great wisdom.
> Those who harbor evil designs,
> I can figure them out easily—
> As if they were crafty hares,
> Who, though running fast, cannot escape from the hounds.

When Kong made a commentary on the first two lines above, however, he added:

It is the moral person
Who plans, supervises, and upholds the curriculum [*ke cheng*].
That is legitimate.

(As quoted in Li, 1999, p. 758)

It was the first time in China's history that *ke cheng* appeared as a single term. In this context, *ke cheng* is directly related to the construction of the magnificent temple by the moral person, and indirectly related to the great way of rites and music, which has "benevolence" (*ren*) as its core. In Confucian culture, *temple* and *rites and music* are all interrelated. *Temple* references the physical culture, and *rites and music* describe the spiritual culture. Rites and music are the content of the temple; the temple is the embodiment and symbol of rites and music. Both have their own intrinsic laws or working "way." Constructing the temple or the performing of rites and music must follow the Tao, the Way. Therefore, *ke cheng* here means the working way of the temple or rites and music, and their construction or process of creation. Furthermore, the subject who makes and supervises ke cheng is a "moral person" (*jun zi*). Only the moral person can understand and live the Tao, and is qualified to develop ke cheng. In sum, the word *ke cheng* has historically possessed moral and spiritual meanings.

If Kong Yingda created the word *ke cheng*, it is believed that Zhu Xi first introduced it to schools and made it the content that was taught by teachers and learned by students. Zhu (1130–1200 C.E.), a well-known Confucian in China, was born in the time of the Northern Song dynasty. Experienced in creating academies of classical learning and in teaching students, he could give a new meaning—an educational meaning—to *ke cheng*. For example, when Zhu talked about learning (Zhu, 1986, p. 165), he said,

The time devoted to ke cheng should be sufficient; And *ke cheng* must be arduously studied.
Develop a little ke cheng, but use much time and energy to implement it.

In Zhu Xi's view, implementing curriculum (*ke cheng*) means esteeming morality and doing inquiry learning. So, for Zhu, curriculum is also a moral event: morality is its core. There is an interesting historical anecdote. Once, Zhu's brother-in-law used "Doing Inquiry Learning" as his study's name, and asked Zhu to write a motto for him. Zhu answered him at once: "'You should change "Doing Inquiry Learning" into "Esteeming Morality" as your study's name, because esteeming morality is the aim of doing inquiry learning'" (as quoted in Qian, 2002, p. 148). It is clear that Zhu regards morality as the soul of curriculum and learning.

Toward a Contemporary Moral Creativity-Based Curriculum

Since China entered the modern era, curriculum as a concept has lost its moral meaning or value implications, and has become a procedural arrangement of learning content. This change is reflected in two contemporary Chinese dictionaries. In *The Origin of Chinese Words* (in Chinese, *Ci Yuan*), *ke cheng* is defined as

1. Work or study course, regulated by a certain amount of time and contents.
2. Levy taxes according to tax rate. (*Origin*, 1983, p. 2904)

The first meaning is much earlier than the second one. During the Jin dynasty (1115–1234 C.E.), *ke cheng* started to have the meaning "taxation." *The Sea of Chinese Words* (in Chinese, *Ci Hai*), one of the most authoritative dictionaries in China, describes *ke cheng* as follows:

1. The study course of lessons.
2. Broadly speaking, it means the scope, structure, and course of educational content set in order to realize the educational aims of schools at all levels; narrowly speaking, it means one subject matter in the determined teaching plan.
3. The general name of many kinds of business taxes in the Yuan dynasty (1271–1368 C.E.). (Xia, 1999, p. 1144)

The Origin of Chinese Words and *The Sea of Chinese Words* are very modern texts, the former first appearing in 1915, and the latter in 1979. In these two dictionaries it is difficult to find the moral meaning of curriculum. On the contrary, a Western conventional understanding of curriculum is predominant.

From the late 19th century on, Western culture has increasingly influenced China. The famous May Fourth Movement of 1919 is also known as the New Culture Movement, with so-called new culture actually being Western culture. The main themes of this movement were democracy and science, the latter of which was strongly colored with Enlightenment reasoning. The Western Enlightenment movement, with its emphasis on reason, objectivity, and science, played a role in the devaluation of Confucian morality in schooling and society. When creativity is separated from morality, it becomes a "stray lamb" that loses its way. If creativity loses its way, it might serve evil and give rise to endless ruin in the world. From my point of view, the most serious crisis in today's world is spiritual, the core of which is moral.

On May 17, 2000, the Chinese philosopher Cheng Zhongying interviewed the well-known contemporary German philosopher Hans-Georg Gadamer. When they talked about the future of the world, Gadamer said, quite seriously, "It is very difficult to avoid World War III." When Cheng asked him the reasons for this prediction, Gadamer said, "First, modern science and technology have been ruining the world dramatically. Second, the conflicts among different civilizations are getting increasingly fierce" (Cheng, 2002, pp. 8–9). The following year 9/11 happened, and this signified a new stage in a worldwide moral and spiritual crisis. However, as Gadamer has suggested in the interview, we must have a consciousness of crisis on the one hand while holding an optimistic attitude toward the future of the world on the other. To step out of crisis, we need to recover the ontological position of morality and promote continuous and fruitful dialogue among different civilizations based on hermeneutic wisdom.

Let's turn to the field of curriculum. During the 20th century there were two worldwide curriculum reforms. The first is generally known as the New Education Movement, which happened also in Europe and America in the late 19th and early 20th centuries. The second is generally known as the Curriculum Reform Movement, or the Structure of the Disciplines Movement, which started in America in the late 1950s and spread to Europe and Eastern Asia in the 1960s and 1970s. For the former, John Dewey's theory is regarded as representative. For the latter, Jerome Bruner's theory is considered key. Although there are many debates on the relationship between Dewey and Bruner (see, e.g., Fox, 1969; Young, 1972), there is at least one commonality between them: both of them explored *problem questions* sufficiently, but overlooked *meaning questions*. They explored "problem solving," "reflective thinking," "discovery learning," "active occupations," "spiral curriculum," and so on, in order to find a way to achieve "excellence of intelligence" or creativity. But they overlooked the following questions: Where does creativity come from? What is the relationship between creativity and morality? What is the lived meaning of problem solving?

I think there is an urgent need for a moral creativity–based curriculum in today's world. In order to construct it, maybe we can be inspired by the primordial meaning of curriculum in China ("sharing") and the long Chinese curriculum tradition. We can benefit from returning to a notion of curriculum that is rooted in a Confucian understanding of moral creativity. In the Chinese curriculum tradition, curriculum was essentially created by conversations between teachers and students. In ancient China, the teacher was the model of morality in society. In my opinion, over the past 2,000 years Confucius has remained the best teacher. In China, it is very important to distinguish between two kinds of teachers: the teacher of moral persons (*ren shi*) and the teacher of classics (*jing shi*). The former is the ideal for teachers to pursue. If a teacher is the teacher of moral persons, she always embodies what she teaches, and curriculum is the natural expression of her spiritual life. And the spiritual life is known as the "teacher's way" (*shi tao*). This is very different from the concepts of the West. For example, Aristotle said, "I love my teacher Plato, but I love truth much more" (as quoted in Qian, 2001, p. 173). In Aristotle's mind, what the teacher teaches is separated from the teacher himself. In contrast, Mencius once said, "The greatest wish in my whole life is to learn from Confucius"[5] (Mencius 3, chapter 2). Confucius, as the model of the teacher of moral persons, is at one with the curriculum he teaches.

What is the role of the student? In the Chinese curriculum tradition, the student is the converser of the teacher and the sharer of the teacher's way. Yan Hui, one of Confucius's students, has remained a model of the best student. Confucius said, "Yan Hui sees me as his father, but I see him as my close friend" (Analects 11, chapter 10). Yan Hui is the most qualified conversationalist, and the best sharer and developer of Confucius's way. When Yan Hui died at the age of 40, Confucius cried out, "God killed me! God killed me!" (Analects 11, chapter 8). The teacher and the student share common learning, common causes, common feelings, common beings, and common lives. As the famous Chinese historian Qian Mu has said, "Teaching and learning are equal, sharing one common cause. The teacher and the student are also equal, sharing one common life" (Qian, 2001, p. 178). In the process of sharing between teachers and students, curriculum is generated. This is, once again, *curriculum as sharing.*

The ultimate aim of a curriculum of moral creativity is the development of personhood. If we are to sum up the long tradition of Confucianism in a few words, we can put it this way: It is transforming knowledge into wisdom, and integrating wisdom with morality. The educational aim of Confucianism is to cultivate a whole person in whom morality is central. Thus, Confucian education can be called "education for a whole person." Contemporary Chinese philosopher Feng has generalized the ideal personality of Confucianism as a "popularized free personality" (Feng, 1994, p. 652). Here personality (*ren ge*) and morality (*de xing*) have the same meaning. People with such a personality can think independently, critically, and creatively because they are free. Everyone can attain this vision because it is popular.

A moral creativity–based curriculum integrates *problem questions* with *meaning questions*. *Meaning questions* explore how human beings live together with nature and others peacefully and in harmony. For Confucianism, the principle of benevolence (*ren*)—from which two related principles, nature and humanism, derive—is the ultimate ground on which to seek meaning. As has already been suggested, the ultimate vision of meaning seeking is the unity between human beings and heaven. Problem questions explore what difficulties we might encounter when we interact with the world. As I have noted elsewhere, there are four relationships between meaning questions and problem questions:

1. Some problem questions have no meanings.
2. Some problem questions have meanings.
3. Some meaning questions are dependent on problem solving.
4. Some meaning questions are independent of problem solving. (Zhang, 2003)

A moral creativity–based curriculum is based on meaning questions, with an effort to integrate them with problem questions.

In summary, Confucianism opens up a new horizon with which to understand curriculum: the essence of curriculum can be revealed through moral creativity. Constructing a moral creativity–based curriculum is a means by which to escape the current curriculum trap of technical rationality and utilitarianism.

A Curriculum of Lived Experience

Confucianism is not only an axiology but also a methodology. In the 1950s, Feng set as his life principle the transforming of theory into morality and into method—a principle that, in my opinion, embodies the basic qualities of Confucianism. And it is also true for curriculum research. According to William F. Pinar, "the educational possibility for curriculum theory is to help you reflect more profoundly, and not without humor on occasion, on your individual, specific situation" (Pinar 1995, p. 9). This indicates that curriculum theory can be transformed into a process through which the curriculum scholar may seek lived meaning.

The contemporary Chinese philosopher Chen Lai (1998) has used the phrase "metaphysics of lived experience," which can be used to generalize Confucian methodology. A metaphysics of lived experience is the confluence of the Confucian cultivation of morality, Taoist tranquil observation (*jing guan*) and profound insight (*xuan lan*), and Buddhist enlightenment (*dun wu*). When Confucianism stepped into the new stage of neo-Confucianism during the Song dynasty (951–1279 C.E.) and the Ming dynasty (1368–1644 C.E.), this methodology developed into its peak. Lived experience involves intellectual intuition. In the Western world, Immanuel Kant trusted the intellectual world to God and the sensible world to human beings. But according to Chinese philosophy, human beings have intellectual intuition—the insight of infinity and absoluteness in vivid events and passing moments. It is obtained by human beings' encounter with the superlogical sphere. It is the embodiment of moral creativity, and must be justified by life practice.

A metaphysics of lived experience as a methodology recognizes curriculum research to be:

1. A process of moral experience in the curriculum field. As the great Confucian Wang Yangming (1472–1529) has put it, "seeking conscience" (*zhi liang zhi*) in the curriculum field is our commitment.
2. A process of reflection and sharing in which "reflection" means "reflecting on one's own mind" (*fan qiu zhu ji*). As Mencius has said, "All the world is in myself. When I reflect on it and find it, how happy I am!" (Mencius, book 13, chapter 4). Sharing means that the researcher and the researched share a cause and a life.
3. The embodiment of the researcher's life practice.
4. A holistic, dynamic, and organic observation of curriculum.

As I have discussed elsewhere, the metaphysics of lived experience is not only a method for undertaking curriculum research, but can also be a method for teaching. If teaching is based on the lived experiences of teachers and students, the meaning of teaching will be found and promoted (Zhang, 2000).

Conclusion: Toward Confucianism in Day-to-Day Life

As early as the pre-Qin period, Confucianism put forward a well-known proposition: Everyone can be Yao and Shun (two legendary sagelike kings in remote antiquity). Confucianism has never been separated from everyday life; that is why it has been such an influential philosophy in Chinese culture. During the long period of autocratic monarchy, Confucianism became "the school of the internal sage and external controller" and became the main ideology and the principle for governing the country. When Confucianism developed into neo-Confucianism during the Ming Dynasty, especially in Wang Yangming's neo-Confucian school, it experienced a big shift—a shift to day-to-day life. Wang Yangming said, "The pursuit of conscience is never separated from everyday life." The Yangming School in Taizhou proposed a well-known idea: "Every-one on the street is a sage" (as quoted in Yu, 1998, p. 245). This signified that Confucianism started to step out of the so-called "internal sage and external controller" (*nei sheng wai wang*) pattern and turn to the ordinary person's everyday life. After the end of the institutionalization of Confucianism in the early 20th century, everyday life has been the only medium for the influence of Confucianism.

The Confucian shift to everyday life involves a popularizing process. This means that the ideal of the "popularized free personality" has been rooted in Confucianism. To understand curriculum as a Confucian text is to look for the Confucian spirit in the ordinary lives of students, teachers, schools, fami-lies, and communities, and to nurture a "popularized free personality."

Notes

This chapter was supported by the Program for New Century Excellent Talents in University in China.

1. For the main arguments on "Westernization" and "anti-Western Westernization," see Von Laue, 1987.
2. Jaspers formulated his theory of the "axial period" in 1949, noting, "Mankind always lives in dependence on what people thought and created in the axial period, and people tend to review this period at every new leap forward and they are rekindled by it. After that, so always is the case, the revival of and the return to the potentiality of the axial period, or its renaissance, always provides us with some new spiritual impetus" (Jaspers, 1949, p. 4).
3. King Wen was one of most famous kings in ancient China, and lived during the Shang dynasty (ca.1600—1100 B.C.E.) and the Zhou dynasty (1100—221 B.C.E.). He was the founder of the Western Zhou dynasty (ca. 1100—771 B.C.E.)
4. Here I use the translation "gentleman" to indicate the Confucian ideal, since historically it was the man who had institutional and intellectual access to claim such an ideal in the Confucian world. This aspect of the Confucian heritage has been criticized in contempo-rary times.
5. Mencius (ca. 385—304 B.C.E.) was one of the most important Confucians in the pre-Qin period. He lived during the Warring States period (475—221 B.C.E.) of the Eastern Zhou dynasty.

References

Chen, L. (1998). On the mysticism in Confucian tradition. In Center for Study of Traditional Chinese Culture at Peking University (Ed.), *Selections of national learning for the centennial of Beijing University: Philosophy* (pp. 540–541). Beijing, China: Beijing University Press.

Cheng, Z. (Ed.). (2002). *Ontological hermeneutics*. Beijing, China: Beijing University Press.

Feng, Q. (1997). *Toward wisdom*. Shanghai, China: East China Normal University Press.

Fox, J. T. (1969). Epistemology, psychology and their relevance for education in Bruner and Dewey. *Educational Theory, 19*, 58–75.

Jaspers, K. T. (1953). *The origin and goal of history* (M. Bullock, Trans.). New Haven: Yale University Press.

Li, X. (Ed.). (1999). *Interpretations of thirteen classics: A hermeneutic of the Book of Songs* (vol. 2). Beijing, China: Beijing University Press.

Mu, Z. (1997). *Nineteen lectures on Chinese philosophy*. Shanghai, China: Shanghai Classics Press.

Origin. (1983). *The Origin of Chinese words* (vol. 4). Shanghai, China: Commercial Publishing House.

Pinar, W. F. (with Reynolds, W. M., Slattery, P., and Taubman, P. M.). (1995). *Understanding curriculum*. New York: Lang.

Qian, M. (2001). *On modern Chinese disciplines*. Beijing, China: Sanlian Book Store.

Qian, M. (2002). *Outline of Zhu Xi's scholarship*. Beijing, China: Sanlian Book Store.

Von Laue, T. H. (1987). *The world revolution of Westernization: The twentieth century in global perspective*. Oxford, England: Oxford University Press.

Xia, Z. (1999). *The sea of Chinese words*. Shanghai, China: Dictionary Publishing House.

Xu, S. (1963). *Exploring the etymology of Chinese words*. Beijing, China: China Publishing House.

Xu, S. (2002). *New translations of exploring the etymology of Chinese words* (K. Tang, Trans.). Changsha, China: Yuelu Publishing House.

Young, E. L. (1972). Dewey and Bruner: A Common Ground? *Educational Theory, 22*(1), 58-68.

Yu, Y. (1998). *Modern Confucianism*. Shanghai, China: People's Publishing House.

Zhang, H. (2000). *Research on experience curriculum*. Shanghai, China: Educational Publishing House.

Zhang, H. (2003). Research-based learning and life. *Exploring Education Development, 24*(6), 17–21.

Zhang, H., & Zhong Q. (2003). Curriculum studies in China: Retrospect and prospect. In Pinar, W. F. (Ed.), *International handbook of curriculum research* (pp. 253–270). Mahwah, NJ: Erlbaum.

Zhu, X. (1983). *Interpretations of four classics*. Beijing, China: China's Publishing House. (Original work composed during the Song dynasty)

Zhu, X. (1986). *Zhu Xi's recorded discourses* (vol. 1). Beijing, China: China's Publishing House.

AFTERWORD: TEACHING ALONG THE WAY

This book lingers. The thoughts contained within its pages not only intercon-nect chapter with chapter, they seep into my actions as person, as teacher. I am intrigued from the very start of this reading with, for instance, the notion that there are many Easts and Wests, that no amount of training can produce good character, that compassion (suffering with) is both simple and complex, that the true nature of thought itself is empty and transient. I carry these ideas into the classroom with peril, knowing that clarity and power point are prized tools for students in the information age. But information, this book makes clear, is not wisdom; no amount of information can shape the soul or stop World War III. Perhaps Gertrude Stein was more Zen than Dada when she claimed that nobody teaches anybody anything; perhaps nothingness offers a necessary empty space for engagement.

Information that reaches too quickly for answers are what evaluation forms with boxes prize. Check it off: the teacher was clear and precise; class time was used efficiently; the instructor had command of the subject matter. I read none of those words—*command, precision, efficiency*—as positives in the pages of this book. What a relief, a delicious sense of breath this book offers: a real alternative to education-as-assessment. I am struck with the healthy disregard for boxes and either/or thinking that these educators share. Having sprung free of the trap of literalism, the writers in this volume offer the classroom as a place for walking the way of life. Rather than charting lesson plans or chant-ing George W. Bush mantras, they engage the whole reader in what for me has become a process of radical unlearning.

My remarks are intended to suggest an after-thinking, not a comprehensive commentary. To do the latter would be to crush the spirit the text releases. Let me say, simply, that the educational insights from a study of thinkers famil-iar with Eastern thought are refreshing, important, and laced with forgotten truths. They urge engagement in elementary awareness, attention, and appreciation for dailiness; spontaneity, laughter, and openness to contradiction. The chapters repeat and reinforce without repetition and enforcement. The ideas and the expression of the ideas celebrate fluidity, the very thing labels and boxes can never contain.

Just yesterday I had occasion to put my new unlearning to the test, as it were. I forgot to bring the book we were studying. I came to class with the wrong text. I also brought the wrong video, which I intended as a visual restatement of the text I wanted to discuss. Me, me, me.

Perfect.

After a momentary panic (the class, after all is two and a half hours clock time), I knew I simply had to (a) be honest, (b) leave a lot up to the students, (c) listen more closely to what was *not* being said, (d) reveal my foolishness, and (e) forget myself. I cannot account for the students' reaction, but I can say that the hours went by in a totally different way. I saw no eyes flying to the clock. Why? What was different? To quote Hongyu Wang, I offered myself as a "meandering contradiction"—which, she writes, is essential for understanding subjectivity and education. No longer the professor, I was immediately disrobed, all props removed. I was one of the circle and together we were looking at the text; or rather, I was listening to the text in a new way since I was "unprepared." The video I showed was not at all wonderful, but the mistake was hilarious. We read out loud. We wondered out loud. A new emphasis was taking place, one that depended less on the eye, more on the ear; less on talking points, more on questionings. For me, the experience was exhilarating. But to make that an everyday plan would be to turn a surprise into a project. The different sense of the classroom is what I think Kaustuv Roy means as a different time movement, one that offers "incandescence within the daily act of learning."

A fear factor, however, prevents us educators from revealing ourselves to each other (students included in the "each" of "other"), especially in a situation where podium establishes procedure. And, of course, some students do not like it at all when the classroom becomes a bit like life, messy and unpredictable. Here, again, is where Eastern thought has important things to say, disabusing us of poses. The Buddhist idea of impermanence and change, as foundational aspects of life, offers counterpoint to the odd notion of the teacher as "expert." Experts don't forget their books or have memory lapses; experts have talking points. Claudia Eppert addresses the problem of the fear factor when she discusses Jiddu Krishnamurti's understanding that "fear blocks the intelligent understanding of life." What the fearful educator does by arming herself with dazzling efficiency and zip-zap technology is comparable, Eppert suggests, to world leaders arming their arsenals or high school students coming to school armed. Fear prevents movement, reifies positions, and instantiates labels. Fear ultimately causes destruction, the implications of which for a world ticking toward nuclear midnight are unspeakable.

To deliteralize in a climate of extreme literalism is, to put it mildly, difficult. But that is what this book urges by way of introducing the wisdom traditions of the East. The education of most worth today is not that which can be described by clarity or control but rather by paying attention, attending, and respecting the tension that comes from another way of living.

Mary Aswell Doll
Savannah College of Art and Design

CONTRIBUTORS

Heesoon Bai has been studying Buddhism and Daoism for close to three decades, and since her appointment to the faculty of education at Simon Fraser University she has been applying Buddhist and Daoist thoughts and practices, such as mindfulness, nonduality, and *Qi* philosophy, to education. For her publications and teaching, see http://www.educ.sfu.ca/fri/Bai/.

Avraham Cohen is an educator and a psychotherapist. He has been involved in spiritual practices for over 30 years, and practices and teaches whole-person meditation, which developed out of his experiences of the Subud latihan, Buddhist mindfulness, and Sufi heart rhythm meditation; his background in Aikido is also a strong influence on his work. In his teaching of master's degree students, counseling psychology students, and in his private practice he works extensively with humanistic, transpersonal, process-oriented ideas and a living experience of Daoism with its emphasis on *Qi* energy. He has published a number of articles in counseling and psychotherapy journals.

Mary Aswell Doll, professor of liberal arts at Savannah College of Art and Design, teaches courses in world mythology, British literature, Southern U.S. literature, absurdist literature, and women in literature. Although her main concerns are with fiction, poetry, and drama, she has had an interest in Eastern thought ever since the publication of her book *Like Letters in Running Water: A Mythopoetics of Curriculum* (Lawrence Erlbaum Associates, 2000), inspired by finding *The Teaching of Buddha* in her hotel room while visiting Japan. In addition, her work in Jungian thought has been a constant in her approaches to scholarship and teaching. She is the author of three books and coeditor of two books, as well as the author of chapters in books and articles in the *Journal of Beckett Studies*, the *Journal of Mental Imagery*, *Soundings*, the *Dictionary of Literary Biography Yearbook*, and the *Journal of Curriculum Theorizing*. Her latest coauthored book is *Triple Takes on Curricular Worlds* (State University of New York Press, 2006).

Claudia Eppert taught at Louisiana State University for eight years and is now associate professor of English Language Arts Education at the University of Alberta. These last seven years she has been immersed in studies of Eastern thought and contemplative practices in order to further her understanding of the complexities and possibilities of witnessing social suffering through literature, media, and the arts. She is coeditor with Roger I. Simon and Sharon Rosenberg of *Between Hope and Despair: Pedagogy and the Remembrance of Historical Trauma* (Rowman and Littlefield, 2000). Her work has also appeared in such journals as *New German Critique*; the *JCT: Journal of Curriculum Theorizing*; the *Review of Education/Pedagogy/Cultural Studies*; *JAC: A Quarterly Journal for the Interdisciplinary Study of Rhetoric, Writing, Multiple Literacies, and Politics*; *Taboo: Journal of Culture and Education*; and in several edited books, including *Difficult Memories: Talk in a Post-Holocaust Era* (Peter Lang, 2002) and *Spirituality and Ethics in Education: Philosophical, Theological, and Radical Perspectives* (Sussex Academic Press, 2004).

Robert Hattam is an associate professor in the Hawke Research Institute and the School of Education at the University of South Australia. His research interests include social theory, critical pedagogy, engaged Buddhism, and Tibetan Buddhism. His publications include *Awakening Struggle: Towards a Buddhist Critical Social Theory* (PostPressed, 2004), a coauthored book titled *Teachers' Work in a Globalising Economy* (Falmer, 2000), and a coedited book titled *Schooling for a Fair Go* (Federation Press, 1998). He is currently corecipient of the Australian Research Council funded grants Rethinking, Reconciliation and Pedagogy in Unsettling Times and Schooling, Globalisation and Refugees in Australia.

Petra Munro Hendry is a professor in the Department of Curriculum and Instruction at Louisiana State University, where she is codirector of the Curriculum Theory Project and a member of the women's and gender studies faculty. Her research interests are the narrative analysis of women educators' life histories, curriculum history, and discourses of qualitative research. She is currently completing her book *Engendering Curriculum History*. Her interest in Eastern thought emerged from her research on European medieval religious women and their philosophies of embodied knowing. Hendry is author of *Subject to Fiction: Women Teachers' Life History Narratives and the Cultural Politics of*

Resistance (Open University, 1998) and coauthor of *Pedagogies of Resistance: Women Educator Activists 1880–1960* (Teachers College Press, 1999).

jan jagodzinski is a professor in the Department of Secondary Education at the University of Alberta in Edmonton, Alberta, Canada where he teaches visual art education and curricular issues as they relate to postmodern concerns of gender politics, cultural studies, and the media (film and television). He is a founding member of the *Journal of Social Theory in Art Education*; the editor of *JSTAE: Journal of Social Theory in Art Education;* past president of SIG Media, Culture, and Curriculum; author of *The Anamorphic I/i,* (Duval, 1996), *Postmodern Dilemmas: Outrageous Essays in Art and Art Education* (Lawrence Erlbaum Associates, 1997); *Pun(k) Deconstruction: Experifigural Writings in Art and Art Education* (Lawrence Erlbaum Associates, 1997); *Youth Fantasies: The Perverse Landscape of the Media* (Palgrave, 2004); *Music in Youth Culture: A Lacanian Approach* (Palgrave, 2005); *The Oral Eye* (Hamstead, in press); and *Television Culture* (Palgrave, in press), and the editor of *Pedagogical Desire: Transference, Seduction, Authority and the Question of Ethics* (Bergin and Garvey, 2001).

David Jardine is a professor of education at the University of Calgary. Alan Watts's *The Book* was the first book he read from cover to cover, sometime in 1968, back in the days when there were angels. His latest publication is a coauthored text titled *Curriculum in Abundance* (Lawrence Erlbaum Associates, 2006), which in part toys with the Buddhist insight of emptiness.

Takuya Kaneda is an associate professor of art education at Otsuma Women's University in Tokyo. He has traveled extensively in Asia, incuding some years spent in Nepal and India, and has engaged in making video documentaries on Buddhist rituals in Kathmandu. He was a visiting instructor at Jiddu Krishnamurti's Rishi Valley School in India in 1999. He is also very active as the representative of the International Children's Peace Mural Project and has organized many workshops for children in different parts of the world to grow peace consciousness through art. He is the coauthor of *Peaceful Children: Beyond War, Violence and Bullying* (Seseragi-Shuppan, 2004) and has written many articles on education including a book chapter in Japanese, "Ravindranath Tagore: Education for Spiritual Fulfillment and the Concept of Freedom in Art Education in Japan," published in *Nurturing Our Wholeness: Perspectives on Spirituality in Education* (Foundations for Educational Renewal, 2002), coedited by J. Miller and Y. Nakagawa.

Xin Li is a professor in the Department of Teacher Education at California State University–Long Beach. Her research interests include narrative inquiry of cross-cultural experiences. She approaches Taoism as a philosophy that provides guidance for surviving social-cultural vicissitudes, living meaningful lives in interruption, and cultivating cultural creativity in diversity. Her recent publications on the topic include *The Tao of Life Stories: Chinese Language, Poetry, and Culture in Education* (Lang, 2002), and the articles "A Tao of Narrative: Dynamic Splicing of Teacher Stories" (*Curriculum Inquiry*, 2005), and "Becoming Taoist I and Thou: Identity-Making of Opposite Cultures" (*Journal of Curriculum and Pedagogy*, 2006). She teaches graduate courses in cross-cultural education and literacy, and credential courses in cultural and linguistic diversity.

Yoshiharu Nakagawa is a professor of education at Ritsumeikan University in Kyoto, Japan. He received his Ph.D. from the Ontario Institute for Studies in Education at the University of Toronto, where his doctoral thesis "Eastern Philosophy and Holistic Education" was focused on a theoretical foundation for holistic education from diverse perspectives of Eastern philosophy. This work was later published as *Education for Awakening: An Eastern Approach to Holistic Education* (Foundation for Educational Renewal, 2000). He is the coeditor of *Nurturing Our Wholeness: Perspectives on Spirituality in Education* (Foundation for Educational Renewal, 2002). Recently, he contributed a chapter, "The Child as Compassionate Bodhisattva and as Human Sufferer/Spiritual Seeker: Intertwined Buddhist Images," to *Nurturing Child and Adolescent Spirituality: Perspectives from the World's Religious Traditions* (Rowman and Littlefield, 2006). He is also the author of a Japanese book, *Holistic Clinical Pedagogy* (Seseragi-Shuppan, 2005).

Jane Piirto is a Trustees Professor at Ashland University in Ashland, Ohio. She wrote the chapter in this volume after a research visit to India, where she was researching indigenous schools for talented students in Chennai, Mumbai, Pune, and Trivandrum. Piirto's books include *Understanding Creativity* (Great Potential, 2004), *"My Teeming Brain": Understanding Creative Writers* (Hampton Press, 2002), and *Talented Children and Adults* (Great Potential, 2003). She is an award-winning poet and novelist.

Kaustuv Roy's principal research interest is in political philosophy and theory and the New Left. He also writes on micropolitical praxis. He is the author of *Teachers in Nomadic Spaces: Deleuze and Curriculum* (Lang, 2003).

David Geoffrey Smith is a professor of education at the University of Alberta in Edmonton, Alberta, Canada. He teaches and researches in the areas of curriculum studies, globalization theory, and religious education. A special interest is a graduate seminar he conducts called Teaching as the Practice of Wisdom. Collections of his published papers are available in *Pedagon: Interdisciplinary Studies in the Human Sciences, Pedagogy and Culture* (Peter Lang, 1999), and *Trying to Teach in a Season of Great Untruth* (SensePublishing, 2006). Born in China and raised in Africa, Smith characterizes his work as a hermeneutic of encounter at the interfaces of global culture.

Daniel Vokey is an associate professor in the Department of Educational Studies at the University of British Columbia, where he recently offered the graduate course Spirituality and Education in a Pluralistic World. He has pursued his interest in transformative education through a B.A. and an M.A. in religious studies, an M.Ed in curriculum and instruction, and a Ph.D. in philosophy of education. Since 1989 he has been a Mahāyāna practitioner in the Shambhala Buddhist tradition, offering introductory courses and meditation instruction for newer students in the sangha and integrating the results of his study of Buddhist philosophy into his academic publications. Vokey draws inspiration from many contemplative traditions, and in 1994 was an enthusiastic participant in Inner Peace, Active Love: An Interfaith Meditation Retreat held to correspond with the Dalai Lama's roundtable dialogue in Vancouver, Balancing Educating the Mind with Educating the Heart.

Hongyu Wang is associate professor in curriculum studies at Oklahoma State University. She received her Ph.D. in curriculum theory from Louisiana State University, and has coauthored books and published articles both in Chinese and in English. She is coeditor, with Donna Trueit, William E. Doll, Jr., and William F. Pinar, of *The Internationalization of Curriculum Studies* (Lang, 2003) and author of *The Call from the Stranger on a Journey Home: Curriculum in a Third Space* (Lang, 2004), which provides a critical analysis of the writings of Eastern and Western philosophers, principally Confucius, Michel Foucault, and Julia Kristeva. She teaches graduate courses in curriculum research, multicultural education, and intercultural curriculum dialogues. Translator of William E. Doll Jr.'s *A Post-modern Perspective on Curriculum* (Teachers College Press, 1993), she has worked on introducing North American curriculum texts into the Chinese educational field.

Hua Zhang is a professor at the Institute of Curriculum and Instruction, East China Normal University (ECNU). He also serves as a consultant for the National Educational Ministry in current national curriculum reform. He is the vice president of the International Association for the Advancement of Curriculum Studies (IAACS). He received his Ph.D. from ECNU in 1998. He is the editor of the journal *Global Education,* and also the editor of the upcoming journal *IAACS Transnational Curriculum Inquiry.* His research includes Confucian–Taoist–Buddhist orientation in curriculum studies, phenomenological–existentialist–hermeneutic studies in curriculum studies, educational philosophy, and moral education. He has published 6 books and more than 90 papers in academic journals.

NAME INDEX

A

Abe, M., 233
Abraham, N., 82
Abu-Lughod, L., 2
Adhe, T., 130
Adorno, T., 74
Agger, B., 111, 127
Ahluwalia, P., 131
Ahmed, S., 159
Aiello, P., 130
Aitken, R., 123
Alexander, 8, 10, 239, 240
Alfassa, M., 180
Allan, S., 321
Ames, R., 41, 49
Amin, S., 8
Amore, R., 10
Aoki, T. T., xviii, xx, xxi, 329, 330
Arabi, I., 231
Arends, T., 13
Arendt, H., 74
Aristotle, 8, 288, 291, 300, 306, 343
Arnold, E., 18
Ashoka, 10
Aston, R., 71
Atkinson, S., 131
Atmaswarupananda, S., 26, 27, 28
Attridge, D., 95
Atwell-Vasey, W., 331
Augustine, 12
Aung, S. S. K., 130
Aurobindo, Sri, xx, 172, 176, 179–181, 187–190, 270
Ayers, W., 331

B

Bacon, F., 16, 75, 143
Bai, H., 35
Bakhtin, M., 91
Ban Zhao, 319, 325, 327
Barthes, R., 81
Bartlett, E., 208, 217
Basham, A., 11
Bastian, G., 130
Batchelor, S., 18, 19, 21, 112, 124, 130
Bateson, G., 22
Bauman, Z., 110
Baumann, M., 83
Beaud, M., 5
Beck, U., 110
Behn, A., 143
Behre, W., 71
Behrendt, L., 109
Benhabib, S., 111
Bennett, W., 70, 73
Benz, S., 58
Bercovitch, S., 67
Bergson, H., 267, 269–276, 280–284
Berlak, A., 58
Berrigan, D., 123, 130
Berry, P., 87
Berry, T., 38
Besant, A., 254–257, 260, 261
Best, S., 111
Bhikkhu, S., 130
Bishop, P., 131
Blascovich, J., 141, 142
Blavatsky, H., 19, 254
Blofeld, J., 212, 217
Bogdan, D., 68
Bohm, D., 22

SUBJECT INDEX